HISTORY OF
ENGLISH LITERATURE

HISTORY OF
English Literature

VOLUME II

Hippolyte A. Taine

FREDERICK UNGAR PUBLISHING CO.
NEW YORK

Translated from the French by H. Van Laun

Republished 1965

Reprinted from the 1883 edition

34272

Printed in the United States of America

Library of Congress Catalog Card No. 65-20501

CONTENTS.

BOOK II.—THE RENAISSANCE.

CHAPTER III.

Ben Jonson.

		PAGE
I.	The masters of the school, in the school and in their age—Jonson—His mood—Character—Education—First efforts—Struggles—Poverty—Sickness—Death	1
II.	Learning—Classical tastes—Didactic characters—Good management of his plots—Freedom and precision of his style—Vigour of his will and passion	6
III.	Dramas—*Catiline* and *Sejanus*—How he was able to depict the personages and the passions of the Roman decadence	14
IV.	Comedies—His reformation and theory of the theatre—Satirical comedies—*Volpone*—Why these comedies are serious and warlike—How they depict the passions of the Renaissance—His farces—*The Silent Woman*—Why these comedies are energetic and rude—How they conform with the tastes of the Renaissance	21
V.	Limits of his talent—Wherein he is inferior to Molière—Want of higher philosophy and comic	

vi CONTENTS.

PAGE

gaiety—His imagination and Fancy—*The Staple of News* and *Cynthia's Revels*—How he treats the comedy of society, and lyrical comedy—His smaller poems—His masques—Theatrical and picturesque manners of the court—*The Sad Shepherd*—How Jonson remains a poet to his death 38

VI. General idea of Shakspeare—The fundamental idea in Shakspeare—Conditions of human reason—Shakspeare's master faculty—Conditions of exact representation 45

CHAPTER IV.

Shakspeare.

I. Life and character of Shakspeare—Family—Youth—Marriage—He becomes an actor—*Adonis*—Sonnets—Loves—Humour—Conversation—Melancholy—The constitution of the productive and sympathetic character—Prudence—Fortune—Retirement 50

II. Style—Images—Excesses—Incongruities—Copiousness—Difference between the creative and analytic conception 67

III. Manners—Familiar intercourse—Violent bearing—Harsh language—Conversation and action—Agreement of manners and style . . . 74

IV. The *dramatis personæ*—All of the same family—Brutes and idiots—Caliban, Ajax, Cloten, Polonius, the Nurse—How the mechanical imagination can precede or survive reason 83

V. Men of wit—Difference between the wit of reasoners and of artists—Mercutio, Beatrice, Rosalind, Benedict, the clowns—Falstaff . . . 90

CONTENTS. vii

PAGE

VI. Women—Desdemona, Virginia, Juliet, Miranda, Imogen, Cordelia, Ophelia, Volumnia—How Shakspeare represents love—Why he bases virtue on instinct or passion 96
VII. Villains—Iago, Richard III.—How excessive lusts and the lack of conscience are the natural province of the impassioned imagination . . 101
VIII. Principal characters—Excess and disease of the imagination—Lear, Othello, Cleopatra, Coriolanus, Macbeth, Hamlet—Comparison of Shakspeare's psychology with that of the French tragic authors 104
IX. Fancy—Agreement of imagination with observation in Shakspeare—Interesting nature of sentimental and romantic comedy—*As you like it*—Idea of existence—*Midsummer Night's Dream*—Idea of love—Harmony of all parts of the work—Harmony between the artist and his work . 124

CHAPTER V.

The Christian Renaissance.

I. Vices of the Pagan Renaissance—Decay of the Southern civilisations 142
II. The Reformation—Aptitude of the Germanic races, and suitability of Northern climates—Albert Durer's bodies and souls—His martyrdoms and last judgments—Luther—His idea of justice—Construction of Protestantism—Crisis of the conscience—Renewal of heart—Suppression of ceremonies—Transformation of the clergy . 148
III. Reformation in England—Tyranny of the ecclesiastical courts—Disorders of the clergy—Irritation of the people—The interior of a diocese—Perse-

CONTENTS.

cutions and convulsions—The translation of the Bible—How biblical events and Hebraic sentiments are in accordance with contemporary manners and with the English character—*The Prayer Book*—Moral and manly feeling of the prayers and church service—Preaching—Latimer—His education—Character—Familiar and persuasive eloquence—Death—The martyrs under Mary—England thenceforth Protestant . . 158

IV. The Anglicans—Close connection between religion and society—How the religious sentiment penetrates literature—How the sentiment of the beautiful subsists in religion—Hooker—His breadth of mind and the fulness of his style—Hales and Chillingworth—Praise of reason and tolerance—Jeremy Taylor—His learning, imagination, and poetic feeling 186

V. The Puritans—Opposition of religion and the world—Dogmas—Morality—Scruples—Their triumph and enthusiasm—Their work and practical sense 202

VI. Bunyan—His life, spirit, and poetical work—The Prospect of Protestantism in England . . 221

CHAPTER VI.

Milton.

I. General idea of his mind and character—Family—Education—Studies—Travels—Return to England 240

II. Effects of a concentrated and solitary character—Austerity—Inexperience—Marriage—Children—Domestic Troubles 246

CONTENTS.

		PAGE
III.	Combative energy—Polemic against the bishops—Against the king—Enthusiasm and sternness—Theories on government, church, and education—Stoicism and virtue—Old age, occupations, person	249
IV.	Milton's residence in London and the country—General appearance	257
V.	Milton as a prose-writer—Changes during three centuries in countenances and ideas—Heaviness of his logic—*The Doctrine and Discipline of Divorce*—Heavy Humour—*Animadversions upon the Remonstrant's Defence*—Clumsiness of discussion—*Defensio Populi Anglicani*—Violence of his animosities—*The reason of Church Government*—*Eikonoklastes*—Liberality of Doctrines—*Of Reformation*—*Areopagitica*—Style—Breadth of eloquence—Wealth of imagery—Lyric sublimity of diction	258
VI.	Milton as a poet—How he approaches and is distinct from the poets of the Renaissance—How he gives poetry a moral tone—Profane poems—*L'Allegro* and *Il Penseroso*—*Comus*—*Lycidas*—Religious poems—*Paradise Lost*—Conditions of a genuine epic—They are not to be met with in the age or in the poet—Comparison of Adam and Eve with an English family—Comparison of God and the angels to a monarch's court—The rest of the poem—Comparison between the sentiments of Satan and the republican passions—Lyrical and moral character of the scenery—Loftiness and sense of the moral ideas—Situation of the poet and the poem between two ages—Composition of his genius and his work	279

BOOK III.—THE CLASSIC AGE.

CHAPTER I.

The Restoration.

I. THE ROISTERERS.

		PAGE
I.	The excesses of Puritanism—How they induce excesses of sensuality	320
II.	Picture of these manners by a stranger—The *Mémoires de Grammont*—Difference of debauchery in France and England	324
III.	Butler's *Hudibras*—Platitude of his comic style, and harshness of his rancorous style . . .	328
IV.	Baseness, cruelty, brutality, debauchery, of the court —Rochester, his life, poems, style, morals .	332
V.	Philosophy consonant with these manners—Hobbes, his spirit and his style—His curtailments and his discoveries—His mathematical method— In how much he resembles Descartes—His morality, æsthetics, politics, logic, psychology, metaphysics—Spirit and aim of his philosophy .	342
VI.	The theatre—Alteration in taste, and in the public— Audiences before and after the Restoration .	350
VII.	Dryden—Disparity of his comedies—Unskilfulness of his indecencies—How he translates Molière's *Amphitryon*	353
VIII.	Wycherley—Life—Character—Melancholy, greed, immodesty—*Love in a Wood*, *Country Wife*, *Dancing Master*—Licentious pictures, and repugnant details—His energy and realism—Parts of Olivia and Manly in his *Plain Dealer*— Certain words of Milton's *Paradise Lost* . .	357

CONTENTS.

2. THE WORLDLINGS.

I. Appearance of the worldly life in Europe—Its conditions and causes—How it was established in England—Etiquette, amusements, conversations, manners, and talents of the drawing-room . 371
II. Dawn of the classic spirit in Europe—Its origin—Its nature—Difference of conversation under Elizabeth and Charles II. 375
III. Sir William Temple—His life, character, spirit, and style 378
IV. Writers of fashion—Their correct language and gallant bearing—Sir Charles Sedley, the Earl of Dorset, Edmund Waller—His opinions and style—Wherein consists his polish—Wherein he is not sufficiently polished—Culture of style—Lack of poetry—Character of monarchical and classic style 385
V. Sir John Denham—His poem of *Cooper's Hill*—Oratorical swell of his verse—English seriousness of his moral preoccupations—How people of fashion and literary men followed then the fashions of France 395
VI. The comic-authors—Comparison of this theatre with that of Molière—Arrangement of ideas in Molière—General ideas in Molière—How in Molière the odious is concealed, while the truth is depicted—How in Molière the honest man is still the man of the world—How the respectable man of Molière is a French type 399
VII. Action—Complication of intrigues—Frivolity of purpose—Crudeness of the characters—Grossness of manners—Wherein consists the talent of Wycherley, Congreve, Vanbrugh, and Farquhar—Kind of characters they are able to produce . 409

PAGE

VIII. Natural characters—*Sir John Brute*, the husband; *Squire Sullen*—*Sir Tunbelly*, the father—*Miss Hoyden*, the young lady—*Squire Humphry*, the young gentleman—Idea of nature according to this theatre 414

IX. Artificial characters—Women of the world—*Miss Prue, Lady Wishfort, Lady Pliant, Mrs. Millamant*—Men of the world—*Mirabell*—Idea of society according to this theatre—Why this culture and this literature have not produced durable works—Wherein they are opposed to the English character—Transformation of taste and manners 419

X. The continuation of comedy—Sheridan—Life—Talent—*The School for Scandal*—How comedy degenerates and is extinguished—Causes of the decay of the theatre in Europe and in England . 432

HISTORY OF ENGLISH LITERATURE.

BOOK II.
THE RENAISSANCE.

CHAPTER III.
Ben Jonson.

I.

WHEN a new civilisation brings a new art to light, there are about a dozen men of talent who partly express the general idea, surrounding one or two men of genius who express it thoroughly. Guillen de Castro, Perez de Montalvan, Tirzo de Molina, Ruiz de Alarcon, Agustin Moreto, surrounding Calderon and Lope de Vega; Crayer, Van Oost, Rombouts, Van Thulden, Van Dyck, Honthorst, surrounding Rubens; Ford, Marlowe, Massinger, Webster, Beaumont, Fletcher, surrounding Shakspeare and Ben Jonson. The first constitute the chorus, the others are the leading men. They sing the same piece together, and at times the chorist is equal to the solo artist; but only at times. Thus, in the dramas which I have just referred to, the poet occasionally reaches the summit of his art, hits upon a complete character, a burst of sublime passion;

then he falls back, gropes amid qualified successes, rough sketches, feeble imitations, and at last takes refuge in the tricks of his trade. It is not in him, but in great men like Ben Jonson and Shakspeare, that we must look for the attainment of his idea and the fulness of his art. "Numerous were the wit-combats," says Fuller, "betwixt him (Shakspeare) and Ben Jonson, which two I behold like a Spanish great galleon and an English man-of-war. Master Jonson (like the former) was built far higher in learning; solid, but slow in his performances. Shakspeare, with the English man-of-war, lesser in bulk, but lighter in sailing, could turn with all tides, tack about and take advantage of all winds, by the quickness of his wit and invention."[1] Such was Ben Jonson physically and morally, and his portraits do but confirm this just and animated outline: a vigorous, heavy, and uncouth person; a broad and long face, early disfigured by scurvy, a square jaw, large cheeks; his animal organs as much developed as those of his intellect: the sour aspect of a man in a passion or on the verge of a passion; to which add the body of an athlete, about forty years of age, "mountain belly, ungracious gait." Such was the outside, and the inside is like it. He was a genuine Englishman, big and coarsely framed, energetic, combative, proud, often morose, and prone to strange splenetic imaginations. He told Drummond that for a whole night he imagined "that he saw the Carthaginians and Romans fighting on his great toe."[2] Not that he is melancholic by nature; on the contrary, he loves to escape from him-

---

[1] Fuller's *Worthies*, ed. Nuttall, 1840, 3 vols. iii. 284.

[2] There is a similar hallucination to be met with in the life of Lord Castlereagh, who afterwards committed suicide.

self by free and noisy, unbridled merriment, by copious and varied converse, assisted by good Canary wine, which he imbibes, and which ends by becoming a necessity to him. These great phlegmatic butchers' frames require a generous liquor to give them a tone, and to supply the place of the sun which they lack. Expansive moreover, hospitable, even lavish, with a frank imprudent spirit,[1] making him forget himself wholly before Drummond, his Scotch host, an over rigid and malicious pedant, who has marred his ideas and vilified his character.[2] What we know of his life is in harmony with his person: he suffered much, fought much, dared much. He was studying at Cambridge, when his stepfather, a bricklayer, recalled him, and taught him to use the trowel. He ran away, enlisted as a common soldier, and served in the English army, at that time engaged against the Spaniards in the Low Countries, killed and despoiled a man in single combat, "in the view of both armies." He was a man of bodily action, and he exercised his limbs in early life.[3] On his return to England, at the age of nineteen, he went on the stage for his livelihood, and occupied himself also in touching up dramas. Having been challenged, he fought a duel, was seriously wounded, but killed

[1] His character lies between those of Fielding and Dr. Johnson.

[2] Mr. David Laing remarks, however, in Drummond's defence, that as "Jonson died August 6, 1637, Drummond survived till December 4, 1649, and no portion of these Notes (Conversations) were made public till 1711, or sixty-two years after Drummond's death, and seventy-four after Jonson's, which renders quite nugatory all Gifford's accusations of Drummond's having published them 'without shame.' As to Drummond decoying Jonson under his roof with any premeditated design on his reputation, as Mr. Campbell has remarked, no one can seriously believe it."—*Archæologica Scotica*, vol. iv. page 243.—TR.

[3] At the age of forty-four he went to Scotland on foot.

his adversary; for this he was cast into prison, and found himself "nigh the gallows." A catholic priest visited and converted him; quitting his prison penniless, at twenty years of age, he married. At last, four years later, his first successful play was acted. Children came, he must earn bread for them; and he was not inclined to follow the beaten track to the end, being persuaded that a fine philosophy—a special nobleness and dignity—ought to be introduced into comedy,— that it was necessary to follow the example of the ancients, to imitate their severity and their accuracy, to be above the theatrical racket and the common improbabilities in which the vulgar delighted. He openly proclaimed his intention in his prefaces, sharply railed at his rivals, proudly set forth on the stage [1] his doctrines, his morality, his character. He thus made bitter enemies, who defamed him outrageously and before their audiences, whom he exasperated by the violence of his satires, and against whom he struggled without intermission to the end. He did more, he constituted himself a judge of the public corruption, sharply attacked the reigning vices, "fearing no strumpet's drugs, nor ruffian's stab." [2] He treated his hearers like schoolboys, and spoke to them always like a censor and a master. If necessary, he ventured further. His companions, Marston and Chapman, had been committed to prison for some reflections on the Scotch in one of their pieces called "Eastward-Hoe;" and the report spreading that they were in danger of losing their noses and ears, Jonson, who had written part of the piece, voluntarily surrendered himself a prisoner, and obtained

---

[1] Parts of *Crites* and *Asper.*
[2] *Every Man out of his Humour,* i.; Gifford's *Jonson,* p. 30.

their pardon. On his return, amid the feasting and rejoicing, his mother showed him a violent poison which she intended to put into his drink, to save him from the execution of the sentence; and "to show that she was not a coward," adds Jonson, "she had resolved to drink first." We see that in vigorous actions he found examples in his own family. Toward the end of his life, money was scarce with him; he was liberal, improvident; his pockets always had holes in them, and his hand was always ready to give; though he had written a vast quantity, he was still obliged to write in order to live. Paralysis came on, his scurvy became worse, dropsy set in. He could not leave his room, nor walk without assistance. His last plays did not succeed. In the epilogue to the *New Inn* he says:

"If you expect more than you had to-night,
The maker is sick and sad. . . .
All that his faint and falt'ring tongue doth crave,
Is, that you not impute it to his brain,
That's yet unhurt, altho' set round with pain,
It cannot long hold out."

His enemies brutally insulted him:

"Thy Pegasus . . .
He had bequeathed his belly unto thee,
To hold that little learning which is fled
Into thy guts from out thy emptye head."

Inigo Jones, his colleague, deprived him of the patronage of the court. He was obliged to beg a supply of money from the Lord Treasurer, then from the Earl of Newcastle:

> "Disease, the enemy, and his engineers,
> Want, with the rest of his concealed compeers,
> Have cast a trench about me, now five years. . . .
> The muse not peeps out, one of hundred days;
> But lies blocked up and straitened, narrowed in,
> Fixed to the bed and boards, unlike to win
> Health, or scarce breath, as she had never been." [1]

His wife and children were dead; he lived alone, forsaken, waited on by an old woman. Thus almost always sadly and miserably, is dragged out and ends the last act of the human comedy. After so many years, after so many sustained efforts, amid so much glory and genius, we find a poor shattered body, drivelling and suffering, between a servant and a priest.

II.

This is the life of a combatant, bravely endured, worthy of the seventeenth century by its crosses and its energy; courage and force abounded throughout. Few writers have laboured more, and more conscientiously; his knowledge was vast, and in this age of eminent scholars he was one of the best classics of his time, as deep as he was accurate and thorough, having studied the most minute details and understood the true spirit of ancient life. It was not enough for him to have stored his mind from the best writers, to have their whole works continually in his mind, to scatter his pages whether he would or no, with recollections of them. He dug into the orators, critics, scholiasts, grammarians, and compilers of inferior rank; he picked up

---

[1] Ben Jonson's *Poems*, ed. Bell, *An Epistle Mendicant*, to Richard, Lord Weston, Lord High Treasurer (1631), p. 244.

stray fragments; he took characters, jokes, refinements, from Athenæus, Libanius, Philostratus. He had so well entered into and digested the Greek and Latin ideas, that they were incorporated with his own. They enter into his speech without incongruity; they spring forth in him as vigorous as at their first birth; he originates even when he remembers. On every subject he had this thirst for knowledge, and this gift of mastering knowledge. He knew alchemy when he wrote the *Alchemist*. He is familiar with alembics, retorts, receivers, as if he had passed his life seeking after the philosopher's stone. He explains incineration, calcination, imbibition, rectification, reverberation, as well as Agrippa and Paracelsus. If he speaks of cosmetics,[1] he brings out a shopful of them; we might make out of his plays a dictionary of the oaths and costumes of courtiers; he seems to have a specialty in all branches. A still greater proof of his force is, that his learning in nowise mars his vigour; heavy as is the mass with which he loads himself, he carries it without stooping. This wonderful mass of reading and observation suddenly begins to move, and falls like a mountain on the overwhelmed reader. We must hear Sir Epicure Mammon unfold the vision of splendours and debauchery, in which he means to plunge, when he has learned to make gold. The refined and unchecked impurities of the Roman decadence, the splendid obscenities of Heliogabalus, the gigantic fancies of luxury and lewdness, tables of gold spread with foreign dainties, draughts of dissolved pearls, nature devastated to provide a single dish, the many crimes committed by sensuality against nature, reason, and justice, the delight in defying and

---

[1] *The Devil is an Ass.*

outraging law,—all these images pass before the eyes with the dash of a torrent and the force of a great river. Phrase follows phrase without intermission, ideas and facts crowd into the dialogue to paint a situation, to give clearness to a character, produced from this deep memory, directed by this solid logic, launched by this powerful reflection. It is a pleasure to see him advance weighted with so many observations and recollections, loaded with technical details and learned reminiscences, without deviation or pause, a genuine literary Leviathan, like the war elephants which used to bear towers, men, weapons, machines, on their backs, and ran as swiftly with their freight as a nimble steed.

In the great dash of this heavy attempt, he finds a path which suits him. He has his style. Classical erudition and education made him a classic, and he writes like his Greek models and his Roman masters. The more we study the Latin races and literatures in contrast with the Teutonic, the more fully we become convinced that the proper and distinctive gift of the first is the art of development, that is, of drawing up ideas in continuous rows, according to the rules of rhetoric and eloquence, by studied transitions, with regular progress, without shock or bounds. Jonson received from his acquaintance with the ancients the habit of decomposing ideas, unfolding them bit by bit in natural order, making himself understood and believed. From the first thought to the final conclusion, he conducts the reader by a continuous and uniform ascent. The track never fails with him as with Shakspeare. He does not advance like the rest by abrupt intuitions, but by consecutive deductions; we can walk with him without need of bounding, and we are continually kept upon the straight path: antithesis of words unfolds antithesis of thoughts; symmetrical phrases guide the mind through difficult ideas; they are like barriers set on either side of the road to prevent our falling into the ditch. We do not meet on our way extraordinary, sudden, gorgeous images, which might dazzle or delay us; we travel on, enlightened by moderate and sustained metaphors. Jonson has all the methods of Latin art; even, when he wishes it, especially on Latin subjects, he has the last and most erudite, the brilliant conciseness of Seneca and Lucan, the squared equipoised, filed off antithesis, the most happy and studied artifices of oratorical architecture.[1] Other poets are nearly visionaries; Jonson is almost a logician.

Hence his talent, his successes, and his faults: if he has a better style and better plots than the others, he is not, like them, a creator of souls. He is too much of a theorist, too preoccupied by rules. His argumentative habits spoil him when he seeks to shape and motion complete and living men. No one is capable of fashioning these unless he possesses, like Shakspeare, the imagination of a seer. The human being is so complex that the logician who perceives his different elements in succession can hardly study them all, much less gather them all in one flash, so as to produce the dramatic response or action in which they are concentrated and which should manifest them. To discover such actions and responses, we need a kind of inspiration and fever. Then the mind works as in a dream. The characters move within the poet, almost involuntarily: he waits for them to speak, he remains motionless, hearing their voices, wholly wrapt in contemplation, in

[1] *Sejanus, Catilina, passim.*

order that he may not disturb the inner drama which they are about to act in his soul. That is his artifice: to let them alone. He is quite astonished at their discourse; as he observes them, he forgets that it is he who invents them. Their mood, character, education, disposition of mind, situation, attitude, and actions, form within him so well-connected a whole, and so readily unite into palpable and solid beings, that he dares not attribute to his reflection or reasoning a creation so vast and speedy. Beings are organised in him as in nature, that is, of themselves, and by a force which the combinations of his art could not replace.[1] Jonson has nothing wherewith to replace it but these combinations of art. He chooses a general idea—cunning, folly, severity—and makes a person out of it. This person is called Crites, Asper, Sordido, Deliro, Pecunia, Subtil, and the transparent name indicates the logical process which produced it. The poet took an abstract quality, and putting together all the actions to which it may give rise, trots it out on the stage in a man's dress. His characters, like those of la Bruyère and Theophrastus, were hammered out of solid deductions. Now it is a vice selected from the catalogue of moral philosophy, sensuality thirsting for gold: this perverse double inclination becomes a personage, Sir Epicure Mammon; before the alchemist, before the famulus, before his friend, before his mistress, in public or alone, all his words denote a greed of pleasure and of gold, and they express nothing more.[2] Now it is a mania

---

[1] Alfred de Musset, preface to *La Coupe et les Lèvres*. Plato: *Ion*.
[2] Compare Sir Epicure Mammon with Baron Hulot from Balzac's *Cousine Bette*. Balzac, who is learned like Jonson, creates real beings like Shakspeare.

gathered from the old sophists, a babbling with horror of noise; this form of mental pathology becomes a personage, Morose; the poet has the air of a doctor who has undertaken to record exactly all the desires of speech, all the necessities of silence, and to record nothing else. Now he picks out a ridicule, an affectation, a species of folly, from the manners of the dandies and the courtiers; a mode of swearing, an extravagant style, a habit of gesticulating, or any other oddity contracted by vanity or fashion. The hero whom he covers with these eccentricities, is overloaded by them. He disappears beneath his enormous trappings; he drags them about with him everywhere; he cannot get rid of them for an instant. We no longer see the man under the dress; he is like a mannikin, oppressed under a cloak, too heavy for him. Sometimes, doubtless, his habits of geometrical construction produce personages almost life-like. Bobadil, the grave boaster; Captain Tucca, the begging bully, inventive buffoon, ridiculous talker; Amorphus the traveller, a pedantic doctor of good manners, laden with eccentric phrases, create as much illusion as we can wish; but it is because they are flitting comicalities and low characters. It is not necessary for a poet to study such creatures; it is enough that he discovers in them three or four leading features; it is of little consequence if they always present themselves with the same attitudes; they produce laughter, like the *Countess d'Escarbagnas* or any of the *Fâcheux* in Molière; we want nothing else of them. On the contrary, the others weary and repel us. They are stage-masks, not living figures. Having acquired a fixed expression, they persist to the end of the piece in their unvarying grimace or their eternal frown. A man is not an abstract passion. He stamps the vices and virtues which he possesses with his individual mark. These vices and virtues receive, on entering into him, a bent and form which they have not in others. No one is unmixed sensuality. Take a thousand sensualists, and you will find a thousand different modes of sensuality; for there are a thousand paths, a thousand circumstances and degrees, in sensuality. If Jonson wanted to make Sir Epicure Mammon a real being, he should have given him the kind of disposition, the species of education, the manner of imagination, which produce sensuality. When we wish to construct a man, we must dig down to the foundations of mankind; that is, we must define to ourselves the structure of his bodily machine, and the primitive gait of his mind. Jonson has not dug sufficiently deep, and his constructions are incomplete; he has built on the surface, and he has built but a single story. He was not acquainted with the whole man, and he ignored man's basis; he put on the stage and gave a representation of moral treatises, fragments of history, scraps of satire; he did not stamp new beings on the imagination of mankind.

He possesses all other gifts, and in particular the classical; first of all, the talent for composition. For the first time we see a connected, well-contrived plot, a complete intrigue, with its beginning, middle, and end, subordinate actions well arranged, well combined; an interest which grows and never flags; a leading truth which all the events tend to demonstrate; a ruling idea which all the characters unite to illustrate; in short, an art like that which Molière and Racine were about to apply and teach. He does not, like Shak speare, take a novel from Greene, a chronicle from Holinshed, a life from Plutarch, such as they are, to cut them into scenes, irrespective of likelihood, indifferent as to order and unity, caring only to set up men, at times wandering into poetic reveries, at need finishing up the piece abruptly with a recognition or a butchery. He governs himself and his characters; he wills and he knows all that they do, and all that he does. But beyond his habits of Latin regularity, he possesses the great faculty of his age and race,—the sentiment of nature and existence, the exact knowledge of precise detail, the power in frankly and boldly handling frank passions. This gift is not wanting in any writer of the time; they do not fear words that are true, shocking, and striking details of the bedchamber or medical study; the prudery of modern England and the refinement of monarchical France veil not the nudity of their figures, or dim the colouring of their pictures. They live freely, amply, amidst living things; they see the ins and outs of lust raging without any feeling of shame, hypocrisy, or palliation; and they exhibit it as they see it, Jonson as boldly as the rest, occasionally more boldly than the rest, strengthened as he is by the vigour and ruggedness of his athletic temperament, by the extraordinary exactness and abundance of his observations and his knowledge. Add also his moral loftiness, his asperity, his powerful chiding wrath, exasperated and bitter against vice, his will strengthened by pride and by conscience:

> " With an armed and resolved hand,
> I'll strip the ragged follies of the time
> Naked as at their birth . . . and with a whip of steel,
> Print wounding lashes in their iron ribs.

> I fear no mood stampt in a private brow,
> When I am pleas'd t' unmask a public vice.
> I fear no strumpet's drugs, nor ruffian's stab,
> Should I detect their hateful luxuries;"[1]

above all, a scorn of base compliance, an open disdain for

> "Those jaded wits
> That run a broken pace for common hire,"—[2]

an enthusiasm, or deep love of

> "A happy muse,
> Borne on the wings of her immortal thought,
> That kicks at earth with a disdainful heel,
> And beats at heaven gates with her bright hoofs."[3]

Such are the energies which he brought to the drama and to comedy; they were great enough to ensure him a high and separate position.

III.

For whatever Jonson undertakes, whatever be his faults, haughtiness, rough-handling, predilection for morality and the past, antiquarian and censorious instincts, he is never little or dull. It signifies nothing that in his Latinised tragedies, *Sejanus, Catiline,* he is fettered by the worship of the old worn models of the Roman decadence; nothing that he plays the scholar, manufactures Ciceronian harangues, hauls in choruses imitated from Seneca, holds forth in the style of Lucan and the rhetors of the empire; he more than once attains a genuine accent; through his pedantry, heaviness, literary adoration of the ancients, nature forces its

---

[1] *Every Man out of his Humour,* Prologue.
[2] *Poetaster,* i. 1. [3] *Ibid.*

way; he lights, at his first attempt, on the crudities, horrors, gigantic lewdness, shameless depravity of imperial Rome; he takes in hand and sets in motion the lusts and ferocities, the passions of courtesans and princesses, the daring of assassins and of great men, which produced Messalina, Agrippina, Catiline, Tiberius.[1] In the Rome which he places before us we go boldly and straight to the end; justice and pity oppose no barriers. Amid these customs of victors and slaves, human nature is upset; corruption and villany are held as proofs of insight and energy. Observe how, in *Sejanus*, assassination is plotted and carried out with marvellous coolness. Livia discusses with Sejanus the methods of poisoning her husband, in a clear style, without circumlocution, as if the subject were how to gain a lawsuit or to serve up a dinner. There are no equivocations, no hesitation, no remorse in the Rome of Tiberius. Glory and virtue consist in power; scruples are for base minds; the mark of a lofty heart is to desire all and to dare all. Macro says rightly:

"Men's fortune there is virtue; reason their will;
Their license, law; and their obscrvance, skill.
Occasion is their foil; conscience, their stain;
Profit, their lustre; and what else is, vain."[2]

Sejanus addresses Livia thus:

"Royal lady, . . .
Yet, now I see your wisdom, judgment, strength,
Quickness, and will, to apprehend the means
To your own good and greatness, I protest
Myself through rarified, and turn'd all flame
In your affection."[3]

[1] See the second Act of *Catiline*.
[2] *The Fall of Sejanus*, iii. last Scene.   [3] *Ibid.* ii.

These are the loves of the wolf and his mate; he praises her for being so ready to kill. And observe in one moment the morals of a prostitute appear behind the manners of the poisoner. Sejanus goes out, and immediately, like a courtesan, Livia turns to her physician, saying:

" How do I look to-day ?

 Eudemus. Excellent clear, believe it. This same fucus
Was well laid on.
 Livia.   Methinks 'tis here not white.
 E. Lend me your scarlet, lady. 'Tis the sun
Hath giv'n some little taint unto the ceruse,
You should have us'd of the white oil I gave you.
Sejanus, for your love ! His very name
Commandeth above Cupid or his shafts. . . .
         [*Paints her cheeks.*]
    " Tis now well, lady, you should
Use of the dentifrice I prescrib'd you too,
To clear your teeth, and the prepar'd pomatum,
To smooth the skin. A lady cannot be
Too curious of her form, that still would hold
The heart of such a person, made her captive,
As you have his : who, to endear him more
In your clear eye, hath put away his wife . . .
Fair Apicata, and made spacious room
To your new pleasures.
 L.   Have not we return'd
That with our hate to Drusus, and discovery
Of all his counsels ? . . .
 E. When will you take some physic, lady ?
 L.   When
I shall, Eudemus : but let Drusus' drug
Be first prepar'd.
 E. Were Lygdus made, that's done. . .
I'll send you a perfume, first to resolve

> And procure sweat, and then prepare a bath
> To cleanse and clear the cutis; against when
> I'll have an excellent new fucus made
> Resistive 'gainst the sun, the rain or wind,
> Which you shall lay on with a breath or oil,
> As you best like, and last some fourteen hours.
> This change came timely, lady, for your health." [1]

He ends by congratulating her on her approaching change of husbands; Drusus was injuring her complexion; Sejanus is far preferable; a physiological and practical conclusion. The Roman apothecary kept on the same shelf his medicine-chest, his chest of cosmetics, and his box of poisons.[2]

After this we find one after another all the scenes of Roman life unfolded, the bargain of murder, the comedy of justice, the shamelessness of flattery, the anguish and vacillation of the senate. When Sejanus wishes to buy a conscience, he questions, jokes, plays round the offer he is about to make, throws it out as if in pleasantry, so as to be able to withdraw it, if need be; then, when the intelligent look of the rascal, whom he is trafficking with, shows that he is understood:

> "Protest not,
> Thy looks are vows to me. . . .
> Thou art a man, made to make consuls. Go." [3]

Elsewhere, the senator Latiaris in his own house storms before his friend Sabinus, against tyranny, openly expresses a desire for liberty, provoking him to speak.

---

[1] *The Fall of Sejanus*, ii.
[2] See *Catiline*, Act ii.; a very fine scene, no less plain spoken and animated, on the dissipation of the higher ranks in Rome.
[3] *The Fall of Sejanus*, i.

Then two spies who were hid "between the roof and ceiling," cast themselves on Sabinus, crying, "Treason to Cæsar!" and drag him, with his face covered, before the tribunal, thence to "be thrown upon the Gemonies."[1] So, when the senate is assembled, Tiberius has chosen beforehand the accusers of Silius, and their parts distributed to them. They mumble in a corner, whilst aloud is heard, in the emperor's presence:

> "Cæsar,
> Live long and happy, great and royal Cæsar;
> The gods preserve thee and thy modesty,
> Thy wisdom and thy innocence. . . .
>   Guard
> His meekness, Jove, his piety, his care,
> His bounty."[2]

Then the herald cites the accused; Varro, the consul, pronounces the indictment; Afer hurls upon them his bloodthirsty eloquence: the senators get excited; we see laid bare, as in Tacitus and Juvenal, the depths of Roman servility, hypocrisy, insensibility, the venomous craft of Tiberius. At last, after so many others, the turn of Sejanus comes. The fathers anxiously assemble in the temple of Apollo; for some days past Tiberius has seemed to be trying to contradict himself; one day he appoints the friends of his favourite to high places, and the next day sets his enemies in eminent positions. The senators mark the face of Sejanus, and know not what to anticipate; Sejanus is troubled, then after a moment's cringing is more arrogant than ever. The plots are confused, the rumours contradictory. Macro alone is in the confidence of Tiberius, and soldiers are

---

[1] *The Fall of Sejanus*, iv.   [2] *Ibid.* iii.

seen, drawn up at the porch of the temple, ready to enter at the slightest commotion. The formula of convocation is read, and the council marks the names of those who do not respond to the summons; then Regulus addresses them, and announces that Cæsar

> " Propounds to this grave senate, the bestowing
> Upon the man he loves, honour'd Sejanus,
> The tribunitial dignity and power :
> Here are his letters, signed with his signet.
> What pleaseth now the Fathers to be done ? "
>   " *Senators.* Read, read them, open, publicly read them.
>   *Cotta.* Cæsar hath honour'd his own greatness much
> In thinking of this act.
>   *Trio.*   It was a thought
> Happy, and worthy Cæsar.
>   *Latiaris.*   And the lord
> As worthy it, on whom it is directed !
>   *Haterius.* Most worthy !
>   *Sanquinius.* Rome did never boast the virtue
> That could give envy bounds, but his : Sejanus—
>   1*st Sen.* Honour'd and noble !
>   2*d Sen.* Good and great Sejanus !
>   *Præcones.* Silence ! " [1]

Tiberius' letter is read. First, long obscure and vague phrases, mingled with indirect protestations and accusations, foreboding something and revealing nothing. Suddenly comes an insinuation against Sejanus. The fathers are alarmed, but the next line reassures them. A word or two further on, the same insinuation is repeated with greater exactness. "Some there be that would interpret this his public severity to be particular ambition; and that, under a pretext of service to

[1] *The Fall of Sejanus,* v.

us, he doth but remove his own lets: alleging the strengths he hath made to himself, by the prætorian soldiers, by his faction in court and senate, by the offices he holds himself, and confers on others, his popularity and dependents, his urging (and almost driving) us to this our unwilling retirement, and lastly, his aspiring to be our son-in-law." The fathers rise: "This is strange!" Their eager eyes are fixed on the letter, on Sejanus, who perspires and grows pale; their thoughts are busy with conjectures, and the words of the letter fall one by one, amidst a sepulchral silence, caught up as they fall with all devouring and attentive eagerness. The senators anxiously weigh the value of these shifty expressions, fearing to compromise themselves with the favourite or with the prince, all feeling that they must understand, if they value their lives.

"'*Your wisdoms, conscript fathers, are able to examine, and censure these suggestions. But, were they left to our absolving voice, we durst pronounce them, as we think them, most malicious.*'

Senator. O, he has restor'd all; list.

Præco. '*Yet are they offered to be averr'd, and on the lives of the informers.*'"[1]

At this word the letter becomes menacing. Those next Sejanus forsake him. "Sit farther. . . . Let's remove!" The heavy Sanquinius leaps panting over the benches. The soldiers come in; then Macro. And now, at last, the letter orders the arrest of Sejanus.

"*Regulus.* Take him hence;
And all the gods guard Cæsar!
　Trio. Take him hence.
　Haterius. Hence.

[1] *The Fall of Sejanus.* v.

Cotta. To the dungeon with him.
Sanquinius. He deserves it.
Senator. Crown all our doors with bays.
San. And let an ox,
  With gilded horns and garlands, straight be led
  Unto the Capitol.
Hat. And sacrific'd
  To Jove, for Cæsar's safety.
Tri. All our gods
  Be present still to Cæsar ! . . .
Cot. Let all the traitor's titles be defac'd.
Tri. His images and statues be pull'd down. . . .
Sen. Liberty, liberty, liberty ! Lead on,
  And praise to Macro that hath saved Rome !" [1]

It is the baying of a furious pack of hounds, let loose at last on him, under whose hand they had crouched, and who had for a long time beaten and bruised them. Jonson discovered in his own energetic soul the energy of these Roman passions; and the clearness of his mind, added to his profound knowledge, powerless to construct characters, furnished him with general ideas and striking incidents, which suffice to depict manners.

IV.

Moreover, it was to this that he turned his talent. Nearly all his work consists of comedies, not sentimental and fanciful as Shakspeare's, but imitative and satirical, written to represent and correct follies and vices. He introduced a new model; he had a doctrine; his masters were Terence and Plautus. He observes the unity of time and place, almost exactly. He ridicules the authors who, in the same play,

[1] *The Fall of Sejanus,* v.

> "Make a child now swaddled, to proceed
> Man, and then shoot up, in one beard and weed,
> Past threescore years ; or, with three rusty swords,
> And help of some few foot and half-foot words,
> Fight over York and Lancaster's long jars. . . .
> He rather prays you will be pleas'd to see."[1]

He wishes to represent on the stage

> "One such to-day, as other plays shou'd be ;
> Where neither chorus wafts you o'er the seas,
> Nor creaking throne comes down the boys to please :
> Nor nimble squib is seen to make afeard
> The gentlewomen. . . .
> But deeds, and language, such as men do use. . . .
> You, that have so grac'd monsters, may like men."[2]

Men, as we see them in the streets, with their whims and humours—

> "When some one peculiar quality
> Doth so possess a man, that it doth draw
> All his affects, his spirits, and his powers
> In their confluctions, all to run one way,
> This may be truly said to be a humour."[3]

It is these humours which he exposes to the light, not with the artist's curiosity, but with the moralist's hate.

> "I will scourge those apes,
> And to these courteous eyes oppose a mirror,
> As large as is the stage whereon we act ;
> Where they shall see the time's deformity
> Anatomized in every nerve, and sinew,
> With constant courage, and contempt of fear. . . .
>   My strict hand
> Was made to seize on vice, and with a gripe

---

[1] *Every Man in his Humour*, Prologue.
[2] *Ibid.*   [3] *Ibid.*

> Squeeze out the humour of such spongy souls,
> As lick up every idle vanity."[1]

Doubtless a determination so strong and decided does violence to the dramatic spirit. Jonson's comedies are not rarely harsh; his characters are too grotesque, laboriously constructed, mere automatons; the poet thought less of producing living beings than of scotching a vice; the scenes get arranged, or are confused together in a mechanical manner; we see the process, we feel the satirical intention throughout; delicate and easy-flowing imitation is absent, as well as the graceful fancy which abounds in Shakspeare. But if Jonson comes across harsh passions, visibly evil and vile, he will derive from his energy and wrath the talent to render them odious and visible, and will produce a *Volpone*, a sublime work, the sharpest picture of the manners of the age, in which is displayed the full brightness of evil lusts, in which lewdness, cruelty, love of gold, shamelessness of vice, display a sinister yet splendid poetry, worthy of one of Titian's bacchanals.[2] All this makes itself apparent in the first scene, when Volpone says:

> " Good morning to the day; and next, my gold !——
> Open the shrine, that I may see my saint."

This saint is his piles of gold, jewels, precious plate:

> " Hail the world's soul, and mine ! . . . O thou son of Sol,
> But brighter than thy father, let me kiss,
> With adoration, thee, and every relick
> Of sacred treasure in this blessed room."[3]

[1] *Every Man out of his Humour*, Prologue.
[2] Compare *Volpone* with Regnard's *Légataire*; the end of the sixteenth with the beginning of the eighteenth century.
[3] *Volpone*, i. 1.

Presently after, the dwarf, the eunuch, and the hermaphrodite of the house sing a sort of pagan and fantastic interlude; they chant in strange verses the metamorphoses of the hermaphrodite, who was first the soul of Pythagoras. We are at Venice, in the palace of the magnifico Volpone. These deformed creatures, the splendour of gold, this strange and poetical buffoonery, carry the thought immediately to the sensual city, queen of vices and of arts.

The rich Volpone lives like an ancient Greek or Roman. Childless and without relatives, playing the invalid, he makes all his flatterers hope to be his heir, receives their gifts,

> "Letting the cherry knock against their lips,
> And draw it by their mouths, and back again." [1]

Glad to have their gold, but still more glad to deceive them, artistic in wickedness as in avarice, and just as pleased to look at a contortion of suffering as at the sparkle of a ruby.

The advocate Voltore arrives, bearing a "huge piece of plate." Volpone throws himself on his bed, wraps himself in furs, heaps up his pillows, and coughs as if at the point of death:

> "*Volpone.* I thank you, signior Voltore,
> Where is the plate? mine eyes are bad. . . . Your love
> Hath taste in this, and shall not be unanswer'd . . .
> I cannot now last long. . . I feel me going,—
> Uh, uh, uh, uh!" [2]

He closes his eyes, as though exhausted:

[1] *Volpone*, i. 1.   [2] *Ibid.* i. 3.

"*Voltore.* Am I inscrib'd his heir for certain?
   Mosca (*Volpone's Parasite*).   Are you!
I do beseech you, sir, you will vouchsafe
To write me in your family. All my hopes
Depend upon your worship: I am lost,
Except the rising sun do shine on me.
   Volt. It shall both shine and warm thee, Mosca.
   M.   Sir,
I am man, that hath not done your love
All the worst offices: here I wear your keys,
See all your coffers and your caskets lock'd,
Keep the poor inventory of your jewels,
Your plate and monies; am your steward, sir,
Husband your goods here.
   Volt. But am I sole heir?
   M. Without a partner, sir; confirm'd this morning:
The wax is warm yet, and the ink scarce dry
Upon the parchment.
   Volt.   Happy, happy, me!
By what good chance, sweet Mosca?
   M.   Your desert, sir;
I know no second cause."[1]

And he details the abundance of the wealth in which Voltore is about to revel, the gold which is to pour upon him, the opulence which is to flow in his house as a river:

"When will you have your inventory brought, sir?
  Or see a copy of the will?"

The imagination is fed with precise words, precise details. Thus, one after another, the would-be heirs come like beasts of prey. The second who arrives is an old miser, Corbaccio, deaf, "impotent," almost dying,

---

[1] *Volpone*, i. 3.

who nevertheless hopes to survive Volpone. To make more sure of it, he would fain have Mosca give his master a narcotic. He has it about him, this excellent opiate: he has had it prepared under his own eyes, he suggests it. His joy on finding Volpone more ill than himself is bitterly humorous:

"*Corbaccio.* How does your patron? . . .
 Mosca.   His mouth
Is ever gaping, and his eyelids hang.
 C. Good.
 M. A freezing numbness stiffens all his joints,
And makes the colour of his flesh like lead.
 C. 'Tis good.
 M. His pulse beats slow, and dull.
 C.   Good symptoms still.
 M. And from his brain—
 C.   I conceive you; good.
 M. Flows a cold sweat, with a continual rheum,
Forth the resolved corners of his eyes.
 C. Is't possible? Yet I am better, ha!
How does he, with the swimming of his head?
 M. O, sir, 'tis past the scotomy; he now
Hath lost his feeling, and hath left to snort:
You hardly can perceive him, that he breathes.
 C. Excellent, excellent! sure I shall outlast him:
This makes me young again, a score of years."[1]

If you would be his heir, says Mosca, the moment is favourable; but you must not let yourself be forestalled. Voltore has been here, and presented him with this piece of plate:

"*C.*   See, Mosca, look,
Here, I have brought a bag of bright chequines,
Will quite weigh down his plate. . . .

[1] *Volpone*, i. 4.

M. Now, would I counsel you, make home with speed;
There, frame a will; whereto you shall inscribe
My master your sole heir. . . .
    C.   This plot
Did I think on before. . . .
    M. And you so certain to survive him—
    C.   Ay.
    M. Being so lusty a man—
    C.   'Tis true." [1]

And the old man hobbles away, not hearing the insults and ridicule thrown at him, he is so deaf.

When he is gone the merchant Corvino arrives, bringing an orient pearl and a splendid diamond:

" *Corvino.* Am I his heir?
    Mosca. Sir, I am sworn, I may not show the will
Till he be dead; but here has been Corbaccio,
Here has been Voltore, here were others too,
I cannot number 'em, they were so many;
All gaping here for legacies : but I,
Taking the vantage of his naming you,
Signior Corvino, Signior Corvino, took
Paper, and pen, and ink, and there I asked him,
Whom he would have his heir? *Corvino.* Who
Should be executor? *Corvino.* And,
To any question he was silent to,
I still interpreted the nods he made,
Through weakness, for consent : and sent home th' others,
Nothing bequeath'd them, but to cry and curse.
    Cor. O my dear Mosca ! . . . Has he children?
    M. Bastards,
Some dozen, or more, that he begot on beggars,
Gypsies, and Jews, and black-moors, when he was drunk. . . .

[1] *Volpone*, i. 4.

> Speak out:
> You may be louder yet. . . .
> Faith, I could stifle him rarely with a pillow,
> As well as any woman that should keep him.
>   *C.* Do as you will; but I'll begone." [1]

Corvino presently departs; for the passions of the time have all the beauty of frankness. And Volpone, casting aside his sick man's garb, cries:

> "My divine Mosca!
> Thou hast to-day out gone thyself. . . . Prepare
> Me music, dances, banquets, all delights;
> The Turk is not more sensual in his pleasures,
> Than will Volpone." [2]

On this invitation, Mosca draws a most voluptuous portrait of Corvino's wife, Celia. Smitten with a sudden desire, Volpone dresses himself as a mountebank, and goes singing under her windows with all the sprightliness of a quack; for he is naturally a comedian, like a true Italian, of the same family as Scaramouch, as good an actor in the public square as in his house. Having once seen Celia, he resolves to obtain her at any price:

> "Mosca, take my keys,
> Gold, plate, and jewels, all's at thy devotion;
> Employ them how thou wilt; nay, coin me too:
> So thou, in this, but crown my longings, Mosca." [3]

Mosca then tells Corvino that some quack's oil has cured his master, and that they are looking for a

---

[1] *Volpone*, i. 5.   [2] *Ibid.*   [3] *Ibid.* ii. 2.

"young woman, lusty and full of juice," to complete the cure:

"Have you no kinswoman?
Odso—Think, think, think, think, think, think, think, sir.
One o' the doctors offer'd there his daughter.
Corvino. How!
Mosca.　　　　Yes, signior Lupo, the physician.
C. His daughter!
M.　　　　　　And a virgin, sir. . . .
C.　　　　　　Wretch!
Covetous wretch."[1]

Though unreasonably jealous, Corvino is gradually induced to offer his wife. He has given too much already, and would not lose his advantage. He is like a half-ruined gamester, who with a shaking hand throws on the green cloth the remainder of his fortune. He brings the poor sweet woman, weeping and resisting. Excited by his own hidden pangs, he becomes furious:

"Be damn'd!
Heart, I will drag thee hence, home, by the hair;
Cry thee a strumpet through the streets; rip up
Thy mouth unto thine ears; and slit thy nose;
Like a raw rochet!—Do not tempt me; come,
Yield, I am loth—Death! I will buy some slave
Whom I will kill, and bind thee to him, alive;
And at my window hang you forth, devising
Some monstrous crime, which I, in capital letters,
Will eat into thy flesh with aquafortis,
And burning corsives, on this stubborn breast.
Now, by the blood thou hast incensed, I'll do it!
Celia. Sir, what you please, you may, I am your martyr.
Corvino. Be not thus obstinate, I have not deserv'd it:

[1] *Volpone*, ii. 2.

Think who it is intreats you. Prithee, sweet ;—
Good faith thou shalt have jewels, gowns, attires,
What thou wilt think, and ask. Do but go kiss him,
Or touch him, but. For my sake.—At my suit.—
This once.—No! not! I shall remember this.
Will you disgrace me thus? Do you thirst my undoing?" [1]

Mosca turned a moment before, to Volpone:

"Sir,
Signior Corvino . . . hearing of the consultation had
So lately, for your health, is come to offer,
Or rather, sir, to prostitute.—
Corvino.   Thanks, sweet Mosca.
Mosca. Freely, unask'd, or unintreated.
C.   Well.
Mosca. As the true fervent instance of his love,
His own most fair and proper wife; the beauty
Only of price in Venice.—
C.   'Tis well urg'd." [2]

Where can we see such blows launched and driven hard, full in the face, by the violent hand of satire? Celia is alone with Volpone, who, throwing off his feigned sickness, comes upon her, "as fresh, as hot, as high, and in as jovial plight," as on the gala-days of the Republic, when he acted the part of the lovely Antinous. In his transport he sings a love song; his voluptuousness culminates in poetry; for poetry was then in Italy the blossom of vice. He spreads before her pearls, diamonds, carbuncles. He is in raptures at the sight of the treasures, which he displays and sparkles before her eyes:

---

[1] *Volpone*, iii. 5. We pray the reader to pardon us for Ben Jonson's broadness. If I omit it, I cannot depict the sixteenth century. Grant the same indulgence to the historian as to the anatomist.

[2] *Volpone*, iii.

"Take these,
And wear, and lose them: yet remains an ear-ring
To purchase them again, and this whole state.
A gem but worth a private patrimony,
Is nothing: we will eat such at a meal,
The heads of parrots, tongues of nightingales,
The brains of peacocks, and of estriches,
Shall be our food. . . .
   Conscience? 'Tis the beggar's virtue. . . .
Thy baths shall be the juice of July flowers,
Spirit of roses, and of violets,
The milk of unicorns, and panthers' breath
Gather'd in bags, and mixt with Cretan wines.
Our drink shall be prepared gold and amber;
Which we will take, until my roof whirl round
With the vertigo: and my dwarf shall dance,
My eunuch sing, my fool make up the antic,
Whilst we, in changed shapes, act Ovid's tales,
Thou, like Europa now, and I like Jove,
Then I like Mars, and thou like Erycine;
So, of the rest, till we have quite run through,
And wearied all the fables of the gods." [1]

We recognise Venice in this splendour of debauchery —Venice, the throne of Aretinus, the country of Tintoretto and Giorgione. Volpone seizes Celia: "Yield, or I'll force thee!" But suddenly Bonario, disinherited son of Corbaccio, whom Mosca had concealed there with another design, enters violently, delivers her, wounds Mosca, and accuses Volpone before the tribunal, of imposture and rape.

The three rascals who aim at being his heirs, work together to save Volpone. Corbaccio disavows his son,

[1] *Volpone*, iii. 5.

and accuses him of parricide. Corvino declares his wife an adulteress, the shameless mistress of Bonario. Never on the stage was seen such energy of lying, such open villany. The husband, who knows his wife to be innocent, is the most eager:

> " This woman (please your fatherhoods) is a whore,
> Of most hot exercise, more than a partrich,
> Upon record.
>   1*st Advocate.* No more.
>   *Corvino.* Neighs like a jennet.
>   *Notary.* Preserve the honour of the court.
>   *C.*   I shall,
> And modesty of your most reverend ears.
> And yet I hope that I may say, these eyes
> Have seen her glued unto that piece of cedar,
> That fine well-timber'd gallant; and that here
> The letters may be read, thorough the horn,
> That make the story perfect. . . .
>   3*d Adv.* His grief hath made him frantic. (*Celia swoons.*)
>   *C.* Rare! Prettily feign'd! again!"[1]

They have Volpone brought in, like a dying man; manufacture false " testimony," to which Voltore gives weight with his advocate's tongue, with words worth a sequin apiece. They throw Celia and Bonario into prison, and Volpone is saved. This public imposture is for him only another comedy, a pleasant pastime, and a masterpiece.

> " *Mosca.* To gull the court.
>   *Volpone.* And quite divert the torrent
> Upon the innocent. . . .
>   *M.* You are not taken with it enough, methinks.
>   *V.* O, more than if I had enjoy'd the wench?"[2]

---

[1] *Volpone,* iv. 1.   [2] *Ibid.* v. 1.

To conclude, he writes a will in Mosca's favour, has his death reported, hides behind a curtain, and enjoys the looks of the would-be heirs. They had just saved him from being thrown into prison, which makes the fun all the better; the wickedness will be all the greater and more exquisite. "Torture 'em rarely," Volpone says to Mosca. The latter spreads the will on the table, and reads the inventory aloud. "Turkey carpets nine. Two cabinets, one of ebony, the other mother-of-pearl. A perfum'd box, made of an onyx." The heirs are stupefied with disappointment, and Mosca drives them off with insults. He says to Corvino:

" Why should you stay here? with what thought, what promise?
  Hear you; do you not know, I know you an ass,
  And that you would most fain have been a wittol,
  If fortune would have let you? That you are
  A declar'd cuckold, on good terms? This pearl,
  You'll say, was yours? Right: this diamond?
  I'll not deny't, but thank you. Much here else?
  It may be so. Why, think that these good works
  May help to hide your bad. [*Exit Corvino.*] . . .
     Corbaccio. I am cozen'd, cheated, by a parasite slave;
  Harlot, thou hast gull'd me.
     Mosca.   Yes, sir. Stop your mouth,
  Or I shall draw the only tooth is left.
  Are not you he, that filthy covetous wretch,
  With the three legs, that here, in hope of prey,
  Have, any time this three years, snufft about,
  With your most grov'ling nose, and would have hir'd
  Me to the pois'ning of my patron, sir?
  Are not you he that have to-day in court
  Profess'd the disinheriting of your son?
  Perjur'd yourself? Go home, and die, and stink."[1]

[1] *Volpone*, v. 1.

Volpone goes out disguised, comes to each of them in turn, and succeeds in wringing their hearts. But Mosca, who has the will, acts with a high hand, and demands of Volpone half his fortune. The dispute between the two rascals discovers their impostures, and the master, the servant, with the three would-be heirs, are sent to the galleys, to prison, to the pillory—as Corvino says, to

> "Have mine eyes beat out with stinking fish,
> Bruis'd fruit, and rotten eggs.—'Tis well. I'm glad,
> I shall not see my shame yet." [1]

No more vengeful comedy has been written, none more persistently athirst to make vice suffer, to unmask, triumph over, and punish it.

Where can be the gaiety of such a theatre? In caricature and farce. There is a rough gaiety, a sort of physical, external laughter which suits this combative, drinking, blustering mood. It is thus that this mood relaxes from war-waging and murderous satire; the pastime is appropriate to the manners of the time, excellent to attract men who look upon hanging as a good joke, and laugh to see the Puritan's ears cut. Put yourself for an instant in their place, and you will think like them, that *The Silent Woman* is a masterpiece. Morose is an old monomaniac, who has a horror of noise, but loves to speak. He inhabits a street so narrow that a carriage cannot enter it. He drives off with his stick the bear-leaders and sword-players, who venture to pass under his windows. He has sent away his servant whose shoes creaked; and Mute, the new one, wears slippers "soled with wool," and only speaks in a whisper

---

[1] *Volpone*, v. 8.

through a tube. Morose ends by forbidding the whisper, and makes him reply by signs. He is also rich, an uncle, and he ill-treats his nephew Sir Dauphine Eugenie, a man of wit, but who lacks money. We anticipate all the tortures which poor Morose is to suffer. Sir Dauphine finds him a supposed silent woman, the beautiful Epicœne. Morose, enchanted by her brief replies and her voice, which he can hardly hear, marries her, to play his nephew a trick. It is his nephew who has played him a trick. As soon as she is married, Epicœne speaks, scolds, argues as loud and as long as a dozen women:—" Why, did you think you had married a statue? or a motion only? one of the French puppets, with the eyes turn'd with a wire? or some innocent out of the hospital, that would stand with her hands thus, and a plaise mouth, and look upon you?"[1]

She orders the servants to speak louder; she opens the doors wide to her friends. They arrive in shoals, offering their noisy congratulations to Morose. Five or six women's tongues overwhelm him all at once with compliments, questions, advice, remonstrances. A friend of Sir Dauphine comes with a band of music, who play all together, suddenly, with their whole force. Morose says, " O, a plot, a plot, a plot, a plot, upon me! This day I shall be their anvil to work on, they will grate me asunder. 'Tis worse than the noise of a saw."[2] A procession of servants is seen coming, with dishes in their hands; it is the racket of a tavern which Sir Dauphine is bringing to his uncle. The guests clash the glasses, shout, drink healths; they have with them a drum and trumpets which make great noise. Morose flees to the top of the house, puts

[1] *Epicœne*, iii. 2.   [2] *Ibid.* iii. 2.

"a whole nest of night-caps" on his head and stuffs up his ears. Captain Otter cries, "Sound, Tritons o' the Thames! *Nunc est bibendum, nunc pede libero.*" "Villains, murderers, sons of the earth and traitors," cries Morose from above, "what do you there?" The racket increases. Then the captain, somewhat "jovial," maligns his wife, who falls upon him and gives him a good beating. Blows, cries, music, laughter, resound like thunder. It is the poetry of uproar. Here is a subject to shake coarse nerves, and to make the mighty chests of the companions of Drake and Essex shake with uncontrollable laughter. "Rogues, hell-hounds, Stentors! . . . They have rent my roof, walls, and all my windows asunder, with their brazen throats!" Morose casts himself on his tormentors with his long sword, breaks the instruments, drives away the musicians, disperses the guests amidst an inexpressible uproar, gnashing his teeth, looking haggard. Afterwards they pronounce him mad, and discuss his madness before him.[1] The disease in Greek is called μανία, in Latin *insania, furor, vel ecstasis melancholica* that is, *egressio*, when a man *ex melancholico evadit fanaticus.* . . . But he may be but *phreneticus* yet, mistress; and *phrenetis* is only *delirium,* or so." They talk of the books which he must read aloud to cure him. They add by way of consolation, that his wife talks in her sleep, "and snores like a porpoise." "O redeem me, fate; redeem me, fate!" cries the poor man.[2] "For how many causes may a man be divorc'd, nephew?" Sir Dauphine chooses two knaves, and disguises them, one as a priest, the other as a lawyer, who launch at his head Latin terms of civil and canon law, explain to Morose the twelve cases of nullity,

---

[1] Compare M. de Pourceaugnac in Molière.   [2] *Epicœne,* iv. 1, 2.

jingle in his ears one after another the most barbarous words in their obscure vocabulary, wrangle, and make between them as much noise as a couple of bells in a belfry. Following their advice he declares himself impotent. The wedding-guests propose to toss him in a blanket; others demand an immediate inspection. Fall after fall, shame after shame; nothing serves him; his wife declares that she consents to "take him with all his faults." The lawyer proposes another legal method; Morose shall obtain a divorce by proving that his wife is faithless. Two boasting knights, who are present, declare that they have been her lovers. Morose, in raptures, throws himself at their knees, and embraces them. Epicœne weeps, and Morose seems to be delivered. Suddenly the lawyer decides that the plan is of no avail, the infidelity having been committed before the marriage. "O, this is worst of all worst worsts that hell could have devis'd! marry a whore, and so much noise!" There is Morose then, declared impotent and a deceived husband, at his own request, in the eyes of the whole world, and moreover married for ever. Sir Dauphine comes in like a clever rascal, and as a succouring deity. "Allow me but five hundred during life, uncle," and I free you. Morose signs the deed of gift with alacrity; and his nephew shows him that Epicœne is a boy in disguise.[1] Add to this enchanting farce the funny parts of the two accomplished and gallant knights who, after having boasted of their bravery, receive gratefully, and before the ladies, flips and kicks.[2] Never was coarse physical laughter more adroitly produced.

[1] *Epicœne*, v.
[2] Compare Polichinelle in *Le Malade imaginaire*; Géronte in *Les Fourberies de Scapin*.

In this broad coarse gaiety, this excess of noisy transport, you recognise the stout roysterer, the stalwart drinker who swallowed hogsheads of Canary, and made the windows of the Mermaid shake with his bursts of humour.

V.

Jonson did not go beyond this; he was not a philosopher like Molière, able to grasp and dramatise the crisis of human life, education, marriage, sickness, the chief characters of his country and century, the courtier, the tradesman, the hypocrite, the man of the world.[1] He remained on a lower level, in the comedy of plot,[2] the painting of the grotesque,[3] the representation of too transient subjects of ridicule,[4] too general vices.[5] If at times, as in the *Alchemist*, he has succeeded by the perfection of plot and the vigour of satire, he has miscarried more frequently by the ponderousness of his work and the lack of comic lightness. The critic in him mars the artist; his literary calculations strip him of spontaneous invention; he is too much of a writer and moralist, not enough of a mimic and an actor. But he is loftier from another side, for he is a poet; almost all writers, prose-authors, preachers even, were so at the time we speak of. Fancy abounded, as well as the perception of colours and forms, the need and wont of enjoying through the imagination and the eyes. Many of Jonson's pieces, the *Staple of News*, *Cynthia's Revels*,

---

[1] Compare *l'Ecole des Femmes*, *Tartuffe*, *Le Misanthrope*, *Le Bourgeois-gentilhomme*, *Le Malade imaginaire*, *Georges Dandin*.
[2] Compare *les Fourberies de Scapin*.
[3] Compare *les Fâcheux*.
[4] Compare *les Précieuses Ridicules*.
[5] Compare the plays of Destouches.

are fanciful and allegorical comedies like those of Aristophanes. He there dallies with the real, and beyond the real, with characters who are but theatrical masks, abstractions personified, buffooneries, decorations, dances, music, pretty laughing whims of a picturesque and sentimental imagination. Thus, in *Cynthia's Revels*, three children come on " pleading possession of the cloke" of black velvet, which an actor usually wore when he spoke the prologue. They draw lots for it; one of the losers, in revenge, tells the audience beforehand the incidents of the piece. The others interrupt him at every sentence, put their hands on his mouth, and taking the cloak one after the other, begin to criticise the spectators and authors. This child's play, these gestures and loud voices, this little amusing dispute, divert the public from their serious thoughts, and prepare them for the oddities which they are to look upon.

We are in Greece, in the valley of Gargaphie, where Diana[1] has proclaimed "a solemn revels." Mercury and Cupid have come down, and begin by quarrelling; the latter says: "My light feather-heel'd coz, what are you any more than my uncle Jove's pander? a lacquey that runs on errands for him, and can whisper a light message to a loose wench with some round volubility? . . . One that sweeps the gods' drinking-room every morning, and sets the cushions in order again, which they threw one at another's head over night?"[2]

They are good-tempered gods. Echo, awoke by Mercury weeps for the " too beauteous boy Narcissus":

" That trophy of self-love, and spoil of nature,
  Who, now transformed into this drooping flower,

[1] By Diana, Queen Elizabeth is meant.   [2] *Cynthia's Revels*, i. 1.

> Hangs the repentant head, back from the stream. . . .
> Witness thy youth's dear sweets, here spent untasted,
> Like a fair taper, with his own flame wasted ! . . .
> And with thy water let this curse remain,
> As an inseparate plague, that who but taste
> A drop thereof, may, with the instant touch,
> Grow doatingly enamour'd on themselves." [1]

The courtiers and ladies drink thereof, and behold, a sort of a review of the follies of the time, arranged, as in Aristophanes, in an improbable farce, a brilliant show. A silly spendthrift, Asotus, wishes to become a man of the court and of fashionable manners; he takes for his master Amorphus, a learned traveller, expert in gallantry, who, to believe himself, is

> "An essence so sublimated and refined by travel . . . able . . . to speak the mere extraction of language; one that . . . was your first that ever enrich'd his country with the true laws of the duello; whose optics have drunk the spirit of beauty in some eight-score and eighteen princes' courts, where I have resided, and been there fortunate in the amours of three hundred forty and five ladies, all nobly if not princely descended, . . . in all so happy, as even admiration herself doth seem to fasten her kisses upon me." [2]

Asotus learns at this good school the language of the court, fortifies himself like other people with quibbles, learned oaths, and metaphors; he fires off in succession supersubtle tirades, and duly imitates the grimaces and tortuous style of his masters. Then, when he has drunk the water of the fountain, becoming suddenly pert and rash, he proposes to all comers a tournament of "court compliment." This odd tournament

---

[1] *Cynthia's Revels*, i. 1.   [2] *Ibid.*

is held before the ladies; it comprises four jousts, and at each the trumpets sound. The combatants perform in succession "the BARE ACCOST;" "the BETTER REGARD;" "the SOLEMN ADDRESS;" and "the PERFECT CLOSE."[1] In this grave buffoonery the courtiers are beaten. The severe Crites, the moralist of the play, copies their language, and pierces them with their own weapons. Already, with grand declamation, he had rebuked them thus:

> " O vanity,
> How are thy painted beauties doated on,
> By light, and empty idiots! how pursu'd
> With open and extended appetite!
> How they do sweat, and run themselves from breath,
> Rais'd on their toes, to catch thy airy forms,
> Still turning giddy, till they reel like drunkards,
> That buy the merry madness of one hour,
> With the long irksomeness of following time!"[2]

To complete the overthrow of the vices, appear two symbolical masques, representing the contrary virtues. They pass gravely before the spectators, in splendid array, and the noble verses exchanged by the goddess and her companions raise the mind to the lofty regions of serene morality, whither the poet desires to carry us:

> " Queen, and huntress, chaste and fair,
>   Now the sun is laid to sleep,
> Seated in thy silver chair,
>   State in wonted manner keep. . .
> Lay thy bow of pearl apart,
>   And thy crystal shining quiver;
> Give unto the flying hart
>   Space to breathe, how short soever."[3]

[1] *Cynthia's Revels*, v. 2.   [2] *Ibid.* i. 1.   [3] *Cynthia's Revels*, v. 3.

In the end, bidding the dancers to unmask, Cynthia shows that the vices have disguised themselves as virtues. She condemns them to make fit reparation, and to bathe themselves in Helicon. Two by two they go off singing a palinode, whilst the chorus sings the supplication " Good Mercury defend us."[1] Is it an opera or a comedy? It is a lyrical comedy; and if we do not discover in it the airy lightness of Aristophanes, at least we encounter, as in the *Birds* and the *Frogs*, the contrasts and medleys of poetic invention, which, through caricature and ode, the real and the impossible, the present and the past, sent forth to the four quarters of the globe, simultaneously unites all kinds of incompatibilities, and culls all flowers.

Jonson went further than this, and entered the domain of pure poetry. He wrote delicate, voluptuous, charming love poems, worthy of the ancient idyllic muse.[2] Above all, he was the great, the inexhaustible inventor of Masques, a kind of masquerades, ballets, poetic choruses, in which all the magnificence and the imagination of the English Renaissance is displayed. The Greek gods, and all the ancient Olympus, the allegorical personages whom the artists of the time delineate in their pictures; the antique heroes of popular legends; all worlds, the actual, the abstract, the divine, the human, the ancient, the modern, are searched by his hands, brought on the stage to furnish costumes, harmonious groups, emblems, songs, whatever can excite, intoxicate the artistic sense. The *élite*, moreover, of the kingdom is there on the stage. They are not mountebanks moving about in borrowed clothes, clumsily

---

[1] *Cynthia's Revels*, last scene.
[2] *Celebration of Charis—Miscellaneous Poems.*

worn, for which they are still in debt to the tailor; they are ladies of the court, great lords, the queen, in all the splendour of their rank and pride, with real diamonds, bent on displaying their riches, so that the whole splendour of the national life is concentrated in the opera which they enact, like jewels in a casket. What dresses! what profusion of splendours! what medley of strange characters, gipsies, witches, gods, heroes, pontiffs, gnomes, fantastic beings! How many metamorphoses, jousts, dances, marriage songs! What variety of scenery, architecture, floating isles, triumphal arches, symbolic spheres! Gold glitters; jewels flash; purple absorbs the lustre-lights in its costly folds; streams of light shine upon the crumpled silks; diamond necklaces, darting flame, clasp the bare bosoms of the ladies; strings of pearls are displayed, loop after loop, upon the silver-sown brocaded dresses; gold embroidery, weaving whimsical arabesques, depicts upon their dresses flowers, fruits, and figures, setting picture within picture. The steps of the throne bear groups of Cupids, each with a torch in his hand.[1] On either side the fountains cast up plumes of pearls; musicians, in purple and scarlet, laurel-crowned, make harmony in the bowers. The trains of masques cross, commingling their groups; "the one half in orange-tawny and silver, the other in sea-green and silver. The bodies and short skirts (were of) white and gold to both."

Such pageants Jonson wrote year after year, almost to the end of his life, true feasts for the eyes, like the processions of Titian. Even when he grew to be old, his imagination, like that of Titian, remained abundant and fresh. Though forsaken, lying gasping on his bed, feel-

[1] *Masque of Beauty.*

ing the approach of death, in his supreme bitterness he did not lose his faculties, but wrote *The Sad Shepherd*, the most graceful and pastoral of his pieces. Consider that this beautiful dream arose in a sick-chamber, amidst medicine bottles, physic, doctors, with a nurse at his side, amidst the anxieties of poverty and the choking-fits of a dropsy! He is transported to a green forest, in the days of Robin Hood, amidst the gay chase and the great barking greyhounds. There are the malicious fairies, who like Oberon and Titania, lead men to flounder in mishaps. There are open-souled lovers, who like Daphne and Chloe, taste with awe the painful sweetness of the first kiss. There lived Earine, whom the stream has "suck'd in," whom her lover, in his madness, will not cease to lament:

" Earine,
Who had her very being, and her name
With the first knots or buddings of the spring,
Born with the primrose or the violet,
Or earliest roses blown : when Cupid smil'd,
And Venus led the graces out to dance,
And all the flowers and sweets in nature's lap
Leap'd out, and made their solemn conjuration
To last but while she liv'd ! " . . . [1]
" But she, as chaste as was her name, Earine,
Died undeflower'd : and now her sweet soul hovers
Here in the air above us." [2]

Above the poor old paralytic artist, poetry still hovers like a haze of light. Yes, he had cumbered himself with science, clogged himself with theories, constituted himself theatrical critic and social censor,

[1] *The Sad Shepherd*, i. 2.   [2] *Ibid.* iii. 2.

filled his soul with unrelenting indignation, fostered a combative and morose disposition; but divine dreams never left him. He is the brother of Shakspeare.

VI.

So now at last we are in the presence of one, whom we perceived before us through all the vistas of the Renaissance, like some vast oak to which all the forest ways converge. I will treat of Shakspeare by himself. In order to take him in completely, we must have a wide and open space. And yet how shall we comprehend him? how lay bare his inner constitution? Lofty words, eulogies, are all used in vain; he needs no praise, but comprehension merely; and he can only be comprehended by the aid of science. As the complicated revolutions of the heavenly bodies become intelligible only by use of a superior calculus, as the delicate transformations of vegetation and life need for their explanation the intervention of the most difficult chemical formulas, so the great works of art can be interpreted only by the most advanced psychological systems; and we need the loftiest of all these to attain to Shakspeare's level—to the level of his age and his work, of his genius and of his art.

After all practical experience and accumulated observations of the soul, we find as the result that wisdom and knowledge are in man only effects and fortuities. Man has no permanent and distinct force to secure truth to his intelligence, and common sense to his conduct. On the contrary, he is naturally unreasonable and deceived. The parts of his inner mechanism are like the wheels of clock-work, which go of themselves, blindly, carried away by impulse and weight, and which yet sometimes, by virtue of a certain unison, end by indicating the hour. This final intelligent motion is not natural, but fortuitous; not spontaneous, but forced; not innate, but acquired. The clock did not always go regularly; on the contrary, it had to be regulated little by little, with much difficulty. Its regularity is not ensured; it may go wrong at any time. Its regularity is not complete; it only approximately marks the time. The mechanical force of each piece is always ready to drag all the rest from their proper action, and to disarrange the whole agreement. So ideas, once in the mind, pull each their own way blindly and separately, and their imperfect agreement threatens confusion every moment. Strictly speaking, man is mad, as the body is ill, by nature; reason and health come to us as a momentary success, a lucky accident.[1] If we forget this, it is because we are now regulated, dulled, deadened, and because our internal motion has become gradually, by friction and reparation, half harmonised with the motion of things. But this is only a semblance; and the dangerous primitive forces remain untamed and independent under the order which seems to restrain them. Let a great danger arise, a revolution take place, they will break out and explode, almost as terribly as in earlier times. For an idea is not a mere inner mark, employed to designate one aspect of things, inert, always ready to fall into order with other similar ones, so as to make an exact whole. However it may be reduced and disciplined, it still retains a sensible tinge which shows

[1] This idea may be expanded psychologically: external perception, memory, are real hallucinations, etc. This is the analytical aspect: under another aspect reason and health are the natural goals.

its likeness to an hallucination; a degree of individual persistence which shows its likeness to a monomania; a network of singular affinities which shows its likeness to the ravings of delirium. Being such, it is beyond question the rudiment of a nightmare, a habit, an absurdity. Let it become once developed in its entirety, as its tendency leads it,[1] and you will find that it is essentially an active and complete image, a vision drawing along with it a train of dreams and sensations, which increases of itself, suddenly, by a sort of rank and absorbing growth, and which ends by possessing, shaking, exhausting the whole man. After this, another, perhaps entirely opposite, and so on successively: there is nothing else in man, no free and distinct power; he is in himself but the process of these headlong impulses and swarming imaginations: civilisation has mutilated, attenuated, but not destroyed them; shocks, collisions, transports, sometimes at long intervals a sort of transient partial equilibrium: this is his real life, the life of a lunatic, who now and then simulates reason, but who is in reality "such stuff as dreams are made on;"[2] and this is man, as Shakspeare has conceived him. No writer, not even Molière, has penetrated so far beneath the semblance of common sense and logic in which the human machine is enclosed, in order to disentangle the brute powers which constitute its substance and its mainspring.

How did Shakspeare succeed? and by what extraordinary instinct did he divine the remote conclusions, the deepest insights of physiology and psychology? He had a complete imagination; his whole genius lies

[1] See Spinoza and Dugald Stewart: Conception in its natural state is belief.   [2] *Tempest*, iv. 1.

in that complete imagination. These words seem commonplace and void of meaning. Let us examine them closer, to understand what they contain. When we think a thing, we, ordinary men, we only think a part of it; we see one side, some isolated mark, sometimes two or three marks together; for what is beyond, our sight fails us; the infinite network of its infinitely-complicated and multiplied properties escapes us; we feel vaguely that there is something beyond our shallow ken, and this vague suspicion is the only part of our idea which at all reveals to us the great beyond. We are like tyro-naturalists, quiet people of limited understanding, who, wishing to represent an animal, recall its name and ticket in the museum, with some indistinct image of its hide and figure; but their mind stops there. If it so happens that they wish to complete their knowledge, they lead their memory, by regular classifications, over the principal characters of the animal, and slowly, discursively, piecemeal, bring at last the bare anatomy before their eyes. To this their idea is reduced, even when perfected; to this also most frequently is our conception reduced, even when elaborated. What a distance there is between this conception and the object, how imperfectly and meanly the one represents the other, to what extent this mutilates that; how the consecutive idea, disjointed in little, regularly arranged and inert fragments, resembles but slightly the organised, living thing, created simultaneously, ever in action, and ever transformed, words cannot explain. Picture to yourself, instead of this poor dry idea, propped up by a miserable mechanical linkwork of thought, the complete idea, that is, an inner representation, so abundant and full, that it exhausts all the properties and relations of the object, all its inward and outward aspects; that it exhausts them instantaneously; that it conceives of the entire animal, its colour, the play of the light upon its skin, its form, the quivering of its outstretched limbs, the flash of its eyes, and at the same time its passion of the moment, its excitement, its dash; and beyond this its instincts, their composition, their causes, their history; so that the hundred thousand characteristics which make up its condition and its nature find their analogues in the imagination which concentrates and reflects them: there you have the artist's conception, the poet's—Shakspeare's; so superior to that of the logician, of the mere savant or man of the world, the only one capable of penetrating to the very essence of existences, of extricating the inner from beneath the outer man, of feeling through sympathy, and imitating without effort, the irregular oscillation of human imaginations and impressions, of reproducing life with its infinite fluctuations, its apparent contradictions, its concealed logic; in short, to create as nature creates. This is what is done by the other artists of this age; they have the same kind of mind, and the same idea of life: you will find in Shakspeare only the same faculties, with a still stronger impulse; the same idea, with a still more prominent relief.

CHAPTER IV.

Shakspeare.

I AM about to describe an extraordinary species of mind, perplexing to all the French modes of analysis and reasoning, all-powerful, excessive, master of the sublime as well as of the base; the most creative mind that ever engaged in the exact copy of the details of actual existence, in the dazzling caprice of fancy, in the profound complications of superhuman passions; a nature poetical, immoral, inspired, superior to reason by the sudden revelations of its seer's madness; so extreme in joy and grief, so abrupt of gait, so agitated and impetuous in its transports, that this great age alone could have cradled such a child.

I.

Of Shakspeare all came from within—I mean from his soul and his genius; circumstances and the externals contributed but slightly to his development.[1] He was intimately bound up with his age; that is, he knew by experience the manners of country, court, and town; he had visited the heights, depths, the middle ranks of mankind; nothing more. In all other respects, his life was commonplace; its irregularities, troubles, passions, suc-

[1] Halliwell's *Life of Shakspeare*.

cesses, were, on the whole, such as we meet with everywhere else.[1] His father, a glover and wool-stapler, in very easy circumstances, having married a sort of country heiress, had become high-bailiff and chief alderman in his little town; but when Shakspeare was nearly fourteen he was on the verge of ruin, mortgaging his wife's property, obliged to resign his municipal offices, and to remove his son from school to assist him in his business. The young fellow applied himself to it as well as he could, not without some scrapes and frolics: if we are to believe tradition, he was one of the thirsty souls of the place, with a mind to support the reputation of his little town in its drinking powers. Once, they say, having been beaten at Bideford in one of these ale-bouts, he returned staggering from the fight, or rather could not return, and passed the night with his comrades under an apple-tree by the roadside. Without doubt he had already begun to write verses, to rove about like a genuine poet, taking part in the noisy rustic feasts, the gay allegorical pastorals, the rich and bold outbreak of pagan and poetical life, as it was then to be found in an English village. At all events, he was not a pattern of propriety, and his passions were as precocious as they were imprudent. While not yet nineteen years old, he married the daughter of a substantial yeoman, about eight years older than himself— and not too soon, as she was about to become a mother.[2] Other of his outbreaks were no more fortunate. It

[1] Born 1564, died 1616. He adapted plays as early as 1591. The first play entirely from his pen appeared in 1593.—PAYNE COLLIER.

[2] Mr. Halliwell and other commentators try to prove that at this time the preliminary trothplight was regarded as the real marriage; that this trothplight had taken place, and that there was therefore no irregularity in Shakspeare's conduct.

seems that he was fond of poaching, after the manner of the time, being "much given to all unluckinesse in stealing venison and rabbits," says the Rev. Richard Davies;[1] "particularly from Sir Thomas Lucy, who had him oft whipt and sometimes imprisoned, and at last made him fly the country; . . . but his revenge was so great, that he is his Justice Clodpate." Moreover, about this time Shakspeare's father was in prison, his affairs were not prosperous, and he himself had three children, following one close upon the other; he must live, and life was hardly possible for him in his native town. He went to London, and took to the stage: took the lowest parts, was a "servant" in the theatre, that is, an apprentice, or perhaps a supernumerary. They even said that he had begun still lower, and that to earn his bread he had held gentlemen's horses at the door of the theatre.[2] At all events he tasted misery, and felt, not in imagination, but in fact, the sharp thorn of care, humiliation, disgust, forced labour, public discredit, the power of the people. He was a comedian, one of "His Majesty's poor players,"[3] —a sad trade, degraded in all ages by the contrasts and the falsehoods which it allows: still more degraded then by the brutalities of the crowd, who not seldom would stone the actors, and by the severities of the magistrates, who would sometimes condemn them to lose their ears. He felt it, and spoke of it with bitterness:

[1] Halliwell, 123.
[2] All these anecdotes are traditions, and consequently more or less doubtful; but the other facts are authentic.
[3] Terms of an extant document. He is named along with Burbadge and Greene.

> "Alas, 'tis true I have gone here and there
> And made myself a motley to the view,
> Gored mine own thoughts, sold cheap what is most dear."[1]

And again :

> "When in disgrace with fortune[2] and men's eyes,
> I all alone beweep my outcast state,
> And trouble deaf heaven with my bootless cries,
> And look upon myself and curse my fate,
> Wishing me like to one more rich in hope,
> Featured like him, like him with friends possessed. . . .
> With what I most enjoy contented least ;
> Yet in those thoughts myself almost despising."[3]

We shall find further on the traces of this long-enduring disgust, in his melancholy characters, as where he says :

> "For who would bear the whips and scorns of time,
> The oppressor's wrong, the proud man's contumely,
> The pangs of despised love, the law's delay,
> The insolence of office and the spurns
> That patient merit of the unworthy takes,
> When he himself might his quietus make
> With a bare bodkin ?"[4]

But the worst of this undervalued position is, that it eats into the soul. In the company of actors we become actors : it is vain to wish to keep clean, if you live in a dirty place; it cannot be. No matter if a man braces himself; necessity drives him into a corner and sullies

---

[1] *Sonnet* 110.
[2] See *Sonnets* 91 and 111 ; also *Hamlet*, iii. 2. Many of Hamlet's words would come better from the mouth of an actor than a prince. See also the 66th *Sonnet*, "Tired with all these."
[3] *Sonnet* 29. [4] *Hamlet*. iii. 1.

him. The machinery of the decorations, the tawdriness and medley of the costumes, the smell of the tallow and the candles, in contrast with the parade of refinement and loftiness, all the cheats and sordidness of the representation, the bitter alternative of hissing or applause, the keeping of the highest and lowest company, the habit of sporting with human passions, easily unhinge the soul, drive it down the slope of excess, tempt it to loose manners, green-room adventures, the loves of strolling actresses. Shakspeare escaped them no more than Molière, and grieved for it, like Molière:

" O, for my sake do you with Fortune chide,
 The guilty goddess of my harmful deeds,
 That did not better for my life provide
 Than public means which public manners breeds." [1]

They used to relate in London, how his comrade Burbadge, who played Richard III., having a rendezvous with the wife of a citizen, Shakspeare went before, was well received, and was pleasantly occupied, when Burbadge arrived, to whom he sent the message, that William the Conqueror came before Richard III.[2] We may take this as an example of the tricks and somewhat coarse intrigues which are planned, and follow in quick succession, on this stage. Outside the theatre he lived with fashionable young nobles, Pembroke, Montgomery, Southampton,[3] and others, whose hot and licentious youth gratified his imagination and senses by the example of Italian pleasures and elegancies.

[1] *Sonnet* 111.
[2] Anecdote written in 1602 on the authority of Tooley the actor.
[3] The Earl of Southampton was nineteen years old when Shakspeare dedicated his *Adonis* to him.

Add to this the rapture and transport of poetical nature, and this kind of afflux, this boiling over of all the powers and desires which takes place in brains of this kind, when the world for the first time opens before them, and you will understand the *Venus and Adonis,* "the first heir of his invention." In fact, it is a first cry, a cry in which the whole man is displayed. Never was seen a heart so quivering to the touch of beauty, of beauty of every kind, so delighted with the freshness and splendour of things, so eager and so excited in adoration and enjoyment, so violently and entirely carried to the very essence of voluptuousness. His Venus is unique; no painting of Titian's has a more brilliant and delicious colouring;[1] no strumpet-goddess of Tintoretto or Giorgione is more soft and beautiful:

"With blindfold fury she begins to forage,
Her face doth reek and smoke, her blood doth boil. . . .

And glutton-like she feeds, yet never filleth;
Her lips are conquerors, his lips obey,
Paying what ransom the insulter willeth;
Whose vulture thought doth pitch the price so high,
That she will draw his lips' rich treasure dry."[2]

"Even as an empty eagle, sharp by fast,
Tires with her beak on feathers, flesh and bone,
Shaking her wings, devouring all in haste,
Till either gorge be stuff'd or prey be gone;
Even so she kiss'd his brow, his cheek, his chin,
And where she ends she doth anew begin."[3]

All is taken by storm, the senses first, the eyes dazzled by carnal beauty, but the heart also from whence the

[1] See Titian's picture, Loves of the Gods, at Blenheim.
[2] *Venus and Adonis.* l. 548-553. [3] *Ibid.* l. 55-60.

poetry overflows: the fulness of youth inundates even inanimate things; the country looks charming amidst the rays of the rising sun, the air, saturated with brightness, makes a gala-day;

> "Lo, here the gentle lark, weary of rest,
> From his moist cabinet mounts up on high,
> And wakes the morning, from whose silver breast
> The sun ariseth in his majesty;
> Who doth the world so gloriously behold
> That cedar-tops and hills seem burnish'd gold."[1]

An admirable debauch of imagination and rapture, yet disquieting; for such a mood will carry one a long way.[2] No fair and frail dame in London was without *Adonis* on her table.[3] Perhaps Shakspeare perceived that he had transcended the bounds, for the tone of his next poem, the *Rape of Lucrece,* is quite different; but as he had already a mind liberal enough to embrace at the same time, as he did afterwards in his dramas, the two extremes of things, he continued none the less to follow his bent. The "sweet abandonment of love" was the great occupation of his life; he was tender-hearted, and he was a poet: nothing more is required to be smitten, deceived, to suffer, to traverse without pause the circle of illusions and troubles, which whirls and whirls round, and never ends.

He had many loves of this kind, amongst others one for a sort of Marion Delorme,[4] a miserable deluding de-

[1] *Venus and Adonis, l.* 853-858.

[2] Compare the first pieces of Alfred de Musset, *Contes d'Italie et d'Espagne.*

[3] Crawley, quoted by Ph. Chasles, *Etudes sur Shakspeare.*

[4] A famed French courtesan (1613-1650), the heroine of a drama of that name, by Victor Hugo, having for its subject-matter: "Love purifies everything."—Tr.

spotic passion, of which he felt the burden and the shame, but from which nevertheless he could not and would not free himself. Nothing can be sadder than his confessions, or mark better the madness of love, and the sentiment of human weakness:

> "When my love swears that she is made of truth,
> I do believe her, though I know she lies." [1]

So spoke Alceste of Célimène;[2] but what a soiled Célimène is the creature before whom Shakspeare kneels, with as much of scorn as of desire!

> "Those lips of thine,
> That have profaned their scarlet ornaments
> And seal'd false bonds of love as oft as mine,
> Robb'd others' beds' revenues of their rents.
> Be it lawful I love thee, as thou lov'st those
> Whom thine eyes woo as mine importune thee." [3]

This is plain-speaking and deep shamelessness of soul, such as we find only in the stews; and these are the intoxications, the excesses, the delirium into which the most refined artists fall, when they resign their own noble hand to these soft, voluptuous, and clinging ones. They are higher than princes, and they descend to the lowest depths of sensual passion. Good and evil then lose their names; all things are inverted:

> "How sweet and lovely dost thou make the shame
> Which, like a canker in the fragrant rose,
> Doth spot the beauty of thy budding name!
> O, in what sweets dost thou thy sins enclose!

---

[1] *Sonnet* 138.
[2] Two characters in Molière's *Misanthrope*. The scene referred to is Act v. sc. 7.—TR.
[3] *Sonnet* 142.

> That tongue that tells the story of thy days,
> Making lascivious comments on thy sport,
> Cannot dispraise but in a kind of praise;
> Naming thy name blesses an ill report." [1]

What are proofs, the will, reason, honour itself, when the passion is so absorbing? What can be said further to a man who answers, "I know all that you are going to say, and what does it all amount to?" Great loves are inundations, which drown all repugnance and all delicacy of soul, all preconceived opinions and all received principles. Thenceforth the heart is dead to all ordinary pleasures: it can only feel and breathe on one side. Shakspeare envies the keys of the instrument over which his mistress' fingers run. If he looks at flowers, it is she whom he pictures beyond them; and the extravagant splendours of dazzling poetry spring up in him repeatedly, as soon as he thinks of those glowing black eyes:

> "From you have I been absent in the spring,
> When proud-pied April dress'd in all his trim,
> Hath put a spirit of youth in every thing,
> That heavy Saturn laugh'd and leap'd with him." [2]

He saw none of it:

> "Nor did I wonder at the lily's white,
> Nor praise the deep vermilion in the rose." [3]

All this sweetness of spring was but her perfume and her shade:

> "The forward violet thus I did chide:
> 'Sweet thief, whence didst thou steal thy sweet that smells,
> If not from my love's breath? The purple pride,

---

[1] *Sonnet* 95. [2] *Sonnet* 98. [3] *Ibid.*

Which on thy soft cheek for complexion dwells
In my love's veins thou hast too grossly dyed.'
The lily I condemned for thy hand,
And buds of marjoram had stol'n thy hair:
The roses fearfully on thorns did stand,
One blushing shame, another white despair:
A third, nor red nor white, had stol'n of both
And to his robbery had annex'd thy breath; . . .
More flowers I noted, yet I none could see
But sweet or colour it had stol'n from thee." [1]

Passionate archness, delicious affectations, worthy of Heine and the contemporaries of Dante, which tell us of long rapturous dreams concentrated on one object. Under a sway so imperious and sustained, what sentiment could maintain its ground? That of family? He was married and had children,—a family which he went to see "once a year;" and it was probably on his return from one of these journeys that he used the words above quoted. Conscience? "Love is too young to know what conscience is." Jealousy and anger?

"For, thou betraying me, I do betray
My nobler part to my gross body's treason." [2]

Repulses?

"He is contented thy poor drudge to be
To stand in thy affairs, fall by thy side." [3]

He is no longer young; she loves another, a handsome, young, light-haired fellow, his own dearest friend, whom he has presented to her, and whom she wishes to seduce:

[1] *Sonnet* 99.   [2] *Sonnet* 151.   [3] *Ibid.*

> " Two loves I have of comfort and despair,
> Which like two spirits do suggest me still:
> The better angel is a man right fair,
> The worser spirit a woman colour'd ill.
> To win me soon to hell, my female evil
> Tempteth my better angel from my side." [1]

And when she has succeeded in this,[2] he dares not confess it to himself, but suffers all, like Molière. What wretchedness is there in these trifles of every-day life! How man's thoughts instinctively place by Shakspeare's side the great unhappy French poet (Molière), also a philosopher by nature, but more of a professional laugher, a mocker of old men in love, a bitter railer at deceived husbands, who, after having played in one of his most approved comedies, said aloud to a friend, "My dear fellow, I am in despair; my wife does not love me!" Neither glory, nor work, nor invention satisfy these vehement souls: love alone can gratify them, because, with their senses and heart, it contents also their brain; and all the powers of man, imagination like the rest, find in it their concentration and their employment. "Love is my sin," he said, as did Musset and Heine; and in the *Sonnets* we find traces of yet other passions, equally abandoned; one in particular, seemingly for a great lady. The first half of his dramas, *Midsummer Night's Dream*, *Romeo and Juliet*, the *Two Gentlemen of Verona*, preserve the warm imprint more completely; and we have only to

---

[1] *Sonnet* 144; also the *Passionate Pilgrim*, 2.
[2] This new interpretation of the *Sonnets* is due to the ingenious and learned conjectures of M. Ph. Chasles.—For a short history of these *Sonnets*, see Dyce's *Shakspeare*, i. pp. 96–102. This learned editor says: "I contend that allusions scattered through the whole series are not to be hastily referred to the personal circumstances of Shakspeare."—TR.

consider his latest women's character,[1] to see with what exquisite tenderness, what full adoration, he loved them to the end.

In this is all his genius; his was one of those delicate souls which, like a perfect instrument of music, vibrate of themselves at the slightest touch. This fine sensibility was the first thing observed in him. "My darling Shakspeare," "Sweet Swan of Avon:" these words of Ben Johnson only confirm what his contemporaries reiterate. He was affectionate and kind, "civil in demeanour, and excellent in the qualitie he professes;"[2] if he had the impulse, he had also the effusion of true artists; he was loved, men were delighted in his company; nothing is more sweet or winning than this charm, this half-feminine abandonment in a man. His wit in conversation was ready, ingenious, nimble; his gaiety brilliant; his imagination fluent, and so copious, that, as his friends tell us, he never erased

---

[1] Miranda, Desdemona, Viola. The following are the first words of the Duke in *Twelfth Night*:—

"If music be the food of love, play on;
Give me excess of it, that, surfeiting,
The appetite may sicken, and so die.
That strain again! it had a dying fall:
O, it came o'er my ear like the sweet south,
That breathes upon a bank of violets,
Stealing and giving odour! Enough; no more:
'Tis not so sweet now as it was before.
O spirit of love! how quick and fresh art thou,
That, notwithstanding thy capacity
Receiveth as the sea, nought enters there,
Of what validity and pitch soever,
But falls into abatement and low price,
Even in a minute: so full of shapes is fancy
That it alone is high-fantastical."

[2] H. Chettle, in repudiating Greene's sarcasm, attributed to him.

what he had written;—at least when he wrote out a scene for the second time, it was the idea which he would change, not the words, by an after-glow of poetic thought, not with a painful tinkering of the verse. All these characteristics are combined into a single one: he had a sympathetic genius; I mean that naturally he knew how to forget himself and become transfused into all the objects which he conceived. Look around you at the great artists of your time, try to approach them, to become acquainted with them, to see them as they think, and you will observe the full force of this word. By an extraordinary instinct, they put themselves at once in a position of existences; men, animals, flowers, plants, landscapes, whatever the objects are, living or not, they feel by intuition the forces and tendencies which produce the visible external; and their soul, infinitely complex, becomes by its ceaseless metamorphoses, a sort of abstract of the universe. This is why they seem to live more than other men; they have no need to be taught, they divine. I have seen such a man, apropos of a piece of armour, a costume, a collection of furniture, enter into the middle-age more fully than three savants together. They reconstruct, as they build, naturally, surely, by an inspiration which is a winged chain of reasoning. Shakspeare had only an imperfect education, "small Latin and less Greek," barely French and Italian,[1] nothing else; he had not travelled, he had only read the current literature of his day, he had picked up a few law words in the court of his little town: reckon up, if you can, all that he knew of man and of history. These men see more objects

---

[1] Dyce, *Shakspeare*, i. 27 : "Of French and Italian, I apprehend, he knew but little."—Tr.

at a time; they grasp them more closely than other men, more quickly and thoroughly; their mind is full, and runs over. They do not rest in simple reasoning; at every idea their whole being, reflections, images, emotions, are set aquiver. See them at it; they gesticulate, mimic their thought, brim over with comparisons; even in their talk they are imaginative and original, with familiarity and boldness of speech, sometimes happily, always irregularly, according to the whims and starts of the adventurous improvisation. The animation, the brilliancy of their language is marvellous; so are their fits, the wide leaps with which they couple widely-removed ideas, annihilating distance, passing from pathos to humour, from vehemence to gentleness. This extraordinary rapture is the last thing to quit them. If perchance ideas fail, or if their melancholy is too violent, they still speak and produce, even if it be nonsense: they become clowns, though at their own expense, and to their own hurt. I know one of these men who will talk nonsense when he thinks he is dying, or has a mind to kill himself; the inner wheel continues to turn, even upon nothing, that wheel which man must needs see ever turning, even though it tear him as it turns; his buffoonery is an outlet: you will find him, this inextinguishable urchin, this ironical puppet, at Ophelia's tomb, at Cleopatra's death-bed, at Juliet's funeral. High or low, these men must always be at some extreme. They feel their good and their ill too deeply; they expatiate too abundantly on each condition of their soul, by a sort of involuntary novel. After the traducings and the disgusts by which they debase themselves beyond measure, they rise and become exalted in a marvellous fashion, even trembling with pride and joy. "Haply," says Shakspeare, after one of these dull moods:

> "Haply I think on thee, and then my state,
> Like to the lark at break of day arising
> From sullen earth, sings hymns at heaven's gate."[1]

Then all fades away, as in a furnace where a stronger flare than usual has left no substance fuel behind it.

> "That time of year thou mayst in me behold
> When yellow leaves, or none, or few, do hang
> Upon those boughs which shake against the cold,
> Bare ruin'd choirs, where late the sweet birds sang.
> In me thou see'st the twilight of such day
> As after sunset fadeth in the west,
> Which by and by black night doth take away,
> Death's second self, that seals up all in rest."[2] . . .

> "No longer mourn for me when I am dead
> Than you shall hear the surly sullen bell
> Give warning to the world that I am fled
> From this vile world, with vilest worms to dwell:
> Nay, if you read this line, remember not
> The hand that writ it; for I love you so,
> That I in your sweet thoughts would be forgot
> If thinking on me then should make you woe."[3]

These sudden alternatives of joy and sadness, divine transports and grand melancholies, exquisite tenderness and womanly depressions, depict the poet, extreme in emotions, ceaselessly troubled with grief or merriment, feeling the slightest shock, more strong, more dainty in enjoyment and suffering than other men, capable of more intense and sweeter dreams, within whom is

[1] *Sonnet* 29. [2] *Sonnet* 73. [3] *Sonnet* 71.

stirred an imaginary world of graceful or terrible beings, all impassioned like their author.

Such as I have described him, however, he found his resting-place. Early, at least what regards outward appearances, he settled down to an orderly, sensible, almost humdrum existence, engaged in business, provident of the future. He remained on the stage for at least seventeen years, though taking secondary parts;[1] he sets his wits at the same time to the touching up of plays with so much activity, that Greene called him " an upstart crow beautified with our feathers; . . . an absolute *Johannes factotum*, in his owne conceyt the onely shake-scene in a countrey."[2] At the age of thirty-three he had amassed money enough to buy at Stratford a house with two barns and two gardens, and he went on steadier and steadier in the same course. A man attains only to easy circumstances by his own labour; if he gains wealth, it is by making others labour for him. This is why, to the trades of actor and author, Shakspeare added those of manager and director of a theatre. He acquired a share in the Blackfriars and Globe theatres, farmed tithes, bought large pieces of land, more houses, gave a dowry to his daughter Susanna, and finally retired to his native town on his property, in his own house, like a good landlord, an honest citizen, who manages his fortune fitly, and takes his share of municipal work. He had an income of two or three hundred pounds, which would be equivalent to about eight or twelve hundred at the present time, and according to tradition, lived cheerfully and on good terms with his neighbours; at all events, it

[1] The part in which he excelled was that of the ghost in *Hamlet*.
[2] Greene's *A Groatsworth of Wit*, etc.

does not seem that he thought much about his literary glory, for he did not even take the trouble to collect and publish his works. One of his daughters married a physician, the other a wine merchant; the last did not even know how to sign her name. He lent money, and cut a good figure in this little world. Strange close; one which at first sight resembles more that of a shopkeeper than of a poet. Must we attribute it to that English instinct which places happiness in the life of a country gentleman and a landlord with a good rent-roll, well connected, surrounded by comforts, who quietly enjoys his undoubted respectability,[1] his domestic authority, and his county standing? Or rather, was Shakspeare, like Voltaire, a common-sense man, though of an imaginative brain, keeping a sound judgment under the sparkling of his genius, prudent from scepticism, saving through a desire for independence, and capable, after going the round of human ideas, of deciding with Candide,[2] that the best thing one can do in this world is " to cultivate one's garden?" I had rather think, as his full and solid head suggests,[3] that by the mere force of his overflowing imagination he escaped, like Goethe, the perils of an overflowing imagination; that in depicting passion, he succeeded, like Goethe, in deadening passion; that the fire did not break out in his conduct, because it found issue in his poetry; that his theatre kept pure his life; and that, having passed, by sympathy, through every kind of folly and wretchedness that is incident to human ex-

[1] "He was a respectable man." "A good word; what does it mean?" "He kept a gig."—(From Thurtell's trial for the murder of Weare.)
[2] The model of an optimist, the hero of one of Voltaire's tales.—Tr.
[3] See his portraits, and in particular his bust.

istence, he was able to settle down amidst them with a calm and melancholic smile, listening, for the sake of relaxation, to the aerial music of the fancies in which he revelled.[1] I am willing to believe, lastly, that in frame as in other things, he belonged to his great generation and his great age; that with him, as with Rabelais, Titian, Michel Angelo, and Rubens, the solidity of the muscles was a counterpoise to the sensibility of the nerves; that in those days the human machine, more severely tried and more firmly constructed, could withstand the storms of passion and the fire of inspiration; that soul and body were still at equilibrium; that genius was then a blossom, and not, as now, a disease. We can but make conjectures about all this: if we would become acquainted more closely with the man, we must seek him in his works.

II.

Let us then look for the man, and in his style. The style explains the work; whilst showing the principal features of the genius, it infers the rest. When we have once grasped the dominant faculty, we see the whole artist developed like a flower.

Shakspeare imagines with copiousness and excess; he scatters metaphors profusely over all he writes; every instant abstract ideas are changed into images; it is a series of paintings which is unfolded in his mind. He does not seek them, they come of themselves; they crowd within him, covering his arguments; they dim with their brightness the pure light of logic. He does not labour to explain or prove; picture on picture, image on image, he is for ever copying the strange and splendid

[1] Especially in his later plays: *Tempest, Twelfth Night.*

visions which are engendered one after another, and are heaped up within him. Compare to our dull writers this passage, which I take at hazard from a tranquil dialogue :

> " The single and peculiar life is bound,
> With all the strength and armour of the mind,
> To keep itself from noyance; but much more
> That spirit upon whose weal depend and rest
> The lives of many. The cease of majesty
> Dies not alone; but, like a gulf, doth draw
> What's near it with it: it is a massy wheel,
> Fix'd on the summit of the highest mount,
> To whose huge spokes ten thousand lesser things
> Are mortised and adjoin'd ; which, when it falls,
> Each small annexment, petty consequence,
> Attends the boisterous ruin. Never alone
> Did the king sigh, but with a general groan."[1]

Here we have three successive images to express the same thought. It is a whole blossoming; a bough grows from the trunk, from that another, which is multiplied into numerous fresh branches. Instead of a smooth road, traced by a regular line of dry and cunningly-fixed landmarks, you enter a wood, crowded with interwoven trees and luxuriant bushes, which conceal and prevent your progress, which delight and dazzle your eyes by the magnificence of their verdure and the wealth of their bloom. You are astonished at first, modern mind that you are, business man, used to the clear dissertations of classical poetry; you become cross; you think the author is amusing himself, and that through conceit and bad taste he is misleading you and himself in his garden thickets. By no means; if he

[1] *Hamlet,* iii. 3.

speaks thus, it is not from choice, but of necessity; metaphor is not his whim, but the form of his thought In the height of passion, he imagines still. When Hamlet, in despair, remembers his father's noble form, he sees the mythological pictures with which the taste of the age filled the very streets:

> " A station like the herald Mercury
> New lighted on a heaven-kissing hill." [1]

This charming vision, in the midst of a bloody invective proves that there lurks a painter underneath the poet. Involuntarily and out of season, he tears off the tragic mask which covered his face; and the reader discovers, behind the contracted features of this terrible mask, a graceful and inspired smile which he did not expect to see.

Such an imagination must needs be vehement. Every metaphor is a convulsion. Whosoever involuntarily and naturally transforms a dry idea into an image, has his brain on fire; true metaphors are flaming apparitions, which are like a picture in a flash of lightning. Never, I think, in any nation of Europe, or in any age of history, has so grand a passion been seen. Shakspeare's style is a compound of frenzied expressions. No man has submitted words to such a contortion. Mingled contrasts, tremendous exaggerations, apostrophes, exclamations the whole fury of the ode, confusion of ideas, accumulation of images, the horrible and the divine, jumbled into the same line; it seems to my fancy as though he never writes a word without shouting it. 'What have I done?' the queen asks Hamlet. He answers:

[1] Act iii. Sc. 4.

> "Such an act
> That blurs the grace and blush of modesty,
> Calls virtue hypocrite, takes off the rose
> From the fair forehead of an innocent love,
> And sets a blister there, makes marriage-vows
> As false as dicers' oaths : O, such a deed
> As from the body of contraction plucks
> The very soul, and sweet religion makes
> A rhapsody of words : Heaven's face doth glow;
> Yea, this solidity and compound mass,
> With tristful visage, as against the doom,
> Is thought-sick at the act." [1]

It is the style of phrensy. Yet I have not given all. The metaphors are all exaggerated, the ideas all verge on the absurd. All is transformed and disfigured by the whirlwind of passion. The contagion of the crime, which he denounces, has marred all nature. He no longer sees anything in the world but corruption and lying. To vilify the virtuous were little; he vilifies virtue herself. Inanimate things are sucked into this whirlpool of grief. The sky's red tint at sunset, the pallid darkness spread by night over the landscape, become the blush and the pallor of shame, and the wretched man who speaks and weeps sees the whole world totter with him in the dimness of despair.

Hamlet, it will be said, is half-mad; this explains the vehemence of his expressions. The truth is that Hamlet, here, is Shakspeare. Be the situation terrible or peaceful, whether he is engaged on an invective or a conversation, the style is excessive throughout. Shakspeare never sees things tranquilly. All the powers of his mind are concentrated in the present

[1] Act iii. Sc. 4.

image or idea. He is buried and absorbed in it. With such a genius, we are on the brink of an abyss; the eddying water dashes in headlong, swallowing up whatever objects it meets, and only bringing them to light transformed and mutilated. We pause stupefied before these convulsive metaphors, which might have been written by a fevered hand in a night's delirium, which gather a pageful of ideas and pictures in half a sentence, which scorch the eyes they would enlighten. Words lose their meaning; constructions are put out of joint; paradoxes of style, apparently false expressions, which a man might occasionally venture upon with diffidence in the transport of his rapture, become the ordinary language. Shakspeare dazzles, repels, terrifies, disgusts, oppresses; his verses are a piercing and sublime song, pitched in too high a key, above the reach of our organs, which offends our ears, of which our mind alone can divine the justice and beauty.

Yet this is little; for that singular force of concentration is redoubled by the suddenness of the dash which calls it into existence. In Shakspeare there is no preparation, no adaptation, no development, no care to make himself understood. Like a too fiery and powerful horse, he bounds, but cannot run. He bridges in a couple of words an enormous interval; is at the two poles in a single instant. The reader vainly looks for the intermediate track; dazed by these prodigious leaps, he wonders by what miracle the poet has entered upon a new idea the very moment when he quitted the last, seeing perhaps between the two images a long scale of transitions, which we mount with difficulty step by step, but which he has spanned in a stride. Shakspeare flies, we creep. Hence comes a style made up of conceits, bold images shattered in an instant by others still bolder, barely indicated ideas completed by others far removed, no visible connection, but a visible incoherence; at every step we halt, the track failing; and there, far above us, lo, stands the poet, and we find that we have ventured in his footsteps, through a craggy land, full of precipices, which he threads, as if it were a straightforward road, but on which our greatest efforts barely carry us along.

What will you think, further, if we observe that these vehement expressions, so natural in their up-welling, instead of following one after the other, slowly and with effort, are hurled out by hundreds, with an impetuous ease and abundance, like the bubbling waves from a welling spring, which are heaped together, rise one above another, and find nowhere room enough to spread and exhaust themselves? You may find in *Romeo and Juliet* a score of examples of this inexhaustible inspiration. The two lovers pile up an infinite mass of metaphors, impassioned exaggerations, clenches contorted phrases, amorous extravagances. Their language is like the trill of nightingales. Shakspeare's wits, Mercutio, Beatrice, Rosalind, his clowns, buffoons, sparkle with far-fetched jokes, which rattle out like a volley of musketry. There is none of them but provides enough play on words to stock a whole theatre. Lear's curses, or Queen Margaret's, would suffice for all the madmen in an asylum, or all the oppressed of the earth. The sonnets are a delirium of ideas and images, laboured at with an obstinacy enough to make a man giddy. His first poem, *Venus and Adonis*, is the sensual ecstasy of a Correggio, insatiable and excited. This exuberant fecundity intensifies qualities already in excess, and multiplies a hundred-fold the luxuriance of metaphor, the incoherence of style, and the unbridled vehemence of expression.[1]

All that I have said may be compressed into a few words. Objects were taken into his mind organised and complete; they pass into ours disjointed, decomposed, fragmentarily. He thought in the lump, we think piecemeal; hence his style and our style—two languages not to be reconciled. We, for our part, writers and reasoners, can note precisely by a word each isolated fraction of an idea, and represent the due order of its parts by the due order of our expressions. We advance gradually; we follow the filiations, refer continually to the roots, try and treat our words as numbers, our sentences as equations; we employ but general terms, which every mind can understand, and regular constructions, into which any mind can enter; we attain justness and clearness, not life. Shakspeare lets justness and clearness look out for themselves, and attains life. From amidst his complex conception and his coloured semi-vision he grasps a fragment, a quivering fibre, and shows it; it is for you, from this fragment, to divine the rest. He, behind the word, has a whole picture, an attitude, a long argument abridged, a mass of swarming ideas; you know them, these abbreviative, condensive words: these are they which we launch out amidst the fire of invention, in a fit of passion—words of slang or of fashion, which appeal to local memory or individual experience;[2]

[1] This is why, in the eyes of a writer of the seventeenth century, Shakspeare's style is the most obscure, pretentious, painful, barbarous, and absurd, that could be imagined.

[2] Shakspeare's vocabulary is the most copious of all. It comprises about 15,000 words; Milton's only 8000.

little desultory and incorrect phrases, which, by their irregularity, express the suddenness and the breaks of the inner sensation; trivial words, exaggerated figures.[1] There is a gesture beneath each, a quick contraction of the brows, a curl of laughing lips, a clown's trick, an unhinging of the whole machine. None of them mark ideas, all suggest images; each is the extremity and issue of a complete mimic action; none is the expression and definition of a partial and limited idea. This is why Shakspeare is strange and powerful, obscure and creative, beyond all the poets of his or any other age; the most immoderate of all violators of language, the most marvellous of all creators of souls, the farthest removed from regular logic and classical reason, the one most capable of exciting in us a world of forms and of placing living beings before us.

III.

Let us reconstruct this world, so as to find in it the imprint of its creator. A poet does not copy at random the manners which surround him; he selects from this vast material, and involuntarily brings upon the stage the habits of the heart and conduct which best suit his talent. If he is a logician, a moralist, an orator, as, for instance, one of the French great tragic poets (Racine) of the seventeenth century, he will only represent noble manners; he will avoid low characters; he will have a horror of menials and the plebs; he will observe the greatest decorum amidst the strongest outbreaks of passion; he will reject as scandalous every low or inde-

---

[1] See the conversation of Laertes and his sister, and of Laertes and Polonius, in *Hamlet*. The style is foreign to the situation; and we see here plainly the natural and necessary process of Shakspeare's thought.

cent word; he will give us reason, loftiness, good taste throughout; he will suppress the familiarity, childishness, artlessness, gay banter of domestic life; he will blot out precise details, special traits, and will carry tragedy into a serene and sublime region, where his abstract personages, unencumbered by time and space, after an exchange of eloquent harangues and able dissertations, will kill each other becomingly, and as though they were merely concluding a ceremony. Shakspeare does just the contrary, because his genius is the exact opposite. His master faculty is an impassioned imagination, freed from the shackles of reason and morality. He abandons himself to it, and finds in man nothing that he would care to lop off. He accepts nature and finds it beautiful in its entirety. He paints it in its littlenesses, its deformities, its weaknesses, its excesses, its irregularities, and in its rages; he exhibits man at his meals, in bed, at play, drunk, mad, sick; he adds that which ought not to be seen to that which passes on the stage. He does not dream of ennobling, but of copying human life, and aspires only to make his copy more energetic and more striking than the original.

Hence the morals of this drama; and first, the want of dignity. Dignity arises from self-command. A man selects the most noble of his acts and attitudes, and allows himself no other. Shakspeare's characters select none, but allow themselves all. His kings are men, and fathers of families. The terrible Leontes who is about to order the death of his wife and his friend, plays like a child with his son: caresses him, gives him all the pretty pet names which mothers are wont to employ; he dares be trivial; he gabbles like a nurse; he has her language and fulfils her duties:

> "*Leontes.* What, hast smutch'd thy nose?
> They say it is a copy out of mine. Come, captain,
> We must be neat; not neat, but cleanly, captain : . . .
> Come, sir page,
> Look on me with your welkin eye : sweet villain !
> Most dear'st ! my collop . . . Looking on the lines
> Of my boy's face, methoughts I did recoil
> Twenty-three years, and saw myself unbreech'd,
> In my green velvet coat, my dagger muzzled,
> Lest it should bite its master. . . .
> How like, methought, I then was to this kernel,
> This squash, this gentleman ! . . . My brother,
> Are you so fond of your young prince as we
> Do seem to be of ours ?
>   *Polixenes.* If at home, sir,
> He's all my exercise, my mirth, my matter,
> Now my sworn friend and then mine enemy,
> My parasite, my soldier, statesman, all :
> He makes a July's day short as December,
> And with his varying childness cures in me
> Thoughts that would thick my blood." [1]

There are a score of such passages in Shakspeare. The great passions, with him as in nature, are preceded or followed by trivial actions, small-talk, commonplace sentiments. Strong emotions are accidents in our life : to drink, to eat, to talk of indifferent things, to carry out mechanically an habitual duty, to dream of some stale pleasure or some ordinary annoyance, that is in which we employ all our time. Shakspeare paints us as we are; his heroes bow, ask people for news, speak of rain and fine weather, as often and as casually as ourselves, on the very eve of falling into the extremity of misery, or of plunging into fatal resolutions. Hamlet asks

[1] *Winter's Tale,* i. 2.

what's o'clock, finds the wind biting, talks of feasts and music heard without; and this quiet talk, so unconnected with the action, so full of slight, insignificant facts, which chance alone has raised up and guided, lasts until the moment when his father's ghost, rising in the darkness, reveals the assassination which it is his duty to avenge.

Reason tells us that our manners should be measured; this is why the manners which Shakspeare paints are not so. Pure nature is violent, passionate: it admits no excuses, suffers no middle course, takes no count of circumstances, wills blindly, breaks out into railing, has the irrationality, ardour, anger of children. Shakspeare's characters have hot blood and a ready hand. They cannot restrain themselves, they abandon themselves at once to their grief, indignation, love, and plunge desperately down the steep slope, where their passion urges them. How many need I quote? Timon, Posthumus, Cressida, all the young girls, all the chief characters in the great dramas; everywhere Shakspeare paints the unreflecting impetuosity of the impulse of the moment. Capulet tells his daughter Juliet that in three days she is to marry Earl Paris, and bids her be proud of it; she answers that she is not proud of it, and yet she thanks the earl for this proof of love. Compare Capulet's fury with the anger of Orgon,[1] and you may measure the difference of the two poets and the two civilisations:

> "*Capulet.* How now, how now, chop-logic! What is this?
> 'Proud,' and 'I thank you,' and 'I thank you not;'
> And yet 'not proud,' mistress minion, you,
> Thank me no thankings, nor proud me no prouds,

[1] One of Molière's characters in *Tartuffe*.—Tr.

But fettle your fine joints 'gainst Thursday next,
To go with Paris to Saint Peter's church,
Or I will drag thee on a hurdle thither.
Out, you green-sickness carrion! out, you baggage!
You tallow-face!

   Juliet. Good father, I beseech you on my knees,
Hear me with patience but to speak a word.

   C. Hang thee, young baggage! disobedient wretch
I tell thee what: get thee to church o' Thursday,
Or never after look me in the face:
Speak not, reply not, do not answer me;
My fingers itch. . . .

   Lady C. You are too hot.

   C. God's bread! it makes me mad:
Day, night, hour, tide, time, work, play,
Alone, in company, still my care hath been
To have her match'd: and having now provided
A gentleman of noble parentage,
Of fair demesnes, youthful, and nobly train'd,
Stuff'd, as they say, with honourable parts,
Proportion'd as one's thought would wish a man;
And then to have a wretched puling fool,
A whining mammet, in her fortune's tender,
To answer, '*I'll not wed; I cannot love,
I am too young; I pray you, pardon me,*"—
But, an you will not wed, I'll pardon you:
Graze where you will, you shall not house with me:
Look to't, think on't, I do not use to jest.
Thursday is near; lay hand on heart, advise:
An you be mine, I'll give you to my friend;
An you be not, hang, beg, starve, die in the streets,
For, by my soul, I'll ne'er acknowledge thee."[1]

This method of exhorting one's child to marry is peculiar to Shakspeare and the sixteenth century.

[1] *Romeo and Juliet,* iii. 5.

Contradiction to these men was like a red rag to a bull; it drove them mad.

We might be sure that in this age, and on this stage, decency was a thing unknown. It is wearisome, being a check; men got rid of it, because it was wearisome. It is a gift of reason and morality; as indecency is produced by nature and passion. Shakspeare's words are too indecent to be translated. His characters call things by their dirty names, and compel the thoughts to particular images of physical love. The talk of gentlemen and ladies is full of coarse allusions; we should have to find out an alehouse of the lowest description to hear like words nowadays.[1]

It would be in an alehouse too that we should have to look for the rude jests and brutal kind of wit which form the staple of these conversations. Kindly politeness is the slow fruit of advanced reflection; it is a sort of humanity and kindliness applied to small acts and everyday discourse; it bids man soften towards others, and forget himself for the sake of others; it constrains genuine nature, which is selfish and gross. This is why it is absent from the manners of the drama we are considering. You will see carmen, out of sportiveness and good humour, deal one another hard blows; so it is pretty well with the conversation of the lords and ladies of Shakspeare who are in a sportive mood; for instance, Beatrice and Benedick, very well bred folk as things go,[2] with a great reputation for wit and politeness, whose smart retorts create amusement

---

[1] *Henry VIII.* ii. 3, and many other scenes.
[2] *Much Ado about Nothing.* See also the manner in which Henry V. in Shakspeare's *King Henry V.* pays court to Katharine of France (v. 2).

for the bystanders. These "skirmishes of wit" consist in telling one another plainly: You are a coward, a glutton, an idiot, a buffoon, a rake, a brute! You are a parrot's tongue, a fool, a . . . (the word is there). Benedick says:

> "I will go . . . to the Antipodes . . . rather than hold three words' conference with this harpy. . . . I cannot endure my Lady Tongue. . . .
> *Don Pedro.* You have put him down, lady, you have put him down.
> *Beatrice.* So I would not he should do me, my lord, lest I should prove the mother of fools." [1]

We can infer the tone they use when in anger. Emilia, in *Othello,* says:

> " He call'd her whore ; a beggar in his drink
> Could not have laid such terms upon his callat." [2]

They have a vocabulary of foul words as complete as that of Rabelais, and they exhaust it. They catch up handfuls of mud, and hurl it at their enemy, not conceiving themselves to be smirched.

Their actions correspond. They go without shame or pity to the limits of their passion. They kill, poison, violate, burn; the stage is full of abominations. Shakspeare lugs upon the stage all the atrocious deeds of the civil wars. These are the ways of wolves and hyænas. We must read of Jack Cade's sedition[3] to gain an idea of this madness and fury. We might imagine we were seeing infuriated beasts, the murderous recklessness of a wolf in a sheepfold, the brutality of a hog fouling and rolling himself in filth and blood.

---

[1] *Much Ado about Nothing*, ii. 1. [2] Act iv. 2.
[3] *Second Part of Henry VI.* iv. 6.

They destroy, kill, butcher each other; with their feet in the blood of their victims, they call for food and drink; they stick heads on pikes and make them kiss one another, and they laugh.

"*Jack Cade.* There shall be in England seven halfpenny loaves sold for a penny. . . . There shall be no money ; all shall eat and drink on my score, and I will apparel them all in one livery. . . . And here sitting upon London-stone, I charge and command that, of the city's cost, the pissing-conduit run nothing but claret wine this first year of our reign. . . . Away, burn all the records of the realm : my mouth shall be the parliament of England. . . . And henceforth all things shall be in common. . . . What canst thou answer to my majesty for giving up of Normandy unto Mounsieur Basimecu, the dauphin of France ? . . . The proudest peer in the realm shall not wear a head on his shoulders, unless he pay me tribute ; there shall not a maid be married, but she shall pay to me her maidenhead ere they have it. (*Re-enter rebels with the heads of Lord Say and his son-in-law.*) But is not this braver ? Let them kiss one another, for they loved well when they were alive." [1]

Man must not be let loose; we know not what lusts and rage may brood under a sober guise. Nature was never so hideous, and this hideousness is the truth.

Are these cannibal manners only met with among the scum ? Why, the princes are worse. The Duke of Cornwall orders the old Earl of Gloucester to be tied to a chair, because, owing to him King Lear has escaped :

" Fellows, hold the chair.
Upon these eyes of thine I'll set my foot.
(*Gloucester is held down in the chair, while Cornwall plucks out one of his eyes, and sets his foot on it.*)

[1] *Henry VI.* 2d part, iv. 2, 6, 7.

Gloster. He that will think to live till he be old,
Give me some help! O cruel: O you gods!
   Regan. One side will mock another; the other too.
   Cornwall. If you see vengeance,—
   Servant.   Hold your hand, my lord:
I have served you ever since I was a child;
But better service have I never done you,
Than now to bid you hold.
   Regan. How now, you dog!
   Serv. If you did wear a beard upon your chin,
I'd shake it on this quarrel. What do you mean?
   Corn. My villain!   *Draws and runs at him.*)
   Serv. Nay, then, come on, and take the chance of anger.
              (*Draws; they fight; Cornwall is wounded.*)
   Regan. Give me thy sword. A peasant stand up thus.
              (*Snatches a sword, comes behind, and stabs him.*)
   Serv. O, I am slain! My lord, you have one eye left
To see some mischief on him. O!   (*Dies.*)
   Corn. Lest it see more, prevent it. Out, vile jelly!
Where is thy lustre now?
   Gloster. All dark and comfortless. Where's my son? . . .
   Regan. Go thrust him out at gates, and let him smell
His way to Dover."[1]

Such are the manners of that stage. They are unbridled, like those of the age, and like the poet's imagination. To copy the common actions of every-day life, the puerilities and feeblenesses to which the greatest continually sink, the outbursts of passion which degrade them, the indecent, harsh, or foul words, the atrocious deeds in which licence revels, the brutality and ferocity of primitive nature, is the work of a free and unencumbered imagination. To copy this hideousness and these excesses with a selection of such familiar, signi-

[1] *King Lear*, iii. 7.

ficant, precise details, that they reveal under every word of every personage a complete civilisation, is the work of a concentrated and all-powerful imagination. This species of manners and this energy of description indicate the same faculty, unique and excessive, which the style had already indicated.

IV.

On this common background stands out in striking relief a population of distinct living figures, illuminated by an intense light. This creative power is Shakspeare's great gift, and it communicates an extraordinary significance to his words. Every phrase pronounced by one of his characters enables us to see, besides the idea which it contains and the emotion which prompted it, the aggregate of the qualities and the entire character which produced it—the mood, physical attitude, bearing, look of the man, all instantaneously, with a clearness and force approached by no one. The words which strike our ears are not the thousandth part of those we hear within; they are like sparks thrown off here and there; the eyes catch rare flashes of flame; the mind alone perceives the vast conflagration of which they are the signs and the effect. He gives us two dramas in one: the first strange, convulsive, curtailed, visible; the other consistent, immense, invisible; the one covers the other so well, that as a rule we do not realise that we are perusing words: we hear the roll of those terrible voices, we see contracted features, glowing eyes, pallid faces; we see the agitation, the furious resolutions which mount to the brain with the feverish blood, and descend to the sharp-strung nerves. This property possessed by every phrase to exhibit a world of sentiments and forms, comes from the fact that the phrase is actually caused by a world of emotions and images. Shakspeare, when he wrote, felt all that we feel, and much besides. He had the prodigious faculty of seeing in a twinkling of the eye a complete character, body, mind, past and present, in every detail and every depth of his being, with the exact attitude and the expression of face, which the situation demanded. A word here and there of Hamlet or Othello would need for its explanation three pages of commentaries; each of the half-understood thoughts, which the commentator may have discovered, has left its trace in the turn of the phrase, in the nature of the metaphor, in the order of the words; nowadays, in pursuing these traces, we divine the thoughts. These innumerable traces have been impressed in a second, within the compass of a line. In the next line there are as many, impressed just as quickly, and in the same compass. You can gauge the concentration and the velocity of the imagination which creates thus.

These characters are all of the same family. Good or bad, gross or delicate, witty or stupid, Shakspeare gives them all the same kind of spirit which is his own. He has made of them imaginative people, void of will and reason, impassioned machines, vehemently jostled one against another, who were outwardly whatever is most natural and most abandoned in human nature. Let us act the play to ourselves, and see in all its stages this clanship of figures, this prominence of portraits.

Lowest of all are the stupid folk, babbling or brutish. Imagination already exists there, where reason is not yet born; it exists also there where reason is dead. The idiot and the brute blindly follow the phantoms which exist in their benumbed or mechanical brains.

No poet has understood this mechanism like Shakspeare. His Caliban, for instance, a deformed savage, fed on roots, growls like a beast under the hand of Prospero, who has subdued him. He howls continually against his master, though he knows that every curse will be paid back with "cramps and aches." He is a chained wolf, trembling and fierce, who tries to bite when approached, and who crouches when he sees the lash raised. He has a foul sensuality, a loud base laugh, the gluttony of degraded humanity. He wished to violate Miranda in her sleep. He cries for his food, and gorges himself when he gets it. A sailor who had landed in the island, Stephano, gives him wine; he kisses his feet, and takes him for a god; he asks if he has not dropped from heaven, and adores him. We find in him rebellious and baffled passions, which are eager to rise again and to be satiated. Stephano had beaten his comrade. Caliban cries, "Beat him enough: after a little time I'll beat him too." He prays Stephano to come with him and murder Prospero in his sleep; he thirsts to lead him there, dances through joy and sees his master already with his "weasand" cut, and his brains scattered on the earth:

> "Prithee, my king, be quiet. See'st thou here,
> This is the mouth o' the cell: no noise, and enter.
> Do that good mischief which may make this island
> Thine own for ever, and I, thy Caliban,
> For aye thy foot-licker."[1]

Others, like Ajax and Cloten, are more like men, and yet it is pure mood that Shakspeare depicts in them, as in Caliban. The clogging corporeal machine, the

[1] *The Tempest*, iv. 1.

mass of muscles, the thick blood sluggishly moving along in the veins of these fighting men, oppress the intelligence, and leave no life but for animal passions. Ajax uses his fists, and devours meat; that is his existence; if he is jealous of Achilles, it is pretty much as a bull is jealous of his fellow. He permits himself to be restrained and led by Ulysses, without looking before him: the grossest flattery decoys him. The Greeks have urged him to accept Hector's challenge. Behold him puffed up with pride, scorning to answer anyone, not knowing what he says or does. Thersites cries, "Good-morrow, Ajax;" and he replies, "Thanks, Agamemnon." He has no further thought than to contemplate his enormous frame, and roll majestically his big stupid eyes. When the day of the fight has come, he strikes at Hector as on an anvil. After a good while they are separated. "I am not warm yet," says Ajax, "let us fight again." [1] Cloten is less massive than this phlegmatic ox; but he is just as idiotic, just as vainglorious, just as coarse. The beautiful Imogen, urged by his insults and his scullion manners, tells him that his whole body is not worth as much as Posthumus' meanest garment. He is stung to the quick, repeats the word several times; he cannot shake off the idea, and runs at it again and again with his head down, like an angry ram:

"*Cloten.* 'His garment?' Now, the devil—

Imogen. To Dorothy my woman hie thee presently—

C. 'His garment?' . . . You have abused me: 'His meanest garment!' . . . I'll be revenged: 'His meanest garment!' Well." [2]

[1] See *Troilus and Cressida*, ii. 3, the jesting manner in which the generals drive on this fierce brute.   [2] *Cymbeline*, ii 3.

He gets some of Posthumus' garments, and goes to Milford Haven, expecting to meet Imogen there. On his way he mutters thus:

"With that suit upon my back, will I ravish her: first kill him, and in her eyes; there shall she see my valour, which will then be a torment to her contempt. He on the ground, my speech of insultment ended on his dead body, and when my lust has dined,—which, as I say, to vex her I will execute in the clothes that she so praised,—to the court I'll knock her back, foot her home again." [1]

Others again, are but babblers: for example, Polonius, the grave brainless counsellor; a great baby, not yet out of his "swathing clouts;" a solemn booby, who rains on men a shower of counsels, compliments, and maxims; a sort of court speaking-trumpet, useful in grand ceremonies, with the air of a thinker, but fit only to spout words. But the most complete of all these characters is that of the nurse in Romeo and Juliet, a gossip, loose in her talk, a regular kitchen oracle, smelling of the stew-pan and old boots, foolish, impudent, immoral, but otherwise a good creature, and affectionate to her nurse-child. Mark this disjointed and never-ending gossip's babble:

"*Nurse.* 'Faith I can tell her age unto an hour.
Lady Capulet. She's not fourteen. . . .
Nurse. Come Lammas-eve at night shall she be fourteen.
Susan and she—God rest all Christian souls!—
Were of an age: well, Susan is with God;
She was too good for me: but, as I said,
On Lammas-eve at night shall she be fourteen;
That shall she, marry; I remember it well.

[1] *Cymbeline*, iii. 5.

> 'Tis since the earthquake now eleven years;
> And she was wean'd,—I never shall forget it,—
> Of all the days of the year, upon that day:
> For I had then laid wormwood to my dug,
> Sitting in the sun under the dove-house wall;
> My lord and you were then at Mantua:—
> Nay, I do bear a brain:—but, as I said,
> When it did taste the wormwood on the nipple
> Of my dug and felt it bitter, pretty fool,
> To see it tetchy and fall out with the dug!
> Shake, quoth the dove-house: 'twas no need, I trow,
> To bid me trudge:
> And since that time it is eleven years;
> For then she could stand alone; nay, by the rood,
> She could have run and waddled all about;
> For even the day before, she broke her brow." [1]

Then she tells an indecent anecdote, which she begins over again four times. She is silenced: what then? She has her anecdote in her head, and cannot cease repeating it and laughing to herself. Endless repetitions are the mind's first step. The vulgar do not pursue the straight line of reasoning and of the story; they repeat their steps, as it were merely marking time: struck with an image, they keep it for an hour before their eyes, and are never tired of it. If they do advance, they turn aside to a hundred subordinate ideas before they get at the phrase required. They allow themselves to be diverted by all the thoughts which come across them. This is what the nurse does; and when she brings Juliet news of her lover, she torments and wearies her, less from a wish to tease than from a habit of wandering from the point:

[1] *Romeo and Juliet*, i. 3.

"*Nurse.* Jesu, what haste? can you not stay awhile?
Do you not see that I am out of breath?
Juliet. How art thou out of breath, when thou hast breath
To say to me that thou art out of breath?
Is thy news good, or bad? answer to that;
Say either, and I'll stay the circumstance:
Let me be satisfied: is't good or bad?
N. Well, you have made a simple choice; you know not how to choose a man: Romeo! no, not he: though his face be better than any man's, yet his leg excels all men's; and for a hand and a foot, and a body, though they be not to be talked on, yet they are past compare: he is not the flower of courtesy, but, I'll warrant him, as gentle as a lamb. Go thy ways, wench; serve God. What, have you dined at home?
J. No, no: but all this did I know before.
What says he of our marriage? what of that?
N. Lord, how my head aches! what a head have I!
It beats as it would fall in twenty pieces.
My back o' t'other side,—O, my back, my back!
Beshrew your heart for sending me about,
To catch my death with jaunting up and down!
J. I' faith, I am sorry that thou art not well.
Sweet, sweet, sweet nurse, tell me, what says my love?
N. Your love says, like an honest gentleman, and a courteous, and a kind, and a handsome, and, I warrant, a virtuous,—Where is your mother?"[1]

It is never-ending. Her gabble is worse when she comes to announce to Juliet the death of her cousin and the banishment of Romeo. It is the shrill cry and chatter of an overgrown asthmatic magpie. She laments, confuses the names, spins roundabout sentences, ends by asking for *aqua-vitæ*. She curses Romeo, then brings him to Juliet's chamber. Next day Juliet is

[1] *Romeo and Juliet*, ii. 5.

ordered to marry Earl Paris; Juliet throws herself into her nurse's arms, praying for comfort, advice, assistance. The other finds the true remedy: Marry Paris,

> "O, he's a lovely gentleman!
> Romeo's a dishclout to him: an eagle, madam,
> Hath not so green, so quick, so fair an eye
> As Paris hath. Beshrew my very heart,
> I think you are happy in this second match,
> For it excels your first." [1]

This cool immorality, these weather-cock arguments, this fashion of estimating love like a fishwoman, completes the portrait.

V.

The mechanical imagination produces Shakspeare's fool-characters: a quick venturesome dazzling, unquiet imagination, produces his men of wit. Of wit there are many kinds. One, altogether French, which is but reason, a foe to paradox, scorner of folly, a sort of incisive common sense, having no occupation but to render truth amusing and evident, the most effective weapon with an intelligent and vain people: such was the wit of Voltaire and the drawing-rooms. The other, that of improvisatores and artists, is a mere inventive rapture, paradoxical, unshackled, exuberant, a sort of self-entertainment, a phantasmagoria of images, flashes of wit, strange ideas, dazing and intoxicating, like the movement and illumination in a ball-room. Such is the wit of Mercutio, of the clowns, of Beatrice, Rosalind, and Benedick. They laugh, not from a sense of the ridiculous, but from the desire to laugh. You must

[1] *Romeo and Juliet,* iii. 5.

look elsewhere for the campaigns which aggressive reason makes against human folly. Here folly is in its full bloom. Our folk think of amusement, and nothing more. They are good-humoured; they let their wit prance gaily over the possible and the impossible. They play upon words, contort their sense, draw absurd and laughable inferences, send them back to one another, and without intermission, as if with shuttlecocks, and vie with each other in singularity and invention. They dress all their ideas in strange or sparkling metaphors. The taste of the time was for masquerades; their conversation is a masquerade of ideas. They say nothing in a simple style; they only seek to heap together subtle things, far-fetched, difficult to invent and to understand; all their expressions are over-refined, unexpected, extraordinary; they strain their thought, and change it into a caricature. " Alas, poor Romeo!" says Mercutio, " he is already dead; stabbed with a white wench's black eye; shot through the ear with a love-song, the very pin of his heart cleft with the blind bow-boy's butt-shaft."[1] Benedick relates a conversation he has just held with his mistress : " O, she misused me past the endurance of a block! an oak, but with one green leaf on it would have answered her; my very visor began to assume life, and scold with her."[2] These gay and perpetual extravagances show the bearing of the speakers. They do not remain quietly seated in their chairs, like the Marquesses in the *Misanthrope;* they whirl round, leap, paint their faces, gesticulate boldly their ideas; their wit-rockets end with a song. Young folk, soldiers and artists, they let off their fireworks of phrases, and gambol round about. " There

[1] *Romeo and Juliet*, ii. 4.   [2] *Much Ado about Nothing*, ii. 1.

was a star danced, and under that was I born."[1] This expression of Beatrice's aptly describes the kind of poetical, sparkling, unreasoning, charming wit, more akin to music than to literature, a sort of dream, which is spoken out aloud, and whilst wide awake, not unlike that described by Mercutio:

> " O, then, I see Queen Mab hath been with you.
>   She is the fairies' midwife; and she comes
>   In shape no bigger than an agate-stone
>   On the fore-finger of an alderman,
>   Drawn with a team of little atomies
>   Athwart men's noses as they lie asleep;
>   Her waggon-spokes made of long spinners' legs,
>   The cover of the wings of grasshoppers,
>   The traces of the smallest spider's web,
>   The collars of the moonshine's watery beams,
>   Her whip of cricket's bone, the lash of film,
>   Her waggoner a small grey-coated gnat,
>   Not half so big as a round little worm
>   Prick'd from the lazy finger of a maid;
>   Her chariot is an empty hazel-nut,
>   Made by the joiner squirrel or old grub,
>   Time out o' mind the fairies' coachmakers.
>   And in this state she gallops night by night
>   Through lovers' brains, and then they dream of love:
>   O'er courtiers' knees, that dream on court'sies straight,
>   O'er lawyers' fingers, who straight dream on fees,
>   O'er ladies' lips, who straight on kisses dream. . . .
>   Sometime she gallops o'er a courtier's nose,
>   And then dreams he of smelling out a suit;
>   And sometime comes she with a tithe-pig's tail
>   Tickling a parson's nose as a' lies asleep,
>   Then dreams he of another benefice:

[1] *Much ado About Nothing*, ii. 1.

> Sometime she driveth o er a soldier's neck,
> And then dreams he of cutting foreign throats,
> Of breaches, ambuscadoes, Spanish blades,
> Of healths five-fathom deep ; and then anon
> Drums in his ear, at which he starts and wakes,
> And being thus frighted swears a prayer or two
> And sleeps again. This is that very Mab
> That plats the manes of horses in the night,
> And bakes the elf-locks in foul sluttish hairs,
> Which once untangled much misfortune bodes. . . .
> This is she"[1] . . .

Romeo interrupts him, or he would never end. Let the reader compare with the dialogue of the French theatre this little poem,

> " Child of an idle brain,
> Begot of nothing but vain fantasy,"[2]

introduced without incongruity in the midst of a conversation of the sixteenth century, and he will understand the difference between the wit which devotes itself to reasoning, or to record a subject for laughter, and that imagination which is self-amused with its own act.

Falstaff has the passions of an animal, and the imagination of a man of wit. There is no character which better exemplifies the fire and immorality of Shakspeare. Falstaff is a great supporter of disreputable places, swearer, gamester, idler, wine-bibber, as low as he well can be. He has a big belly, bloodshot eyes, bloated face, shaking legs; he spends his life with his elbows among the tavern-jugs, or asleep on the ground behind the arras; he only wakes to curse, lie, brag, and steal

[1] *Romeo and Juliet*, i. 4. *Ibid.*

He is as big a swindler as Panurge, who had sixty-three ways of making money, "of which the honestest was by sly theft." And what is worse, he is an old man, a knight, a courtier, and well educated. Must he not be odious and repulsive? By no means; we cannot help liking him. At bottom, like his brother Panurge, he is "the best fellow in the world." He has no malice in his composition; no other wish than to laugh and be amused. When insulted, he bawls out louder than his attackers, and pays them back with interest in coarse words and insults; but he owes them no grudge for it. The next minute he is sitting down with them in a low tavern, drinking their health like a brother and comrade. If he has vices, he exposes them so frankly that we are obliged to forgive him them. He seems to say to us "Well, so I am, what then? I like drinking: isn't the wine good? I take to my heels when hard hitting begins; don't blows hurt? I get into debt, and do fools out of their money; isn't it nice to have money in your pocket? I brag; isn't it natural to want to be well thought of?"—"Dost thou hear, Hal? thou knowest, in the state of innocency, Adam fell; and what should poor Jack Falstaff do in the days of villany? Thou seest I have more flesh than another man, and therefore more frailty."[1] Falstaff is so frankly immoral, that he ceases to be so. Conscience ends at a certain point; nature assumes its place, and man rushes upon what he desires, without more thought of being just or unjust than an animal in the neighbouring wood. Falstaff, engaged in recruiting, has sold exemptions to all the rich people, and only enrolled starved and half-naked wretches. There's but a shirt

---

[1] First Part of *King Henry IV.*, iii. 3.

and a half in all his company: that does not trouble him. Bah: "they'll find linen enough on every hedge." The prince, who has seen them, says, "I did never see such pitiful rascals." "Tut, tut," answers Falstaff, "good enough to toss; food for powder; they'll fill a pit as well as better; tush, man, mortal men, mortal men."[1] His second excuse is his unfailing spirit. If ever there was a man who could jabber, it is he. Insults and oaths, curses, jobations, protests, flow from him as from an open barrel. He is never at a loss; he devises a shift for every difficulty. Lies sprout out of him, fructify, increase, beget one another, like mushrooms on a rich and rotten bed of earth. He lies still more from his imagination and nature than from interest and necessity. It is evident from the manner in which he strains his fictions. He says he has fought alone against two men. The next moment it is four. Presently we have seven, then eleven, then fourteen. He is stopped in time, or he would soon be talking of a whole army. When unmasked, he does not lose his temper, and is the first to laugh at his boastings. "Gallants, lads, boys, hearts of gold. . . . What, shall we be merry? shall we have a play extempore?"[2] He does the scolding part of King Henry with so much truth, that we might take him for a king, or an actor. This big pot-bellied fellow, a coward, a cynic, a brawler, a drunkard, a lewd rascal, a pothouse poet, is one of Shakspeare's favourites. The reason is, that his morals are those of pure nature, and Shakspeare's mind is congenial with his own.

[1] First Part of *King Henry IV.*, iv. 2. [2] *Ibid.* ii. 4.

VI.

Nature is shameless and gross amidst this mass of flesh, heavy with wine and fatness. It is delicate in the delicate body of women, but as unreasoning and impassioned in Desdemona as in Falstaff. Shakspeare's women are charming children, who feel in excess and love passionately. They have unconstrained manners, little rages, nice words of friendship, a coquettish rebelliousness, a graceful volubility, which recall the warbling and the prettiness of birds. The heroines of the French stage are almost men; these are women and in every sense of the word. More imprudent than Desdemona a woman could not be. She is moved with pity for Cassio, and asks a favour for him passionately, recklessly, be the thing just or no, dangerous or no. She knows nothing of man's laws, and does not think of them. All that she sees is, that Cassio is unhappy:—

> " Be thou assured, good Cassio . . . My lord shall never rest;
> I'll watch him, tame and talk him out of patience;
> His bed shall seem a school, his board a shrift;
> I'll intermingle everything he does
> With Cassio's suit." [1]

She asks her favour:

> "*Othello.* Not now, sweet Desdemona; some other time.
> *Desdemona.* But shall't be shortly?
> *O.* The sooner, sweet, for you.
> *Des.* Shall't be to-night at supper?
> *O.* No, not to-night.
> *Des.* To-morrow dinner, then?
> *O.* I shall not dine at home;
> I meet the captains at the citadel.

[1] *Othello*, iii. 3.

> *Des.* Why, then, to-morrow night; or Tuesday morn;
> On Tuesday noon, or night; on Wednesday morn;
> I prithee, name the time, but let it not
> Exceed three days: in faith, he's penitent." [1]

She is somewhat astonished to see herself refused: she scolds Othello. He yields: who would not yield seeing a reproach in those lovely sulking eyes? O, says she, with a pretty pout:

> "This is not a boon;
> 'Tis as I should entreat you wear your gloves,
> Or feed on nourishing dishes, or keep you warm,
> Or sue to you to do peculiar profit
> To your own person." [2]

A moment after, when he prays her to leave him alone for a while, mark the innocent gaiety, the ready curtsy, the playful child's tone:

> "Shall I deny you? no: farewell, my lord. . . .
> Emilia, come: Be as your fancies teach you;
> Whate'er you be, I am obedient." [3]

This vivacity, this petulance, does not prevent shrinking modesty and silent timidity: on the contrary, they spring from a common cause, extreme sensibility. She who feels much and quickly has more reserve and more passion than others; she breaks out or is silent; she says nothing or everything. Such is this Imogen

> "So tender of rebukes that words are strokes,
> And strokes death to her." [4]

Such is Virgilia, the sweet wife of Coriolanus; her heart is not a Roman one; she is terrified at her husband's victories: when Volumnia describes him

---

[1] *Othello*, iii. 3. [2] *Ibid.* [3] *Ibid.* [4] *Cymbeline.* iii. 5.

stamping on the field of battle, and wiping his bloody brow with his hand, she grows pale:

> "His bloody brow! O Jupiter, no blood! . . .
> Heavens bless my lord from fell Aufidius!"[1]

She wishes to forget all that she knows of these dangers; she dare not think of them. When asked if Coriolanus does not generally return wounded, she cries, "O, no, no, no." She avoids this cruel picture, and yet nurses a secret pang at the bottom of her heart. She will not leave the house: "I'll not over the threshold till my lord return."[2] She does not smile, will hardly admit a visitor; she would blame herself, as for a lack of tenderness, for a moment's forgetfulness or gaiety. When he does return, she can only blush and weep. This exalted sensibility must needs end in love. All Shakspeare's women love without measure, and nearly all at first sight. At the first look Juliet casts on Romeo, she says to the nurse:

> "Go, ask his name: if he be married,
> My grave is like to be my wedding bed."[3]

It is the revelation of their destiny. As Shakspeare has made them, they cannot but love, and they must love till death. But this first look is an ecstasy: and this sudden approach of love is a transport. Miranda seeing Fernando, fancies that she sees "a thing divine." She halts motionless, in the amazement of this sudden vision, at the sound of these heavenly harmonies which rise from the depths of her heart. She weeps, on seeing him drag the heavy logs; with her slender white hands she would do the work whilst he reposed. Her compassion and tenderness carry her away; she is no longer

---

[1] *Coriolanus*, i. 3.   [2] *Ibid.*   [3] *Romeo and Juliet*, i. 5.

mistress of her words, she says what she would not, what her father has forbidden her to disclose, what an instant before she would never have confessed. The too full heart overflows unwittingly, happy, and ashamed at the current of joy and new sensations with which an unknown feeling has flooded her:

"*Miranda.* I am a fool to weep at what I am glad of. . . .
Fernando. Wherefore weep you?
M. At mine unworthiness that dare not offer
What I desire to give, and much less take
What I shall die to want. . . .
I am your wife, if you will marry me;
If not, I'll die your maid."[1]

This irresistible invasion of love transforms the whole character. The shrinking and tender Desdemona, suddenly, in full senate, before her father, renounces her father; dreams not for an instant of asking his pardon, or consoling him. She will leave for Cyprus with Othello, through the enemy's fleet and the tempest. Everything vanishes before the one and adored image which has taken entire and absolute possession of her whole heart. So, extreme evils, bloody resolves, are only the natural sequence of such love. Ophelia becomes mad, Juliet commits suicide; no one but looks upon such madness and death as necessary. You will not then discover virtue in these souls, for by virtue is implied a determinate desire to do good, and a rational observance of duty. They are only pure through delicacy or love. They recoil from vice as a gross thing, not as an immoral thing. What they feel is not respect for the marriage vow, but adoration of their husband.

[1] *The Tempest*, iii. 1.

"O sweetest, fairest lily!" So Cymbeline speaks of one of these frail and lovely flowers which cannot be torn from the tree to which they have grown, whose least impurity would tarnish their whiteness. When Imogen learns that her husband means to kill her as being faithless, she does not revolt at the outrage; she has no pride, but only love. "False to his bed!" She faints at the thought that she is no longer loved. When Cordelia hears her father, an irritable old man, already almost insane, ask her how she loves him, she cannot make up her mind to say aloud the flattering protestations which her sisters have been lavishing. She is ashamed to display her tenderness before the world, and to buy a dowry by it. He disinherits her, and drives her away: she holds her tongue. And when she afterwards finds him abandoned and mad, she goes on her knees before him, with such a touching emotion, she weeps over that dear insulted head with so gentle a pity, that you might fancy it was the tender voice of a desolate but delighted mother, kissing the pale lips of her child:

> "O you kind gods,
> Cure this great breach in his abused nature!
> The untuned and jarring senses, O, wind up
> Of this child-changed father! . . .
> O my dear father! Restoration hang
> Thy medicine on my lips; and let this kiss
> Repair those violent harms that my two sisters
> Have in thy reverence made! . . . Was this a face
> To be opposed against the warring winds?
> . . . Mine enemy's dog,
> Though he had bit me, should have stood that night
> Against my fire. . . .
> How does my royal lord? How fares your majesty?"[1]

[1] *King Lear*, iv. 7.

If, in short, Shakspeare comes across a heroic character, worthy of Corneille, a Roman, such as the mother of Coriolanus, he will explain by passion, what Corneille would have explained by heroism. He will depict it violent and thirsting for the violent feelings of glory. She will not be able to refrain herself. She will break out into accents of triumph when she sees her son crowned; into imprecations of vengeance when she sees him banished. She will descend to the vulgarities of pride and anger; she will abandon herself to mad effusions of joy, to dreams of an ambitious fancy,[1] and will prove once more that the impassioned imagination of Shakspeare has left its trace in all the creatures whom it has called forth.

VII.

Nothing is easier to such a poet than to create perfect villains. Throughout he is handling the unruly passions which make their character, and he never hits upon the moral law which restrains them; but at the same time, and by the same faculty, he changes the inanimate masks, which the conventions of the stage mould on an identical pattern, into living and illusory figures.

---

[1] " O ye're well met : the hoarded plague o' the gods
Requite your love !
If that I could for weeping, you should hear—
Nay, and you shall hear some. . . .
I'll tell thee what ; yet go :
Nay but thou shalt stay too : I would my son
Were in Arabia, and thy tribe before him,
His good sword in his hand."—*Coriolanus*, iv. 2.
See again, *Coriolanus*, i. 3, the frank and abandoned triumph of a woman of the people ; " I sprang not more in joy at first hearing he was a man-child than now in first seeing he had proved himself a man."

How shall a demon be made to look as real as a man? Iago is a soldier of fortune who has roved the world from Syria to England, who, nursed in the lowest ranks, having had close acquaintance with the horrors of the wars of the sixteenth century, had drawn thence the maxims of a Turk and the philosophy of a butcher; principles he has none left. "O my reputation, my reputation!" cries the dishonoured Cassio. "As I am an honest man," says Iago, "I thought you had received some bodily wound; there is more sense in that than in reputation."[1] As for woman's virtue, he looks upon it like a man who has kept company with slave-dealers. He estimates Desdemona's love as he would estimate a mare's: that sort of thing lasts so long—then . . . And then he airs an experimental theory with precise details and nasty expressions like a stud doctor. "It cannot be that Desdemona should long continue her love to the Moor, nor he his to her. . . . These Moors are changeable in their wills; . . . the food that to him now is as luscious as locusts, shall be to him shortly as bitter as coloquintida. She must change for youth: when she is sated with his body, she will find the error of her choice."[2] Desdemona on the shore, trying to forget her cares, begs him to sing the praises of her sex. For every portrait he finds the most insulting insinuations. She insists, and bids him take the case of a deserving woman. "Indeed" he replies, "She was a wight, if ever such wight were, . . . to suckle fools and chronicle small beer."[3] He also says, when Desdemona asks him what he would write in praise of her: "O gentle lady do not put me to't; for I am nothing, if not critical."[4] This is the key to his char-

---

[1] *Othello*, ii. 3. [2] *Ibid.* i. 3. [3] *Ibid.* ii. 1. [4] *Ibid.*

acter. He despises man; to him Desdemona is a little wanton wench, Cassio an elegant word-shaper, Othello a mad bull, Roderigo an ass to be basted, thumped, made to go. He diverts himself by setting these passions at issue; he laughs at it as at a play. When Othello, swooning, shakes in his convulsions, he rejoices at this capital result: "Work on, my medicine, work! Thus credulous fools are caught."[1] You would take him for one of the poisoners of the time, studying the effect of a new potion on a dying dog. He only speaks in sarcasms: he has them ready for every one, even for those whom he does not know. When he wakes Brabantio to inform him of the elopement of his daughter, he tells him the matter in coarse terms, sharpening the sting of the bitter pleasantry, like a conscientious executioner, rubbing his hands when he hears the culprit groan under the knife. "Thou art a villain!" cries Brabantio. "You are — a senator!" answers Iago. But the feature which really completes him, and makes him take rank with Mephistopheles, is the atrocious truth and the cogent reasoning by which he likens his crime to virtue.[2] Cassio, under his advice, goes to see Desdemona, to obtain her intercession for him; this visit is to be the ruin of Desdemona and Cassio. Iago, left alone, hums for an instant quietly, then cries:

> "And what's he then that says I play the villain?
> When this advice is free I give and honest,
> Probal to thinking and indeed the course
> To win the Moor again."[3]

[1] *Othello*, iv. 1.
[2] See the like cynicism and scepticism in Richard III. Both begin by slandering human nature, and both are misanthropical of *malice prepense*.
[3] *Othello*, ii. 3.

To all these features must be added a diabolical energy,[1] an inexhaustible inventiveness in images, caricatures, obscenity, the manners of a guard-room, the brutal bearing and tastes of a trooper, habits of dissimulation, coolness, hatred, and patience, contracted amid the perils and devices of a military life, and the continuous miseries of long degradation and frustrated hope; you will understand how Shakspeare could transform abstract treachery into a concrete form, and how Iago's atrocious vengeance is only the natural consequence of his character, life, and training.

VIII.

How much more visible is this impassioned and unfettered genius of Shakspeare in the great characters which sustain the whole weight of the drama! The startling imagination, the furious velocity of the manifold and exuberant ideas, passion let loose, rushing upon death and crime, hallucinations, madness, all the ravages of delirium bursting through will and reason: such are the forces and ravings which engender them. Shall I speak of dazzling Cleopatra, who holds Antony in the whirlwind of her devices and caprices, who fascinates and kills, who scatters to the winds the lives of men as a handful of desert dust, the fatal Eastern sorceress who sports with love and death, impetuous, irresistible, child of air and fire, whose life is but a tempest, whose thought, ever barbed and broken, is like the crackling of a lightning flash? Of Othello, who, beset by the graphic picture of physical adultery, cries at every word of Iago like a man on the rack;

[1] See his conversation with Brabantio, then with Roderigo, Act i.

who, his nerves hardened by twenty years of war and shipwreck, grows mad and swoons for grief, and whose soul, poisoned by jealousy, is distracted and disorganised in convulsions and in stupor? Or of old King Lear, violent and weak, whose half-unseated reason is gradually toppled over under the shocks of incredible treacheries, who presents the frightful spectacle of madness, first increasing, then complete, of curses, howlings, superhuman sorrows, into which the transport of the first access of fury carries him, and then of peaceful incoherence, chattering imbecility, into which the shattered man subsides; a marvellous creation, the supreme effort of pure imagination, a disease of reason, which reason could never have conceived?[1] Amid so many portraitures let us choose two or three to indicate the depth and nature of them all. The critic is lost in Shakspeare, as in an immense town; he will describe a couple of monuments, and entreat the reader to imagine the city.

Plutarch's Coriolanus is an austere, coldly haughty patrician, a general of the army. In Shakspeare's hands he becomes a coarse soldier, a man of the people as to his language and manners, an athlete of war, with a voice like a trumpet; whose eyes by contradiction are filled with a rush of blood and anger, proud and terrible in mood, a lion's soul in the body of a bull. The philosopher Plutarch told of him a lofty philosophic action, saying that he had been at pains to save his landlord in the sack of Corioli. Shakspeare's Coriolanus has indeed the same disposition, for he is really a good fellow; but when Lartius asks him the name

[1] See again, in Timon, and Hotspur more particularly, perfect examples of vehement and unreasoning imagination.

of this poor Volscian, in order to secure his liberty, he yawns out:

> "By Jupiter! forgot.
> I am weary; yea, my memory is tired.
> Have we no wine here?"[1]

He is hot, he has been fighting, he must drink; he leaves his Volscian in chains, and thinks no more of him. He fights like a porter, with shouts and insults, and the cries from that deep chest are heard above the din of the battle like the sounds from a brazen trumpet. He has scaled the walls of Corioli, he has butchered till he is gorged with slaughter. Instantly he turns to the army of Cominius, and arrives red with blood, "as he were flay'd." "Come I too late?" Cominius begins to compliment him. "Come I too late?" he repeats. The battle is not yet finished: he embraces Cominius:

> "O! let me clip ye
> In arms as sound as when I woo'd, in heart
> As merry as when our nuptial day was done."[2]

For the battle is a real holiday to him. Such senses, such a strong frame, need the outcry, the din of battle, the excitement of death and wounds. This haughty and indomitable heart needs the joy of victory and destruction. Mark the display of his patrician arrogance and his soldier's bearing, when he is offered the tenth of the spoils:

> "I thank you, general;
> But cannot make my heart consent to take
> A bribe to pay my sword."[3]

[1] *Coriolanus*, i. 9.   [2] *Ibid.* i. 6.   [3] *Ibid.* i. 9.

The soldiers cry, Marcius! Marcius! and the trumpets sound. He gets into a passsion: rates the brawlers:

> "No more, I say! For that I have not wash'd
> My nose that bled, or foil'd some debile wretch,—
> ... You shout me forth
> In acclamations hyperbolical;
> As if I loved my little should be dieted
> In praises sauced with lies." [1]

They are reduced to loading him with honours: Cominius gives him a war-horse; decrees him the cognomen of Coriolanus: the people shout Caius Marcius Coriolanus! He replies:

> "I will go wash;
> And when my face is fair, you shall perceive
> Whether I blush or no: howbeit, I thank you.
> I mean to stride your steed." [2]

This loud voice, loud laughter, blunt acknowledgment, of a man who can act and shout better than speak, foretell the mode in which he will treat the plebeians. He loads them with insults; he cannot find abuse enough for the cobblers, tailors, envious cowards, down on their knees for a coin. "To beg of Hob and Dick!" "Bid them wash their faces and keep their teeth clean." But he must beg, if he would be consul; his friends constrain him. It is then that the passionate soul, incapable of self-restraint, such as Shakspeare knew how to paint, breaks forth without hindrance. He is there in his candidate's gown, gnashing his teeth, and getting up his lesson in this style:

[1] *Coriolanus*, i. 9.   [2] *Ibid.*

> "What must I say?
> 'I pray, sir'—Plague upon't! I cannot bring
> My tongue to such a pace:—'Look, sir, my wounds!
> I got them in my country's service, when
> Some certain of your brethren roar'd and ran
> From the noise of our own drums.'"[1]

The tribunes have no difficulty in stopping the election of a candidate who begs in this fashion. They taunt him in full senate, reproach him with his speech about the corn. He repeats it, with aggravations. Once roused, neither danger nor prayer restrains him:

> "His heart's his mouth:
> And, being angry, 'does forget that ever
> He heard the name of death."[2]

He rails against the people, the tribunes, ediles, flatterers of the plebs. "Come, enough," says his friend Menenius. "Enough, with over-measure," says Brutus the tribune. He retorts:

> "No, take more:
> What may be sworn by, both divine and human,
> Seal what I end withal! . . . At once pluck out
> The multitudinous tongue; let them not lick
> The sweet which is their poison."[3]

The tribune cries, Treason! and bids seize him. He cries:

> "Hence, old goat! . . .
> Hence, rotten thing! or I shall shake thy bones
> Out of thy garments!"[4]

He strikes him, drives the mob off: he fancies himself amongst Volscians. "On fair ground I could beat forty of them!" And when his friends hurry him off, he threatens still, and

[1] *Coriolanus*, ii. 3.   [2] *Ibid.* iii. 1.   [3] *Ibid.*   [4] *Ibid.*

"Speak(s) o' the people,
As if you (he) were a god to punish, not
A man of their infirmity."[1]

Yet he bends before his mother, for he has recognised in her a soul as lofty and a courage as intractable as his own. He has submitted from his infancy to the ascendency of this pride which he admires. Volumnia reminds him: "My praises made thee first a soldier." Without power over himself, continually tost on the fire of his too hot blood, he has always been the arm, she the thought. He obeys from involuntary respect, like a soldier before his general, but with what effort!

"*Coriolanus.* The smiles of knaves
Tent in my cheeks, and schoolboys' tears take up
The glances of my sight! a beggar's tongue
Make motion through my lips, and my arm'd knees
Who bow'd but in my stirrup, bend like his
That hath received an alms!—I will not do't. . . .
    Volumnia.   . . . Do as thou list.
Thy valiantness was mine, thou suck'dst it from me,
But owe thy pride thyself.
    Cor. Pray, be content:
Mother, I am going to the market-place;
Chide me no more. I'll mountebank their loves,
Cog their hearts from them, and come home beloved
Of all the trades in Rome."[2]

He goes, and his friends speak for him. Except a few bitter asides, he appears to be submissive. Then the tribunes pronounce the accusation, and summon him to answer as a traitor:

[1] *Coriolanus*, iii. 1. [2] *Ibid.* iii. 2.

> "*Cor.* How! traitor!
> *Men.* Nay, temperately: your promise.
> *Cor.* The fires i' the lowest hell fold-in the people!
> Call me their traitor! Thou injurious tribune!
> Within thine eyes sat twenty thousand deaths,
> In thy hands clutch'd as many millions, in
> Thy lying tongue both numbers, I would say,
> 'Thou liest,' unto thee with a voice as free
> As I do pray the gods."[1]

His friends surround him, entreat him: he will not listen; he foams at the mouth, he is like a wounded lion:

> "Let them pronounce the steep Tarpeian death,
> Vagabond exile, flaying, pent to linger.
> But with a grain a day, I would not buy
> Their mercy at the price of one fair word."[2]

The people vote exile, supporting by their shouts the sentence of the tribune:

> "*Cor.* You common cry of curs! whose breath I hate
> As reek o' the rotten fens, whose love I prize
> As the dead carcasses of unburied men
> That do corrupt my air, I banish you. . . . Despising,
> For you, the city, thus I turn my back:
> There is a world elsewhere."[3]

Judge of his hatred by these raging words. It goes on increasing whilst waiting for vengeance. We find him next with the Volscian army before Rome. His friends kneel before him, he lets them kneel. Old Menenius, who had loved him as a son, only comes now to be driven away   "Wife, mother, child, I know not."[4]

---

[1] *Coriolanus*, iii. 3.   [2] *Ibid.*   [3] *Ibid.*   [4] *Ibid.* v. 2

He knows not himself. For this strength of hating in a noble heart is the same as the force of loving. He has transports of tenderness as of rage, and can contain himself no more in joy than in grief. He runs, spite of his resolution, to his wife's arms; he bends his knee before his mother. He had summoned the Volscian chiefs to make them witnesses of his refusals; and before them, he grants all, and weeps. On his return to Corioli, an insulting word from Aufidius maddens him, and drives him upon the daggers of the Volscians. Vices and virtues, glory and misery, greatness and feebleness, the unbridled passion which composes his nature, endowed him with all.

If the life of Coriolanus is the history of a mood, that of Macbeth is the history of a monomania. The witches' prophecy has sunk into his mind at once, like a fixed idea. Gradually this idea corrupts the rest, and transforms the whole man. He is haunted by it; he forgets the thanes who surround him and "who stay upon his leisure;" he already sees in the future an indistinct chaos of images of blood:

> . . . "Why do I yield to that suggestion
> Whose horrid image doth unfix my hair
> And make my seated heart knock at my ribs ? . . .
> My thought, whose murder yet is but fantastical,
> Shakes so my single state of man that function
> Is smother'd in surmise, and nothing is
> But what is not." [1]

This is the language of hallucination. Macbeth's hallucination becomes complete when his wife has persuaded him to assassinate the king. He sees in the air a blood-stained dagger, "in form as palpable, as this

[1] *Macbeth*, i. 3.

which now I draw." His whole brain is filled with grand and terrible phantoms, which the mind of a common murderer could never have conceived: the poetry of which indicates a generous heart, enslaved to an idea of fate, and capable of remorse:

> . . . " Now o'er the one half world
> Nature seems dead, and wicked dreams abuse
> The curtain'd sleep; witchcraft celebrates
> Pale Hecate's offerings, and wither'd murder,
> Alarum'd by his sentinel, the wolf,
> Whose howl's his watch, thus with his stealthy pace,
> With Tarquin's ravishing strides, towards his design
> Moves like a ghost. . . .   (*A bell rings.*)
> I go, and it is done; the bell invites me.
> Hear it not, Duncan; for it is a knell
> That summons thee to heaven or to hell." [1]

He has done the deed, and returns tottering, haggard, like a drunken man. He is horrified at his bloody hands, "these hangman's hands." Nothing now can cleanse them. The whole ocean might sweep over them, but they would keep the hue of murder. "What hands are here? ha, they pluck out mine eyes!" He is disturbed by a word which the sleeping chamberlains uttered:

> "One cried, 'God bless us!' and 'Amen' the other;
> As they had seen me with these hangman's hands.
> Listening their fear, I could not say 'Amen,'
> When they did say, 'God bless us!' . . .
> But wherefore could not I pronounce 'Amen!'
> I had most need of blessing, and 'Amen'
> Stuck in my throat." [2]

[1] *Macbeth*, ii. 1.   [2] *Ibid.* ii. 2

Then comes a strange dream; a frightful vision of the punishment that awaits him descends upon him.

Above the beating of his heart, the tingling of the blood which seethes in his brain, he had heard them cry:

> "'Sleep no more!
> Macbeth does murder sleep,' the innocent sleep,
> Sleep that knits up the ravell'd sleave of care,
> The death of each day's life, sore labour's bath,
> Balm of hurt minds, great nature's second course,
> Chief nourisher in life's feast."[1]

And the voice, like an angel's trumpet, calls him by all his titles:

> "'Glamis hath murder'd sleep, and therefore Cawdor
> Shall sleep no more; Macbeth shall sleep no more!'"[2]

This idea, incessantly repeated, beats in his brain, with monotonous and quick strokes, like the tongue of a bell. Insanity begins; all the force of his mind is occupied by keeping before him, in spite of himself, the image of the man whom he has murdered in his sleep:

> " To know my deed, 'twere best not know myself. (*Knock.*)
> Wake Duncan with thy knocking! I would thou couldst!"[3]

Thenceforth, in the rare intervals in which the fever of his mind is assuaged, he is like a man worn out by a long malady. It is the sad prostration of maniacs worn out by their fits of rage:

> " Had I but died an hour before this chance,
> I had lived a blessed time; for, from this instant
> There's nothing serious in mortality:

---

[1] *Macbeth*, ii. 2.   [2] *Ibid.*   [3] *Ibid.* ii. 3.

> All is but toys : renown and grace is dead ;
> The wine of life is drawn, and the mere lees
> Is left this vault to brag of." [1]

When rest has restored some force to the human machine, the fixed idea shakes him again, and drives him onward, like a pitiless horseman, who has left his panting horse only for a moment, to leap again into the saddle, and spur him over precipices. The more he has done, the more he must do :

> " I am in blood
> Stepp'd in so far that, should I wade no more,
> Returning were as tedious as go o'er." [2] . . .

He kills in order to preserve the fruit of his murders. The fatal circlet of gold attracts him like a magic jewel ; and he beats down, from a sort of blind instinct, the heads which he sees between the crown and him :

> " But let the frame of things disjoint, both the worlds suffer,
>   Ere we will eat our meal in fear and sleep
>   In the affliction of these terrible dreams
>   That shake us nightly : better be with the dead,
>   Whom we, to gain our peace, have sent to peace,
>   Than on the torture of the mind to lie
>   In restless ecstasy. Duncan is in his grave ;
>   After life's fitful fever he sleeps well ;
>   Treason has done his worst : nor steel, nor poison,
>   Malice domestic, foreign levy, nothing,
>   Can touch him further." [3]

Macbeth has ordered Banquo to be murdered, and in the midst of a great feast he is informed of the success of his plan. He smiles, and proposes Banquo's

---

[1] *Macbeth*, ii. 3. [2] *Ibid.* iii. 4. [3] *Ibid.* iii. 2.

health. Suddenly, conscience-smitten, he sees the ghost of the murdered man; for this phantom, which Shakspeare summons, is not a mere stage-trick: we feel that here the supernatural is unnecessary, and that Macbeth would create it, even if hell would not send it. With muscles twitching, dilated eyes, his mouth half open with deadly terror, he sees it shake its bloody head, and cries with that hoarse voice which is only to be heard in maniacs' cells:

> "Prithee, see there ! Behold ! look ! lo ! how say you ?
> Why, what care I ? If thou canst nod, speak too.
> If charnel-houses and our graves must send
> Those that we bury back, our monuments
> Shall be the maws of kites. . . .
> Blood hath been shed ere now, i' the olden time, . . .
> Ay, and since too, murders have been perform'd
> Too terrible for the ear: the times have been,
> That, when the brains were out, the man would die,
> And there an end ; but now they rise again,
> With twenty mortal murders on their crowns,
> And push us from our stools : . . .
> Avaunt ! and quit my sight ! let the earth hide thee !
> Thy bones are marrowless, thy blood is cold ;
> Thou hast no speculation in those eyes
> Which thou dost glare with ! "[1]

His body trembling like that of an epileptic, his teeth clenched, foaming at the mouth, he sinks on the ground, his limbs writhe, shaken with convulsive quiverings, whilst a dull sob swells his panting breast, and dies in his swollen throat. What joy can remain for a man beset by such visions ? The wide dark country, which he surveys from his towering castle, is but a field of

[1] *Macbeth*, iii. 4.

death, haunted by ominous apparitions; Scotland, which he is depopulating, a cemetery,

> "Where . . . the dead man's knell
> Is there scarce ask'd for who; and good men's lives
> Expire before the flowers in their caps,
> Dying or ere they sicken." [1]

His soul is "full of scorpions." He has "supp'd full with horrors," and the loathsome odour of blood has disgusted him with all else. He goes stumbling over the corpses which he has heaped up, with the mechanical and desperate smile of a maniac-murderer. Thenceforth death, life, all is one to him; the habit of murder has placed him out of the pale of humanity. They tell him that his wife is dead:

> "*Macbeth.* She should have died hereafter;
> There would have been a time for such a word.
> To-morrow, and to-morrow, and to-morrow,
> Creeps in this petty pace from day to day
> To the last syllable of recorded time,
> And all our yesterdays have lighted fools
> The way to dusty death. Out, out, brief candle!
> Life's but a walking shadow; a poor player
> That struts and frets his hour upon the stage,
> And then is heard no more: it is a tale
> Told by an idiot, full of sound and fury,
> Signifying nothing." [2]

There remains for him the hardening of the heart in crime, the fixed belief in destiny. Hunted down by his enemies, "bear-like, tied to a stake," he fights, troubled only by the prediction of the witches, sure of being invulnerable so long as the man whom they have

[1] *Macbeth*, iv. 3.   [2] *Ibid.* v. 5.

described, does not appear. Henceforth his thoughts dwell in a supernatural world, and to the last he walks with his eyes fixed on the dream, which has possessed him, from the first.

The history of Hamlet, like that of Macbeth, is a story of moral poisoning. Hamlet has a delicate soul, an impassioned imagination, like that of Shakspeare. He has lived hitherto, occupied in noble studies, skilful in mental and bodily exercises, with a taste for art, loved by the noblest father, enamoured of the purest and most charming girl, confiding, generous, not yet having perceived, from the height of the throne to which he was born, aught but the beauty, happiness, grandeur of nature and humanity.[1] On this soul, which character and training make more sensitive than others, misfortune suddenly falls, extreme, overwhelming, of the very kind to destroy all faith and every motive for action: with one glance he has seen all the vileness of humanity; and this insight is given him in his mother. His mind is yet intact; but judge from the violence of his style, the crudity of his exact details, the terrible tension of the whole nervous machine, whether he has not already one foot on the verge of madness :

> " O that this too, too solid flesh would melt,
> Thaw and resolve itself into a dew !
> Or that the Everlasting had not fix'd
> His canon 'gainst self-slaughter ! O God ! God !
> How weary, stale, flat and unprofitable,
> Seem to me all the uses of this world !
> Fie on't ! ah fie ! 'tis an unweeded garden,
> That grows to seed ; things rank and gross in nature

[1] Goethe, *Wilhelm Meister.*

> Possess it merely.   That it should come to this !
> But two months dead : nay, not so much, not two :
> So excellent a king, . . . so loving to my mother
> That he might not let e'en the winds of heaven
> Visit her face too roughly.   Heaven and earth !
>   . . . And yet, within a month,—
> Let me not think on't—Frailty, thy name is woman !—
> A little month, or ere those shoes were old
> With which she follow'd my poor father's body, . . .
> Ere yet the salt of most unrighteous tears
> Had left the flushing in her galled eyes,
> She married.   O, most wicked speed, to post
> With such dexterity to incestuous sheets !
> It is not nor it cannot come to good !
> But break, my heart ; for I must hold my tongue !" [1]

Here already are contortions of thought, a beginning of hallucination, the symptoms of what is to come after. In the middle of conversation the image of his father rises before his mind. He thinks he sees him. How then will it be when the "canonised bones have burst their cerements," "the sepulchre hath oped his ponderous and marble jaws," and when the ghost comes in the night, upon a high "platform" of land, to tell him of the tortures of his prison of fire, and of the fratricide, who has driven him thither ? Hamlet grows faint, but grief strengthens him, and he has a desire for living :

> "Hold, hold, my heart ;
> And you my sinews, grow not instant old,
> But bear me stiffly up !   Remember thee !
> Ay, thou poor ghost, while memory holds a seat
> In this distracted globe.—Remember thee ?

[1] *Hamlet,* i. 2.

Yea, from the table of my memory
I'll wipe away all trivial fond records,
All saws of books, all forms, all pressures past, . . .
And thy commandment all alone shall live. . . .
O villain, villain, smiling, damned villain !
My tables,—meet it is I set it down,
That one may smile, and smile, and be a villain ;
At least I'm sure it may be so in Denmark :
So, uncle, there you are." [1]   (*writing.*)

This convulsive outburst, this fevered writing hand, this frenzy of intentness, prelude the approach of a kind of monomania. When his friends come up, he treats them with the speeches of a child or an idiot. He is no longer master of his words ; hollow phrases whirl in his brain, and fall from his mouth as in a dream. They call him ; he answers by imitating the cry of a sportsman whistling to his falcon : " Hillo, ho, ho, boy ! come, bird, come." Whilst he is in the act of swearing them to secrecy, the ghost below repeats " Swear." Hamlet cries, with a nervous excitement and a fitful gaiety :

" Ah ha, boy ! say'st thou so ? art thou there, truepenny ?
Come on—you hear this fellow in the cellarage,—
Consent to swear. . . .
  Ghost (*beneath*).   Swear.
  Hamlet. Hic et ubique ? then we'll shift our ground.
Come hither, gentlemen. . . . Swear by my sword.
  Ghost (*beneath*).   Swear.
  Ham. Well said, old mole ! canst work i' the earth so fast ?
A worthy pioner ! " [2]

Understand that as he says this his teeth chatter,

[1] *Hamlet*, i. 5.   [2] *Ibid.*

"pale as his shirt, his knees knocking each other." Intense anguish ends with a kind of laughter, which is nothing else than a spasm. Thenceforth Hamlet speaks as though he had a continuous nervous attack. His madness is feigned, I admit; but his mind, as a door whose hinges are twisted, swings and bangs with every wind with a mad haste and with a discordant noise. He has no need to search for the strange ideas, apparent incoherencies, exaggerations, the deluge of sarcasms which he accumulates. He finds them within him; he does himself no violence, he simply gives himself up to himself. When he has the piece played which is to unmask his uncle, he raises himself, lounges on the floor, lays his head in Ophelia's lap; he addresses the actors, and comments on the piece to the spectators; his nerves are strung, his excited thought is like a surging and crackling flame, and cannot find fuel enough in the multitude of objects surrounding it, upon all of which it seizes. When the king rises unmasked and troubled, Hamlet sings, and says, "Would not this, sir, and a forest of feathers—if the rest of my fortunes turn Turk with me—with two Provincial roses on my razed shoes, get me a fellowship in a cry of players, sir!"[1] And he laughs terribly, for he is resolved on murder. It is clear that this state is a disease, and that the man will not survive it.

In a soul so ardent of thought, and so mighty of feeling, what is left but disgust and despair? We tinge all nature with the colour of our thoughts; we shape the world according to our own ideas; when our soul is sick, we see nothing but sickness in the universe:

[1] *Hamlet*, iii. 2.

"This goodly frame, the earth, seems to me a sterile promontory, this most excellent canopy, the air, look you, this brave o'erhanging firmament, this majestical roof fretted with golden fire, why, it appears no other thing to me than a foul and pestilent congregation of vapours. What a piece of work is a man! how noble in reason! how infinite in faculty! in form and moving how express and admirable! in action how like an angel! in apprehension how like a god! the beauty of the world! the paragon of animals! And yet, to me, what is this quintessence of dust? man delights not me: no, nor woman neither." [1]

Henceforth his thought sullies whatever it touches. He rails bitterly before Ophelia against marriage and love. Beauty! Innocence! Beauty is but a means of prostituting innocence: "Get thee to a nunnery: why wouldst thou be a breeder of sinners?... What should such fellows as I do crawling between earth and heaven? We are arrant knaves, all; believe none of us." [2]

When he has killed Polonius by accident, he hardly repents it; it is one fool less. He jeers lugubriously:

"*King.* Now Hamlet, where's Polonius?

Hamlet. At supper.

K. At supper! where?

H. Not where he eats, but where he is eaten: a certain convocation of politic worms are e'en at him." [3]

And he repeats in five or six fashions these gravedigger jests. His thoughts already inhabit a churchyard; to this hopeless philosophy a genuine man is a corpse. Public functions, honours, passions, pleasures, projects, science, all this is but a borrowed mask, which death

[1] *Hamlet*, ii. 2.   [2] *Ibid.* iii. 1.   [3] *Ibid.* iv. 3.

removes, so that people may see what we are, an evil-smelling and grinning skull. It is this sight he goes to see by Ophelia's grave. He counts the skulls which the gravedigger turns up; this was a lawyer's, that a courtier's. What bows, intrigues, pretensions, arrogance! And here now is a clown knocking it about with his spade, and playing "at loggats with 'em." Cæsar and Alexander have turned to clay and make the earth fat; the masters of the world have served to "patch a wall." "Now get you to my lady's chamber, and tell her, let her paint an inch thick, to this favour she must come; make her laugh at that."[1] When a man has come to this, there is nothing left but to die.

This heated imagination, which explains Hamlet's nervous disease and his moral poisoning, explains also his conduct. If he hesitates to kill his uncle, it is not from horror of blood or from our modern scruples. He belongs to the sixteenth century. On board ship he wrote the order to behead Rosencrantz and Guildenstern, and to do so without giving them "shriving-time." He killed Polonius, he caused Ophelia's death, and has no great remorse for it. If for once he spared his uncle, it was because he found him praying, and was afraid of sending him to heaven. He thought he was killing him, when he killed Polonius. What his imagination robs him of, is the coolness and strength to go quietly and with premeditation to plunge a sword into a breast. He can only do the thing on a sudden suggestion; he must have a moment of enthusiasm; he must think the king is behind the arras, or else, seeing that he himself is poisoned, he must find his victim under his foil's point. He is not master of his acts;

[1] *Hamlet*, v. 1.

opportunity dictates them; he cannot plan a murder, but must improvise it. A too lively imagination exhausts the will, by the strength of images which it heaps up, and by the fury of intentness which absorbs it. You recognise in him a poet's soul, made not to act, but to dream, which is lost in contemplating the phantoms of its creation, which sees the imaginary world too clearly to play a part in the real world; an artist whom evil chance has made a prince, whom worse chance has made an avenger of crime, and who, destined by nature for genius, is condemned by fortune to madness and unhappiness. Hamlet is Shakspeare, and, at the close of this gallery of portraits which have all some features of his own, Shakspeare has painted himself in the most striking of all.

If Racine or Corneille had framed a psychology, they would have said, with Descartes: Man is an incorporeal soul, served by organs, endowed with reason and will, dwelling in palaces or porticos, made for conversation and society, whose harmonious and ideal action is developed by discourse and replies, in a world constructed by logic beyond the realms of time and place.

If Shakspeare had framed a psychology, he would have said, with Esquirol:[1] Man is a nervous machine, governed by a mood, disposed to hallucinations, carried away by unbridled passions, essentially unreasoning, a mixture of animal and poet, having instead of mind rapture, instead of virtue sensibility, imagination for prompter and guide, and led at random, by the most determinate and complex circumstances, to sorrow, crime, madness, and death.

[1] A French physician (1772–1844), celebrated for his endeavours to improve the treatment of the insane.—TR.

IX.

Could such a poet always confine himself to the imitation of nature? Will this poetical world which is going on in his brain, never break loose from the laws of the world of reality? Is he not powerful enough to follow his own laws? He is; and the poetry of Shakspeare naturally finds an outlet in the fantastical. This is the highest grade of unreasoning and creative imagination. Despising ordinary logic, it creates another; it unites facts and ideas in a new order, apparently absurd, in reality regular; it lays open the land of dreams, and its dreams seem to us the truth.

When we enter upon Shakspeare's comedies, and even his half-dramas,[1] it is as though we met him on the threshold, like an actor to whom the prologue is committed, to prevent misunderstanding on the part of the public, and to tell them: "Do not take too seriously what you are about to hear: I am amusing myself. My brain, being full of fancies, desired to array them, and here they are. Palaces, distant landscapes, transparent clouds which blot in the morning the horizon with their grey mists, the red and glorious flames into which the evening sun descends, white cloisters in endless vista through the ambient air, grottos, cottages, the fantastic pageant of all human passions, the irregular sport of unlooked-for adventures,—this is the medley of forms, colours, sentiments, which I let become entangled and confused in my presence, a many-tinted skein of glistening silks, a slender arabesque, whose

---

[1] *Twelfth Night, As you Like it, Tempest, Winter's Tale*, etc., *Cymbeline, Merchant of Venice,* etc.

sinuous curves, crossing and mingled, bewilder the mind by the whimsical variety of their infinite complications. Don't regard it as a picture. Don't look for a precise composition, a sole and increasing interest, the skilful management of a well-ordered and congruous plot. I have tales and novels before me which I am cutting up into scenes. Never mind the *finis*, I am amusing myself on the road. It is not the end of the journey which pleases me, but the journey itself. Is there any need in going so straight and quick? Do you only care to know whether the poor merchant of Venice will escape Shylock's knife? Here are two happy lovers, seated under the palace walls on a calm night; wouldn't you like to listen to the peaceful reverie which rises like a perfume from the bottom of their hearts?

> " How sweet the moonlight sleeps upon this bank!
> Here will we sit and let the sounds of music
> Creep in our ears : soft stillness and the night
> Become the touches of sweet harmony.
> Sit, Jessica. Look how the floor of heaven
> Is thick inlaid with patines of bright gold :
> There's not the smallest orb which thou behold'st,
> But in his motion like an angel sings,
> Still quiring to the young-eyed cherubims ;
> Such harmony is in immortal souls ;
> But whilst this muddy vesture of decay
> Doth grossly close it in, we cannot hear it.
>   (*Enter musicians.*)
> Come, ho ! and wake Diana with a hymn :
> With sweetest touches pierce your mistress' ear,
> And draw her home with music.
> *Jessica.* I am never merry when I hear sweet music." [1]

[1] *Merchant of Venice*, v. 1.

"Have I not the right, when I see the big laughing face of a clownish servant, to stop near him, see him gesticulate, frolic, gossip, go through his hundred pranks and his hundred grimaces, and treat myself to the comedy of his spirit and gaiety? Two fine gentlemen pass by. I hear the rolling fire of their metaphors, and I follow their skirmish of wit. Here in a corner is the artless arch face of a young wench. Do you forbid me to linger by her, to watch her smiles, her sudden blushes, the childish pout of her rosy lips, the coquetry of her pretty motions? You are in a great hurry if the prattle of this fresh and musical voice can't stop you. Is it no pleasure to view this succession of sentiments and faces? Is your fancy so dull, that you must have the mighty mechanism of a geometrical plot to shake it? My sixteenth century playgoers were easier to move. A sunbeam that had lost its way on an old wall, a foolish song thrown into the middle of a drama, occupied their mind as well as the blackest of catastrophes. After the horrible scene in which Shylock brandished his butcher's knife before Antonio's bare breast, they saw just as willingly the petty household wrangle, and the amusing bit of raillery which ends the piece. Like soft moving water, their soul rose and sank in an instant to the level of the poet's emotion, and their sentiments readily flowed in the bed he had prepared for them. They let him stray here and there on his journey, and did not forbid him to make two voyages at once. They allowed several plots in one. If but the slightest thread united them it was sufficient. Lorenzo eloped with Jessica, Shylock was frustrated in his revenge, Portia's suitors failed in the test imposed upon them; Portia, disguised as a doctor of laws, took from her husband the ring which he had promised never to part with; these three or four comedies, disunited, mingled, were shuffled and unfolded together, like an unknotted skein in which threads of a hundred colours are entwined. Together with diversity, my spectators allowed improbability. Comedy is a slight winged creature, which flutters from dream to dream, whose wings you would break if you held it captive in the narrow prison of common sense. Do not press its fictions too hard; do not probe their contents. Let them float before your eyes like a charming swift dream. Let the fleeting apparition plunge back into the bright misty land from whence it came. For an instant it deluded you; let it suffice. It is sweet to leave the world of realities behind you; the mind rests amidst impossibilities. We are happy when delivered from the rough chains of logic, to wander amongst strange adventures, to live in sheer romance, and know that we are living there. I do not try to deceive you, and make you believe in the world where I take you. A man must disbelieve it in order to enjoy it. We must give ourselves up to illusion, and feel that we are giving ourselves up to it. We must smile as we listen. We smile in *The Winter's Tale*, when Hermione descends from her pedestal, and when Leontes discovers his wife in the statue, having believed her to be dead. We smile in *Cymbeline*, when we see the lone cavern in which the young princes have lived like savage hunters. Improbability deprives emotions of their sting. The events interest or touch us without making us suffer. At the very moment when sympathy is too intense, we remind ourselves that it is all a fancy. They become like distant objects, whose distance softens their outline, and wraps them in a luminous veil of blue air. Your true comedy is an opera. We listen to sentiments without thinking too much of plot. We follow the tender or gay melodies without reflecting that they interrupt the action. We dream elsewhere on hearing music; here I bid you dream on hearing verse."

Then the speaker of the prologue retires, and the actors come on.

As you Like it is a caprice,[1] Action there is none; interest barely; likelihood still less. And the whole is charming. Two cousins, princes' daughters, come to a forest with a court clown, Celia disguised as a shepherdess, Rosalind as a boy. They find here the old duke, Rosalind's father, who, driven out of his duchy, lives with his friends like a philosopher and a hunter. They find amorous shepherds, who with songs and prayers pursue intractable shepherdesses. They discover or they meet with lovers who become their husbands. Suddenly it is announced that the wicked Duke Frederick, who had usurped the crown, has just retired to a cloister, and restored the throne to the old exiled duke. Every one gets married, every one dances, everything ends with a "rustic revelry." Where is the pleasantness of these puerilities? First, the fact of its being puerile; the absence of the serious is refreshing. There are no events, and there is no plot. We gently follow the easy current of graceful or melancholy emotions, which takes us away and moves us about without wearying. The place adds to the illusion and charm. It is

---

[1] In English, a word is wanting to express the French *fantaisie* used by M. Taine, in describing this scene: what in music is called a *capriccio*. Tennyson calls the *Princess* a medley, but it is ambiguous. —Tr.

an autumn forest, in which the sultry rays permeate the blushing oak leaves, or the half-stript ashes tremble and smile to the feeble breath of evening. The lovers wander by brooks that "brawl" under antique roots. As you listen to them, you see the slim birches, whose cloak of lace grows glossy under the slant rays of the sun that gilds them, and the thoughts wander down the mossy vistas in which their footsteps are not heard. What better place could be chosen for the comedy of sentiment and the play of heart-fancies? Is not this a fit spot in which to listen to love-talk? Some one has seen Orlando, Rosalind's lover, in this glade; she hears it and blushes. "Alas the day! . . . What did he, when thou sawest him? What said he? How looked he? Wherein went he? What makes he here? Did he ask for me? Where remains he? How parted he with thee? and when shalt thou see him again?" Then, with a lower voice, somewhat hesitating: "Looks he as freshly as he did the day he wrestled?" She is not yet exhausted: "Do you not know I am a woman? When I think, I must speak. Sweet, say on."[1] One question follows another, she closes the mouth of her friend, who is ready to answer. At every word she jests, but agitated, blushing, with a forced gaiety; her bosom heaves, and her heart beats. Nevertheless she is calmer when Orlando comes; bandies words with him; sheltered under her disguise, she makes him confess that he loves Rosalind. Then she plagues him, like the frolic, the wag, the coquette she is. "Why, how now, Orlando, where have you been all this while? You a lover?" Orlando repeats that he loves Rosalind, and she pleases herself by making him repeat it more

[1] *As you Like it*, iii. 2.

than once. She sparkles with wit, jests, mischievous pranks; pretty fits of anger, feigned sulks, bursts of laughter, deafening babble, engaging caprices. " Come, woo me, woo me; for now I am in a holiday humour, and like enough to consent. What would you say to me now, an I were your very very Rosalind?" And every now and then she repeats with an arch smile, " And I am your Rosalind; am I not your Rosalind?"[1] Orlando protests that he would die. Die! Who ever thought of dying for love! Leander? He took one bath too many in the Hellespont; so poets have said he died for love. Troilus? A Greek broke his head with a club; so poets have said he died for love. Come, come, Rosalind will be softer. And then she plays at marriage with him, and makes Celia pronounce the solemn words. She irritates and torments her pretended husband; tells him all the whims she means to indulge in, all the pranks she will play, all the teasing he will have to endure. The retorts come one after another like fireworks. At every phrase we follow the looks of these sparkling eyes, the curves of this laughing mouth, the quick movements of this supple figure. It is a bird's petulance and volubility. "O coz, coz, coz, my pretty little coz, that thou didst know how many fathom deep I am in love." Then she provokes her cousin Celia, sports with her hair, calls her by every woman's name. Antitheses without end, words all a-jumble, quibbles, pretty exaggerations, word-racket; as you listen, you fancy it is the warbling of a nightingale. The trill of repeated metaphors, the melodious roll of the poetical gamut, the summer-warbling rustling under the foliage, change the piece into a veritable opera.

[1] *As you Like it*, iv. 1.

The three lovers end by chanting a sort of trio. The first throws out a fancy, the others take it up. Four times this strophe is renewed; and the symmetry of ideas, added to the jingle of the rhymes, makes of a dialogue a concerto of love:

> "*Phebe.* Good shepherd, tell this youth what 'tis to love.
> *Silvius.* It is to be all made of sighs and tears;
> And so am I for Phebe.
> *P.* And I for Ganymede.
> *Orlando.* And I for Rosalind.
> *Rosalind.* And I for no woman. . . .
> *S.* It is to be all made of fantasy,
> All made of passion, and all made of wishes,
> All adoration, duty, and observance,
> All humbleness, all patience and impatience,
> All purity, all trial, all observance;
> And so I am for Phebe.
> *P.* And so am I for Ganymede.
> *O.* And so am I for Rosalind.
> *R.* And so am I for no woman." [1]

The necessity of singing is so urgent, that a minute later songs break out of themselves. The prose and the conversation end in lyric poetry. We pass straight on into these odes. We do not find ourselves in a new country. We feel the emotion and foolish gaiety as if it were a holiday. We see the graceful couple whom the song of the two pages brings before us, passing in the misty light " o'er the green corn-field," amid the hum of sportive insects, on the finest day of the flowering spring-time. Unlikelihood grows natural, and we are not astonished when we see Hymen

[1] *As you Like it*, v. 2.

leading the two brides by the hand to give them to their husbands.

Whilst the young folks sing, the old folk talk. Their life also is a novel, but a sad one. Shakspeare's delicate soul, bruised by the shocks of social life, took refuge in contemplations of solitary life. To forget the strife and annoyances of the world, he must bury himself in a wide silent forest, and

> "Under the shade of melancholy boughs,
> Loose and neglect the creeping hours of time."[1]

We look at the bright images which the sun carves on the white beech-boles, the shade of trembling leaves flickering on the thick moss, the long waves of the summit of the trees; then the sharp sting of care is blunted; we suffer no more, simply remembering that we suffered once; we feel nothing but a gentle misanthropy, and being renewed, we are the better for it. The old duke is happy in his exile. Solitude has given him rest, delivered him from flattery, reconciled him to nature. He pities the stags which he is obliged to hunt for food:

> "Come, shall we go and kill us venison?
> And yet it irks me the poor dappled fools,
> Being native burghers of this desert city,
> Should in their own confines with forked heads
> Have their round haunches gored."[2]

Nothing sweeter than this mixture of tender compassion, dreamy philosophy, delicate sadness, poetical complaints, and rustic songs. One of the lords sings:

[1] *As you Like it*, ii. 7. [2] *Ibid.* ii. 1.

> "Blow, blow, thou winter wind,
>   Thou art not so unkind
>   As man's ingratitude;
>   Thy tooth is not so keen,
>   Because thou art not seen,
>   Although thy breath be rude.
> Heigh-ho! sing, heigh-ho! unto the green holly:
> Most friendship is feigning, most loving mere folly:
>   Then, heigh-ho, the holly!
>   This life is most jolly."[1]

Amongst these lords is found a soul that suffers more, Jacques the melancholy, one of Shakspeare's best-loved characters, a transparent mask behind which we perceive the face of the poet. He is sad because he is tender; he feels the contact of things too keenly, and what leaves others indifferent, makes him weep.[2] He does not scold, he is sad; he does not reason, he is moved; he has not the combative spirit of a reforming moralist; his soul is sick and weary of life. Impassioned imagination leads quickly to disgust. Like opium, it excites and shatters. It leads man to the loftiest philosophy, then lets him down to the whims of a child. Jacques leaves other men abruptly, and goes to the quiet nooks to be alone. He loves his sadness, and would not exchange it for joy. Meeting Orlando, he says:

> "Rosalind is your love's name?
> *Orlando.* Yes, just.
> *Jacques.* I do not like her name."[3]

He has the fancies of a nervous woman. He is scandalised because Orlando writes sonnets on the forest

---

[1] *As you Like it*, ii. 7.

[2] Compare Jacques with the Alceste of Molière. It is the contrast between a misanthrope through reasoning and one through imagination.

[3] *As you Like it*, iii. 2.

trees. He is eccentric, and finds subjects of grief and gaiety, where others would see nothing of the sort:

> "A fool, a fool! I met a fool i' the forest,
> A motley fool; A miserable world!
> As I do live by food, I met a fool;
> Who laid him down and bask'd him in the sun,
> And rail'd on Lady Fortune in good terms,
> In good set terms and yet a motley fool. . .

Jacques hearing him moralise in such a manner begins to laugh "sans intermission" that a fool could be so meditative:

> O noble fool; A worthy fool! Motley's the only wear. . . .
> O that I were a fool!
> I am ambitious for a motley coat."[1]

The next minute he returns to his melancholy dissertations, bright pictures whose vivacity explains his character, and betrays Shakspeare, hiding under his name

> "All the world's a stage,
> And all the men and women merely players:
> They have their exits and their entrances;
> And one man in his time plays many parts,
> His acts being seven ages. At first the infant,
> Mewling and puking in the nurse's arms.
> And then the whining schoolboy, with his satchel,
> And shining morning face, creeping like snail
> Unwillingly to school. And then the lover,
> Sighing like furnace, with a woeful ballad
> Made to his mistress' eyebrow. Then a soldier,
> Full of strange oaths and bearded like the pard,
> Jealous in honour, sudden and quick in quarrel,
> Seeking the bubble reputation
> Even in the cannon's mouth. And then the justice,

[1] *As you Like it*, ii. 7.

"In fair round belly with good capon lined,
With eyes severe and beard of formal cut,
Full of wise saws and modern instances;
And so he plays his part. The sixth age shifts
Into the lean and slipper'd pantaloon,
With spectacles on nose and pouch on side,
His youthful hose, well saved, a world too wide
For his shrunk shank; and his big manly voice,
Turning again toward childish treble, pipes
And whistles in his sound. Last scene of all,
That ends this strange eventful history,
Is second childishness and mere oblivion,
Sans teeth, sans eyes, sans taste, sans everything." [1]

As you Like it is a half dream. *Midsummer Night's Dream* is a complete one.

The scene, buried in the far-off mist of fabulous antiquity, carries us back to Theseus, Duke of Athens, who is preparing his palace for his marriage with the beautiful queen of the Amazons. The style, loaded with contorted images, fills the mind with strange and splendid visions, and the airy elf-world divert the comedy into the fairy-land from whence it sprung.

Love is still the theme: of all sentiments, is it not the greatest fancy-weaver? But love is not heard here in the charming prattle of Rosalind; it is glaring, like the season of the year. It does not brim over in slight conversations, in supple and skipping prose; it breaks forth into big rhyming odes, dressed in magnificent metaphors, sustained by impassioned accents, such as a warm night, odorous and star-spangled, inspires in a poet and a lover. Lysander and Hermia agree to meet.

[1] *As you Like it*, ii. 7.

> "*Lysander.* To-morrow night when Phœbe doth behold
> Her silver visage in the watery glass,
> Decking with liquid pearl the bladed grass,
> A time that lovers' flights doth still conceal,
> Through Athens' gates have we devised to steal.
>   *Hermia.* And in the wood, where often you and I
> Upon faint primrose-beds were wont to lie. . . .
> There my Lysander and myself shall meet." [1]

They get lost, and fall asleep, wearied, under the trees. Puck squeezes in the youth's eyes the juice of a magic flower, and changes his heart. Presently, when he awakes, he will become enamoured of the first woman he sees. Meanwhile Demetrius, Hermia's rejected lover, wanders with Helena, whom he rejects, in the solitary wood. The magic flower changes him in turn: he now loves Helena. The lovers flee and pursue one another, beneath the lofty trees, in the calm night. We smile at their transports, their complaints, their ecstasies, and yet we join in them. This passion is a dream, and yet it moves us. It is like those airy webs which we find at morning on the crest of the hedgerows where the dew has spread them, and whose weft sparkles like a jewel-casket. Nothing can be more fragile, and nothing more graceful. The poet sports with emotions; he mingles, confuses, redoubles, interweaves them; he twines and untwines these loves like the mazes of a dance, and we see the noble and tender figures pass by the verdant bushes, beneath the radiant eyes of the stars, now wet with tears, now bright with rapture. They have the abandonment of true love, not the grossness of sensual love. Nothing causes us to fall from the ideal world in which Shak-

---

[1] *Midsummer Night's Dream*, i. 1.

speare conducts us. Dazzled by beauty, they adore it, and the spectacle of their happiness, their emotion, and their tenderness, is a kind of enchantment.

Above these two couples flutters and hums the swarm of elves and fairies. They also love. Titania, their queen, has a young boy for her favourite, son of an Indian king, of whom Oberon, her husband, wishes to deprive her. They quarrel, so that the elves creep for fear into the acorn cups, in the golden primroses. Oberon, by way of vengeance, touches Titania's sleeping eyes with the magic flower, and thus on waking the nimblest and most charming of the fairies finds herself enamoured of a stupid blockhead with an ass's head. She kneels before him; she sets on his " hairy temples a coronet of fresh and fragrant flowers:"

> " And that same dew, which sometime on the buds
> Was wont to swell like round and orient pearls,
> Stood now within the pretty floweret's eyes,
> Like tears that did their own disgrace bewail." [1]

She calls round her all her fairy attendants;

> " Be kind and courteous to this gentleman;
> Hop in his walks, and gambol in his eyes;
> Feed him with apricocks and dewberries,
> With purple grapes, green figs, and mulberries;
> The honey-bags steal from the humble-bees,
> And for night-tapers crop their waxen thighs
> And light them at the fiery glow-worm's eyes,
> To have my love to bed and to arise;
> And pluck the wings from painted butterflies
> To fan the moonbeams from his sleeping eyes. . . .
> Come, wait upon him; lead him to my bower.

[1] *Midsummer Night's Dream*, iv. 1.

> The moon, methinks, looks with a watery eye;
> And when she weeps, weeps every little flower,
> Lamenting some enforced chastity.
> Tie up my love's tongue, bring him silently."[1]

It was necessary, for her love brayed horribly, and to all the offers of Titania, replied with a petition for hay. What can be sadder and sweeter than this irony of Shakspeare? What raillery against love, and what tenderness for love! The sentiment is divine: its object unworthy. The heart is ravished, the eyes blind. It is a golden butterfly, fluttering in the mud; and Shakspeare, whilst painting its misery, preserves all its beauty:

> " Come, sit thee down upon this flowery bed,
>   While I thy amiable cheeks do coy,
>   And stick musk-roses in thy sleek smooth head,
>   And kiss thy fair large ears, my gentle joy. . . .
>   Sleep thou, and I will wind thee in my arms. . . .
>   So doth the woodbine the sweet honeysuckle
>   Gently entwist; the female ivy so
>   Enrings the barky fingers of the elm.
>   O, how I love thee! how I dote on thee!"[2]

At the return of morning, when

> "The eastern gate, all fiery red,
> Opening on Neptune with fair blessed beams,
> Turns into yellow gold his salt green streams,"[3]

the enchantment ceases, Titania awakes on her couch of wild thyme and drooping violets. She drives the monster away; her recollections of the night are effaced in a vague twilight:

---

[1] *Midsummer Night's Dream*, iii. 1.   [2] *Ibid.* iv. 1.   [3] *Ibid.* iii. 2.

> "These things seem small and undistinguishable,
> Like far-off mountains turned into clouds." [1]

And the fairies

> "Go seek some dew drops here
> And hang a pearl in every cowslip's ear." [2]

Such is Shakspeare's fantasy, a slight tissue of bold inventions, of ardent passions, melancholy mockery, dazzling poetry, such as one of Titania's elves would have made. Nothing could be more like the poet's mind than these nimble genii, children of air and flame, whose flights "compass the globe" in a second, who glide over the foam of the waves and skip between the atoms of the winds. Ariel flies, an invisible songster, around shipwrecked men to console them, discovers the thoughts of traitors, pursues the savage beast Caliban, spreads gorgeous visions before lovers, and does all in a lightning-flash:

> "Where the bee sucks, there suck I:
> In a cowslip's bell I lie. . . .
> Merrily, merrily shall I live now
> Under the blossom that hangs on the bough. . . .
> I drink the air before me, and return
> Or ere your pulse twice beat." [3]

Shakspeare glides over things on as swift a wing, by leaps as sudden, with a touch as delicate.

What a soul! what extent of action, and what sovereignty of an unique faculty! what diverse creations, and what persistence of the same impress! There they all are united, and all marked by the same

---

[1] *Midsummer Night's Dream*, iv. i.   [2] *Ibid.* ii. 1.
[3] *Tempest*, v. 1.

sign, void of will and reason, governed by mood, imagination, or pure passion, destitute of the faculties contrary to those of the poet, dominated by the corporeal type which his painter's eyes have conceived, endowed by the habits of mind and by the vehement sensibility which he finds in himself.[1] Go through the groups, and you will only discover in them divers forms and divers states of the same power. Here, a herd of brutes, dotards, and gossips, made up of a mechanical imagination; further on, a company of men of wit, animated by a gay and foolish imagination; then, a charming swarm of women whom their delicate imagination raises so high, and their self-forgetting love carries so far; elsewhere a band of villains, hardened by unbridled passions, inspired by artistic rapture; in the centre a mournful train of grand characters, whose excited brain is filled with sad or criminal visions, and whom an inner destiny urges to murder, madness, or death. Ascend one stage, and contemplate the whole scene: the aggregate bears the same mark as the details. The drama reproduces promiscuously uglinesses, basenesses, horrors, unclean details, profligate and ferocious manners, the whole reality of life just as it is, when it is unrestrained by decorum, common sense, reason, and duty. Comedy, led through a phantasmagoria of pictures, gets lost in the likely and the unlikely, with no other connection but the caprice of an amused imagination, wantonly disjointed and romantic, an opera without music, a concerto of melancholy and tender sentiments, which bears the mind into the supernatural world, and brings before our eyes on its fairy-wings the genius

[1] There is the same law in the organic and in the moral world. It is what Geoffrey Saint-Hilaire calls unity of composition.

which has created it. Look now. Do you not see the poet behind the crowd of his creations? They have heralded his approach. They have all shown somewhat of him. Ready, impetuous, impassioned, delicate, his genius is pure imagination, touched more vividly and by slighter things than ours. Hence his style, blooming with exuberant images, loaded with exaggerated metaphors, whose strangeness is like incoherence, whose wealth is superabundant, the work of a mind, which, at the least incitement, produces too much and takes too wide leaps. Hence this involuntary psychology, and this terrible penetration, which instantaneously perceiving all the effects of a situation, and all the details of a character, concentrates them in every response, and gives to a figure a relief and a colouring which create illusion. Hence our emotion and tenderness. We say to him, as Desdemona to Othello: "I love thee for the battles, sieges, fortunes thou hast passed, and for the distressful stroke that thy youth suffered."

CHAPTER V.

The Christian Renaissance.

I.

"I would have my reader fully understand," says Luther in the preface to his complete works, "that I have been a monk and a bigoted Papist, so intoxicated, or rather so swallowed up in papistical doctrines, that I was quite ready, if I had been able, to kill or procure the death of those who should have rejected obedience to the Pope by so much as a syllable. I was not all cold or all ice in the Pope's defence, like Eckius and his like, who veritably seemed to me to constitute themselves his defenders rather for their belly's sake than because they looked at the matter seriously. More, to this day they seem to mock at him, like Epicureans. I for my part proceeded frankly, like a man who has horribly feared the day of judgment, and who yet hoped to be saved with a shaking of all his bones." Again, when he saw Rome for the first time, he prostrated himself, saying, " I salute thee, holy Rome . . . bathed in the blood of so many martyrs." Imagine, if you may, the effect which the shameless paganism of the Italian Renaissance had upon such a mind, so loyal, so Christian. The beauty of art, the charm of a refined and sensuous existence, had taken no hold upon him; he judged morals, and he judged them with his conscience only. He regarded this southern civilisation with the eyes of a man of the north, and understood its vices only, like Ascham, who said he had seen in Venice "more libertie to sinne in IX dayes than ever I heard tell of in our noble Citie of London in IX yeare."[1] Like Arnold and Channing in the present day, like all the men of Germanic[2] race and education, he was horrified at this voluptuous life, now reckless and now licentious, but always void of moral principles, given up to passion, enlivened by irony, caring only for the present, destitute of belief in the infinite, with no other worship than that of visible beauty, no other object than the search after pleasure, no other religion than the terrors of imagination and the idolatry of the eyes.

"I would not," said Luther afterwards, "for a hundred thousand florins have gone without seeing Rome; I should always have doubted whether I was not doing injustice to the Pope. The crimes of Rome are incredible; no one will credit so great a perversity who has not the witness of his eyes, ears, personal knowledge. . . . There reigned all the villanies and infamies, all the atrocious crimes, in particular blind greed, contempt of God, perjuries, sodomy. . . . We Germans swill liquour enough to split us, whilst the Italians are sober. But they are the most impious of men; they make a mock of true religion, they scorn the rest of us Christians, because we believe everything in Scripture. . . . There is a saying in Italy which they make use of when they go to church: 'Come

[1] Roger Ascham, *The Scholemaster* (1570), ed. Arber, 1870, first book, p. 83.
[2] See, in *Corinne*, Lord Nevil's judgment on the Italians.

and let us conform to the popular error.' 'If we were
obliged,' they say again, 'to believe in every word of
God, we should be the most wretched of men, and we
should never be able to have a moment's cheerfulness;
we must put a good face on it, and not believe everything.' This is what Leo X. did, who, hearing a
discussion as to the immortality or mortality of the
soul, took the latter side. 'For,' said he, 'it would
be terrible to believe in a future state. Conscience is
an evil beast, who arms man against himself.' . . . The
Italians are either epicureans or superstitious. The
people fear St. Anthony and St. Sebastian more than
Christ, because of the plagues they send. This is why,
when they want to prevent the Italians from committing a nuisance anywhere, they paint up St. Anthony
with his fiery lance. Thus do they live in extreme
superstition, ignorant of God's word, not believing the
resurrection of the flesh, nor life everlasting, and fearing
only temporal evils. Their blasphemy also is frightful,
. . . and the cruelty of their revenge is atrocious.
When they cannot get rid of their enemies in any
other way, they lay ambush for them in the churches,
so that one man cleft his enemy's head before the altar.
. . . There are often murders at funerals on account
of inheritances. . . . They celebrate the Carnival with
extreme impropriety and folly for several weeks, and
they have made a custom of various sins and extravagances at it, for they are men without conscience, who
live in open sin, and make light of the marriage tie.
. . . We Germans, and other simple nations, are like
a bare clout; but the Italians are painted and speckled
with all sorts of false opinions, and disposed still to
embrace many worse. . . . Their fasts are more splen-

did than our most sumptuous feasts. They dress extravagantly; where we spend a florin on our clothes, they put down ten florins to have a silk coat. . . . When they (the Italians) are chaste, it is sodomy with them. There is no society amongst them. No one trusts another; they do not come together freely, like us Germans; they do not allow strangers to speak publicly with their wives: compared with the Germans, they are altogether men of the cloister." These hard words are weak compared with the facts.[1] Treasons, assassinations, tortures, open debauchery, the practice of poisoning, the worst and most shameless outrages, are unblushingly and publicly tolerated in the open light of heaven. In 1490, the Pope's vicar having forbidden clerics and laics to keep concubines, the Pope revoked the decree, "saying that that was not forbidden, because the life of priests and ecclesiastics was such that hardly one was to be found who did not keep a concubine, or at least who had not a courtesan." Cæsar Borgia at the capture of Capua "chose forty of the most beautiful women, whom he kept for himself; and a pretty large number of captives were sold at a low price at Rome." Under Alexander VI., "all ecclesiastics, from the greatest to the least, have concubines in the place of wives, and that publicly. If God hinder it not," adds the historian, "this corruption will pass to the monks and religious orders, although, to confess the truth, almost all the monasteries of the town have become bawd-houses, without any one to speak against it." With respect to Alexander VI.,

[1] See *Corpus historicorum medii ævi*, G. Eccard, vol. ii.; Joh. Burchardi, high chamberlain to Alexander VI., *Diarium*, p. 2134. Guicciardini, *Dell' istoria d'Italia*, p. 211, ed. Panthéon Littéraire.

who loved his daughter Lucretia, the reader may find in Burchard the description of the marvellous orgies in which he joined with Lucretia and Cæsar, and the enumeration of the prizes which he distributed. Let the reader also read for himself the story of the bestiality of Pietro Luigi Farnese, the Pope's son, how the young and upright Bishop of Fano died from his outrage, and how the Pope, speaking of this crime as "a youthful levity," gave him in this secret bull "the fullest absolution from all the penalties which he might have incurred by human incontinence, in whatever shape or with whatever cause." As to civil security, Bentivoglio caused all the Marescotti to be put to death; Hippolyto d'Este had his brother's eyes put out in his presence; Cæsar Borgia killed his brother; murder is consonant with their public manners, and excites no wonder. A fisherman was asked why he had not informed the governor of the town that he had seen a body thrown into the water; "he replied that he had seen about a hundred bodies thrown into the water during his lifetime in the same place, and that no one had ever troubled himself about it." "In our town," says an old historian, "much murder and pillage was done by day and night, and hardly a day passed but some one was killed." Cæsar Borgia one day killed Peroso, the Pope's favourite, between his arms and under his cloak, so that the blood spurted up to the Pope's face. He caused his sister's husband to be stabbed and then strangled in open day, on the steps of the palace; count, if you can, his assassinations. Certainly he and his father, by their character, morals, complete, open and systematic wickedness, have presented to Europe the two most successful images of the devil. To sum up in a word, it was on the model of this society, and for this society, that Machiavelli wrote his *Prince*. The complete development of all the faculties and all the lusts of man, the complete destruction of all the restraints and all the shame of man, are the two distinguishing marks of this grand and perverse culture. To make man a strong being, endowed with genius, audacity, presence of mind, astute policy, dissimulation, patience, and to turn all this power to the acquisition of every kind of pleasure, pleasures of the body, of luxury, arts, literature, authority; that is, to form and to set free an admirable and formidable animal, very lustful and well armed,—such was his object; and the effect, after a hundred years, is visible. They tore one another to pieces like beautiful lions and superb panthers. In this society, which was turned into an arena, amid so many hatreds, and when exhaustion was setting in, the foreigner appeared: all bent beneath his lash; they were caged, and thus they pine away, in dull pleasures, with low vices, bowing their backs.[1] Despotism, the Inquisition, the Cicisbei, dense ignorance, and open knavery, the shamelessness and the smartness of harlequins and rascals, misery and vermin, —such is the issue of the Italian Renaissance. Like the old civilisations of Greece and Rome,[2] like the modern civilisations of Provence and Spain, like all southern civilisations, it bears in its bosom an irremediable vice, a bad and false conception of man. The Germans of the sixteenth century, like the Germans of

[1] See, in Casanova's *Mémoires*, the picture of this degradation. See also the *Mémoires* of Scipione Rossi, on the convents of Tuscany at the close of the eighteenth century.

[2] From Homer to Constantine, the ancient city was an association of freemen, whose aim was the conquest and destruction of other freemen.

the fourth century, have rightly judged it; with their simple common sense, with their fundamental honesty, they have put their fingers on the secret plague-spot. A society cannot be founded only on the pursuit of pleasure and power; a society can only be founded on the respect for liberty and justice. In order that the great human renovation which in the sixteenth century raised the whole of Europe might be perfected and endure, it was necessary that, meeting with another race, it should develop another culture, and that from a more wholesome conception of existence it might educe a better form of civilisation.

II.

Thus, side by side with the Renaissance, was born the Reformation. It also was in fact a new birth, one in harmony with the genius of the Germanic peoples. The distinction between this genius and others is its moral principles. Grosser and heavier, more given to gluttony and drunkenness,[1] these nations are at the same time more under the influence of conscience, firmer in the observance of their word, more disposed to self-denial and sacrifice. Such their climate has made them; and such they have continued, from Tacitus to Luther, from Knox to Gustavus Adolphus and Kant. In the

[1] *Mémoires de la Margrave de Baireuth.* See also Misson, *Voyage en Italie*, 1700. Compare the manners of the students at the present day. "The Germans are, as you know, wonderful drinkers: no people in the world are more flattering, more civil, more officious; but yet they have terrible customs in the matter of drinking. With them everything is done drinking: they drink in doing everything. There was not time during a visit to say three words, before you were astonished to see the collation arrive, or at least a few jugs of wine, accompanied by a plate of crusts of bread, dished up with pepper and salt; a fatal preparation for bad drinkers. Then you must become acquainted with the

course of time, and beneath the incessant action of the ages, the phlegmatic body, fed on coarse food and strong drink, had become rusty, the nerves less excitable, the muscles less strung, the desires less seconded by action, the life more dull and slow, the soul more hardened and indifferent to the shocks of the body: mud, rain, snow, a profusion of unpleasing and gloomy sights, the want of lively and delicate excitements of the senses, keep man in a militant attitude. Heroes in the barbarous ages, workers to-day, they endure weariness now as they courted wounds then; now, as then, nobility of soul appeals to them; thrown back upon the enjoyments of the soul, they find in these a world, the world of moral beauty. For them the ideal is displaced; it is no longer amidst forms, made up of force and joy, but it is transferred to sentiments, made up of truth, uprightness, attachment to duty, observance of order. What matters it if the storm rages and if it snows, if the wind blusters in the black pine-forests or on the wan sea-surges where the sea-gulls scream, if a man, stiff and blue with cold, shutting himself up in his cottage, have but a dish of sourkrout or a piece of salt beef, under his smoky light and beside his fire of turf; another kingdom opens to reward him, the kingdom of inward contentment: his wife loves him and is faithful; his children round his hearth spell out the old family

laws which are afterwards observed, sacred and inviolable laws. You must never drink without drinking to some one's health; also, after drinking, you must offer the wine to him whose health you have drunk. You must never refuse the glass which is offered to you, and you must naturally drain it to its last drop. Reflect a little, I beseech you, on these customs, and see how it is possible to cease drinking; accordingly, they never cease. In Germany it is a perpetual drinking-bout; to drink in Germany is to drink for ever."

Bible; he is the master in his home, the protector, the benefactor, honoured by others, honoured by himself; and if so be that he needs assistance, he knows that at the first appeal he will see his neighbours stand faithfully and bravely by his side. The reader need only compare the portraits of the time, those of Italy and Germany; he will comprehend at a glance the two races and the two civilisations, the Renaissance and the Reformation: on one side a half-naked condottiere in Roman costume, a cardinal in his robes, amply draped, in a rich arm-chair, carved and adorned with heads of lions, foliage, dancing fauns, he himself full of irony, and voluptuous, with the shrewd and dangerous look of a politician and man of the world, craftily poised and on his guard; on the other side, some honest doctor, a theologian, a simple man, with badly combed locks, stiff as a post, in his simple gown of coarse black serge, with big books of dogma ponderously clasped, a conscientious worker, an exemplary father of a family. See now the great artist of the age, a laborious and conscientious workman, a follower of Luther's, a true Northman —Albert Durer.[1] He also, like Raphael and Titian, has his ideal of man, an inexhaustible ideal, whence spring by hundreds living figures and the representations of manners, but how national and original! He cares not for expansive and happy beauty: to him nude bodies are but bodies undressed: narrow shoulders, prominent stomachs, thin legs, feet weighed down by shoes, his neighbour the carpenter's, or his gossip the sausage-seller's. The heads stand out in his etchings, remorselessly scraped and scooped away, savage or commonplace, often wrinkled by the fatigues of trade,

[1] See his letters, and the sympathy expressed for Luther.

generally sad, anxious, and patient, harshly and wretchedly transformed by the necessities of realistic life. Where is the vista out of this minute copy of ugly truth? To what land will the lofty and melancholy imagination betake itself? The land of dreams, strange dreams swarming with deep thoughts, sad contemplation of human destiny, a vague notion of the great enigma, groping reflection, which in the dimness of the rough woodcuts, amidst obscure emblems and fantastic figures, tries to seize upon truth and justice. There was no need to search so far; Durer had grasped them at the first effort. If there is any decency in the world, it is in the Madonnas which are constantly springing to life under his pencil. He did not begin, like Raphael, by making them nude; the most licentious hand would not venture to disturb one stiff fold of their robes; with an infant in their arms, they think but of him, and will never think of anybody else but him; not only are they innocent, but they are virtuous. The good German housewife, for ever shut up, voluntarily and naturally, within her domestic duties and contentment, breathes out in all the fundamental sincerity, the seriousness, the unassailable loyalty of their attitudes and looks. He has done more; with this peaceful virtue he has painted a militant virtue. There at last is the genuine Christ, the man crucified, lean and fleshless through his agony, whose blood trickles minute by minute, in rarer drops, as the feebler and feebler pulsations give warning of the last throe of a dying life. We do not find here, as in the Italian masters a sight to charm the eyes, a mere flow of drapery, a disposition of groups. The heart, the very heart is wounded by this sight: it is the just man oppressed, who is dying because the world hates justice. The mighty, the men of the age, are there, indifferent, full of irony: a plumed knight, a big-bellied burgomaster, who, with hands folded behind his back, looks on, kills an hour. But the rest weep; above the fainting women, angels full of anguish catch in their vessels the holy blood as it trickles down, and the stars of heaven veil their face not to behold so tremendous an outrage. Other outrages will also be represented; tortures manifold, and the true martyrs beside the true Christ, resigned, silent, with the sweet expression of the earliest believers. They are bound to an old tree, and the executioner tears them with his iron pointed lash. A bishop with clasped hands is praying, lying down, whilst an auger is being screwed into his eye. Above amid the interlacing trees and gnarled roots, a band of men and women, climb under the lash the breast of a hill, and they are hurled from the crest at the lance's point into the abyss; here and there roll heads, lifeless bodies; and by the side of those who are being decapitated, the swollen corpses, impaled, await the croaking ravens. All these sufferings must be undergone for the confession of faith and the establishment of justice. But above there is a guardian, an avenger, an all-powerful Judge, whose day shall come. This day has come, and the piercing rays of the last sun already flash, like a handful of darts, across the darkness of the age. High up in the heavens appears the angel in his shining robe, leading the ungovernable horsemen, the flashing swords, the inevitable arrows of the avengers, who are to trample upon and punish the earth; mankind falls down beneath their charge, and already the jaw of the infernal monster grinds the head of the wicked prelates. This is the popular poem of conscience, and from the days of the apostles, man has not had a more sublime and complete conception.[1]

For conscience, like other things, has its poem; by a natural invasion the all-powerful idea of justice overflows from the soul, covers heaven, and enthrones there a new deity. A formidable deity, who is scarcely like the calm intelligence which serves philosophers to explain the order of things; nor to that tolerant deity, a kind of constitutional king, whom Voltaire discovered at the end of a chain of argument, whom Béranger sings of as of a comrade, and whom he salutes "sans lui demander rien." It is the just Judge, sinless and stern, who demands of man a strict account of his visible actions and of all his invisible feelings, who tolerates no forgetfulness, no dejection, no failing, before whom every approach to weakness or error is an outrage and a treason. What is our justice before this strict justice? People lived in peace in the times of ignorance; at most, when they felt themselves guilty, they went for absolution to a priest; all was ended by their buying a big indulgence; there was a tariff, as there still is; Tetzel the Dominican declares that all sins are blotted out "as soon as the money chinks in the box." Whatever be the crime, there is a quittance; even "*si Dei matrem violavisset*," he might go home clean and sure of heaven. Unfortunately the vendors of pardons did not know that all was changed, and that the intellect was become manly, no longer gabbling words mechanically like a catechism, but probing them anxiously like a truth. In the universal Renaissance, and in the mighty growth of all human ideas,

---

[1] See a collection of Albert Durer's wood-carvings. Remark the resemblance of his *Apocalypse* to Luther's *Table Talk*.

the German idea of duty blooms like the rest. Now, when we speak of justice, it is no longer a lifeless phrase which we repeat, but a living idea which we produce; man sees the object which it represents, and feels the emotion which summons it up; he no longer receives, but he creates it; it is his work and his tyrant; he makes it, and submits to it. "These words *justus* and *justitia Dei*," says Luther, "were a thunder to my conscience. I shuddered to hear them; I told myself, if God is just, He will punish me."[1] For as soon as the conscience discovers again the idea of the perfect model,[2] the smallest failings appeared to be crimes, and man, condemned by his own scruples, fell prostrate, and, "as it were, swallowed up" with horror. "I, who lived the life of a spotless monk," says Luther, "yet felt within me the troubled conscience of a sinner, without managing to assure myself as to the satisfaction

---

[1] Calvin, the logician of the Reformation, well explains the dependence of all the Protestant ideas in his *Institutes of the Christian Religion*, i. (1.) The idea of the perfect God, the stern Judge. (2.) The alarm of conscience. (3.) The impotence and corruption of nature. (4.) The advent of free grace. (5.) The rejection of rites and ceremonies.

[2] "In the measure in which pride is rooted within us, it always appears to us as though we were just and whole, good and holy; unless we are convinced by manifest arguments of our injustice, uncleanness, folly, and impurity. For we are not convinced of it if we turn our eyes to our own persons merely, and if we do not think also of God, who is the only rule by which we must shape and regulate this judgment. . . . And then that which had a fair appearance of virtue will be found to be nothing but weakness.

"This is the source of that horror and wonder by which the Scriptures tell us the saints were afflicted and cast down, when and as often as they felt the presence of God. For we see those who were as it might be far from God, and who were confident and went about with head erect, as soon as He displayed His glory to them, they were shaken and terrified, so much so that they were overwhelmed, nay swallowed up in the horror of death, and that they fainted away."—*Calvin's Institutes*, i.

which I owed to God. . . . Then I said to myself: Am I then the only one who ought to be sad in my spirit? . . . Oh, what horrible spectres and figures I used to see!" Thus alarmed, conscience believes that the terrible day is at hand. "The end of the world is near. . . . Our children will see it; perchance we ourselves." Once in this mood he had terrible dreams for six months at a time. Like the Christians of the Apocalypse he fixes the moment when the world will be destroyed: it will come at Easter, or at the conversion of Saint Paul. One theologian, his friend, thought of giving all his goods to the poor; "but would they receive it?" he said. "To-morrow night we shall be seated in heaven." Under such anguish the body gives way. For fourteen days Luther was in such a condition, that he could neither drink, eat, nor sleep. "Day and night," his eyes fixed on a text of Saint Paul, he saw the Judge, and His inevitable hand. Such is the tragedy which is enacted in all Protestant souls—the eternal tragedy of conscience; and its issue is a new religion.

For nature alone and unassisted cannot rise from this abyss. "By itself it is so corrupted, that it does not feel the desire for heavenly things. . . . There is in it before God nothing but lust." Good intentions cannot spring from it. "For, terrified by the vision of his sin, man could not resolve to do good, troubled and anxious as he is; on the contrary, dejected and crushed by the weight of his sin, he falls into despair and hatred of God, as it was with Cain, Saul, Judas;" so that, abandoned to himself, he can find nothing within him but the rage and the dejection of a despairing wretch or a devil. In vain he might try to redeem himself by good works : our good deeds are not pure; even though pure, they do not wipe out the stain of previous sins, and moreover they do not take away the original corruption of the heart; they are only boughs and blossoms, the inherited poison is in the sap Man must descend to the heart, underneath literal obedience and legal rule; from the kingdom of law he must penetrate into that of grace; from forced righteousness to spontaneous generosity; beneath his original nature, which led him to selfishness and earthly things, a second nature must be developed, leading him to sacrifice and heavenly things. Neither my works, nor my justice, nor the works or justice of any creature or of all creatures, could work in me this wonderful change. One alone can do it, the pure God, the Just Victim, the Saviour, the Redeemer, Jesus, my Christ, by imputing to me His justice, by pouring upon me His merits, by drowning my sin under His sacrifice. The world is a "mass of perdition,"[1] predestined to hell. Lord Jesus, draw me back, select me from this mass. I have no claim to it; there is nothing in me that is not abominable; this very prayer is inspired and formed within me by Thee. But I weep, and my breast heaves, and my heart is broken. Lord, let me feel myself redeemed, pardoned, Thy elect one, Thy faithful one; give me grace, and give me faith! "Then," says Luther, "I felt myself born anew, and it seemed that I was entering the open gates of heaven."

What remains to be done after this renovation of the heart? Nothing: all religion is in that: the rest must be reduced or suppressed; it is a personal affair, an inward dialogue between God and man, where there are

[1] Saint Augustine.

only two things at work,—the very word of God as it is transmitted by Scripture, and the emotions of the heart of man, as the word of God excites and maintains them.[1] Let us do away with the rites that appeal to the senses, wherewith men wished to replace this intercourse between the invisible soul and the visible judge,—mortifications, fasts, corporeal penance, Lent, vows of chastity and poverty, rosaries, indulgences; rites serve only to smother living piety underneath mechanical works. Away with the mediators by which men have attempted to impede the direct intercourse between God and man,—namely, saints, the Virgin, the Pope, the priest; whosoever adores or obeys them is an idolater. Neither saints nor Virgin can convert or save us; God alone by His Christ can convert and save. Neither Pope nor priest can fix our faith or forgive our sins; God alone instructs us by His word, and absolves us by His pardon. No more pilgrimages or relics; no more traditions or auricular confessions. A new church appears, and therewith a new worship; ministers of religion change their tone, the worship of God its form; the authority of the clergy is diminished, and the pomp of services is reduced: they are reduced and diminished the more, because the primitive idea of the new

[1] Melancthon, preface to *Luther's Works*: "It is clear that the works of Thomas, Scotus, and the like, are utterly silent about the element of justification by faith, and contain many errors concerning the most important questions relating to the church. It is clear that the discourses of the monks in their churches almost throughout the world were either fables about purgatory and the saints or else some kind of dogma of law or discipline, without a word of the gospel concerning Christ, or else were vain trifles about distinctions in the matter of food, about feasts, and other human traditions. . . . The gospel is pure, incorruptible, and not diluted with Gentile opinions." See also Fox, *Acts and Monuments*, 8 vols., ed. Townsend, 1843, ii. 42.

theology is more absorbing; so much so, that in certain sects they have disappeared altogether. The priest descends from the lofty position in which the right of forgiving sins and of regulating faith had raised him over the heads of the laity; he returns to civil society, marries like the rest, aims to be once more an equal, is merely a more learned and pious man than others, chosen by themselves and their adviser. The church becomes a temple, void of images, decorations, ceremonies sometimes altogether bare; a simple meeting-house, where, between whitewashed walls, from a plain pulpit, a man in a black gown speaks without gesticulations, reads a passage from the Bible, begins a hymn, which the congregation takes up. There is another place of prayer, as little adorned and not less venerated, the domestic hearth, where every night the father of the family, before his servants and his children, prays aloud and reads the Scriptures. An austere and free religion, purged from sensualism and obedience, inward and personal, which, set on foot by the awakening of the conscience, could only be established among races in which each man found within his nature the conviction that he alone is responsible for his actions, and always bound to the observance of his duty.

III.

It must be admitted that the Reformation entered England by a side door; but it is enough that it came in, whatever the manner: for great revolutions are not introduced by court intrigues and official cleverness, but by social conditions and popular instincts. When five millions of men are converted, it is because five millions

CHAP. V. THE CHRISTIAN RENAISSANCE. 159

of men wish to be converted. Let us therefore leave on one side the intrigues in high places, the scruples and passions of Henry VIII.,[1] the pliability and plausibility of Cranmer, the vacillations and basenesses of Parliament, the oscillation and tardiness of the Reformation, begun, then arrested, then pushed forward, then suddenly, violently pushed back, then spread over the whole nation, and hedged in by a legal establishment, built up from discordant materials, but yet solid and durable. Every great change has its root in the soul, and we have only to look close into this deep soil to discover the national inclinations and the secular irritations from which Protestantism has issued.

A hundred and fifty years before, it had been on the point of bursting forth; Wycliff had appeared, the Lollards had sprung up, the Bible had been translated; the Commons had proposed the confiscation of all ecclesiastical property; then under the pressure of the Church, royalty and aristocracy combined, the growing Reformation being crushed, disappeared underground, only to reappear at distant intervals by the sufferings of its martyrs. The bishops had received the right of imprisoning without trial laymen suspected of heresy; they had burned Lord Cobham alive; the kings chose their ministers from the episcopal bench; settled in authority and pomp, they had made the nobility and people bend under the secular sword which had been entrusted to them, and in their hands the stern network of law, which from the Conquest had compressed the nation in its iron meshes, had become still more stringent and more offensive. Venial acts had been construed into crimes, and the

[1] *See* Froude, *History of England*, i.-vi. The conduct of Henry VIII. is there presented in a new light.

judicial repression, extended to sins as well as to crimes, had changed the police into an inquisition. "'Offences against chastity,' 'heresy,' or 'matter sounding thereunto,' 'witchcraft,' 'drunkenness,' 'scandal,' 'defamation,' 'impatient words,' 'broken promises,' 'untruth,' 'absence from church,' 'speaking evil of saints,' 'nonpayment of offerings,' 'complaints against the constitutions of the courts themselves;'"[1] all these transgressions, imputed or suspected, brought folk before the ecclesiastical tribunals, at enormous expense, with long delays, from great distances, under a captious procedure, resulting in heavy fines, strict imprisonments, humiliating abjurations, public penances, and the menace, often fulfilled, of torture and the stake. Judge from a single fact; the Earl of Surrey, a relative of the king, was accused before one of these tribunals of having neglected a fast. Imagine, if you can, the minute and incessant oppressiveness of such a code; how far the whole of human life, visible actions and invisible thoughts, was surrounded and held down by it; how by enforced accusations it penetrated to every hearth and into every conscience; with what shamelessness it was transformed into a vehicle for extortions; what secret anger it excited in these townsfolk, these peasants, obliged sometimes to travel sixty miles and back to leave in one or other of the numberless talons of the law[2] a part of their savings, sometimes their whole substance and that of their children. A man begins to think when he is thus down-trodden; he asks himself quietly if it is really by divine dispensation that mitred

---

[1] Froude, i. 191. *Petition of Commons.* This public and authentic protest shows up all the details of clerical organisation and oppression.

[2] Froude, i. 26 ; ii. 192.

thieves thus practise tyranny and pillage; he looks more closely into their lives; he wants to know if they themselves practise the regularity which they impose on others; and on a sudden he learns strange things. Cardinal Wolsey writes to the Pope, that "both the secular and regular priests were in the habit of committing atrocious crimes, for which, if not in orders, they would have been promptly executed;[1] and the laity were scandalised to see such persons not only not degraded, but escaping with complete impunity." A priest convicted of incest with the prioress of Kilbourn was simply condemned to carry a cross in a procession, and to pay three shillings and fourpence; at which rate, I fancy, he would renew the practice. In the preceding reign (Henry VII.) the gentlemen and farmers of Carnarvonshire had laid a complaint accusing the clergy of systematically seducing their wives and daughters. There were brothels in London for the especial use of priests. As to the abuse of the confessional, read in the original the familiarities to which it opened the door.[2] The bishops gave livings to their children whilst they were still young. The holy Father Prior of Maiden Bradley hath but six children, and but one daughter married yet of the goods of the monastery; trusting shortly to marry the rest. In the convents the monks used to drink after supper till ten or twelve next morning, and came to matins drunk. They played cards or dice. Some came to service in the afternoons, and only then for fear of corporal punishments. The royal "visitors" found concubines in the secret apart-

[1] In May 1528. Froude, i. 194.
[2] Hale, *Criminal Causes. Suppression of the Monasteries*, Camden Soc. Publications. Froude, i. 194–201.

ments of the abbots. At the nunnery of Sion, the confessors seduced the nuns and absolved them at the same time. There were convents, Burnet tells us, where all the recluses were found pregnant. About "two-thirds" of the English monks lived in such sort, that "when their enormities were first read in the Parliament House, there was nothing but 'down with them!'"[1] What a spectacle for a nation in whom reason and conscience were awakening! Long before the great outburst, public wrath muttered ominously, and was accumulating for a revolt; priests were yelled at in the streets or "thrown into the kennel;" women would not "receive the sacrament from hands which they thought polluted."[2] When the apparitor of the ecclesiastical courts came to serve a process, he was driven away with insults. "Go thy way thou stynkyng knave, ye are but knaves and brybours everych one of you." A mercer broke an apparitor's head with his yard. "A waiter at the sign of the Cock" said "that the sight of a priest did make him sick, and that he would go sixty miles to indict a priest." Bishop Fitz-James wrote to Wolsey, that the juries in London were "so maliciously set *in favorem hæreticæ pravitatis,* that they will cast and condemn any clerk, though he were as innocent as Abel."[3] Wolsey himself spoke to the Pope of the "dangerous spirit" which was spread abroad among the people, and planned a Reformation. When Henry VIII. laid the axe to the tree, and slowly, with mistrust, struck a blow, then a second lopping off the branches, there were a

---

[1] Latimer's *Sermons*.
[2] They called them "*horsyn prestes,*" "*horson,*" or "*whorson knaves.*" Hale, p. 99; quoted by Froude, i. 199.
[3] Froude, i. 101 (1514).

thousand, nay, a hundred thousand hearts which approved of it, and would themselves have struck the trunk.

Consider the internal state of a diocese, that of Lincoln for instance,[1] at this period, about 1521, and judge by this example of the manner in which the ecclesiastical machinery works throughout the whole of England, multiplying martyrs, hatreds, and conversions. Bishop Longland summons the relatives of the accused, brothers, women and children, and administers the oath; as they have already been prosecuted and have abjured, they must make oath, or they are relapsed, and the fagots await them. Then they denounce their kinsman and themselves. One has taught the other in English the Epistle of Saint James. This man, having forgotten several words of the *Pater* and *Credo* in Latin, can only repeat them in English. A woman turned her face from the cross which was carried about on Easter morning. Several at church, especially at the moment of the elevation, would not say their prayers, and remained seated "dumb as beasts." Three men, including a carpenter, passed a night together reading a book of the Scriptures. A pregnant woman went to mass not fasting. A brazier denied the Real Presence. A brick-maker kept the Apocalypse in his possession. A thresher said, as he pointed to his work, that he was going to make God come out of his straw. Others spoke lightly of pilgrimage, or of the Pope, or of relics, or of confession. And then fifty of them were condemned the same year to abjure, to promise to denounce each other, and to do penance all their lives, on pain of being burnt, as relapsed heretics. They were shut

[1] Fox, *Acts and Monuments*, iv. 221.

up in different "monasteries;" there they were to be
maintained by alms, and to work for their support;
they were to appear with a fagot on their shoulders at
market, and in the procession on Sunday. Then in a
general procession, then at the punishment of a heretic;
"they were to fast on bread and ale only every Friday
during their life, and every even of Corpus Christy on
bread and water, and carry a visible mark on their cheek."
Beyond that, six were burnt alive, and the children of
one, John Scrivener, were obliged themselves to set
fire to their father's wood pile. Do you think that a
man, burnt or shut up, was altogether done with?
He is silenced, I admit, or he is hidden; but long
memories and bitter resentments endure under a forced
silence. People saw[1] their companion, relation, brother,
bound by an iron chain, with clasped hands, praying
amid the smoke, whilst the flame blackened his skin
and destroyed his flesh. Such sights are not forgotten;
the last words uttered on the fagot, the last appeals to
God and Christ, remain in their hearts all-powerful
and ineffaceable. They carry them about with them, and
silently ponder over them in the fields, at their labour,
when they think themselves alone; and then, darkly,
passionately, their brains work. For, beyond this universal sympathy which gathers mankind about the
oppressed, there is the working of the religious sentiment. The crisis of conscience has begun which is
natural to this race; they meditate on their salvation,
they are alarmed at their condition: terrified at the
judgments of God, they ask themselves whether, living

[1] See, *passim*, the prints of Fox. All the details which follow are from biographies. See those of Cromwell, by Carlyle, of Fox the Quaker, of Bunyan, and the trials reported at length by Fox.

under imposed obedience and ceremonies, they do not become culpable, and merit damnation. Can this terror be stifled by prisons and torture? Fear against fear, the only question is, which is the strongest! They will soon know it: for the peculiarity of these inward anxieties is that they grow beneath constraint and oppression; as a welling spring which we vainly try to stamp out under stones, they bubble and leap up and swell, until their surplus overflows, disjointing or bursting asunder the regular masonry under which men endeavoured to bury them. In the solitude of the fields, or during the long winter nights, men dream; soon they fear, and become gloomy. On Sunday at church, obliged to cross themselves, to kneel before the cross, to receive the host, they shudder, and think it a mortal sin. They cease to talk to their friends, remain for hours with bowed heads, sorrowful; at night their wives hear them sigh; unable to sleep they rise from their beds. Picture such a wan face, full of anguish, nourishing under its sternness and calmness a secret ardour: it is still to be found in England in the poor shabby dissenter, who, Bible in hand, stands up suddenly to preach at a street corner; in those long-faced men who, after the service, not having had enough of prayers, sing a hymn in the street. The sombre imagination has started, like a woman in labour, and its conception swells day by day, tearing him who contains it. Through the long muddy winter, the howling of the wind sighing among the ill-fitting rafters, the melancholy of the sky, continually flooded with rain or covered with clouds, add to the gloom of the lugubrious dream. Thenceforth man has made up his mind; he will be saved at all costs. At the peril of his life, he obtains one of the books which teach the way of salvation,

Wycliff's *Wicket Gate, The Obedience of a Christian,* or sometimes Luther's *Revelation of Antichrist,* but above all some portion of the word of God, which Tyndale had just translated. One man hid his books in a hollow tree; another learned by heart an epistle or a gospel, so as to be able to ponder it to himself even in the presence of his accusers. When sure of his neighbour, he speaks with him in private; and peasant talking to peasant, labourer to labourer—you know what the effect will be. It was the yeomen's sons, as Latimer said, who more than all others maintained the faith of Christ in England;[1] and it was with the yeomen's sons that Cromwell afterwards reaped his Puritan victories. When such words are whispered through a nation, all official voices clamour in vain: the nation has found its poem, it stops its ears to the troublesome would-be distractors, and presently sings it out with a full voice and from a full heart.

But the contagion had even reached the men in office, and Henry VIII. at last permitted the English Bible to be published.[2] England had her book. Every one, says Strype, who could buy this book either read it assiduously, or had it read to him by others, and many well advanced in years learned to read with the same object. On Sunday the poor folk gathered at the bottom of the churches to hear it read. Maldon, a young man, afterwards related that he had clubbed his savings with an apprentice to buy a New Testament, and that for fear of his father, they had hidden it in their straw mattress. In vain the king in his pro-

---

[1] Froude, ii. 33 : "The bishops said in 1529, 'In the crime of heresy thanked be God, there hath no notable person fallen in our time.'"

[2] In 1536. Strype's *Memorials*, appendix. Froude, iii. ch. 12.

clamation had ordered people not to rest too much upon their own sense, ideas, or opinions; not to reason publicly about it in the public taverns and alehouses, but to have recourse to learned and authorised men; the seed sprouted, and they chose rather to take God's word in the matter than men's. Maldon declared to his mother that he would not kneel to the crucifix any longer, and his father in a rage beat him severely, and was ready to hang him. The preface itself invited men to independent study, saying that "the Bishop of Rome has studied long to keep the Bible from the people, and specially from princes, lest they should find out his tricks and his falsehoods; . . . knowing well enough, that if the clear sun of God's word came over the heat of the day, it would drive away the foul mist of his devilish doctrines."[1] Even on the admission, then, of official voices, they had there the pure and the whole truth, not merely speculative but moral truth, without which we cannot live worthily or be saved. Tyndale, the translator, says:

"The right waye (yea and the onely waye) to understand the Scripture unto salvation, is that we ernestlye and above all thynge serche for the profession of our baptisme or covenauntes made betwene God and us. As for an example. Christe sayth, Mat. v., Happy are the mercyfull, for they shall obtayne mercye. Lo, here God hath made a covenaunt wyth us, to be mercyfull unto us, yf we wyll be mercyfull one to another."

What an expression! and with what ardour men pricked by the ceaseless reproaches of a scrupulous conscience, and the presentiment of the dark future, will devote on these pages the whole attention of eyes and heart!

[1] Coverdale. Froude, iii. 81.

I have before me one of these great old folios,[1] in black letter, in which the pages, worn by horny fingers have been patched together, in which an old engraving figures forth to the poor folk the deeds and menaces of the God of Israel, in which the preface and table of contents point out to simple people the moral which is to be drawn from each tragic history, and the application which is to be made of each venerable precept. Hence have sprung much of the English language, and half of the English manners; to this day the country is biblical;[2] it was these big books which had transformed Shakspeare's England. To understand this great change, try to picture these yeomen, these shopkeepers, who in the evening placed this Bible on their table, and bareheaded, with veneration, heard or read one of its chapters. Think that they have no other books, that theirs was a virgin mind, that every impression would make a furrow, that the monotony of mechanical existence rendered them entirely open to new emotions, that they opened this book not for amusement, but to discover in it their doom of life and death; in brief, that the sombre and impassioned imagination of the race raised them to the level of the grandeurs and terrors which were to pass before their eyes. Tyndale, the translator, wrote with such sentiments, condemned, hunted, in concealment, his mind full of the idea of a speedy death, and of the great God for whom at last he mounted the funeral pyre; and the spectators who had seen the remorse of Macbeth[3] and the murders of

[1] 1549. Tyndale's translation.
[2] An expression of Stendhal's; it was his general impression.
[3] The time of which M. Taine speaks, and the translation of Tyndale precede by at least fifty years the appearance of *Macbeth* (1606). Shakspeare's audience read the present authorised translation.—Tr.

Shakspeare can listen to the despair of David, and the massacres accumulated in the books of Judges and Kings. The short Hebrew verse-style took hold upon them by its uncultivated austerity. They have no need, like the French, to have the ideas developed, explained in fine clear language, to be modified and connected.[1] The serious and pulsating tone shakes them at once; they understand it with the imagination and the heart; they are not, like Frenchmen, enslaved to logical regularity; and the old text, so free, so lofty and terrible, can retain in their language its wildness and its majesty. More than any people in Europe, by their inner concentration and rigidity, they realise the Semitic conception of the solitary and almighty God; a strange conception, which we, with all our critical methods, have hardly reconstructed within ourselves at the present day. For the Jew, for the powerful minds who wrote the Pentateuch,[2] for the prophets and authors of the Psalms, life as we conceive it, was secluded from living things, plants, animals, firmament, sensible objects, to be carried and concentrated entirely in the one Being of whom they are the work and the puppets. Earth is the footstool of this great God, heaven is His garment. He is in the world, amongst His creatures, as an Oriental king in his tent, amidst his arms and his carpets. If you enter this tent, all vanishes before the absorbing idea of the master; you see but him; nothing has an individual and independent existence: these arms are but made for his hands, these carpets for his foot; you imagine them only as spread for him and trodden by him.

[1] See Lemaistre de Sacy's French translation of the Bible, so slightly biblical.
[2] See Ewald, *Geschichte des Volks Israel*, his apostrophe to the third writer of the Pentateuch, *Erhabener Geist*, etc.

The awe-inspiring face and the menacing voice of the irresistible lord appear behind his instruments. And in a similar manner, for the Jew, nature and men are nothing of themselves; they are for the service of God; they have no other reason for existence; no other use; they vanish before the vast and solitary Being who extended and set high as a mountain before human thought, occupies and covers in Himself the whole horizon. Vainly we attempt, we seed of the Aryan race, to represent to ourselves this devouring God; we always leave some beauty, some interest, some part of free existence to nature; we but half attain to the Creator, with difficulty, after a chain of reasoning, like Voltaire and Kant; more readily we make Him into an architect; we naturally believe in natural laws; we know that the order of the world is fixed; we do not crush things and their relations under the burden of an arbitrary sovereignty; we do not grasp the sublime sentiment of Job, who sees the world trembling and swallowed up at the touch of the strong hand; we cannot endure the intense emotion or repeat the marvellous accent of the psalms, in which, amid the silence of beings reduced to atoms, nothing remains but the heart of man speaking to the eternal Lord. These Englishmen, in the anguish of a troubled conscience, and the oblivion of sensible nature, renew it in part. If the strong and harsh cheer of the Arab, which breaks forth like the blast of a trumpet at the sight of the rising sun and of the bare solitudes,[1] if the mental trances, the short visions of a luminous and grand landscape, if the Semitic colouring are wanting, at least the seriousness and

[1] See Ps. civ. in Luther's admirable translation and in the English translation.

simplicity have remained; and the Hebraic God brought into the modern conscience, is no less a sovereign in this narrow precinct than in the deserts and mountains from which He sprang. His image is reduced, but His authority is entire; if He is less poetical, He is more moral. Men read with awe and trembling the history of His Works, the tables of His law, the archives of His vengeance, the proclamation of His promises and menaces; they are filled with them. Never has a people been seen so deeply imbued by a foreign book, has let it penetrate so far into its manners and writings, its imagination and language. Thenceforth they have found their King, and will follow Him; no word, lay or ecclesiastic, shall prevail over His word; they have submitted their conduct to Him, they will give body and life for Him; and if need be, a day will come when, out of fidelity to Him, they will overthrow the State.

It is not enough to hear this King, they must answer Him; and religion is not complete until the prayer of the people is added to the revelation of God. In 1548, at last, England received her prayer-book[1] from the hands of Cranmer, Peter Martyr, Bernard Ochin, Melanchthon; the chief and most ardent reformers of Europe were invited to compose a body of doctrines conformable to Scripture, and to express a body of sentiments conformable to the true Christian faith. This prayer-book is an admirable book, in which the full spirit of the Reformation breathes out, where, beside the moving tenderness of the gospel, and the manly

[1] The first Primer of note was in 1545; Froude, v. 141. The Prayer-book underwent several changes in 1552, others under Elizabeth, and a few, lastly, at the Restoration.

accents of the Bible, throb the profound emotion, the grave eloquence, the noble-mindedness, the restrained enthusiasm of the heroic and poetic souls who had re-discovered Christianity, and had passed near the fire of martyrdom.

"Almighty and most merciful Father; We have erred, and strayed from Thy ways like lost sheep. We have followed too much the devices and desires of our own hearts. We have offended against Thy holy laws. We have left undone those things which we ought to have done; And we have done those things which we ought not to have done; And there is no health in us. But Thou, O Lord, have mercy upon us, miserable offenders. Spare Thou them, O God, which confess their faults. Restore Thou them that are penitent; According to Thy promises declared unto mankind in Christ Jesu our Lord. And grant, O most merciful Father, for His sake; That we may hereafter live a godly, righteous, and sober life."

"Almighty and everlasting God, who hatest nothing that Thou hast made, and dost forgive the sins of all them that are penitent; Create and make in us new and contrite hearts, that we worthily lamenting our sins, and acknowledging our wretchedness, may obtain of Thee, the God of all mercy, perfect remission and forgiveness."

The same idea of sin, repentance, and moral renovation continually recurs; the master-thought is always that of the heart humbled before invisible justice, and only imploring His grace in order to obtain His relief. Such a state of mind ennobles man, and introduces a sort of impassioned gravity in all the important actions of his life. Listen to the liturgy of the deathbed, of baptism, of marriage; the latter first:

"Wilt thou have this woman to be thy wedded wife, to live together after God's ordinance, in the holy state of Matrimony?

Wilt thou love her, comfort her, honour, and keep her in sickness and in health; and, forsaking all other, keep thee only unto her, so long as ye both shall live?"

These are genuine, honest, and conscientious words. No mystic languor, here or elsewhere. This religion is not made for women who dream, yearn, and sigh, but for men who examine themselves, act and have confidence, confidence in some one more just than themselves. When a man is sick, and his flesh is weak, the priest comes to him, and says:

"Dearly beloved, know this, that Almighty God is the Lord of life and death, and of all things to them pertaining, as youth strength, health, age, weakness, and sickness. Wherefore, whatsoever your sickness is, know you certainly, that it is God's visitation. And for what cause soever this sickness is sent unto you; whether it be to try your patience for the example of others, . . . or else it be sent unto you to correct and amend in you whatsoever doth offend the eyes of your heavenly Father; know you certainly, that if you truly repent you of your sins, and bear your sickness patiently, trusting in God's mercy, . . . submitting yourself wholly unto His will, it shall turn to your profit, and help you forward in the right way that leadeth unto everlasting life."

A great mysterious sentiment, a sort of sublime epic, void of images, shows darkly amid these probings of the conscience; I mean a glimpse of the divine government and of the invisible world, the only existences, the only realities, in spite of bodily appearances and of the brute chance, which seems to jumble all things together. Man sees this beyond at distant intervals, and raises himself out of his mire, as though he had suddenly breathed a pure and strengthening atmosphere. Such are the effects of public prayer restored to the people; for this had been taken from the Latin and rendered into the vulgar tongue: there is a revolution in this very word. Doubtless routine, here as with the ancient missal, will gradually do its sad work; by repeating the same words, man will often do nothing but repeat words; his lips will move whilst his heart remains inert. But in great anguish, in the confused agitations of a restless and hollow mind, at the funerals of his relatives, the strong words of the book will find him in a mood to feel; for they are living,[1] and do not stay in the ears like those of a dead language; they enter the soul; and as soon as the soul is stirred and worked upon, they take root there. If you go and hear these words in England itself, and if you listen to the deep and pulsating accent with which they are pronounced, you will see that they constitute there a national poem, always understood and always efficacious. On Sunday, when all business and pleasure is suspended, between the bare walls of the village church, where no image, no *ex-voto*, no accessory worship distracts the eyes, the seats are full; the powerful Hebraic verses knock like the strokes of a battering-ram at the door of every soul; then the liturgy unfolds its imposing supplications; and at intervals the song of the congregation, combined with the organ, sustains

[1] "To make use of words in a foreign language, merely with a sentiment of devotion, the mind taking no fruit, could be neither pleasing to God, nor beneficial to man. The party that understood not the pith or effectualness of the talk that he made with God, might be as a harp or pipe, having a sound, but not understanding the noise that itself had made; a Christian man was more than an instrument; and he had therefore provided a determinate form of supplication in the English tongue, that his subjects might be able to pray like reasonable beings in their own language."—*Letter of Henry VIII. to Cranmer.* Froude, iv. 486.

the people's devotion. There is nothing graver and more simple than this singing by the people; no scales, no elaborate melody; it is not calculated for the gratification of the ear, and yet it is free from the sickly sadness, from the gloomy monotony which the middle-age has left in the chanting in Roman Catholic churches; neither monkish nor pagan, it rolls like a manly yet sweet melody, neither contrasting with nor obscuring the words which accompany it; these words are psalms translated into verse, yet lofty; diluted, but not embellished. Everything harmonises—place, music, text, ceremony— to place every man, personally and without a mediator, in presence of a just God, and to form a moral poetry which shall sustain and develop the moral sense.[1]

[1] Bishop John Fisher's *Funeral Oration of the Countess of Richmond* (ed. 1711) shows to what practices this religion succeeded. The Countess was the mother of Henry VII., and translated the *Myrroure of Golde*, and *The Forthe Boke of the Followinge Jesus Chryst* :—

"As for fastynge, for age, and feebleness, albeit she were not bound yet those days that by the Church were appointed, she kept them diligently and seriously, and in especial the holy Lent, throughout that she restrained her appetite till one meal of fish on the day; besides her other peculiar fasts of devotion, as St. Anthony, St. Mary Magdalene, St. Catherine, with other; and throughout all the year the Friday and Saturday she full truly observed. As to hard clothes wearing, she had her shirts and girdles of hair, which, when she was in health, every week she failed not certain days to wear, sometime the one, sometime the other, that full often her skin, as I heard say, was pierced therewith.

"In prayer, every day at her uprising, which commonly was not long after five of the clock, she began certain devotions, and so after them, with one of her gentlewomen, the matins of our Lady; which kept her to then, she came into her closet, where then with her chaplain she said also matins of the day; and after that, daily heard four or five masses upon her knees; so continuing in her prayers and devotions unto the hour of dinner, which of the eating day was ten of the clocks, and upon the fasting day eleven. After dinner full truly she would go her stations to three altars daily; daily her dirges and commendations she would say, and her even songs before supper, both of the day

One detail is still needed to complete this manly religion—human reason. The minister ascends the pulpit and speaks: he speaks coldly, I admit, with literary comments and over-long demonstrations; but solidly, seriously, like a man who desires to convince, and that by honest means, who addresses only the reason, and discourses only of justice. With Latimer and his contemporaries, preaching, like religion, changes its object and character; like religion, it becomes popular and moral, and appropriate to those who hear it, to recall them to their duties. Few men have deserved better of their fellows, in life and word, than he. He was a genuine Englishman, conscientious, courageous, a man of common sense and practical, sprung from the labouring and independent class, the very heart and sinews of the nation. His father, a brave yeoman, had a farm of about four pounds a year, on which he employed half a dozen men, with thirty cows which his wife milked, a good soldier of the king, keeping equipment for himself and his horse so as to join the army if need were,

and of our Lady, beside many other prayers and psalters of David throughout the year ; and at night before she went to bed, she failed not to resort unto her chapel, and there a large quarter of an hour to occupy her devotions. No marvel, though all this long time her kneeling was to her painful, and so painful that many times it caused in her back pain and disease. And yet nevertheless, daily, when she was in health, she failed not to say the crown of our lady, which, after the manner of Rome, containeth sixty and three aves, and at every ave, to make a kneeling. As for meditation, she had divers books in French, wherewith she would occupy herself when she was weary of prayer. Wherefore divers she did translate out of the French into English. Her marvellous weeping they can bear witness of, which here before have heard her confession, which be divers and many, and at many seasons in the year, lightly every third day. Can also record the same those that were present at any time when she was houshylde, which was full nigh a dozen times every year, what floods of tears there issued forth of her eyes !"

training his son to use the bow, making him buckle on his breastplate, and finding a few nobles at the bottom of his purse wherewith to send him to school, and thence to the university.[1] Little Latimer studied eagerly, took his degrees, and continued long a good Catholic, or, as he says, "in darckense and in the shadow of death." At about thirty, having often heard Bilney the martyr, and having, moreover, studied the world and thought for himself, he, as he tells us, "began from that time forward to smell the word of God, and to forsooke the Schoole Doctours, and such fooleries;" presently to preach, and forthwith to pass for a seditious man, very troublesome to those men in authority who did not act with justice. For this was in the first place the salient feature of his eloquence: he spoke to people of their duties, in exact terms. One day, when he preached before the university, the Bishop of Ely came, curious to hear him. Immediately he changed his subject, and drew the portrait of a perfect prelate, a portrait which did not tally well with the bishop's character; and he was denounced for the act. When he was made chaplain of Henry VIII., awe-inspiring as the king was, little as he was himself, he dared to write to him freely to bid him stop the persecution which was set on foot, and to prevent the interdiction of the Bible; verily he risked his life. He had done it before, he did it again; like Tyndale, Knox, all the leaders of the Reformation, he lived in almost ceaseless expectation of death, and in contemplation of the stake. Sick, liable to racking headaches, stomachaches, pleurisy, stone, he wrought a vast work, travelling, writing, preaching, delivering at the age of sixty-seven two sermons every Sunday, and

[1] See vol. i. p. 159, note 1.

generally rising at two in the morning, winter and summer, to study. Nothing can be simpler or more effective than his eloquence; and the reason is, that he never speaks for the sake of speaking, but of doing work. His sermons, amongst others those which he preached before the young king Edward VI., are not, like those of Massillon before the youthful Louis XV., hung in the air, in the calm region of philosophical amplifications: Latimer wishes to correct, and he attacks actual vices, vices which he has seen, which every one can point at with the finger; he too points them out, calls things by their name, and people too, giving facts and details, bravely; and sparing nobody, sets himself without hesitation to denounce and reform iniquity. Universal as his morality is, ancient as is his text, he applies it to his contemporaries, to his audience, at times to the judges who are there "in velvet cotes," who will not hear the poor, who give but a dog's hearing to such a woman in a twelvemonth, and who leave another poor woman in the Fleet, refusing to accept bail;[1] at times to the king's officers, whose thefts he enumerates, whom he sets between hell and restitution, and of whom he obtains, nay extorts, pound for pound, the stolen money.[2] From abstract iniquity he proceeds always to special abuse; for it is abuse which cries out and demands, not a discourser, but a champion. With him theology holds but a secondary place; before all, practice: the true offence against God in his eyes is a bad action; the true service, the suppression of bad deeds. And see by what paths he reaches this. No grand words, no show

[1] Latimer's *Seven Sermons before Edward VI.*, ed. Edward Arber, 1869. Second sermon, pp. 73 and 74.
[2] Latimer's *Sermons.* Fifth sermon, ed. Arber, p. 147.

of style, no exhibition of dialectics. He relates his life, the lives of others, giving dates, numbers, places; he abounds in anecdotes, little obvious circumstances, fit to enter the imagination and arouse the recollections of each hearer. He is familiar, at times humorous, and always so precise, so impressed with real events and particularities of English life, that we might glean from his sermons an almost complete description of the manners of his age and country. To reprove the great, who appropriate common lands by their enclosures, he details the needs of the peasant, without the least care for conventional proprieties; he is not working now for conventionalities, but to produce convictions:—

"A plough land must have sheep; yea, they must have sheep to dung their ground for bearing of corn; for if they have no sheep to help to fat the ground, they shall have but bare corn and thin. They must have swine for their food, to make their veneries or bacon of: their bacon is their venison, for they shall now have *hangum tuum*, if they get any other venison; so that bacon is their necessary meat to feed on, which they may not lack. They must have other cattle: as horses to draw their plough, and for carriage of things to the markets; and kine for their milk and cheese, which they must live upon and pay their rents. These cattle must have pasture, which pasture if they lack, the rest must needs fail them: and pasture they cannot have, if the land be taken in, and enclosed from them." [1]

Another time, to put his hearers on their guard against hasty judgments, he relates that, having entered the gaol at Cambridge to exhort the prisoners, he found a woman accused of having killed her child, who would make no confession:—

[1] Latimer's *Sermons*, ed. Corrie, 1844, 2 vols., *Last Sermon preached before Edward VI.*, i. 249.

"Which denying gave us occasion to search for the matter, and so we did. And at the length we found that her husband loved her not; and therefore he sought means to make her out of the way. The matter was thus: 'a child of hers had been sick by the space of a year, and so decayed as it were in a consumption. At the length it died in harvest-time. She went to her neighbours and other friends to desire their help, to prepare the child to the burial: but there was nobody at home; every man was in the field. The woman, in an heaviness and trouble of spirit, went, and being herself alone, prepared the child to the burial. Her husband coming home, not having great love towards her, accused her of the murder; and so she was taken and brought to Cambridge. But as far forth as I could learn through earnest inquisition, I thought in my conscience the woman was not guilty, all the circumstances well considered. Immediately after this I was called to preach before the king, which was my first sermon that I made before his majesty, and it was done at Windsor; when his majesty, after the sermon was done, did most familiarly talk with me in the gallery. Now, when I saw my time, I kneeled down before his majesty, opening the whole matter; and afterwards most humbly desired his majesty to pardon that woman. For I thought in my conscience she was not guilty; else I would not for all the world sue for a murderer. The king most graciously heard my humble request, insomuch that I had a pardon ready for her at my return homeward. In the mean season that same woman was delivered of a child in the tower at Cambridge, whose godfather I was, and Mistress Cheke was godmother. But all that time I hid my pardon, and told her nothing of it, only exhorting her to confess the truth. At the length the time came when she looked to suffer: I came, as I was wont to do, to instruct her; she made great moan to me, and most earnestly required me that I would find the means that she might be purified before her suffering; for she thought she should have been damned, if she should suffer without purification. . . . So we travailed with this woman till we brought her to a good trade; and at the length shewed her the king's pardon, and let her go.'

"This tale I told you by this occasion, that though some women be very unnatural, and forget their children, yet when we hear anybody so report, we should not be too hasty in believing the tale, but rather suspend our judgments till we know the truth."[1]

When a man preaches thus, he is believed; we are sure that he is not reciting a lesson; we feel that he has seen, that he draws his moral not from books, but from facts; that his counsels come from the solid basis whence everything ought to come,—I mean from manifold and personal experience. Many a time have I listened to popular orators, who address the pocket, and prove their talent by the money they have collected; it is thus that they hold forth, with circumstantial, recent, proximate examples, with conversational turns of speech, setting aside great arguments and fine language. Imagine the ascendency of the Scriptures enlarged upon in such words; to what strata of the people it could descend, what a hold it had upon sailors, workmen, servants! Consider, again, how the authority of these words is doubled by the courage, independence, integrity, unassailable and recognised virtue of him who utters them. He spoke the truth to the king, unmasked robbers, incurred all kind of hate, resigned his see rather than sign anything against his conscience; and at eighty years, under Mary, refusing to recant, after two years of prison and waiting—and what waiting! he was led to the stake. His companion, Ridley, slept the night before as calmly, we are told, as ever

[1] Latimer's *Sermons*, ed. Corrie, *First Sermon on the Lord's Prayer*, i. 335.

he did in his life; and when ready to be chained to the post, said aloud, " O heavenly Father, I give Thee most hearty thanks, for that Thou hast called me to be a professor of Thee, even unto death." Latimer in his turn, when they brought the lighted faggots, cried, "Be of good comfort, Master Ridley, and play the man: we shall this day light such a candle by God's grace, in England, as I trust shall never be put out." He then bathed his hands in the flames, and resigning his soul to God, he expired.

He had judged rightly: it is by this supreme trial that a creed proves its strength and gains its adherents; tortures are a sort of propaganda as well as a testimony, and make converts whilst they make martyrs. All the writings of the time, and all the commentaries which may be added to them, are weak compared to the actions which, one after the other, shone forth at that time from learned and unlearned, down to the most simple and ignorant. In three years, under Mary, nearly three hundred persons, men, women, old and young, some all but children, allowed themselves to be burned alive rather than to abjure. The all-powerful idea of God, and of the faith due to Him, made them resist all the protests of nature, and all the trembling of the flesh. "No one will be crowned," said one of them, " but they who fight like men; and he who endures to the end shall be saved." Doctor Rogers was burned first, in presence of his wife and ten children, one at the breast. He had not been told beforehand, and was sleeping soundly. The wife of the keeper of Newgate woke him, and told him that he must burn that day. "Then," said he, " I need not truss my points." In the midst of the flames he did not seem to suffer.

"His children stood by consoling him, in such a way that he looked as if they were conducting him to a merry marriage."[1] A young man of nineteen, William Hunter, apprenticed to a silk-weaver, was exhorted by his parents to persevere to the end :—

"In the mean time William's father and mother came to him, and desired heartily of God that he might continue to the end in that good way which he had begun : and his mother said to him, that she was glad that ever she was so happy to bear such a child, which could find in his heart to lose his life for Christ's name's sake.

"Then William said to his mother, 'For my little pain which I shall suffer, which is but a short braid, Christ hath promised me, mother (said he), a crown of joy : may you not be glad of that, mother?' With that his mother kneeled down on her knees, saying, 'I pray God strengthen thee, my son, to the end; yea, I think thee as well-bestowed as any child that ever I bare.' . . .

"Then William Hunter plucked up his gown, and stepped over the parlour groundsel, and went forward cheerfully; the sheriff's servant taking him by one arm, and I his brother by another. And thus going in the way, he met with his father according to his dream, and he spake to his son weeping, and saying, 'God be with thee, son William;' and William said, 'God be with you, good father, and be of good comfort; for I hope we shall meet again, when we shall be merry.' His father said, 'I hope so, William;' and so departed. So William went to the place where the stake stood, even according to his dream, where all things were very unready. Then William took a wet broom-faggot, and kneeled down thereon, and read the fifty-first

[1] Noailles, the French (and Catholic) Ambassador. John Fox, *History of the Acts and Monuments of the Church*, ed. Townsend, 1843, 8 vols., vi. 612, says: "His wife and children, being eleven in number, and ten able to go, and one sucking on her breast, met him by the way as he went towards Smithfield."—Tr.

Psalm, till he came to these words, 'The sacrifice of God is a contrite spirit; a contrite and a broken heart, O God, thou wilt not despise.' . . .

"Then said the sheriff, 'Here is a letter from the queen. If thou wilt recant thou shalt live; if not, thou shalt be burned.' 'No,' quoth William, 'I will not recant, God willing.' Then William rose and went to the stake, and stood upright to it. Then came one Richard Ponde, a bailiff, and made fast the chain about William.

"Then said master Brown, 'Here is not wood enough to burn a leg of him.' Then said William, 'Good people! pray for me; and make speed and despatch quickly: and pray for me while you see me alive, good people! and I will pray for you likewise.' 'Now?' quoth master Brown, 'pray for thee! I will pray no more for thee, than I will pray for a dog.' . . .

"Then was there a gentleman which said, 'I pray God have mercy upon his soul.' The people said, 'Amen, Amen.'

"Immediately fire was made. Then William cast his psalter right into his brother's hand, who said, 'William! think on the holy passion of Christ, and be not afraid of death.' And William answered, 'I am not afraid.' Then lift he up his hands to heaven, and said, 'Lord, Lord, Lord, receive my spirit;' and, casting down his head again into the smothering smoke, he yielded up his life for the truth, sealing it with his blood to the praise of God."[1]

When a passion is able thus to subdue the natural affections, it is able also to subdue bodily pain; all the ferocity of the time laboured in vain against inward convictions. Thomas Tomkins, a weaver of Shoreditch, being asked by Bonner if he could stand the fire well, bade him try it. "Bonner took Tomkins by the fingers, and held his hand directly over the flame," to terrify him. But "he never shrank, till the veins

[1] Fox, *History of the Acts*, etc., vi. 727.

shrank and the sinews burst, and the water (blood) did spirt in Mr. Harpsfield's face."[1] "In the Isle of Guernsey, a woman with child being ordered to the fire, was delivered in the flames, and the infant being taken from her, was ordered by the magistrates to be thrown back into the fire."[2] Bishop Hooper was burned three times over in a small fire of green wood. There was too little wood, and the wind turned aside the smoke. He cried out, "For God's love, good people, let me have more fire." His legs and thighs were roasted; one of his hands fell off before he expired; he endured thus three-quarters of an hour; before him in a box was his pardon, on condition that he would retract. Against long sufferings in mephitic prisons, against everything which might unnerve or seduce, these men were invincible: five died of hunger at Canterbury; they were in irons night and day, with no covering but their clothes, on rotten straw; yet there was an understanding amongst them, that the "cross of persecution" was a blessing from God, "an inestimable jewel, a sovereign antidote, well-approved, to cure love of self and earthly affection." Before such examples the people were shaken. A woman wrote to Bishop Bonner, that there was not a child but called him Bonner the hangman, and knew on his fingers, as well as he knew his pater, the exact number of those he had burned at the stake, or suffered to die of hunger in prison these nine months. "You have lost the hearts of twenty thousand persons who were inveterate Papists a year ago." The spectators encouraged the martyrs, and cried out to them that their

[1] Fox, *History of the Acts*, etc., vi. 719.
[2] Neal, *History of the Puritans*, ed. Toulmin, 5 vols., 1793, i. 96.

cause was just. The Catholic envoy Renard wrote to Charles V. that it was said that several had desired to take their place at the stake, by the side of those who were being burned. In vain the queen had forbidden, on pain of death, all marks of approbation. "We know that they are men of God," cried one of the spectators; "that is why we cannot help saying, God strengthen them." And all the people answered, "Amen, Amen." What wonder if, at the coming of Elizabeth, England cast in her lot with Protestantism? The threats of the Armada urged her on still further; and the Reformation became national under the pressure of foreign hostility, as it had become popular through the triumph of its martyrs.

IV.

Two distinct branches receive the common sap,— one above, the other beneath: one respected, flourishing, shooting forth in the open air; the other despised, half buried in the ground, trodden under foot by those who would crush it: both living, the Anglican as well as the Puritan, the one in spite of the effort made to destroy it, the other in spite of the care taken to develop it.

The court has its religion, like the country—a sincere and winning religion. Amid the pagan poetry which up to the Revolution always had the ear of the world, we find gradually piercing through and rising higher a grave and grand idea which sent its roots to the depth of the public mind. Many poets, Drayton, Davies, Cowley, Giles Fletcher, Quarles, Crashaw, wrote sacred histories, pious or moral verses, noble stanzas on death and the immortality of the soul, on the frailty of things human, and on the supreme providence in which alone man finds the support of his weakness and the consolation of his sufferings. In the greatest prose writers, Bacon, Burton, Sir Thomas Browne, Raleigh, we see spring up the fruits of veneration, thoughts about the obscure beyond; in short, faith and prayer. Several prayers written by Bacon are amongst the finest known; and the courtier Raleigh, whilst writing of the fall of empires, and how the barbarous nations had destroyed this grand and magnificent Roman Empire, ended his book with the ideas and tone of a Bossuet.[1] Picture Saint Paul's in London, and the fashionable people who used to meet there; the gentlemen who noisily made the rowels of their spurs resound on entering, looked around and carried on conversation during service, who swore by God's eyes, God's eyelids, who amongst the vaults and chapels showed off their beribboned shoes, their chains, scarves, satin doublets, velvet cloaks, their braggadocio manners and stage attitudes. All this was very free, very loose, very far from our modern decency. But pass over youthful bluster; take man in his great moments, in prison, in danger, or indeed when old age arrives, when he has come to judge of life; take him, above all, in the country, on his estate, far from any town, in the church of the village where he is lord; or again, when he is alone in the evening, at his table, listening to the prayer offered up by his chaplain, having

---

[1] "O eloquent, just, and mightie Death! whom none could advise, thou hast persuaded; what none hath dared, thou hast done; and whom all the world hath flattered, thou only hast cast out of the world and despised; thou hast drawne together all the farre stretched greatnesse, all the pride, crueltie, and ambition of man, and covered it all over with these two narrow words, *Hic jacet.*"

no books but some big folio of dramas, well dog's-eared by his pages, and his prayer-book and Bible; you may then understand how the new religion tightens its hold on these imaginative and serious minds. It does not shock them by a narrow rigour; it does not fetter the flight of their mind; it does not attempt to extinguish the buoyant flame of their fancy; it does not proscribe the beautiful: it preserves more than any reformed church the noble pomp of the ancient worship, and rolls under the domes of its cathedrals the rich modulations, the majestic harmonies of its grave, organ-led music. It is its characteristic not to be in opposition to the world, but, on the contrary, to draw it nearer to itself, by bringing itself nearer to it. By its secular condition as well as by its external worship, it is embraced by and it embraces it: its head is the Queen, it is a part of the Constitution, it sends its dignitaries to the House of Lords; it suffers its priests to marry; its benefices are in the nomination of the great families; its chief members are the younger sons of these same families: by all these channels it imbibes the spirit of the age. In its hands, therefore, reformation cannot become hostile to science, to poetry, to the liberal ideas of the Renaissance. Nay, in the nobles of Elizabeth and James I., as in the cavaliers of Charles I., it tolerates artistic tastes, philosophical curiosity, the ways of the world, and the sentiment of the beautiful. The alliance is so strong, that, under Cromwell, the ecclesiastics in a mass were dismissed for their king's sake, and the cavaliers died wholesale for the Church. The two societies mutually touch and are confounded together. If several poets are pious, several ecclesiastics are poetical,—Bishop Hall, Bishop

Corbet, Wither a rector, and the preacher Donne. If several laymen rise to religious contemplations, several theologians, Hooker, John Hales, Taylor, Chillingworth, set philosophy and reason by the side of dogma. Accordingly we find a new literature arising, lofty and original, eloquent and moderate, armed at the same time against the Puritans, who sacrifice freedom of intellect to the tyranny of the text, and against the Catholics, who sacrifice independence of criticism to the tyranny of tradition; opposed equally to the servility of literal interpretation, and the servility of a prescribed interpretation. Opposed to the first appears the learned and excellent Hooker, one of the gentlest and most conciliatory of men, the most solid and persuasive of logicians, a comprehensive mind, who in every question ascends to the principles,[1] introduces into controversy general conceptions, and the knowledge of human nature;[2] beyond this, a

[1] Hooker's Works, ed. Keble, 1836, 3 vols., *The Ecclesiastical Polity*.

[2] *Ibid.* i. book i. 249, 258, 312 :—

"That which doth assign unto each thing the kind, that which doth moderate the force and power, that which doth appoint the form and measure of working, the same we term a Law. . . .

"Now if nature should intermit her course, and leave altogether, though it were but for awhile, the observation of her own laws; if those principal and mother elements of the world, whereof all things in this lower world are made, should lose the qualities which now they have; if the frame of that heavenly arch erected over our heads should loosen and dissolve itself; if celestial spheres should forget their wonted motions, . . . if the prince of the lights of heaven, which now as a giant doth run his unwearied course, should as it were through a languishing faintness, begin to stand and to rest himself : . . . what would become of man himself, whom these things now do all serve! See we not plainly that obedience of creatures unto the law of nature is the stay of the whole world? . . .

"Between men and beasts there is no possibility of sociable com-

methodical writer, correct and always ample, worthy of being regarded not only as one of the fathers of the English Church, but as one of the founders of English prose. With a sustained gravity and simplicity, he shows the Puritans that the laws of nature, reason, and society, like the law of Scripture, are of divine institution, that all are equally worthy of respect and obedience, that we must not sacrifice the inner word, by which God reaches our intellect, to the outer word, by which God reaches our senses; that thus the civil constitution of the Church, and the visible ordinance of ceremonies, may be conformable to the will of God, even when they are not justified by a clear text of Scripture; and that the authority of the magistrates, as well as the reason of man, does not exceed its rights in establishing certain uniformities and disciplines on which Scripture is silent, in order that reason may decide:—

"For if the natural strength of man's wit may by experience and study attain unto such ripeness in the knowledge of things

munion because the well-spring of that communion is a natural delight which man hath to transfuse from himself into others, and to receive from others into himself, especially those things wherein the excellency of his kind doth most consist. The chiefest instrument of human communion therefore is speech, because thereby we impart mutually one to another the conceits of our reasonable understanding. And for that cause, seeing beasts are not hereof capable, forasmuch as with them we can use no such conference, they being in degree, although above other creatures on earth to whom nature hath denied sense, yet lower than to be sociable companions of man to whom nature hath given reason; it is of Adam said, that amongst the beasts 'he found not for himself any meet companion.' Civil society doth more content the nature of man than any private kind of solitary living, because in society this good of mutual participation is so much larger than otherwise. Herewith notwithstanding we are not satisfied, but we covet (if it might be) to have a kind of society and fellowship even with all mankind."

human, that men in this respect may presume to build somewhat upon their judgment; what reason have we to think but that even in matters divine, the like wits furnished with necessary helps, exercised in Scripture with like diligence, and assisted with the grace of Almighty God, may grow unto so much perfection of knowledge, that men shall have just cause, when anything pertinent unto faith and religion is doubted of, the more willingly to incline their minds towards that which the sentence of so grave, wise, and learned in that faculty shall judge most sound."[1]

This "natural light" therefore must not be despised, but rather used so as to augment the other, as we put torch to torch; above all, employed that we may live in harmony with each other.[2]

"Far more comfort it were for us (so small is the joy we take in these strifes) to labour under the same yoke, as men that look for the same eternal reward of their labours, to be conjoined with you in bands of indissoluble love and amity, to live as if our persons being many, our souls were but one, rather than in such dismembered sort to spend our few and wretched days in a tedious prosecuting of wearisome contentions."

In fact, the conclusions of the greatest theologians are for such harmony: abandoning an oppressive practice they grasp a liberal spirit. If by its political structure the English Church is persecuting, by its doctrinal structure it is tolerant; it needs the reason of the laity too much to refuse it liberty; it lives in a world too cultivated and thoughtful to proscribe thought and culture. John Hales, its most eminent doctor, declared several

[1] *Ecc. Pol.* i. book ii. ch. vii. 4, p. 405.
[2] See the *Dialogues of Galileo*. The same idea which is persecuted by the church at Rome is at the same time defended by the church in England. See also *Ecc. Pol.* i. book iii. 461-481.

times that he would renounce the Church of England to-morrow if she insisted on the doctrine that other Christians would be damned; and that men believe other people to be damned only when they desire them to be so.[1] It was he again, a theologian, a prebendary, who advises men to trust to themselves alone in religious matters; to leave nothing to authority, or antiquity, or the majority; to use their own reason in believing, as they use "their own legs in walking;" to act and be men in mind as well as in the rest; and to regard as cowardly and impious the borrowing of doctrine and sloth of thought. So Chillingworth, a notably militant and loyal mind, the most exact, the most penetrating, and the most convincing of controversialists, first Protestant, then Catholic, then Protestant again and for ever, has the courage to say that these great changes, wrought in himself and by himself, through study and research, are, of all his actions, those which satisfy him most. He maintains that reason alone applied to Scripture ought to persuade men; that authority has no claim in it; that nothing is more against religion than to force religion; that the great principle of the Reformation is liberty of conscience; and that if the doctrines of the different Protestant sects are not absolutely true, at least they are free from all impiety and from all error damnable in itself, or destructive of salvation. Thus is developed a new school of polemics, a theology, a solid and rational apologetics, rigorous in its arguments, capable of expansion, confirmed by science, and which, authorizing independence of personal judgment at the same time with the inter-

[1] Clarendon. See the same doctrines in Jeremy Taylor, *Liberty of Prophesying*, 1647.

vention of the natural reason, leaves religion within reach of the world and the establishments of the past struggling with the future.

A writer of genius appears amongst these, a prose-poet, gifted with an imagination like Spenser and Shakspeare,—Jeremy Taylor, who, from the bent of his mind as well as from circumstances, was destined to present the alliance of the Renaissance with the Reformation, and to carry into the pulpit the ornate style of the court. A preacher at St. Paul's, appreciated and admired by men of fashion for his youthful and fresh beauty and his graceful bearing, as also for his splendid diction; patronised and promoted by Archbishop Laud, he wrote for the king a defence of episcopacy; became chaplain to the king's army; was taken, ruined, twice imprisoned by the Parliamentarians; married a natural daughter of Charles I.; then, after the Restoration, was loaded with honours; became a bishop, member of the Privy Council, and vice-chancellor of the university of Dublin. In every passage of his life, fortunate or otherwise, private or public, we see that he is an Anglican, a royalist, imbued with the spirit of the cavaliers and courtiers, not with their vices. On the contrary, there was never a better or more upright man, more zealous in his duties, more tolerant by principle; so that, preserving a Christian gravity and purity, he received from the Renaissance only its rich imagination, its classical erudition, and its liberal spirit. But he had these gifts entire, as they existed in the most brilliant and original of the men of the world, in Sir Philip Sidney, Lord Bacon, Sir Thomas Browne, with the graces, splendours, refinements which are characteristic of these sensitive and creative geniuses, and yet with the redundancies, singularities, incongruities inevitable in an age when excess of spirit prevented the soundness of taste. Like all these writers, like Montaigne, he was imbued with classic antiquity; in the pulpit he quotes Greek and Latin anecdotes, passages from Seneca, verses of Lucretius and Euripides, and this side by side with texts from the Bible, from the Gospels, and the Fathers. Cant was not yet in vogue; the two great sources of teaching, Christian and Pagan, ran side by side; they were collected in the same vessel, without imagining that the wisdom of reason and nature could mar the wisdom of faith and revelation. Fancy these strange sermons, in which the two eruditions, Hellenic and Evangelic, flow together with their texts, and each text in its own language; in which, to prove that fathers are often unfortunate in their children, the author brings forward one after the other, Chabrias, Germanicus, Marcus Aurelius, Hortensius, Quintus Fabius Maximus, Scipio Africanus, Moses, and Samuel; where, in the form of comparisons and illustrations is heaped up the spoil of histories, and authorities on botany, astronomy, zoology, which the cyclopædias and scientific fancies at that time poured into the brain. Taylor will relate to you the history of the bears of Pannonia, which, when wounded, will press the iron deeper home; or of the apples of Sodom, which are beautiful to the gaze, but full within of rottenness and worms; and many others of the same kind. For it was a characteristic of men of this age and school, not to possess a mind swept, levelled, regulated, laid out in straight paths, like the seventeenth century writers in France, and like the gardens at Versailles, but full, and crowded with circumstantial facts, complete dramatic scenes, little coloured pictures, pellmell and badly dusted; so that, lost in confusion and dust, the modern spectator cries out at their pedantry and coarseness. Metaphors swarm one above the other, jumbled, blocking each other's path, as in Shakspeare. We think to follow one, and a second begins, then a third cutting into the second, and so on, flower after flower, firework after firework, so that the brightness becomes misty with sparks, and the sight ends in a haze. On the other hand, and just by virtue of this same turn of mind, Taylor imagines objects, not vaguely and feebly, by some indistinct general conception, but precisely, entire, as they are, with their visible colour, their proper form, the multitude of true and particular details which distinguish them in their species. He is not acquainted with them by hearsay; he has seen them. Better, he sees them now and makes them to be seen. Read the following extract, and say if it does not seem to have been copied from a hospital, or from a field of battle :—

"And what can we complain of the weakness of our strengths, or the pressures of diseases, when we see a poor soldier stand in a breach almost starved with cold and hunger, and his cold apt to be relieved only by the heats of anger, a fever, or a fired musket, and his hunger slacked by a greater pain and a huge fear? This man shall stand in his arms and wounds, *patiens luminis atque solis*, pale and faint, weary and watchful; and at night shall have a bullet pulled out of his flesh, and shivers from his bones, and endure his mouth to be sewed up from a violent rent to its own dimensions; and all this for a man whom he never saw, or, if he did, was not noted by him; but one that shall condemn him to the gallows if he runs away from all this misery." [1]

[1] Jeremy Taylor's Works, ed. Eden, 1840, 10 vols., *Holy Dying*, ch. iii. sec. 4, § 3, p. 315.

This is the advantage of a full imagination over ordinary reason. It produces in a lump twenty or thirty ideas, and as many images, exhausting the subject which the other only outlines and sketches. There are a thousand circumstances and shades in every event; and they are all grasped in living words like these:—

"For so have I seen the little purls of a spring sweat through the bottom of a bank, and intenerate the stubborn pavement, till it hath made it fit for the impression of a child's foot; and it was despised, like the descending pearls of a misty morning, till it had opened its way and made a stream large enough to carry away the ruins of the undermined strand, and to invade the neighbouring gardens; but then the despised drops were grown into an artificial river, and an intolerable mischief. So are the first entrances of sin, stopped with the antidotes of a hearty prayer, and checked into sobriety by the eye of a reverend man, or the counsels of a single sermon; but when such beginnings are neglected, and our religion hath not in it so much philosophy as to think anything evil as long as we can endure it, they grow up to ulcers and pestilential evils; they destroy the soul by their abode, who at their first entry might have been killed with the pressure of a little finger." [1]

All extremes meet in that imagination. The cavaliers who heard him, found, as in Ford, Beaumont and Fletcher, the crude copy of the most coarse and unclean truth, and the light music of the most graceful and airy fancies; the smell and horrors of a dissecting room,[2] and all on a sudden the freshness and cheerfulness of smiling dawn; the hateful detail of leprosy, its white spots, its inner rottenness; and then this lovely picture of a lark, rising amid the early perfumes of the fields:—

[1] Sermon xvi., *Of Growth in Sin*.
[2] "We have already opened up this dunghill covered with snow, which was indeed on the outside white as the spots of leprosy."

"For so have I seen a lark rising from his bed of grass, and soaring upwards, singing as he rises, and hopes to get to heaven, and climb above the clouds; but the poor bird was beaten back with the loud sighings of an eastern wind, and his motion made irregular and inconstant, descending more at every breath of the tempest, than it could recover by the vibration and frequent weighing of his wings, till the little creature was forced to sit down and pant, and stay till the storm was over; and then it made a prosperous flight, and did rise and sing, as if it had learned music and motion from an angel, as he passed sometimes through the air, about his ministries here below. So is the prayer of a good man."[1]

And he continues with the charm, sometimes with the very words, of Shakspeare. In the preacher, as well as in the poet, as well as in all the cavaliers and all the artists of the time, the imagination is so full, that it reaches the real, even to its filth, and the ideal as far as its heaven.

How could true religious sentiment thus accommodate itself to such a frank and worldly gait? This, however, is what it has done; and more—the latter has generated the former. With Taylor, as well as with the others, bold poetry leads to profound faith. If this alliance astonishes us to-day, it is because in this respect people have grown pedantic. We take a formal man for a religious man. We are content to see him stiff in his black coat, choked in a white neckerchief, with a prayer-book in his hand. We confound piety with decency, propriety, permanent and perfect regularity. We proscribe to a man of faith all candid speech, all bold gesture, all fire and dash in word or act; we are shocked by Luther's rude words, the bursts of

[1] *Golden Grove Sermons*: V. "The Return of Prayers."

laughter which shook his mighty paunch, his rages like a working-man, his plain and free speaking, the audacious familiarity with which he treats Christ and the Deity.[1] We do not perceive that these freedoms and this recklessness are precisely signs of entire belief, that warm and immoderate conviction is too sure of itself to be tied down to an irreproachable style, that impulsive religion consists not of punctilios but of emotions. It is a poem, the greatest of all, a poem believed in; this is why these men found it at the end of their poesy: the way of looking at the world, adopted by Shakspeare and all the tragic poets, led to it; another step, and Jacques, Hamlet, would be there. That vast obscurity, that black unexplored ocean, "the unknown country," which they saw on the verge of our sad life, who knows whether it is not bounded by another shore? The troubled notion of the shadowy beyond is national, and this is why the national renaissance at this time became Christian. When Taylor speaks of death he only takes up and works out a thought which Shakspeare had already sketched:—

"All the succession of time, all the changes in nature, all the varieties of light and darkness, the thousand thousands of accidents in the world, and every contingency to every man, and to every creature, doth preach our funeral sermon, and calls us to look and see how the old sexton Time throws up the earth, and digs a grave where we must lay our sins or our sorrows, and sow

[1] Luther's *Table Talk*, ed. Hazlitt, No. 187, p. 30 : When Jesus Christ was born, he doubtless cried and wept like other children, and his mother tended him as other mothers tend their children. As he grew up he was submissive to his parents, and waited on them, and carried his supposed father's dinner to him; and when he came back, Mary no doubt often said, "My dear little Jesus, where hast thou been?"

our bodies, till they rise again in a fair or in an intolerable eternity."

For beside this final death, which swallows us whole, there are partial deaths which devour us piecemeal:—

"Every revolution which the sun makes about the world, divides between life and death; and death possesses both those portions by the next morrow; and we are dead to all those months which we have already lived, and we shall never live them over again: and still God makes little periods of our age. First we change our world, when we come from the womb to feel the warmth of the sun. Then we sleep and enter into the image of death, in which state we are unconcerned in all the changes of the world: and if our mothers or our nurses die, or a wild boar destroy our vineyards, or our king be sick, we regard it not, but during that state are as disinterest as if our eyes were closed with the clay that weeps in the bowels of the earth. At the end of seven years our teeth fall and die before us, representing a formal prologue to the tragedy; and still every seven years it is odds but we shall finish the last scene: and when nature, or chance, or vice, takes our body in pieces, weakening some parts and loosing others, we taste the grave and the solemnities of our own funerals, first in those parts that ministered to vice, and next in them that served for ornament, and in a short time even they that served for necessity become useless, and entangled like the wheels of a broken clock. Baldness is but a dressing to our funerals, the proper ornament of mourning, and of a person entered very far into the regions and possession of death: and we have many more of the same signification: gray hairs, rotten teeth, dim eyes, trembling joints, short breath, stiff limbs, wrinkled skin, short memory, decayed appetite. Every day's necessity calls for a reparation of that portion which death fed on all night, when we lay in his lap and slept in his outer chambers. The very spirits of a man prey upon the daily portion of bread and flesh, and every meal is a rescue from one death, and lays up for another; and while we think a thought, we die; and the clock strikes, and reckons on our portion of eternity: we form our words with the breath of our nostrils, we have the less to live upon for every word we speak."[1]

Beyond all these destructions other destructions are at work; chance mows us down as well as nature, and we are the prey of accident as well as of necessity:—

"Thus nature calls us to meditate of death by those things which are the instruments of acting it: and God by all the variety of His providence makes us see death everywhere, in all variety of circumstances, and dressed up for all the fancies, and the expectation of every single person.[2] . . . And how many teeming mothers have rejoiced over their swelling wombs, and pleased themselves in becoming the channels of blessing to a family, and the midwife hath quickly bound their heads and feet and carried them forth to burial?[3] . . . You can go no whither but you tread upon a dead man's bones."[4]

Thus these powerful words roll on, sublime as an organ motett; this universal crushing out of human vanities has the funeral grandeur of a tragedy; piety in this instance proceeds from eloquence, and genius leads to faith. All the powers and all the tenderness of the soul are moved. It is not a cold rigorist who speaks; it is a man, a moved man, with senses and a heart, who has become a Christian not by mortification, but by the development of his whole being:—

"Reckon but from the sprightfulness of youth, and the fair cheeks and full eyes of childhood, from the vigorousness and strong flexture of the joints of five and twenty, to the hollowness and dead paleness, to the loathsomeness and horror of a three

[1] *Holy Dying*, ed. Eden, ch. i. sec. i. p. 267.
[2] *Ibid* 267.   [3] *Ibid* 268.   [4] *Ibid.* 269.

days' burial, and we shall perceive the distance to be very great and very strange. But so have I seen a rose newly springing from the clefts of its hood, and at first it was fair as the morning, and full with the dew of heaven as a lamb's fleece; but when a ruder breath had forced open its virgin modesty, and dismantled its too youthful and unripe retirements, it began to put on darkness, and to decline to softness and the symptoms of a sickly age; it bowed the head, and broke its stalk, and at night having lost some of its leaves and all its beauty, it fell into the portion of weeds and outworn faces. The same is the portion of every man and every woman, the heritage of worms and serpents, rottenness and cold dishonour, and our beauty so changed, that our acquaintance quickly knew us not; and that change mingled with so much horror, or else meets so with our fears and weak discoursings, that they who six hours ago tended upon us either with charitable or ambitious services, cannot without some regret stay in the room alone where the body lies stripped of its life and honour. I have read of a fair young German gentleman who living often refused to be pictured, but put off the importunity of his friends' desire by giving way that after a few days' burial they might send a painter to his vault, and if they saw cause for it draw the image of his death unto the life: they did so, and found his face half eaten, and his midriff and backbone full of serpents; and so he stands pictured among his armed ancestors. So does the fairest beauty change, and it will be as bad with you as me; and then what servants shall we have to wait upon us in the grave? what friends to visit us? what officious people to cleanse away the moist and unwholesome cloud reflected upon our faces from the sides of the weeping vaults, which are the longest weepers for our funeral?"[1]

Brought hither, like Hamlet to the burying-ground, amid the skulls which he recognises, and under the oppression of the death which he touches, man needs

[1] *Holy Dying*, ch. i. sec. ii. p. 270.

but a slight effort to see a new world arise in his heart. He seeks the remedy of his sadness in the idea of eternal justice, and implores it with a breadth of words which makes the prayer a hymn in prose, as beautiful as a work of art:—

"Eternal God, Almighty Father of men and angels, by whose care and providence I am preserved and blessed, comforted and assisted, I humbly beg of Thee to pardon the sins and follies of this day, the weakness of my services, and the strengths of my passions, the rashness of my words, and the vanity and evil of my actions. O just and dear God, how long shall I confess my sins, and pray against them, and yet fall under them? O let it be so no more; let me never return to the follies of which I am ashamed, which bring sorrow and death, and Thy displeasure, worse than death. Give me a command over my inclinations and a perfect hatred of sin, and a love to Thee above all the desires of this world. Be pleased to bless and preserve me this night from all sin and all violence of chance, and the malice of the spirits of darkness: watch over me in my sleep; and whether I sleep or wake, let me be Thy servant. Be Thou first and last in all my thoughts, and the guide and continual assistance of all my actions. Preserve my body, pardon the sin of my soul, and sanctify my spirit. Let me always live holily and soberly; and when I die receive my soul into Thy hands."[1]

V.

This was, however, but an imperfect Reformation, and the official religion was too closely bound up with the world to undertake to cleanse it thoroughly: if it repressed the excesses of vice, it did not attack its source; and the paganism of the Renaissance, following its bent, already under James I. issued in the corruption,

[1] *The Golden Grove.*

THE CHRISTIAN RENAISSANCE.

orgie, disgusting, and drunken habits, provoking and gross sensuality,[1] which subsequently under the Restoration stank like a sewer in the sun. But underneath the established Protestantism was propagated the forbidden Protestantism: the yeomen were settling their faith like the gentlemen, and already the Puritans made headway under the Anglicans.

No culture here, no philosophy, no sentiment of harmonious and pagan beauty. Conscience alone spoke, and its restlessness had become a terror. The sons of the shopkeeper, of the farmer, who read the Bible in the barn or the counting-house, amid the barrels or the wool-bags, did not take matters as a handsome cavalier bred up in the old mythology, and refined by an elegant Italian education. They took them tragically, sternly examined themselves, pricked their hearts with their scruples, filled their imaginations with the vengeance of God and the terrors of the Bible. A gloomy epic, terrible and grand as the *Edda*, was fermenting in their melancholy imaginations. They steeped themselves in texts of Saint Paul, in the thundering menaces of the prophets; they burdened their minds with the pitiless doctrines of Calvin; they admitted that the majority of men were predestined to eternal damnation:[2] many believed that this multitude were criminal before their birth; that God willed, foresaw, provided for their ruin; that He designed their punishment from all eternity;

---

[1] See in Beaumont and Fletcher's *Thierry and Theodoret* the characters of Bawder, Protalyce, and Brunhalt. In *The Custom of the Country*, by the same authors, several scenes represent the inside of an infamous house,—a frequent thing, by the way, in the dramas of that time; but here the boarders in the house are men. See also their *Rule a Wife and have a Wife*.

[2] Calvin, quoted by Haag, ii. 216, *Histoire des Dogmes Chrétiens*.

that He created them simply to give them up to it.[1] Nothing but grace can save the wretched creature, free grace, God's sheer favour, which He only grants to a few, and which He distributes not according to the struggles and works of men, but according to the arbitrary choice of His single and absolute will. We are "children of wrath," plague-stricken, and condemned from our birth; and wherever we look in all the expanse of heaven, we find but thunderbolts flashing to destroy us. Fancy, if you can, the effects of such an idea on solitary and morose minds, such as this race and climate generates. Several persons thought themselves damned, and went groaning about the streets; others hardly ever slept. They were beside themselves, always imagining that they felt the hand of God or the claw of the devil upon them. An extraordinary power, immense means of action, were suddenly opened up in the soul, and there was no barrier in the moral life, and no establishment in civil society which their efforts could not upset.

Forthwith private life was transformed. How could ordinary sentiments, natural and every-day notions of happiness and pleasure, subsist before such a conception? Suppose men condemned to death, not ordinary death, but the rack, torture, an infinitely horrible and infinitely extended torment, waiting for their sentence, and yet knowing that they had one chance in a thousand, in a hundred thousand, of pardon; could they still go on amusing themselves, taking an interest in the business or pleasure of the time? The azure heaven shines not for them, the sun warms them not, the beauty and sweetness of things have no attraction for them; they

[1] These were the Supralapsarians.

have lost the wont of laughter; they fasten inwardly, pale and silent, on their anguish and their expectation; they have but one thought: "Will the judge pardon me?" They anxiously probe the involuntary motions of their heart, which alone can reply, and the inner revelation, which alone can render them certain of pardon or ruin. They think that any other condition of mind is unholy, that recklessness and joy are monstrous, that every worldly recreation or preoccupation is an act of paganism, and that the true mark of a Christian is trepidation at the very idea of salvation. Thenceforth rigour and rigidity mark their manners. The Puritan condemns the stage, the assemblies, the world's pomps and gatherings, the court's gallantry and elegance, the poetical and symbolical festivals of the country, the May-poles days, the merry feasts, bell-ringings, all the outlets by which sensuous or instinctive nature endeavoured to relieve itself. He gives them up, abandons recreations and ornaments, crops his hair closely, wears a simple sombre-hued coat, speaks through his nose, walks stiffly, with his eyes turned upwards, absorbed, indifferent to visible things. The external and natural man is abolished; only the inner and spiritual man survives; there remains of the soul only the ideas of God and conscience,—a conscience alarmed and diseased, but strict in every duty, attentive to the least requirements, disdaining the caution of worldly morality, inexhaustible in patience, courage, sacrifice, enthroning chastity on the domestic hearth, truth before the tribunals, honesty in the counting-house, labour in the workshop, everywhere a fixed determination to bear all and do all rather than fail in the least injunction of moral justice and Bible-law. The stoical energy, the fundamental honesty of the race, were aroused at the appeal of an enthusiastic imagination; and these unbending characteristics were displayed in their entirety in conjunction with abnegation and virtue.

Another step, and this great movement passed from within to without, from individual manners to public institutions. Observe these people in their reading of the Bible, they apply to themselves the commands imposed on the Jews, and the prologues urge them to it. At the beginning of their Bibles the translator [1] places a table of the principal words in the Scripture, each with its definition and texts to support it. They read and weigh these words: "*Abomination* before God are Idoles, Images. Before whom the people do bow them selfes." Is this precept observed? No doubt the images are taken away, but the queen has still a crucifix in her chapel, and is it not a remnant of idolatry to kneel down when taking the sacrament? "*Abrogacion*, that is to abolyshe, or to make of none effecte: And so the lawe of the commandementes whiche was in the decrees and ceremonies, is abolished. The sacrifices, festes, meates, and al outwarde ceremonies are abrogated, and all the order of priesthode is abrogated." Is this so, and how does it happen that the bishops still take upon themselves the right of prescribing faith, worship, and of tyrannising over Christian consciences? And have they not preserved in the organ-music, in the surplice of the priests, in the sign of the cross, in a hundred other practices, all these visible rites which God has declared profane? "*Abuses*. The abuses that

---

[1] *The Byble, nowe lately with greate industry and Diligēce recognised* (by Edm. Becke), Lond., by John Daye and William Seres, 1549, with Tyndale's *Prologues*.

be in the church ought to be corrected by the pryuces. The ministers ought to preache against abuses. Any maner of mere tradicions of man are abuses." What, meanwhile, is their prince doing, and why does he leave abuses in the church? The Christian must rise and protest; we must purge the church from the pagan crust with which tradition has covered it.[1]

Such are the ideas conceived by these uncultivated minds. Fancy the simple folk, more capable by their simplicity of a sturdy faith, these freeholders, these big traders, who have sat on juries, voted at elections, deliberated, discussed in common private and public business, used to examine the law, the comparing of precedents, all the detail of juridical and legal procedure; bringing their lawyer's and pleader's training to bear upon the interpretation of Scripture, who, having once formed a conviction, employ for it the cold passion, the intractable obstinacy, the heroic sternness of the English character. Their precise and combative minds take the business in hand. Every one holds himself bound to be ready, strong, and well prepared to answer all such as shall demand a reason of his faith. Each one has his difficulty and conscientious scruple[2] about some portion of the liturgy or the official hierarchy; about

[1] Examination of Mr. Axton: "I can t consent to wear the surplice, it is against my conscience; I trust, by the help of God, I shall never put on that sleeve, which is a mark of the beast."—Examination of Mr. White, "a substantial citizen of London" (1572), accused of not going to the parish church: "The whole Scriptures are for destroying idolatry, and everything that belongs to it."—"Where is the place where these are forbidden?"—"In Deuteronomy and other places; . . . and God by Isaiah commandeth not to pollute ourselves with the garments of the image."

[2] One expression continually occurs: "Tenderness of conscience" —"a squeamish stomach"—"our weaker brethren."

the dignities of canons and archdeacons, or certain passages of the funeral service; about the sacramental bread or the reading of the apocryphal books in church; about plurality of benefices or the ecclesiastical square cap. They each oppose some point, all together the episcopacy and the retention of Romish ceremonies.[1] Then they are imprisoned, fined, put in the pillory; they have their ears cut off; their ministers are dismissed, hunted out, prosecuted.[2] The law declares that any one above the age of sixteen who for the space of a month shall refuse to attend the established worship, shall be imprisoned until such time as he shall submit; and if he does not submit at the end of three months, he shall be banished the kingdom; and if he returns, put to death. They allow this to go on, and show as much firmness in suffering as scruple in belief; for a tittle about receiving of the communion, sitting rather than kneeling, or standing rather than sitting, they give up their livings, their property, their liberty, their country. One Dr. Leighton was imprisoned fifteen weeks in a dog's kennel, without fire, roof, bed, and in irons: his hair and skin fell off; he was set in the pillory during the November frosts, then whipt, and branded on the forehead; his ears were cut off, his nose slit; he was shut up eight years in the Fleet, and thence cast into the common prison. Many went cheerfully to the stake. Religion with them was a covenant, that is, a treaty made with God, which must be kept in spite of everything, as a written engagement, to the letter, to the last syllable. An admirable and deplorable stiffness of an over-scrupulous conscience,

---

[1] The separation of the Anglicans and dissenters may be dated from 1564.   [2] 1592.

which made cavillers at the same time with believers, which was to make tyrants after it had made martyrs.

Between the two, it made fighting men. These men had become wonderfully wealthy and had increased in numbers in the course of eighty years, as is always the case with men who labour, live honestly, and pass their lives uprightly, sustained by a powerful source of action from within. Thenceforth they are able to resist, and they do resist when driven to extremities; they choose to have recourse to arms rather than be driven back to idolatry and sin. The Long Parliament assembles, defeats the king, purges religion; the dam is broken, the Independents are hurled above the Presbyterians, the fanatics above the mere zealots; irresistible and overwhelming faith, enthusiasm, grow into a torrent, swallow up, or at least disturb the strongest minds, politicians, lawyers, captains. The Commons occupy a day in every week in deliberating on the progress of religion. As soon as they touch upon doctrines they become furious. A poor man, Paul Best, being accused of denying the Trinity, they demand the passing of a decree to punish him with death; James Nayler having imagined that he was God, the Commons devote themselves to a trial of eleven days, with a Hebraic animosity and ferocity: "I think him worse than possessed with the devil. Our God is here supplanted. My ears trembled, my heart shuddered, on hearing this report. I will speak no more. Let us all stop our ears and stone him."[1] Before the House of Commons, publicly, the men in authority had ecstasies. After the expulsion of the Presbyterians, the preacher Hugh Peters started up in the middle of a sermon, and cried out: "Now I have

[1] Burton's *Parliamentary Diary*, ed. by Rutt, 1828, 4 vols. i. 54.

it by Revelation, now I shall tell you. This army must root up Monarchy, not only here, but in France and other kingdoms round about; this is to bring you out of Egypt: this Army is that corner-stone cut out of the Mountaine, which must dash the powers of the earth to pieces. But it is objected, the way we walk in is without president (*sic*); what think you of the Virgin Mary? was there ever any president before, that a Woman should conceive a Child without the company of a Man? This is an Age to make examples and presidents in." [1] Cromwell found prophecies, counsels in the Bible for the present time, positive justifications of his policy. " He looked upon the Design of the Lord in this day to be the freeing of His People from every Burden, and that was now accomplishing what was prophesied in the 110th Psalm; from the Consideration of which he was often encouraged to attend the effecting those Ends, spending at least an hour in the Exposition of that Psalm." [2] Granted that he was a schemer,

[1] Walker's *History of Independency*, 1648, part ii. p. 49.

[2] This passage may serve as an example of the difficulties and perplexities to which a translator of a History of Literature must always be exposed, and this without any fault of the original author. *Ab uno disce omnes.* M. Taine says that Cromwell found justification for his policy in Psalm cxiii., which, on looking out, I found to be "an exhortation to praise God for His excellency and for His mercy,"—a psalm by which Cromwell's conduct could nowise be justified. I opened then Carlyle's *Cromwell's Letters*, etc., and saw, in vol. ii. part vi. p. 157, the same fact stated, but Psalm cx. mentioned and given,— a far more likely psalm to have influenced Cromwell. Carlyle refers to *Ludlow*, i. 319, Taine to Guizot, *Portraits Politiques*, p. 63, and to Carlyle. In looking in Guizot's volume, 5th ed., 1862, I find that this writer also mentions Psalm cxiii.; but on referring finally to the *Memoirs of Edmund Ludlow*, printed at Vivay (*sic*) in the Canton of Bern, 1698, I read, in vol. i. p. 319, the sentence, as given above; therefore Carlyle was right.—Tr.

above all ambitious, yet he was truly fanatical and sincere. His doctor related that he had been very melancholy for years at a time, with strange hallucinations, and the frequent fancy that he was at death's door. Two years before the Revolution he wrote to his cousin : " Truly no poor creature hath more cause to put himself forth in the cause of his God than I. . . . The Lord accept me in His Son, and give me to walk in the light —and give us to walk in the light, as He is the light ! . . . blessed be His Name for shining upon so dark a heart as mine ! " [1] Certainly he must have dreamed of becoming a saint as well as a king, and aspired to salvation as well as to a throne. At the moment when he was proceeding to Ireland, and was about to massacre the Catholics there, he wrote to his daughter-in-law a letter of advice which Baxter or Taylor might willingly have subscribed. In the midst of pressing affairs, in 1651, he thus exhorted his wife : " My dearest, I could not satisfy myself to omit this post, although I have not much to write. . . . It joys me to hear thy soul prospereth : the Lord increase His favours to thee more and more. The great good thy soul can wish is, That the Lord lift upon thee the light of His countenance, which is better than life. The Lord bless all thy good counsel and example to all those about thee, and hear all thy prayers, and accept thee always." [2] Dying, he asked whether grace once received could be lost, and was reassured to learn that it could not, being, as he said, certain that he had once been in a state of grace. He died with this prayer : " Lord, though I am a miserable and wretched creature, I am

---

[1] *Cromwell's Letters and Speeches*, ed. Carlyle, 1866, 3 vols. i. 79.
[2] *Idem*, ii. 273.

in Covenant with Thee through grace. And I may, I will, come to Thee, for Thy People. Thou hast made me, though very unworthy, a mean instrument to do them some good, and Thee service. . . . Lord, however Thou do dispose of me, continue and go on to do good for them . . . and go on . . . with the work of reformation; and make the Name of Christ glorious in the world."[1] Underneath this practical, prudent, worldly spirit, there was an English element of anxious and powerful imagination, capable of engendering an impassioned Calvinism and mystic fears.[2] The same contrasts were jumbled together and reconciled in the other Independents. In 1648, after unsuccessful tactics, they were in danger between the king and the Parliament; then they assembled for several days together at Windsor to confess themselves to God, and seek His assistance; and they discovered that all their evils came from the conferences they had had the weakness to propose to the king. "And in this path the Lord led us," said Adjutant Allen, "not only to see our sin, but also our duty; and this so unanimously set with weight upon each heart that none was able hardly to speak a word to each other for bitter weeping, partly in the sense and shame of our iniquities; of our unbelief, base fear of men, and carnal consultations (as the fruit thereof) with our own wisdoms, and not with the Word of the Lord."[3] Thereupon they resolved to bring the king to judgment and death, and did as they had resolved.

Around them, fanaticism and folly gained ground.

[1] *Cromwell's Letters*, ed. Carlyle, iii. 373.

[2] See his speeches. The style is disjointed, obscure, impassioned, out of the common, like that of a man who is not master of his wits, and who yet sees straight by a sort of intuition.

[3] *Cromwell's Letters*, i. 265.

CHAP. V.   THE CHRISTIAN RENAISSANCE.   213

Independents, Millenarians, Antinomians, Anabaptists, Libertines, Familists, Quakers, Enthusiasts, Seekers, Perfectionists, Socinians, Arians, anti-Trinitarians, anti-Scripturalists, Sceptics ; the list of sects is interminable. Women, soldiers, suddenly got up into the pulpit and preached. The strangest ceremonies took place in public. In 1644, says Dr. Featly, the Anabaptists rebaptised a hundred men and women together at twilight, in streams, in branches of the Thames, and elsewhere, plunging them in the water over head and ears. One Oates, in the county of Essex, was brought before a jury for the murder of Anne Martin, who died a few days after her baptism of a cold which had seized her. George Fox the Quaker spoke with God, and witnessed with a loud voice, in the streets and market-places, against the sins of the age. William Simpson, one of his disciples, "was moved of the Lord to go, at several times, for three years, naked and barefoot before them, as a sign unto them, in the markets, courts, towns, cities, to priests' houses, and to great men's houses, telling them, so shall they all be stripped naked, as he was stripped naked. And sometime he was moved to put on hair sackcloth, and to besmear his face, and to tell them, so would the Lord besmear all their religion as he was besmeared.[1]

" A female came into Whitehall Chapel stark naked, in the midst of public worship, the Lord Protector himself being present. A Quaker came to the door of the Parliament House with a drawn sword, and wounded several who were present, saying that he was inspired by the Holy Spirit to kill every man that sat in the house." The Fifth Monarchy men believed that Christ

---

[1] *A Journal of the Life, etc., of that Ancient, Eminent, and Faithful Servant of Jesus Christ, George Fox*, 6th edit., 1836.

was about to descend to reign in person upon earth for a thousand years, with the saints for His ministers. The Ranters looked upon furious vociferations and contortions as the principal signs of faith. The Seekers thought that religious truth could only be seized in a sort of mystical fog, with doubt and fear. The Muggletonians decided that "John Reeve and Ludovick Muggleton were the two last prophets and messengers of God;" they declared the Quakers possessed of the devil, exorcised him, and prophesied that William Penn would be damned. I have before mentioned James Nayler, an old quartermaster of General Lambert, adored as a god by his followers. Several women led his horse, others cast before him their kerchiefs and scarves, singing, Holy, holy, Lord God. They called him "lovely among ten thousand, the only Son of God, the prophet of the Most High, King of Israel, the eternal Son of Justice, the Prince of Peace, Jesus, him in whom the hope of Israel rests." One of them, Dorcas Erbury, declared that she had lain dead for two whole days in her prison in Exeter Gaol, and that Nayler had restored her to life by laying his hands upon her. Sarah Blackbury finding him a prisoner, took him by the hand and said, "Rise up my love, my dove, my fairest one: why stayest thou among the pots?" Then she kissed his hand and fell down before him. When he was put in the pillory, some of his disciples began to sing, weep, smite their breasts; others kissed his hands, rested on his bosom, and kissed his wounds.[1] Bedlam broken loose could not have surpassed them.

Underneath the surface and these disorderly bubbles

---

[1] Burton's *Parliamentary Diary*, i. 46–173. Neal, *History of the Puritans*, iii., Supplt.

THE CHRISTIAN RENAISSANCE.

the wise and deep strata of the nation had settled, and the new faith was doing its work with them,—a practical and positive, a political and moral work. Whilst the German Reformation, after the German wont, resulted in great volumes and a scholastic system, the English Reformation, after the English wont, resulted in action and establishment. "How the Church of Christ shall be governed;" that was the great question which was discussed among the sects. The House of Commons asked the Assembly of Divines: If the classical, provincial, and local assemblies were *jure divino*, and instituted by the will and appointment of Jesus Christ? If they were all so? If only some were so, and which? If appeals carried by the elders of a congregation to provincial, departmental, and national assemblies were *jure divino*, and according to the will and appointment of Jesus Christ? If some only were *jure divino*? And which? If the power of the assemblies in such appeals was *jure divino*, and by the will and appointment of Jesus Christ? and a hundred other questions of the same kind. Parliament declared that, according to Scripture, the dignities of priest and bishop were equal; it regulated ordinations, convocations, excommunications, jurisdictions, elections; spent half its time and exerted all its power in establishing the Presbyterian Church.[1] So, with the Independents, fervour engendered courage and discipline. "Cromwell's regiment of horse were most of them freeholders' sons, who engaged in the war upon principles of conscience; and that being well armed within, by the satisfaction of their consciences, and without with good iron arms, they would as one man stand firmly and charge desper-

[1] See Neal, *Hist. of the Puritans*, ii. 418-450.

ately."[1] This army, in which inspired corporals preached to lukewarm colonels, acted with the solidity and precision of a Russian regiment: it was a duty, a duty towards God, to fire straight and march in good order; and a perfect Christian made a perfect soldier. There was no separation here between theory and practice, between private and public life, between the spiritual and the temporal. They wished to apply Scripture to "establish the kingdom of heaven upon earth," to institute not only a Christian Church, but a Christian Society, to change the law into a guardian of morals, to compel men to piety and virtue; and for a while they succeeded in it. "Though the discipline of the church was at an end, there was nevertheless an uncommon spirit of devotion among people in the parliament quarters; the Lord's day was observed with remarkable strictness, the churches being crowded with numerous and attentive hearers three or four times in the day; the officers of the peace patrolled the streets, and shut up all publick houses; there was no travelling on the road, or walking in the fields, except in cases of absolute necessity. Religious exercises were set up in private families, as reading the Scriptures, family prayer, repeating sermons, and singing of psalms, which was so universal, that you might walk through the city of London on the evening of the Lord's day, without seeing an idle person, or hearing anything but the voice of prayer or praise from churches and private houses."[2] People would rise before daybreak, and walk a great dis-

[1] Whitelocke's *Memorials*, i. 68.
[2] Neal, ii. 553. Compare with the French Revolution. When the Bastille was demolished, they wrote on the ruins these words: "Ici l'on danse." From this contrast we see the difference between the two systems and the two nations.

tance to be able to hear the word of God. "There were no gaming-houses, or houses of pleasure; no profane swearing, drunkenness, or any kind of debauchery."[1] The Parliamentary soldiers came in great numbers to listen to sermons, spoke of religion, prayed and sang psalms together, when on duty. In 1644 Parliament forbade the sale of commodities on Sunday, and ordained "that no person shall travel, or carry a burden, or do any worldly labour, upon penalty of 10s. for the traveller, and 5s. for every burden. That no person shall on the Lord's day use, or be present at, any wrestling, shooting, fowling, ringing of bells for pleasure, markets, wakes, church-ales, dancing, games or sports whatsoever, upon penalty of 5s. to every one above fourteen years of age. And if children are found offending in the premises, their parents or guardians to forfeit 12d. for every offence. If the several fines above mentioned cannot be levied, the offending party shall be set in the stocks for the space of three hours." When the Independents were in power, severity became still greater. The officers in the army, having convicted one of their quartermasters of blasphemy, condemned him to have his tongue bored with a red-hot iron, his sword broken over his head, and himself to be dismissed from the army. During Cromwell's expedition in Ireland, we read that no blasphemy was heard in the camp; the soldiers spent their leisure hours in reading the Bible, singing psalms, and holding religious controversies. In 1650 the punishments inflicted on Sabbath-breakers were doubled. Stern laws were passed against betting, gallantry was reckoned a crime; the theatres were destroyed, the spectators fined, the actors

[1] Neal, *Hist. of the Puritans*, ii. 555.

whipt at the cart's tail; adultery punished with death: in order to reach crime more surely, they persecuted pleasure. But if they were austere against others, they were so against themselves, and practised the virtues they exacted. After the Restoration, two thousand ministers, rather than conform to the new liturgy, resigned their cures, though they and their families had to die of hunger. Many of them, says Baxter, thinking that they were not justified in quitting their ministry after being set apart for it by ordination, preached to such as would hear them in the fields and in certain houses, until they were seized and thrown into prisons, where a great number of them perished. Cromwell's fifty thousand veterans, suddenly disbanded and without resources, did not bring a single recruit to the vagabonds and bandits. "The Royalists themselves confessed that, in every department of honest industry, the discarded warriors prospered beyond other men, that none was charged with any theft or robbery, that none was heard to ask an alms, and that, if a baker, a mason, or a waggoner, attracted notice by his diligence and sobriety, he was in all probability one of Oliver's old soldiers."[1] Purified by persecution and ennobled by patience, they ended by winning the tolerance of the law and the respect of the public, and raised national morality, as they had saved national liberty. But others, exiles in America, pushed to the extreme this great religious and stoical spirit, with its weaknesses and its power, with its vices and its virtues. Their determination, intensified by a fervent faith, employed in political and practical pursuits, invented the science of emigration, made exile tolerable, drove back the Indians,

[1] Macaulay, *Hist. of England*, ed. Lady Trevelyan, i. 121.

CHAP. V. THE CHRISTIAN RENAISSANCE. 219

fertilised the desert, raised a rigid morality into a civil law, founded and armed a church, and on the Bible as a basis built up a new state.[1]

That was not a conception of life from which a genuine literature might be expected to issue. The idea of the beautiful is wanting, and what is a literature without that? The natural expression of the heart's emotions is proscribed, and what is a literature without that? They abolished as impious the free stage and the rich poesy which the Renaissance had brought them. They rejected as profane the ornate style and copious eloquence which had been established around them by the imitation of antiquity and of Italy. They mistrusted reason, and were incapable of philosophy. They ignored the divine languor of the *Imitatio Christi* and the touching tenderness of the Gospel. Their character exhibits only manliness, their conduct austerity, their mind preciseness. We find amongst them only excited theologians, minute controversialists, energetic men of action, narrow and patient minds, engrossed in positive proofs and practical labours, void of general ideas and refined tastes, dulled by texts, dry and obstinate reasoners, who twisted the Scripture in order to extract from it a form of government or a table of dogma. What could be narrower or more repulsive than these pursuits and wrangles? A pamphlet of the time petitions for liberty of conscience, and draws its arguments (1) from the parable of the wheat and the tares

[1] A certain John Denis was publicly whipt for having sung a profane song. Mathias, a little girl, having given some roasted chestnuts to Jeremiah Boosy, and told him ironically that he might give them back to her in Paradise, was ordered to ask pardon three times in church, and to be three days on bread and water in prison. 1660-1670 ; records of Massachusetts.

which grow together till the harvest; (2) from this maxim of the Apostles, Let every man be thoroughly persuaded in his own mind; (3) from this text, Whatsoever is not of faith is sin; (4) from this divine rule of our Saviour, Do to others what you would they should do unto you. Later, when the angry Commons desired to pass judgment on James Nayler, the trial became entangled in an endless juridical and theological discussion, some declaring that the crime committed was idolatry, others seduction, all emptying out before the House their armoury of commentaries and texts.[1] Seldom has a generation been found more mutilated in all the faculties which produce contemplation and ornament, more reduced to the faculties which nourish discussion and morality. Like a beautiful insect which has become transformed and has lost its wings, so we see the poetic generation of Elizabeth disappear, leaving in its place but a sluggish caterpillar, a stubborn and useful spinner, armed with industrious feet and formidable jaws, spending its existence in eating into old leaves and devouring its enemies. They are without style; they speak like business men; at most, here and there, a pamphlet of Prynne possesses a little vigour. Their histories, like May's for instance, are flat and heavy. Their memoirs, even those of Ludlow and Mrs. Hutchinson, are long, wearisome, mere statements, destitute of personal feelings, void of enthusiasm or entertaining matter; "they seem to ignore themselves, and are engrossed by the general prospects of their

[1] "Upon the common sense of Scripture," said Major-general Disbrowe, "there are few but do commit blasphemy, as our Saviour puts it in Mark: 'sins, blasphemies; if so, then none without blasphemy.' It was charged upon David, and Eli's son, 'thou hast blasphemed, or caused others to blaspheme.' "—Burton's *Diary*, i. 54.

cause."[1] Good works of piety, solid and convincing sermons; sincere, edifying, exact, methodical books, like those of Baxter, Barclay, Calamy, John Owen; personal narratives, like that of Baxter, like Fox's journal, Bunyan's life, a large collection of documents and arguments, conscientiously arranged,—this is all they offer; the Puritan destroys the artist, stiffens the man, fetters the writer; and leaves of artist, man, writer, only a sort of abstract being, the slave of a watchword. If a Milton springs up amongst them, it is because by his great curiosity, his travels, his comprehensive education, above all by his youth saturated in the grand poetry of the preceding age, and by his independence of spirit, haughtily defended even against the sectarians, Milton passes beyond sectarianism. Strictly speaking, the Puritans could but have one poet, an involuntary poet, a madman, a martyr, a hero, and a victim of grace; a genuine preacher, who attains the beautiful by chance, whilst pursuing the useful on principle; a poor tinker, who, employing images so as to be understood by mechanics, sailors, servant-girls, attained, without pretending to it, eloquence and high art.

VI.

Next to the Bible, the book most widely read in England is the *Pilgrim's Progress*, by John Bunyan. The reason is, that the basis of Protestantism is the doctrine of salvation by grace, and that no writer has equalled Bunyan in making this doctrine understood.

To treat well of supernatural impressions, a man must have been subject to them. Bunyan had that kind of

[1] Guizot, *Portraits Politiques*, 5th ed., 1862.

imagination which produces them. Powerful as that of an artist, but more vehement, this imagination worked in the man without his co-operation, and besieged him with visions which he had neither willed nor foreseen. From that moment there was in him as it were a second self, ruling the first, grand and terrible, whose apparitions were sudden, its motions unknown, which redoubled or crushed his faculties, prostrated or transported him, bathed him in the sweat of agony, ravished him with trances of joy, and which by its force, strangeness, independence, impressed upon him the presence and the action of a foreign and superior master. Bunyan, like Saint Theresa, was from infancy "greatly troubled with the thoughts of the fearful torments of hell-fire," sad in the midst of pleasures, believing himself damned, and so despairing, that he wished he was a devil, " supposing they were only tormentors; that if it must needs be that I went thither, I might be rather a tormentor, than be tormented myself."[1] There already was the assault of exact and bodily images. Under their influence reflection ceased, and the man was suddenly spurred into action. The first movement carried him with closed eyes, as down a steep slope, into mad resolutions. One day, " being in the field, with my companions, it chanced that an adder passed over the highway; so I, having a stick, struck her over the back; and having stunned her, I forced open her mouth with my stick, and plucked her sting out with my fingers, by which act, had not God been merciful to me, I might, by my desperateness, have brought myself to my end." [2] In his first approaches to conversion he was extreme in his emotions, and

[1] *Grace Abounding to the Chief of Sinners*, § 7.   [2] *Ibid.* § 12.

penetrated to the heart by the sight of physical objects, "adoring" priest, service, altar, vestment. "This conceit grew so strong upon my spirit, that had I but seen a priest (though never so sordid and debauched in his life), I should find my spirit fall under him, reverence him, and knit unto him; yea, I thought, for the love I did bear unto them (supposing they were the ministers of God), I could have laid down at their feet, and have been trampled upon by them; their name, their garb, and work did so intoxicate and bewitch me."[1] Already his ideas clung to him with that irresistible hold which constitutes monomania; no matter how absurd they were, they ruled him, not by their truth, but by their presence. The thought of an impossible danger terrified him just as much as the sight of an imminent peril. As a man hung over an abyss by a sound rope, he forgot that the rope was sound, and he became giddy. After the fashion of English villagers, he loved bell-ringing; when he became a Puritan, he considered the amusement profane, and gave it up; yet, impelled by his desire, he would go into the belfry and watch the ringers. "But quickly after, I began to think, 'How if one of the bells should fall?' Then I chose to stand under a main beam, that lay overthwart the steeple, from side to side, thinking here I might stand sure; but then I thought again, should the bell fall with a swing, it might first hit the wall, and then rebounding upon me, might kill me for all this beam. This made me stand in the steeple-door; and now, thought I, I am safe enough, for if a bell should then fall, I can slip out behind these thick walls, and so be preserved notwithstanding. So after this I would yet

[1] *Grace Abounding*, § 17.

go to see them ring, but would not go any farther than the steeple-door; but then it came into my head, 'How if the steeple itself should fall?' And this thought (it may, for aught I know, when I stood and looked on) did continually so shake my mind, that I durst not stand at the steeple-door any longer, but was forced to flee, for fear the steeple should fall upon my head."[1] Frequently the mere conception of a sin became for him a temptation so involuntary and so strong, that he felt upon him the sharp claw of the devil. The fixed idea swelled in his head like a painful abscess, full of all sensitiveness and of all his life's blood. "Now no sin would serve but that; if it were to be committed by speaking of such a word, then I have been as if my mouth would have spoken that word whether I would or no; and in so strong a measure was the temptation upon me, that often I have been ready to clap my hands under my chin, to hold my mouth from opening; at other times, to leap with my head downward into some muckhill hole, to keep my mouth from speaking."[2] Later, in the middle of a sermon which he was preaching, he was assailed by blasphemous thoughts; the word came to his lips, and all his power of resistance was barely able to restrain the muscle excited by the tyrannous brain.

Once the minister of the parish was preaching against the sin of dancing, oaths, and games, when he was struck with the idea that the sermon was for him, and returned home full of trouble. But he ate; his stomach being charged, discharged his brain, and his remorse was dispersed. Like a true child, entirely absorbed by the emotion of the moment, he was transported, jumped out,

[1] *Grace Abounding*, §§ 33, 34.   [2] *Ibid.* § 103.

and ran to the sports. He had thrown his ball, and was about to begin again, when a voice from heaven suddenly pierced his soul. "'Wilt thou leave thy sins and go to heaven, or have thy sins and go to hell?' At this I was put to an exceeding maze; wherefore, leaving my cat upon the ground, I looked up to heaven, and was as if I had with the eyes of my understanding, seen the Lord Jesus look down upon me, as being very hotly displeased with me, and as if He did severely threaten me with some grievous punishment for these and other ungodly practices."[1] Suddenly reflecting that his sins were very great, and that he would certainly be damned whatever he did, he resolved to enjoy himself in the meantime, and to sin as much as he could in this life. He took up his ball again, recommenced the game with ardour, and swore louder and oftener than ever. A month afterwards, being reproved by a woman, "I was silenced, and put to secret shame, and that too, as I thought, before the God of heaven: wherefore, while I stood there, hanging down my head, I wished that I might be a little child again, and that my father might learn me to speak without this wicked way of swearing; for, thought I, I am so accustomed to it, that it is in vain to think of a reformation, for that could never be. But how it came to pass I know not, I did from this time forward so leave my swearing, that it was a great wonder to myself to observe it; and whereas before I knew not how to speak unless I put an oath before, and another behind, to make my words have authority, now I could without it speak better, and with more pleasantness, than ever I could before."[2] These sudden alternations, these vehement resolutions,

[1] *Grace Abounding*, § 22.   [2] *Ibid.* §§ 27 and 28.

this unlooked-for renewal of heart, are the products of an involuntary and impassioned imagination, which by its hallucinations, its mastery, its fixed ideas, its mad ideas, prepares the way for a poet, and announces an inspired man.

In him circumstances develop character; his kind of life develops his kind of mind. He was born in the lowest and most despised rank, a tinker's son, himself a wandering tinker, with a wife as poor as himself, so that they had not a spoon or a dish between them. He had been taught in childhood to read and write, but he had since " almost wholly lost what he had learned." Education diverts and disciplines a man; fills him with varied and rational ideas; prevents him from sinking into monomania or being excited by transport; gives him determinate thoughts instead of eccentric fancies, pliable opinions for fixed convictions; replaces impetuous images by calm reasonings, sudden resolves by carefully weighed decisions; furnishes us with the wisdom and ideas of others; gives us conscience and self-command. Suppress this reason and this discipline, and consider the poor ignorant working man at his toil; his head works while his hands work, not ably, with methods acquired from any logic he might have mustered, but with dark emotions, beneath a disorderly flow of confused images. Morning and evening, the hammer which he uses in his trade, drives in with its deafening sounds the same thought perpetually returning and self-communing. A troubled, obstinate vision floats before him in the brightness of the hammered and quivering metal. In the red furnace where the iron is glowing, in the clang of the hammered brass, in the black corners where the damp shadow creeps, he sees the flame and darkness of hell, and the rattling of eternal chains. Next day he sees the same image, the day after, the whole week, month, year. His brow wrinkles, his eyes grow sad, and his wife hears him groan in the night-time. She remembers that she has two volumes in an old bag, *The Plain Man's Pathway to Heaven* and *The Practice of Piety*; he spells them out to console himself; and the printed thoughts, already sublime in themselves, made more so by the slowness with which they are read, sink like an oracle into his subdued faith. The braziers of the devils—the golden harps of heaven—the bleeding Christ on the cross,—each of these deep-rooted ideas sprouts poisonously or wholesomely in his diseased brain, spreads, pushes out and springs higher with a ramification of fresh visions, so crowded, that in his encumbered mind he has no further place nor air for more conceptions. Will he rest when he sets forth in the winter on his tramp? During his long solitary wanderings, over wild heaths, in cursed and haunted bogs, always abandoned to his own thoughts, the inevitable idea pursues him. These neglected roads where he sticks in the mud, these sluggish dirty rivers which he crosses on the cranky ferry-boat, these threatening whispers of the woods at night, when in perilous places the livid moon shadows out ambushed forms,—all that he sees and hears falls into an involuntary poem around the one absorbing idea; thus it changes into a vast body of visible legends, and multiplies its power as it multiplies its details. Having become a dissenter, Bunyan is shut up for twelve years, having no other amusement but the *Book of Martyrs* and the Bible, in one of those pestiferous prisons where the Puritans rotted under the Restoration. There he is, still alone, thrown back upon himself by the monotony of his dungeon, besieged by the terrors of the old Testament, by the vengeful outpourings of the prophets, by the thunder-striking words of Paul, by the spectacle of trances and of martyrs, face to face with God, now in despair, now consoled, troubled with involuntary images and unlooked-for emotions, seeing alternately devil and angels, the actor and the witness of an internal drama whose vicissitudes he is able to relate. He writes them: it is his book. You see now the condition of this inflamed brain. Poor in ideas, full of images, given up to a fixed and single thought, plunged into this thought by his mechanical pursuit, by his prison and his readings, by his knowledge and his ignorance, circumstances, like nature, make him a visionary and an artist, furnish him with supernatural impressions and visible images, teaching him the history of grace and the means of expressing it.

The *Pilgrim's Progress* is a manual of devotion for the use of simple folk, whilst it is an allegorical poem of grace. In it we hear a man of the people speaking to the people, who would render intelligible to all the terrible doctrine of damnation and salvation.[1] According to

---

[1] This is an abstract of the events:—From highest heaven a voice has proclaimed vengeance against the City of Destruction, where lives a sinner of the name of *Christian*. Terrified, he rises up amid the jeers of his neighbours, and departs, for fear of being devoured by the fire which is to consume the criminals. A helpful man, *Evangelist*, shows him the right road. A treacherous man, *Worldlywise*, tries to turn him aside. His companion, *Pliable*, who had followed him at first, gets stuck in the Slough of Despond, and leaves him. He advances bravely across the dirty water and the slippery mud, and reaches the *Strait Gate*, where a wise *Interpreter* instructs him by visible shows, and points out the way to the Heavenly City. He passes before a cross, and the heavy burden of sins, which he carried on his back, is

Bunyan, we are "children of wrath," condemned from our birth, guilty by nature, justly predestined to destruction. Beneath this formidable thought the heart gives way. The unhappy man relates how he trembled in all his limbs, and in his fits it seemed to him as though the bones of his chest would break. "One day," he tells us, "I walked to a neighbouring town, and sat down upon a settle in the street, and fell into a very deep pause about the most fearful state my sin had brought me to ; and after long musing, I lifted up my head, but methought I saw, as if the sun that shineth in the heavens did grudge to give light; and as if the very stones in the street, and tiles upon the houses, did band themselves against me. O how happy now was every creature over I was! For they stood fast, and kept their station, but I was gone and lost."[1] The devils gathered together against the repentant sinner; they

loosened and falls off. He painfully climbs the steep hill of *Difficulty*, and reaches a great castle, where *Watchful*, the guardian, gives him in charge to his good daughters *Piety* and *Prudence*, who warn him and arm him against the monsters of hell. He finds his road barred by one of these demons, *Apollyon*, who bids him abjure obedience to the heavenly King. After a long fight he conquers him. Yet the way grows narrow, the shades fall thicker, sulphurous flames rise along the road : it is the valley of the *Shadow of Death*. He passes it, and arrives at the town of Vanity, a vast fair of business, deceits, and shows, which he walks by with lowered eyes, not wishing to take part in its festivities or falsehoods. The people of the place beat him, throw him into prison, condemn him as a traitor and rebel, burn his companion *Faithful*. Escaped from their hands, he falls into those of *Giant Despair*, who beats him, leaves him in a poisonous dungeon without food, and giving him daggers and cords, advises him to rid himself from so many misfortunes. At last he reaches the *Delectable Mountains*, whence he sees the holy city. To enter it he has only to cross a deep river, where there is no foothold, where the water dims the sight, and which is called the river of Death.

[1] Bunyan's *Grace abounding to the Chief of Sinners*, § 187.

choked his sight, besieged him with phantoms, yelled at his side to drag him down their precipices; and the black valley into which the pilgrim plunges, almost matches by the horror of its symbols the agony of the terrors by which he is assailed:—

"I saw then in my Dream, so far as this Valley reached, there was on the right hand a very deep Ditch; that Ditch is it into which the blind have led the blind in all ages, and have both there miserably perished. Again, behold on the left hand, there was a very dangerous Quag, into which, if even a good man falls, he can find no bottom for his foot to stand on. . . .

"The path-way was here also exceeding narrow, and therefore good Christian was the more put to it; for when he sought in the dark to shun the ditch on the one hand, he was ready to tip over into the mire on the other; also when he sought to escape the mire, without great carefulness he would be ready to fall into the ditch. Thus he went on, and I heard him here sigh bitterly; for, besides the dangers mentioned above, the pathway was here so dark, that ofttimes, when he lift up his foot to set forward he knew not where, or upon what he should set it next.

"About the midst of this Valley, I perceived the mouth of Hell to be, and it stood also hard by the wayside. Now, thought Christian, what shall I do? And ever and anon the flame and smoke would come out in such abundance, with sparks and hideous noises. . . . that he was forced to put up his Sword, and betake himself to another weapon, called All-prayer. So he cried in my hearing: "O Lord, I beseech thee deliver my soul." Thus he went on a great while, yet still the flames would be reaching towards him: Also he heard doleful voices, and rushings to and fro, so that sometimes he thought he should be torn in pieces, or trodden down like mire in the Streets."[1]

[1] *Pilgrim's Progress*, Cambridge 1862, First Part, p. 64.

Against this agony, neither his good deeds, nor his prayers, nor his justice, nor all the justice and all the prayers of all other men, could defend him. Grace alone justifies. God must impute to him the purity of Christ, and save him by a free choice. What can be more full of passion than the scene in which, under the name of his poor pilgrim, he relates his own doubts, his conversion, his joy, and the sudden change of his heart?

"Then the water stood in mine eyes, and I asked further, But, Lord, may such a great sinner as I am be indeed accepted of thee, and be saved by thee? And I heard him say, And him that cometh to me I will in no wise cast out. . . . And now was my heart full of joy, mine eyes full of tears, and mine affections running over with love to the Name, People, and Ways of Jesus Christ. . . .

"It made me see that all the World, notwithstanding all the righteousness thereof, is in a state of condemnation. It made me see that God the Father, though he be just, can justly justify the coming sinner. It made me greatly ashamed of the vileness of my former life, and confounded me with the sense of mine own ignorance; for there never came thought into my heart before now, that shewed me so the beauty of Jesus Christ. It made me love a holy life, and long to do something for the Honour and Glory of the Name of the Lord Jesus; yea, I thought that had I now a thousand gallons of blood in my body, I could spill it all for the sake of the Lord Jesus." [1]

Such an emotion does not weigh literary calculations. Allegory, the most artificial kind, is natural to Bunyan. If he employs it here, it is because he does so throughout; if he employs it throughout, it is from necessity, not choice. As children, countrymen, and all uncultivated minds, he transforms arguments into parables; he

[1] *Pilgrim's Progress*, First Part, p. 160.

only grasps truth when it is clothed in images; abstract terms eludé him; he must touch forms and contemplate colours. Dry general truths are a sort of algebra, acquired by the mind slowly and after much trouble, against our primitive inclination, which is to observe detailed events and visible objects; man being incapable of contemplating pure formulas until he is transformed by ten years' reading and reflection. We understand at once the term purification of heart; Bunyan understands it fully only, after translating it by this fable:—

"Then the Interpreter took Christian by the hand, and led him into a very large Parlour that was full of dust, because never swept; the which after he had reviewed a little while, the Interpreter called for a man to sweep. Now when he began to sweep, the dust began so abundantly to fly about, that Christian had almost therewith been choaked. Then said the Interpreter to a Damsel that stood by, Bring hither the Water, and sprinkle the Room; the which when she had done, it was swept and cleansed with pleasure.

"Then said Christian, What means this?

"The Interpreter answered, This Parlour is the heart of a man that was never sanctified by the sweet Grace of the Gospel: the dust is his Original Sin, and inward Corruptions, that have defiled the whole man. He that began to sweep at first, is the Law; but she that brought water, and did sprinkle it, is the Gospel. Now, whereas thou sawest that so soon as the first began to sweep, the dust did so fly about that the Room by him could not be cleansed, but that thou wast almost choaked there with; this is to shew thee, that the Law, instead of cleansing the heart (by its working) from sin, doth revive, put strength into and increase it in the soul, even as it doth discover and forbid it for it doth not give power to subdue.

"Again, as thou sawest the Damsel sprinkle the room with

CHAP. V.   THE CHRISTIAN RENAISSANCE.   233

Water, upon which it was cleansed with pleasure; this is to shew thee that when the Gospel comes in the sweet and precious influences thereof to the heart, then I say, even as thou sawest the Damsel lay the dust by sprinkling the floor with Water, so is sin vanquished and subdued, and the soul made clean, through the faith of it, and consequently fit for the King of Glory to inhabit."[1]

These repetitions, embarrassed phrases, familiar comparisons, this artless style, whose awkwardness recalls the childish periods of Herodotus, and whose simplicity recalls tales for children, prove that if his work is allegorical, it is so in order that it may be intelligible, and that Bunyan is a poët because he is a child.[2]

If you study him well, however, you will find power under his simplicity, and in his puerility the vision. These allegories are hallucinations as clear, complete, and sound as ordinary perceptions. No one but Spenser is so lucid. Imaginary objects rise of themselves before him. He has no trouble in calling them up or forming them. They agree in all their details with all

[1] *Pilgrim's Progress*, First Part, p. 26.
[2] Here is another of his allegories, almost witty, so just and simple it is. See *Pilgrim's Progress*, First Part, p. 68 : Now I saw in my Dream, that at the end of this Valley lay blood, bones, ashes, and mangled bodies of men, even of Pilgrims that had gone this way formerly ; and while I was musing what should be the reason, I espied a little before me a Cave, where two Giants, *Pope* and *Pagan*, dwelt in old time ; by whose power and tyranny the men whose bones, blood, ashes, etc., lay there, were cruelly put to death. But by this place Christian went without much danger, whereat I somewhat wondered ; but I have learnt since, that *Pagan* has been dead many a day ; and as for the other, though he be yet alive, he is by reason of age, and also of the many shrewd brushes that he met with in his younger days, grown so crazy, and stiff in his joints, that he can now do little more than sit in his Cave's mouth, grinning at Pilgrims as they go by, and biting his nails, because he cannot come at them.

the details of the precept which they represent, as a pliant veil fits the body which it covers. He distinguishes and arranges all the parts of the landscape—here the river, on the right the castle, a flag on its left turret, the setting sun three feet lower, an oval cloud in the front part of the sky—with the preciseness of a land-surveyor. We fancy in reading him that we are looking at the old maps of the time, in which the striking features of the angular cities are marked on the copperplate by a tool as certain as a pair of compasses.[1] Dialogues flow from his pen as in a dream. He does not seem to be thinking; we should even say that he was not himself there. Events and speeches seem to grow and dispose themselves within him, independently of his will. Nothing, as a rule, is colder than the characters in an allegory; his are living. Looking upon these details, so small and familiar, illusion gains upon us. Giant Despair, a simple abstraction, becomes as real in his hands as an English gaoler or farmer. He is heard talking by night in bed with his wife Diffidence, who gives him good advice, because here, as in other households, the strong and brutal animal is the least cunning of the two:—

"Then she counselled him that when he arose in the morning he should (take the two prisoners and) beat them without mercy. So when he arose, he getteth him a grievous Crab-tree Cudgel, and goes down into the Dungeon to them, and there first falls to rating of them as if they were dogs, although they gave him never a word of distaste. Then he falls upon them, and beats them fearfully, in such sort, that they were not able to help themselves, or to turn them upon the floor."[2]

[1] For instance, Hollar's work, *Cities of Germany*.
[2] *Pilgrim's Progress*, First Part, p. 126.

This stick, chosen with a forester's experience, this instinct of rating first and storming to get oneself into trim for knocking down, are traits which attest the sincerity of the narrator, and succeed in persuading the reader. Bunyan has the copiousness, the tone, the ease, and the clearness of Homer; he is as close to Homer as an Anabaptist tinker could be to an heroic singer, a creator of gods.

I err; he is nearer. Before the sentiment of the sublime, inequalities are levelled. The depth of emotion raises peasant and poet to the same eminence; and here also, allegory stands the peasant in stead. It alone, in the absence of ecstasy, can paint heaven; for it does not pretend to paint it: expressing it by a figure, it declares it invisible, as a glowing sun at which we cannot look straight, and whose image we observe in a mirror or a stream. The ineffable world thus retains all its mystery; warned by the allegory, we imagine splendours beyond all which it presents to us; we feel behind the beauties which are opened to us, the infinite which is concealed; and the ideal city, vanishing as soon as it appears, ceases to resemble the material Whitehall imagined for Jehovah by Milton. Read the arrival of the pilgrims in the celestial land. Saint Theresa has nothing more beautiful:—

"Yea, here they heard continually the singing of Birds, and saw every day the Flowers appear in the earth, and heard the voice of the Turtle in the land. In this Country the Sun shineth night and day. . . . Here they were within sight of the City they were going to, also here met them some of the inhabitants thereof; for in this land the Shining Ones commonly walked, because it was upon the borders of Heaven. . . . Here they heard voices from out of the City, loud voices, saying, ' Say ye to the daughter of Zion, Behold thy salvation cometh, behold his reward is with him!' Here all the inhabitants of the Country called them 'The holy People, The redeemed of the Lord, Sought out, etc.'

"Now as they walked in this land, they had more rejoicing than in parts more remote from the Kingdom to which they were bound; and drawing near to the City, they had yet a more perfect view thereof. It was builded of Pearls and Precious Stones, also the Street thereof was paved with gold; so that by reason of the natural glory of the City, and the reflection of the Sun-beams upon it, Christian with desire fell sick; Hopeful also had a fit or two of the same disease. Wherefore here they lay by it a while, crying out because of their pangs, 'If you see my Beloved, tell him that I am sick of love.'[1] . . .

"They therefore went up here with much agility and speed, though the foundation upon which the City was framed was higher than the Clouds. They therefore went up through the Regions of the Air, sweetly talking as they went, being comforted, because they safely got over the River, and had such glorious Companions to attend them.

"The talk that they had with the Shining Ones was about the glory of the place, who told them that the beauty and glory of it was inexpressible. There, said they, is the Mount Sion, the heavenly Jerusalem, the innumerable company of Angels, and the Spirits of just men made perfect. You are going now, said they, to the Paradise of God, wherein you shall see the Tree of Life, and eat of the never-fading fruits thereof; and when you come there, you shall have white Robes given you, and your walk and talk shall be every day with the King, even all the days of Eternity.[2]

"There came out also at this time to meet them, several of the King's Trumpeters, cloathed in white and shining Raiment, who with melodious noises and loud, made even the Heavens to echo with their sound. These Trumpeters saluted Christian

---

[1] *Pilgrim's Progress*, First Part, p. 174.   [2] *Ibid.* p. 179.

and his fellow with ten thousand welcomes from the World, and this they did with shouting and sound of Trumpet.

"This done, they compassed them round on every side; some went before, some behind, and some on the right hand, some on the left (as 't were to guard them through the upper Regions), continually sounding as they went with melodious noise, in notes on high; so that the very sight was to them that could behold it, as if Heaven itself was come down to meet them. . . .

"And now were these two men as 't were in Heaven before they came at it, being swallowed up with the sight of Angels, and with hearing of their melodious notes. Here also they had the City itself in view, and they thought they heard all the Bells therein ring to welcome them thereto. But above all the warm and joyful thoughts that they had about their own dwelling there, with such company, and that for ever and ever. Oh by what tongue or pen can their glorious joy be expressed!"[1] . . .

"Now I saw in my Dream that these two men went in at the Gate; and lo, as they entered, they were transfigured, and they had Raiment put on that shone like Gold. There was also that met them with Harps and Crowns, and gave them to them, the Harps to praise withal, and the Crowns in token of honour. Then I heard in my Dream that all the Bells in the City rang again for joy, and that it was said unto them, 'Enter ye into the joy of your Lord.' I also heard the men themselves, that they sang with a loud voice, saying, 'Blessing, Honour, Glory, and Power, be to him that sitteth upon the Throne, and to the Lamb for ever and ever.'

"Now, just as the Gates were opened to let in the men, I looked in after them, and behold, the City shone like the Sun; the Streets also were paved with Gold, and in them walked many men, with Crowns on their heads, Palms in their hands, and golden Harps to sing praises withal.

"There were also of them that had wings, and they answered one another without intermission, saying, 'Holy, holy, holy, is

[1] *Pilgrim's Progress*, First Part, p. 182.

the Lord.' And after that they shut up the Gates. Which when I had seen, I wished myself among them."[1]

He was imprisoned for twelve years and a half; in his dungeon he made wire-snares to support himself and his family; he died at the age of sixty in 1688. At the same time Milton lingered obscure and blind. The last two poets of the Reformation thus survived, amid the classical coldness which then dried up English literature, and the social excess which then corrupted English morals. " Shorn hypocrites, psalm-singers, gloomy bigots," such were the names by which men who reformed the manners and renewed the constitution of England were insulted. But oppressed and insulted as they were, their work continued of itself and without noise underground ; for the ideal which they had raised was, after all, that which the clime suggested and the race demanded. Gradually Puritanism began to approach the world, and the world to approach Puritanism. The Restoration was to fall into evil odour, the Revolution was to come, and beneath the gradual progress of national sympathy, as well as under the incessant effort of public reflection, parties and doctrines were to rally around a free and moral Protestantism.

[1] *Pilgrim's Progress*, First Part, p. 183, etc.

CHAPTER VI.

Milton.

On the borders of the licentious Renaissance which was drawing to a close, and of the exact school of poetry which was springing up, between the monotonous conceits of Cowley and the correct gallantries of Waller, appeared a mighty and superb mind, prepared by logic and enthusiasm for eloquence and the epic style; liberal, Protestant, a moralist and a poet, adorning the cause of Algernon Sidney and Locke with the inspiration of Spenser and Shakspeare; the heir of a poetical age, the precursor of an austere age, holding his place between the epoch of unselfish dreaming and the epoch of practical action; like his own Adam, who, taking his way to an unfriendly land, heard behind him, in the closed Eden, the dying strains of heaven.

John Milton was not one of those fevered souls void of self-command, whose rapture takes them by fits, whom a sickly sensibility drives for ever to the extreme of sorrow or joy, whose pliability prepares them to produce a variety of characters, whose inquietude condemns them to paint the madness and contradictions of passion. Vast knowledge, close logic, and grand passion; these were his marks. His mind was lucid, his imagination limited. He was incapable of " bating one jot of heart or hope," or of being transformed. He conceived the loftiest of ideal beauties, but he conceived only one. He was not born for the drama, but for the ode. He does not create souls, but constructs arguments, and experiences emotions. Emotions and arguments, all the forces and actions of his soul, assemble and are arranged beneath a unique sentiment, that of the sublime; and the broad river of lyric poetry streams from him, impetuous, with even flow, splendid as a cloth of gold.

I.

This dominant sense constituted the greatness and the firmness of his character. Against external fluctuations he found a refuge in himself; and the ideal city which he had built in his soul, endured impregnable to all assaults. It is too beautiful, this inner city, for him to wish to leave it; it was too solid to be destroyed. He believed in the sublime with the whole force of his nature, and the whole authority of his logic; and with him, cultivated reason strengthened by its tests the suggestions of primitive instinct. With this double armour, man can advance firmly through life. He who is always feeding himself with demonstrations is capable of believing, willing, persevering in belief and will; he does not change with every event and every passion, as that fickle and pliable being whom we call a poet; he remains at rest in fixed principles. He is capable of embracing a cause, and of continuing attached to it, whatever may happen, spite of all, to the end. No seduction, no emotion, no accident, no change alters the stability of his conviction or the lucidity of his knowledge. On the first day, on the last day, during the whole time, he preserves intact the entire system of his clear ideas, and the logical vigour of his brain sustains the manly vigour of his heart. When at length, as here, this close logic is employed in the service of noble ideas, enthusiasm is added to constancy. The man holds his opinions not only as true, but as sacred. He fights for them, not only as a soldier, but as a priest. He is impassioned, devoted, religious, heroic. Rarely is such a mixture seen; but it was fully seen in Milton.

He was of a family in which courage, moral nobility, the love of art, were present to whisper the most beautiful and eloquent words around his cradle. His mother was a most exemplary woman, well known through all the neighbourhood for her benevolence.[1] His father, a student of Christ Church, and disinherited as a Protestant, had made his fortune by his own energies, and, amidst his occupations as a scrivener or writer, had preserved the taste for letters, being unwilling to give up "his liberal and intelligent tastes to the extent of becoming altogether a slave to the world;" he wrote verses, was an excellent musician, one of the best composers of his time; he chose Cornelius Jansen to paint his son's portrait when in his tenth year, and gave his child the widest and fullest literary education.[2] Let the reader try to picture this child, in the street (Bread Street) inhabited by merchants, in this citizen-like and scholarly, religious and poetical family, whose manners were regular and their aspirations lofty, where they set the psalms to music, and wrote madrigals in

[1] Matre probatissimâ et eleemosynis per viciniam potissimum nota.—*Defensio Secunda. Life of Milton*, by Keightley.
[2] "My father destined me while yet a little child for the study of humane letters."—*Life*, by Masson, 1859, i. 51.

honour of Oriana the queen,[1] where vocal music, letters, painting, all the adornments of the beautiful Renaissance, decked the sustained gravity, the hard-working honesty, the deep Christianity of the Reformation. All Milton's genius springs from this; he carried the splendour of the Renaissance into the earnestness of the Reformation, the magnificence of Spenser into the severity of Calvin, and, with his family, found himself at the confluence of the two civilisations which he combined. Before he was ten years old he had a learned tutor, "a puritan, who cut his hair short;" after that he went to Saint Paul's school, then to the University of Cambridge, that he might be instructed in "polite literature;" and at the age of twelve he worked, in spite of his weak eyes and headaches, until midnight and even later. His John the Baptist, a character resembling himself, says:

> "When I was yet a child, no childish play
> To me was pleasing; all my mind was set
> Serious to learn and know, and thence to do,
> What might be public good; myself I thought
> Born to that end, born to promote all truth,
> All righteous things."[2]

At school, afterwards at Cambridge, then with his father, he was strengthening and preparing himself with all his power, free from all blame, and loved by all good men; traversing the vast fields of Greek and Latin literature, not only the great writers, but all the writers, down to the half of the middle-age; and studying simultaneously ancient Hebrew, Syriac and rabbinical He-

---

[1] Queen Elizabeth.
[2] *The Poetical Works of John Milton*, ed. Mitford, *Paradise Regained*, Book i. l. 201-206.

brew, French and Spanish, old English literature, all the Italian literature, with such zeal and profit that he wrote Italian and Latin verse and prose like an Italian or a Roman; in addition to this, music, mathematics, theology, and much besides. A serious thought regulated this great toil. "The church, to whose service, by the intentions of my parents and friends, I was destined of a child, and in mine own resolutions: till coming to some maturity of years, and perceiving what tyranny had invaded the church, that he who would take orders must subscribe slave, and take an oath withal, which unless he took with a conscience that would retch, he must either straight perjure, or split his faith; I thought it better to prefer a blameless silence before the sacred office of speaking bought, and begun with servitude and forswearing."[1]

He refused to be a clergyman from the same feelings that he had wished it; the desire and the renunciation all sprang from the same source—a fixed resolve to act nobly. Falling back into the life of a layman, he continued to cultivate and perfect himself, studying passionately and with method, but without pedantry or rigour: nay, rather, after his master Spenser, in *L'Allegro, Il Penseroso, Comus,* he set forth in sparkling and variegated dress the wealth of mythology, nature, and fancy; then, sailing for the land of science and beauty, he visited Italy, made the acquaintance of Grotius and Galileo, sought the society of the learned, the men of letters, the men of the world, listened to the musicians, steeped himself in all the beauties stored up by the Renaissance at Florence and Rome.

[1] Milton's *Prose Works*, ed. Mitford, 8 vols., *The Reason of Church Government*, i. 150.

Everywhere his learning, his fine Italian and Latin style, secured him the friendship and attentions of scholars, so that, on his return to Florence, he "was as well received as if he had returned to his native country." He collected books and music, which he sent to England, and thought of traversing Sicily and Greece, those two homes of ancient letters and arts. Of all the flowers that opened to the Southern sun under the influence of the two great Paganisms, he gathered freely the balmiest and the most exquisite, but without staining himself with the mud which surrounded them. "I call the Deity to witness," he wrote later, "that in all those places in which vice meets with so little discouragement, and is practised with so little shame, I never once deviated from the paths of integrity and virtue, and perpetually reflected that, though my conduct might escape the notice of men, it could not elude the inspection of God."[1]

Amid the licentious gallantries and inane sonnets like those which the Cicisbei and Academicians lavished forth, he retained his sublime idea of poetry: he thought to choose a heroic subject from ancient English history; and as he says, "I was confirmed in this opinion, that he who would not be frustrate of his hope to write well hereafter in laudable things, ought himself to be a true poem; that is, a composition and pattern of the best and honourablest things; not presuming to sing high praises of heroic men, or famous cities, unless he have in himself the experience and the practice of all that which is praise-

---

[1] Milton's *Prose Works* (Bohn's edition, 1848), *Second Defence of the People of England*, i. 257. See also his *Italian Sonnets*, with their religious sentiment.

worthy."[1] Above all, he loved Dante and Petrarch for their purity, telling himself that "if unchastity in a woman, whom St. Paul terms the glory of man, be such a scandal and dishonour, then certainly in a man, who is both the image and glory of God, it must, though commonly not so thought, be much more deflouring and dishonourable."[2] He thought "that every free and gentle spirit, without that oath, ought to be born a knight," for the practice and defence of chastity, and he kept himself virgin till his marriage. Whatever the temptation might be, whatever the attraction or fear, it found him equally opposed and equally firm. From a sense of gravity and propriety he avoided all religious disputes; but if his own creed were attacked, he defended it "without any reserve or fear," even in Rome, before the Jesuits who plotted against him, within a few paces of the Inquisition and the Vatican. Perilous duty, instead of driving him away, attracted him. When the Revolution began to threaten, he returned, drawn by conscience, as a soldier who hastens to danger when he hears the clash of arms, convinced, as he himself tells us, that it was a shame to him leisurely to spend his life abroad, and for his own pleasure, whilst his fellow-countrymen were striving for their liberty. In battle he appeared in the front ranks as a volunteer, courting danger everywhere. Throughout his education and throughout his youth, in his profane readings and his sacred studies, in his acts and his maxims, already a ruling and permanent thought grew manifest—the resolution to develop and unfold within him the ideal man.

[1] Milton's *Prose Works*, Mitford, *Apology for Smectymnuus*, i. 270.
[2] *Ibid.* 273. See also his *Treatise on Divorce*, which shows clearly Milton's meaning.

II.

Two powers chiefly lead mankind—impulse and idea: the one influencing sensitive, unfettered, poetical souls, capable of transformations, like Shakspeare; the other governing active, combative, heroic souls, capable of immutability, like Milton. The first are sympathetic and effusive; the second are concentrative and reserved.[1] The first give themselves up, the others withhold themselves. These, by reliance and sociability, with an artistic instinct and a sudden imitative comprehension, involuntarily take the tone and disposition of the men and things which surround them, and an immediate counterpoise is effected between the inner and the outer man. Those, by mistrust and rigidity, with a combative instinct and a quick reference to rule, become naturally thrown back upon themselves, and in their narrow limits no longer feel the solicitations and contradictions of their surroundings. They have formed a model, and thenceforth this model like a watchword restrains or urges them on. Like all powers destined to have sway, the inner idea grows and absorbs to its use the rest of their being. They bury it in themselves by meditation, they nourish it with reasoning, they put it in communication with the chain of all their doctrines and all their experiences; so that when a temptation assails them, it is not an isolated principle which it attacks, but it encounters

---

[1] "Though Christianity had been but slightly taught me, yet a certain reservedness of natural disposition and moral discipline, learnt out of the noblest philosophy, was enough to keep me in disdain of far less incontinences than this of the bordello."—*Apology for Smectymnuus*, Mitford, i. 272.

the whole combination of their belief, an infinitely ramified combination, too strong for a sensuous seduction to tear asunder. At the same time a man by habit is upon his guard; the combative attitude is natural to him, and he stands erect, firm in the pride of his courage and the inveteracy of his determination.

A soul thus fortified is like a diver in his bell;[1] it passes through life as he passes through the sea, unstained but isolated. On his return to England, Milton fell back among his books, and received a few pupils, upon whom he imposed, as upon himself, continuous toil, serious reading, a frugal diet, a strict behaviour; the life of a recluse, almost of a monk. Suddenly, in a month, after a country visit, he married.[2] A few weeks afterwards, his wife returned to her father's house, would not come back to him, took no notice of his letters, and sent back his messenger with scorn. The two characters had come into collision. Nothing displeases women more than an austere and self-contained character. They see that they have no hold upon it; its dignity awes them, its pride repels, its preoccupations keep them aloof; they feel themselves of less value, neglected for general interests or speculative curiosities; judged, moreover, and that after an inflexible rule; at most regarded with condescension, as a sort of less reasonable and inferior beings, debarred from the equality which they demand, and the love which alone can reward them for the loss of equality. The "priest" character is made for solitude; the tact, ease, charm, pleasantness, and gentleness necessary to

[1] An expression of Jean Paul Richter. See an excellent article on Milton in the *Nat. Review*, July 1859.
[2] 1643, at the age of 35.

all companionship, is wanting to it; we admire him, but we go no further, especially if, like Milton's wife, we are somewhat dull and commonplace,[1] adding mediocrity of intellect to the repugnance of our hearts. He had, so his biographers say, a certain gravity of nature, or severity of mind which would not condescend to petty things, but kept him in the clouds, in a region which is not that of the household. He was accused of being harsh, choleric; and certainly he stood upon his manly dignity, his authority as a husband, and was not so greatly esteemed, respected, studied, as he thought he deserved to be. In short, he passed the day amongst his books, and the rest of the time his heart lived in an abstracted and sublime world of which few wives catch a glimpse, his wife least of all. He had, in fact, chosen like a student, so much the more at random because his former life had been of "a well-governed and wise appetite." Equally like a man of the closet, he resented her flight, being the more irritated because the world's ways were unknown to him. Without dread of ridicule, and with the sternness of a speculative man suddenly brought into collision with actual life, he wrote treatises on *Divorce*, signed them with his name, dedicated them to Parliament, held himself divorced *de facto*, because his wife refused to return, *de jure* because he had four texts of Scripture for it;

---

[1] *Doctrine and Discipline of Divorce*, Mitford, ii. 27, 29, 32. "Mute and spiritless mate." "The bashful muteness of the virgin may oftentimes hide all the unliveliness and natural sloth which is really unfit for conversation." "A man shall find himself bound fast to an image of earth and phlegm, with whom he looked to be the copartner of a sweet and gladsome society." A pretty woman will say in reply: I cannot love a man who carries his head like the Sacrament.

whereupon he paid court to another young lady, and suddenly, seeing his wife on her knees and weeping, forgave her, took her back, renewed the dry and sad marriage-tie, not profiting by experience, but on the other hand fated to contract two other unions, the last with a wife thirty years younger than himself. Other parts of his domestic life were neither better managed nor happier. He had taken his daughters for secretaries, and made them read languages which they did not understand,— a repelling task, of which they bitterly complained. In return, he accused them of being "undutiful and unkind," of neglecting him, not caring whether they left him alone, of conspiring with the servants to rob him in their purchases, of stealing his books, so that they would have disposed of the whole of them. Mary, the second, hearing one day that he was going to be married, said that his marriage was no news; the best news would be his death. An incredible speech, and one which throws a strange light on the miseries of this family. Neither circumstances nor nature had created him for happiness.

III.

They had created him for strife, and after his return to England he had thrown himself heartily into it, armed with logic, anger, and learning, protected by conviction and conscience. When "the liberty of speech was no longer subject to control, all mouths began to be opened against the bishops. . . . I saw that a way was opening for the establishment of real liberty; that the foundation was laying for the deliverance of man from the yoke of slavery and superstition; . . . and as I had from my youth studied the distinction between religious and civil rights, . . . I determined to relinquish the other pursuits in which I was engaged, and to transfer the whole force of my talents and my industry to this one important object." [1] And thereupon he wrote his *Reformation in England,* jeering at and attacking with haughtiness and scorn the prelacy and its defenders. Refuted and attacked in turn, he became still more bitter, and crushed those whom he had beaten.[2] Transported to the limits of his creed, and like a knight making a rush, and who pierces with a dash the whole line of battle, he hurled himself upon the prince, wrote that the abolition of royalty as well as the overthrow of Episcopacy were necessary; and one month after the death of Charles I., justified his execution, replied to the *Eikon Basilike,* then to Salmasius' *Defence of the King,* with incomparable breadth of style and scorn, like a soldier, like an apostle, like a man who everywhere feels the superiority of his science and logic, who wishes to make it felt, who proudly tramples upon and crushes his adversaries as ignoramuses, inferior minds, base hearts.[3] " Kings most commonly," he says, at the beginning of the *Eikonoklastes,* " though strong in legions, are but weak at arguments; as they who ever have accustomed from their cradle to use their will only as their right hand, their reason always as their left. Whence unexpectedly constrained to that kind of com-

---

[1] *Second Defence of the People of England,* Prose Works (Bohn), i. 257.

[2] *Of Reformation touching Church Discipline in England, and the Causes that hitherto have hindered it. Of Prelatical Episcopacy. The Reason of Church Government urged against Prelaty :* 1641. *Apology for Smectymnuus :* 1642.

[3] *The Tenure of Kings and Magistrates. Eikonoklastes :* 1648–9. *Defensio Populi Anglicani :* 1651. *Defensio Secunda :* 1654. *Authoris pro se defensio. Responsio :* 1655.

bat, they prove but weak and puny adversaries." [1] Yet, for love of those who suffer themselves to be overcome by this dazzling name of royalty, he consents to "take up King Charles's gauntlet," and bangs him with it in a style calculated to make the imprudent men who had thrown it down repent. Far from recoiling at the accusation of murder, he accepts and boasts of it. He vaunts the regicide, sets it on a triumphal car, decks it in all the light of heaven. He relates with the tone of a judge, "how a most potent king, after he had trampled upon the laws of the nation, and given a shock to its religion, and began to rule at his own will and pleasure, was at last subdued in the field by his own subjects, who had undergone a long slavery under him; how afterwards he was cast into prison, and when he gave no ground, either by words or actions, to hope better things of him, was finally by the supreme council of the kingdom condemned to die, and beheaded before the very gates of the royal palace. . . . For what king's majesty sitting upon an exalted throne, ever shone so brightly, as that of the people of England then did, when, shaking off that old superstition, which had prevailed a long time, they gave judgment upon the king himself, or rather upon an enemy who had been their king, caught as it were in a net by his own laws (who alone of all mortals challenged to himself impunity by a divine right), and scrupled not to inflict the same punishment upon him, being guilty, which he would have inflicted upon any other?" [2] After having justified the execution, he sanctified it; consecrated it by decrees of heaven after he had authorised it by the laws

[1] Milton's *Prose Works*, Mitford, vol. i. 329.
[2] *Ibid.* Preface to the *Defence of the People of England*, vi. pp. 1, 2.

of the world; from the support of Law he transferred
it to the support of God. This is the God who "uses
to throw down proud and unruly kings, . . . and
utterly to extirpate them and all their family. By his
manifest impulse being set on work to recover our almost lost liberty, following him as our guide, and adoring the impresses of his divine power manifested upon
all occasions, we went on in no obscure but an illus-
trious passage, pointed out and made plain to us by God
himself."[1] Here the reasoning ends with a song of
triumph, and enthusiasm breaks out through the mail
of the warrior. Such he displayed himself in all his
actions and in all his doctrines. The solid files of
bristling and well-ordered arguments which he disposed
in battle-array were changed in his heart in the moment
of triumph into glorious processions of crowned and resplendent hymns. He was transported by them, he de-

---

[1] Mitford, vi. pp. 2-3. This "Defence" was in Latin. Milton
ends it thus :—

"He (God) has gloriously delivered you, the first of nations, from
the two greatest mischiefs of this life, and most pernicious to virtue,
tyranny and superstition; he has endued you with greatness of mind to
be the first of mankind, who after having conquered their own king,
and having had him delivered into their hands, have not scrupled
to condemn him judicially, and, pursuant to that sentence of condemnation, to put him to death. After the performing so glorious an action
as this, you ought to do nothing that is mean and little, not so much
as to think of, much less to do, anything but what is great and sublime. Which to attain to, this is your only way; as you have subdued
your enemies in the field, so to make appear, that unarmed, and in the
highest outward peace and tranquillity, you of all mankind are best
able to subdue ambition, avarice, the love of riches, and can best avoid
the corruptions that prosperity is apt to introduce (which generally
subdue and triumph over other nations), to show as great justice, temperance, and moderation in the maintaining your liberty, as you have
shown courage in freeing yourselves from slavery."—*Ibid.* vol. vi.
251-2.

luded himself, and lived thus alone with the sublime, like a warrior-pontiff, who in his stiff armour, or his glittering stole, stands face to face with truth. Thus absorbed in strife and in his priesthood, he lived out of the world, as blind to palpable facts as he was protected against the seductions of the senses, placed above the stains and the lessons of experience, as incapable of leading men as of yielding to them. There was nothing in him akin to the devices and delays of the statesman, the crafty schemer, who pauses on his way, experimentalises, with eyes fixed on what may turn up, who gauges what is possible, and employs logic for practical purposes. Milton was speculative and chimerical. Locked up in his own ideas, he sees but them, is attracted but by them. Is he pleading against the bishops? He would extirpate them at once, without hesitation; he demands that the Presbyterian worship shall be at once established, without forethought, contrivance, hesitation. It is the command of God, it is the duty of the faithful; beware how you trifle with God or temporise with faith. Concord, gentleness, liberty, piety, he sees a whole swarm of virtues issue from this new worship. Let the king fear nothing from it, his power will be all the stronger. Twenty thousand democratic assemblies will take care that his rights be not infringed. These ideas make us smile. We recognise the party-man, who, on the verge of the Restoration, when "the whole multitude was mad with desire for a king," published *A Ready and Easy Way to establish a Free Commonwealth,* and described his method at length. We recognise the theorist who, to obtain a law of divorce, only appealed to Scripture, and aimed at transforming the civil constitution of a people by changing the accepted sense of a verse. With closed eyes, sacred text in hand, he advances from consequence to consequence, trampling upon the prejudices, inclinations, habits, wants of men, as if a reasoning or religious spirit were the whole man, as if evidence always created belief, as if belief always resulted in practice, as if, in the struggle of doctrines, truth or justice gave doctrines the victory and sovereignty. To cap all, he sketched out a treatise on education, in which he proposed to teach each pupil every science, every art, and, what is more, every virtue. "He who had the art and proper eloquence . . . might in a short space gain them to an incredible diligence and courage, . . . infusing into their young breasts such an ingenuous and noble ardour as would not fail to make many of them renowned and matchless men."[1] Milton had taught for many years and at various times. A man must be insensible to experience or doomed to illusions who retains such deceptions after such experiences.

But his obstinacy constituted his power, and the inner constitution, which closed his mind to instruction, armed his heart against weaknesses. With men generally, the source of devotion dries up when in contact with life. Gradually, by dint of frequenting the world, we acquire its tone. We do not choose to be dupes, and to abstain from the license which others allow themselves; we relax our youthful strictness; we even smile, attributing it to our heated blood; we know our own motives, and cease to find ourselves sublime. We end by taking it calmly, and we see the world wag, only trying to avoid shocks, picking up here and there a few little comfortable

[1] *Of Education.* Mitford, ii. 385.

pleasures. Not so Milton. He lived complete and pure to the end, without loss of heart or weakness; experience could not instruct nor misfortune depress him; he endured all, and repented of nothing. He lost his sight, by his own fault, by writing, though ill, and against the prohibition of his doctors, to justify the English people against the invectives of Salmasius. He saw the funeral of the Republic, the proscription of his doctrines, the defamation of his honour. Around him ran riot, a distaste for liberty, an enthusiasm for slavery. A whole people threw itself at the feet of a young incapable and treacherous libertine. The glorious leaders of the Puritan faith were condemned, executed, cut down alive from the gallows, quartered amidst insults; others, whom death had saved from the hangman, were dug up and exposed on the gibbet; others, exiles in foreign lands, lived, threatened and attacked by royalist bullies; others again, more unfortunate, had sold their cause for money and titles, and sat amid the executioners of their former friends. The most pious and austere citizens of England filled the prisons, or wandered about in poverty and shame; and gross vice, impudently seated on the throne, rallied around it a herd of unbridled lusts and sensualities. Milton himself had been constrained to hide; his books had been burned by the hand of the hangman; even after the general act of indemnity he was imprisoned; when set at liberty, he lived in the expectation of being assassinated, for private fanaticism might seize the weapon relinquished by public revenge. Other smaller misfortunes came to aggravate by their stings the great wounds which afflicted him. Confiscations, a bankruptcy, finally, the great fire of London, had robbed him of three-fourths of his fortune;[1] his daughters neither esteemed nor respected him; he sold his books, knowing that his family could not profit by them after his death; and amidst so many private and public miseries, he continued calm. Instead of repudiating what he had done, he gloried in it: instead of being cast down, he increased in firmness. He says, in his 22d sonnet:

> " Cyriack, this three years day these eyes, though clear,
> To outward view, of blemish or of spot,
> Bereft of sight, their seeing have forgot;
> Nor to their idle orbs doth day appear
> Of sun, or moon, or star, throughout the year,
> Or man, or woman. Yet I argue not
> Against Heaven's hand or will, nor bate one jot
> Of heart or hope; but still bear up and steer
> Right onward. What supports me, dost thou ask?
> The conscience, friend, to have lost them overplied
> In liberty's defence, my noble task;
> Of which all Europe rings from side to side.
> This thought might lead me through the world's vain mask
> Content though blind, had I no other guide." [2]

That thought was indeed his guide; he was "armed in himself," and that "breastplate of diamond"[3] which had protected him in his prime against the wounds in battle, protected him in his old age against the temptations and doubts of defeat and adversity.

---

[1] A scrivener caused him to lose £2000. At the Restoration he was refused payment of £2000 which he had put into the Excise Office, and deprived of an estate of £50 a year, bought by him from the property of the Chapter of Westminster. His house in Bread Street was burnt in the great fire. When he died he is said to have left about £1500 in money (equivalent to about £5000 now), besides household goods. [I am indebted to the kindness of Professor Masson for the collation of this note.—Tr.]

[2] Milton's *Poetical Works*, Mitford, i. Sonnet xxii.   [3] *Italian Sonnets*.

IV.

Milton lived in a small house in London, or in the country, at Horton, in Buckinghamshire, published his *History of Britain*, his *Logic*, a *Treatise on True Religion and Heresy*, meditated his great *Treatise on Christian Doctrine*. Of all consolations, work is the most fortifying and the most healthy, because it solaces a man not by bringing him ease, but by requiring him to exert himself. Every morning he had a chapter of the Bible read to him in Hebrew, and remained for some time in silence, grave, in order to meditate on what he had heard. He never went to a place of worship. Independent in religion as in all else, he was sufficient to himself; finding in no sect the marks of the true church, he prayed to God alone, without needing others' help. He studied till mid-day; then, after an hour's exercise, he played the organ or the bass-violin. Then he resumed his studies till six, and in the evening enjoyed the society of his friends. When any one came to visit him, he was usually found in a room hung with old green hangings, seated in an arm-chair, and dressed neatly in black; his complexion was pale, says one of his visitors, but not sallow; his hands and feet were gouty; his hair, of a light brown, was parted in the midst and fell in long curls; his eyes, grey and clear, showed no sign of blindness. He had been very beautiful in his youth, and his English cheeks, once delicate as a young girl's, retained their colour almost to the end. His face, we are told, was pleasing; his straight and manly gait bore witness to intrepidity and courage. Something great and proud breathes out yet from all his portraits; and certainly few men have done so much honour to their kind. Thus went out this noble life, like a setting sun, bright and calm. Amid so many trials, a pure and lofty joy, altogether worthy of him, had been granted to him: the poet, buried under the Puritan, had reappeared, more sublime than ever, to give to Christianity its second Homer. The dazzling dreams of his youth and the reminiscences of his ripe age were found in him, side by side with Calvinistic dogmas and the visions of Saint John, to create the Protestant epic of damnation and grace; and the vastness of primitive horizons, the flames of the infernal dungeon, the splendours of the celestial court, opened to the inner eye of the soul unknown regions beyond the sights which the eyes of the flesh had lost.

V.

I have before me the formidable volume in which, some time after Milton's death, his prose works were collected.[1] What a book! The chairs creak when you place it upon them, and a man who had turned its leaves over for an hour, would have less pain in his head than in his arm. As the book, so were the men; from the mere outsides we might gather some notion of the controversialists and theologians whose doctrines they contain. Yet we must conclude that the author was eminently learned, elegant, travelled, philosophic, and a man of the world for his age. We think invol-

---

[1] 3 vols. folio, 1697-8. The titles of Milton's chief writings in prose are these:—*Of Reformation in England; The Reason of Church Government urged against Prelaty; Animadversions upon the Remonstrants' Defence; Doctrine and Discipline of Divorce; Tetrachordon; Tractate on Education; Areopagitica; Tenure of Kings and Magistrates; Eikonoklastes; History of Britain; Defence of the People of England.*

untarily of the portraits of the theologians of those days, severe faces engraved on metal by the hard artists' tool, whose square brows and steady eyes stand out in startling prominence against a dark oak panel. We compare them to modern countenances, in which the delicate and complex features seem to quiver at the varied contact of hardly begun sensations and innumerable ideas. We try to imagine the heavy classical education, the physical exercises, the rude treatment, the rare ideas, the imposed dogmas, which formerly occupied, oppressed, fortified, and hardened the young; and we might fancy ourselves looking at an anatomy of megatheria and mastodons, reconstructed by Cuvier.

The race of living men is changed. Our mind fails us now-a-days at the idea of this greatness and this barbarism; but we discover that the barbarism was then the cause of the greatness. As in other times we might have seen, in the primitive slime and among the colossal ferns, ponderous monsters slowly wind their scaly backs, and tear the flesh from one another's sides with their misshapen talons; so now, at a distance, from the height of our calm civilisation, we see the battles of the theologians, who, armed with syllogisms, bristling with texts, covered one another with filth, and laboured to devour each other.

Milton fought in the front rank, pre-ordained to barbarism and greatness by his individual nature and the manners of the time, capable of displaying in high prominence the logic, style, and spirit of his age. It is drawing-room life which trims men into shape: the society of ladies, the lack of serious interests, idleness, vanity, security, are needed to bring men to elegance, urbanity, fine and light humour, to teach the desire to please, the fear to become wearisome, a perfect clearness.

a finished precision, the art of gradual transitions and delicate tact, a taste for suitable images, continual ease, and choice diversity. Seek nothing like this in Milton. The old scholastic system was not far off; it still weighed on those who were destroying it. Under this secular armour discussion proceeded pedantically, with measured steps. The first thing was to propound a thesis; and Milton writes, in large characters, at the head of his *Treatise on Divorce*, " that indisposition, unfitness, or contrariety of mind, arising from a cause in nature unchangeable, hindering, and ever likely to hinder the main benefits of conjugal society, which are solace and peace, is a greater reason of divorce than natural frigidity, especially if there be no children, and that there be mutual consent." And then follow, legion after legion, the disciplined army of the arguments. Battalion after battalion they pass by, numbered very distinctly. There is a dozen of them together, each with its title in clear characters, and the little brigade of subdivisions which it commands. Sacred texts hold the post of honour. Every word of them is discussed, the substantive after the adjective, the verb after the substantive, the preposition after the verb; interpretations, authorities, illustrations, are summoned up, and ranged between palisades of new divisions. And yet there is a lack of order, the question is not reduced to a single idea; we cannot see our way; proofs succeed proofs without logical sequence; we are rather tired out than convinced. We remember that the author speaks to Oxford men, lay or cleric, trained in pretended discussions, capable of obstinate attention, accustomed to digest indigestible books. They are at home in this thorny thicket of scholastic brambles; they beat a path through, somewhat at hazard, hardened against the hurts which repulse us, and not having the smallest idea of the daylight which we require everywhere now.

With such ponderous reasoners, you must not look for wit. Wit is the nimbleness of victorious reason; here, because everything is powerful, all is heavy. When Milton wishes to joke, he looks like one of Cromwell's pikemen, who, entering a room to dance, should fall upon the floor, and that with the extra weight of his armour. Few things could be more stupid than his *Animadversions upon the Remonstrants' Defence.* At the end of an argument his adversary concludes with this specimen of theological wit: "In the meanwhile see, brethren, how you have with Simon fished all night, and caught nothing." And Milton boastfully replies: "If we, fishing with Simon the apostle, can catch nothing; see what you can catch with Simon Magus; for all his hooks and fishing implements he bequeathed among you." Here a great savage laugh would break out. The spectators saw a charm in this way of insinuating that his adversary was simoniacal. A little before, the latter says: "Tell me, is this liturgy good or evil?" Answer: "It is evil: repair the acheloian horn of your dilemma, how you can, against the next push." The doctors wondered at the fine mythological simile, and rejoiced to see the adversary so neatly compared to an ox, a beaten ox, a pagan ox. On the next page the Remonstrant said, by way of a spiritual and mocking reproach: "Truly, brethren, you have not well taken the heighth of the pole." Answer: "No marvel; there be many more that do not take well the height of your pole, but will take better the declination of your altitude." Three quips of the same savour follow one upon the other; all this looked pretty. Elsewhere, Salmasius exclaiming "that the sun itself never beheld a more outrageous action" than the murder of the king, Milton cleverly answers, "The sun has beheld many things that blind Bernard never saw. But we are content you should mention the sun over and over. And it will be a piece of prudence in you so to do. For though our wickedness does not require it, the coldness of the defence that you are making does."[1] The marvellous heaviness of these conceits betrays minds yet entangled in the swaddling-clothes of learning. The Reformation was the inauguration of free thought, but only the inauguration. Criticism was yet unborn; authority still presses with a full half of its weight upon the freest and boldest minds. Milton, to prove that it was lawful to put a king to death, quotes Orestes, the laws of Publicola, and the death of Nero. His *History of Britain* is a farrago of all the traditions and fables. Under every circumstance he adduces a text of Scripture for proof; his boldness consists in showing himself a bold grammarian, a valorous commentator. He is blindly Protestant as others were blindly Catholic. He leaves in its bondage the higher reason, the mother of principles; he has but emancipated a subordinate reason, an interpreter of texts. Like the vast half shapeless creatures, the birth of early times, he is yet but half man and half mud.

Can we expect urbanity here? Urbanity is the elegant dignity which answers insult by calm irony, and respects man whilst piercing a dogma. Milton coarsely knocks his adversary down. A bristling pedant, born from a Greek lexicon and a Syriac grammar,

[1] *A Defence of the People of England*, Mitford vi. 21.

Salmasius had disgorged upon the English people a vocabulary of insults and a folio of quotations. Milton replies to him in the same style; calling him a buffoon, a mountebank, "*professor triobolaris*," a hired pedant, a nobody, a rogue, a heartless being, a wretch, an idiot, sacrilegious, a slave worthy of rods and a pitchfork. A dictionary of big Latin words passed between them. "You, who know so many tongues, who read so many books, who write so much about them, you are yet but an ass." Finding the epithet good, he repeats and sanctifies it. "Oh most drivelling of asses, you come ridden by a woman, with the cured heads of bishops whom you had wounded, a little image of the great beast of the Apocalypse!" He ends by calling him savage beast, apostate, and devil. "Doubt not that you are reserved for the same end as Judas, and that, driven by despair rather than repentance, self-disgusted, you must one day hang yourself, and like your rival, burst asunder in your belly."[1] We fancy we are listening to the bellowing of two bulls.

They had all a bull's ferocity. Milton was a good hater. He fought with his pen, as the Ironsides with the sword, inch by inch, with a concentrated rancour and a fierce obstinacy. The bishops and the king then suffered for eleven years of despotism. Each man recalled the banishments, confiscations, punishments, the

[1] Mitford, vi. 250. Salmasius said of the death of the king: "Horribilis nuntius aures nostras atroci vulnere, sed magis mentes perculit." Milton replied: "Profecto nuntius iste horribilis aut gladium multo longiorem eo quem strinxit Petrus habuerit oportet, aut aures istæ auritissimæ fuerint, quas tam longinquo vulnere perculerit."

"Oratorem tam insipidum et insulsum ut ne ex lacrymis quidem ejus mica salis exiguissima possit exprimi."

"Salmasius nova quadam metamorphosi salmacis factus est."

law violated systematically and relentlessly, the liberty of the subject attacked by a well-laid plot, Episcopal idolatry imposed on Christian consciences, the faithful preachers driven into the wilds of America, or given up to the executioner and the stocks.[1]   Such reminiscences

[1] I copy from Neal's *History of the Puritans*, ii. ch. vii. 367, one of these sorrows and complaints. By the greatness of the outrage the reader can judge of the intensity of the hatred:—

"The humble petition of (Dr.) Alexander Leighton, Prisoner in the Fleet,—Humbly Sheweth,

"That on Feb. 17, 1630, he was apprehended coming from sermon by a high commission warrant, and dragged along the street with bills and staves to London-house. That the gaoler of Newgate being sent for, clapt him in irons, and carried him with a strong power into a loathsome and ruinous dog-hole, full of rats and mice, that had no light but a little grate, and the roof being uncovered, the snow and rain beat in upon him, having no bedding, nor place to make a fire, but the ruins of an old smoaky chimney. In this woeful place he was shut up for fifteen weeks, nobody being suffered to come near him, till at length his wife only was admitted. That the fourth day after his commitment the pursuivant, with a mighty multitude, came to his house to search for jesuits books, and used his wife in such a barbarous and inhuman manner as he is ashamed to express; that they rifled every person and place, holding a pistol to the breast of a child of five years old, threatening to kill him if he did not discover the books; that they broke open chests, presses, boxes, and carried away everything, even household stuff, apparel, arms, and other things; that at the end of fifteen weeks he was served with a subpœna, on an information laid against him by Sir Robert Heath, attorney-general, whose dealing with him was full of cruelty and deceit; but he was then sick, and, in the opinion of four physicians, thought to be poisoned, because all his hair and skin came off; that in the height of this sickness the cruel sentence was passed upon him mentioned in the year 1630, and executed Nov. 26 following, when he received thirty-six stripes upon his naked back with a threefold cord, his hands being tied to a stake, and then stood almost two hours in the pillory in the frost and snow, before he was branded in the face, his nose slit, and his ears cut off; that after this he was carried by water to the Fleet, and shut up in such a room that he was never well, and after eight years was turned into the common gaol."

arising in powerful minds, stamped them with inexpiable hatred, and the writings of Milton bear witness to a rancour which is now unknown. The impression left by his *Eikonoklastes*[1] is oppressive. Phrase by phrase, harshly, bitterly, the king is refuted and accused to the last, without a minute's respite of accusation, the accused being credited with not the slightest good intention, the slightest excuse, the least show of justice, the accuser never for an instant digressing to or resting upon a general idea. It is a hand-to-hand fight, where every word takes effect, prolonged, obstinate, without dash and without weakness, full of a harsh and fixed hostility, where the only thought is how to wound most severely and to kill surely. Against the bishops, who were alive and powerful, his hatred flowed more violently still, and the fierceness of his envenomed metaphors hardly suffices to express it. Milton points to them "basking in the sunny warmth of wealth and promotion," like a brood of foul reptiles. "The sour leaven of human traditions, mixed in one putrified mass with the poisonous dregs of hypocrisie in the hearts of Prelates, . . . is the serpent's egg that will hatch an antichrist wheresoever, and ingender the same monster as big or little as the lump is which breeds him."[2]

So much coarseness and dulness was as an outer breastplate, the mark and the protection of the superabundant force and life which coursed in those athletic limbs and chests. Now-a-days, the mind being more refined has become feebler; convictions, being less stern, have become less strong. Attention, freed from the heavy scholastic logic and scriptural tyranny, has be-

---

[1] An answer to the *Eikon Basilike*, a work on the king's side, and attributed to the king. [2] *Of Reformation in England*, 4to, 1641, p. 62.

come more inert. Belief and the will, dissolved by universal tolerance and by the thousand opposing shocks of multiplied ideas, have engendered an exact and refined style, an instrument of conversation and pleasure, and have expelled the poetic and rude style, a weapon of war and enthusiasm. If we have effaced ferocity and dulness, we have diminished force and greatness.

Force and greatness are manifested in Milton, displayed in his opinions and his style, the sources of his belief and his talent. This proud reason aspired to unfold itself without shackles; it demanded that reason might unfold itself without shackles. It claimed for humanity what it coveted for itself, and championed every liberty in his every work. From the first he attacked the corpulent bishops, scholastic upstarts, persecutors of free discussion, pensioned tyrants of Christian conscience.[1] Above the clamour of the Protestant Revolution, his voice was heard thundering against tradition and obedience. He sourly railed at the pedantic theologians, devoted worshippers of old texts, who mistook a mouldy martyrology for a solid argument, and answered a demonstration with a quotation. He declared that most of the Fathers were turbulent and babbling intriguers, that they were not worth more collectively than individually, that their councils were but a pack of underhand intrigues and vain disputes; he rejected their authority and their example, and set up logic as the only interpreter of Scripture.[2] A Puritan as against bishops, an Independent as against Presbyterians, he was always master

[1] *Of Reformation in England.*
[2] The loss of Cicero's works alone, or those of Livy, could not be repaired by all the Fathers of the church.

of his thought and the inventor of his own faith. No one better loved, practised, and praised the free and bold use of reason. He exercised it even rashly and scandalously. He revolted against custom, the illegitimate queen of human belief, the born and relentless enemy of truth, raised his hand against marriage, and demanded divorce in the case of incompatibility of temper. He declared that "error supports custom, custom countenances error; and these two between them, . . . with the numerous and vulgar train of their followers, . . . envy and cry down the industry of free reasoning, under the terms of humour and innovation."[1] He showed that truth "never comes into the world, but like a bastard, to the ignominy of him that brought her forth; till Time, the midwife rather than the mother of truth, have washed and salted the infant, declared her legitimate."[2] He stood out in three or four writings against the flood of insults and anathemas, and dared even more; he attacked the censorship before Parliament, though its own work; he spoke as a man who is wounded and oppressed, for whom a public prohibition is a personal outrage, who is himself fettered by the fetters of the nation. He does not want the pen of a paid "licenser," to insult by its approval the first page of his book. He hates this ignorant and imperious hand, and claims liberty of writing on the same grounds as he claims liberty of thought:—

"What advantage is it to be a man, over it is to be a boy at school, if we have only escaped the ferula, to come under the fescue of an imprimatur? If serious and elaborate writings, as if they were no more than the theme of a grammar-lad under his pedagogue, must not be uttered without the cursory eyes of

[1] *Doctrine and Discipline of Divorce*, Mitford, ii. 4.   [2] *Ibid.* 5.

a temporizing and extemporizing licenser? He who is not trusted with his own actions, his drift not being known to be evil, and standing to the hazard of law and penalty, has no great argument to think himself reputed in the commonwealth wherein he was born for other than a fool or a foreigner. When a man writes to the world, he summons up all his reason and deliberation to assist him; he searches, meditates, is industrious, and likely consults and confers with his judicious friends; after all which done, he takes himself to be informed in what he writes, as well as any that wrote before him; if in this, the most consummate act of his fidelity and ripeness, no years, no industry, no former proof of his abilities, can bring him to that state of maturity, as not to be still mistrusted and suspected, unless he carry all his considerate diligence, all his midnight watchings, and expense of Palladian oil, to the hasty view of an unleisured licenser, perhaps much his younger, perhaps far his inferior in judgment, perhaps one who never knew the labour of book writing; and if he be not repulsed, or slighted, must appear in print like a puny with his guardian, and his censor's hand on the back of his title to be his bail and surety, that he is no idiot or seducer; it cannot be but a dishonour and derogation to the author, to the book, to the privilege and dignity of learning."[1]

Throw open, then, all the doors; let there be light; let every man think, and bring his thoughts to the light. Dread not any diversities of opinion, rejoice in this great work; why insult the labourers by the name of schismatics and sectaries?

"Yet these are the men cried out against for schismatics and sectaries, as if, while the temple of the Lord was building, some cutting, some squaring the marble, others hewing the cedars, there should be a sort of irrational men, who could not consider there must be many schisms and many dissections made in the quarry and in the timber ere the house of God can be built.

[1] *Areopagitica*, Mitford. ii. 423-4.

And when every stone is laid artfully together, it cannot be united into a continuity, it can but be contiguous in this world. neither can every piece of the building be of one form; nay, rather the perfection consists in this, that out of many moderate varieties and brotherly dissimilitudes that are not vastly disproportional, arises the goodly and the graceful symmetry that commends the whole pile and structure."[1]

Milton triumphs here through sympathy; he breaks forth into magnificent images, he displays in his style the force which he perceives around him and in himself. He lauds the revolution, and his praises seem like the blast of a trumpet, to come from a brazen throat:—

"Behold now this vast city, a city of refuge, the mansion-house of liberty, encompassed and surrounded with his protection; the shop of war has not there more anvils and hammers working, to fashion out the plates and instruments of armed justice in defence of beleagured truth, than there be pens and heads there, sitting by their studious lamps, musing, searching, revolving new notions and ideas wherewith to present, as with their homage and their feality, the approaching reformation. . . . What could a man require more from a nation so pliant, and so prone to seek after knowledge? What wants there to such a towardly and pregnant soil, but wise and faithful labourers, to make a knowing people, a nation of prophets, of sages, and of worthies?[2] . . . Methinks I see in my mind a noble and puissant nation rousing herself like a strong man after sleep, and shaking her invincible locks: methinks I see her as an eagle mewing her mighty youth, and kindling her undazzled eyes at the full midday beam; purging and unscaling her long-abused sight at the fountain itself of heavenly radiance; while the whole noise of timorous and flocking birds, with those also that love the twilight, flutter about, amazed at what she means, and in their envious gabble would prognosticate a year of sects and schisms."[3]

[1] *Areopagitica*, Mitford, ii. 439.   [2] *Ibid.* 437-8.   [3] *Ibid.* 441.

It is Milton who speaks, and it is Milton whom he unwittingly describes.

With a sincere writer, doctrines foretell the style. The sentiments and needs which form and govern his beliefs, construct and colour his phrases. The same genius leaves once and again the same impress, in the thought and in the form. The power of logic and enthusiasm which explains the opinions of Milton, explains his genius. The sectary and the writer are one man, and we shall find the faculties of the sectary in the talent of the writer.

When an idea is planted in a logical mind, it grows and fructifies there in a multitude of accessory and explanatory ideas which surround it, entangled among themselves, and form a thicket and a forest. The sentences in Milton are immense; page-long periods are necessary to enclose the train of so many linked arguments, and so many metaphors accumulated around the governing thought. In this great travail, heart and imagination are shaken; Milton exults while he reasons, and the words come as from a catapult, doubling the force of their flight by their heavy weight. I dare not place before a modern reader the gigantic periods which commence the treatise *Of Reformation in England*. We no longer possess this power of breath; we only understand little short phrases; we cannot fix our attention on the same point for a page at a time. We require manageable ideas; we have given up the big two-handed sword of our fathers, and we only carry a light foil. I doubt, however, if the piercing phraseology of Voltaire be more mortal than the cleaving of this iron mace:—

"If in less noble and almost mechanick arts he is not

esteemed to deserve the name of a compleat architect, an excellent painter, or the like, that bears not a generous mind above the peasantly regard of wages and hire; much more must we think him a most imperfect and incompleat Divine, who is so far from being a contemner of filthy lucre; that his whole divinity is moulded and bred up in the beggarly and brutish hopes of a fat prebendary, deanery, or bishoprick." [1]

If Michael Angelo's prophets could speak, it would be in this style; and twenty times while reading it, we may discern the sculptor.

The powerful logic which lengthens the periods sustains the images. If Shakspeare and the nervous poets embrace a picture in the compass of a fleeting expression, break upon their metaphors with new ones, and exhibit successively in the same phrase the same idea in five or six different forms, the abrupt motion of their winged imagination authorises or explains these varied colours and these mingling flashes. More connected and more master of himself, Milton develops to the end the threads which these poets break. All his images display themselves in little poems, a sort of solid allegory, of which all the interdependent parts concentrate their light on the single idea which they are intended to embellish or demonstrate :—

"In this manner the prelates, . . . coming from a mean and plebeian life on a sudden to be lords of stately palaces, rich furniture, delicious fare, and princely attendance, thought the plain and homespun verity of Christ's gospel unfit any longer to hold their lordships' acquaintance, unless the poor threadbare matron were put into better clothes : her chaste and modest veil surrounded with celestial beams, they overlaid with wanton tresses, and in a flaring tire bespeckled her with all the gaudy allurements of a whore." [2]

[1] *Animadversions upon Remonstrants' Defence*, Mitford, i. 234-5.
[2] *Of Reformation in England*, first book, Mitford, i. 23.

Politicians reply that this gaudy church supports royalty.

"What greater debasement can there be to royal dignity, whose towering and steadfast height rests upon the unmovable foundations of justice, and heroic virtue, than to chain it in a dependence of subsisting, or ruining, to the painted battlements and gaudy rottenness of prelatry, which want but one puff of the king's to blow them down like a pasteboard house built of court-cards?"[1]

Metaphors thus sustained receive a singular breadth, pomp, and majesty. They are spread forth without clashing together, like the wide folds of a scarlet cloak, bathed in light and fringed with gold.

Do not take these metaphors for an accident. Milton lavishes them, like a priest who in his worship exhibits splendours and wins the eye, to gain the heart. He has been nourished by the reading of Spenser. Drayton, Shakspeare, Beaumont, all the most sparkling poets; and the golden flow of the preceding age, though impoverished all around him and slackened within himself, has become enlarged like a lake through being dammed up in his heart. Like Shakspeare, he imagines at every turn, and even out of turn, and scandalises the classical and French taste.

" . . . As if they could make God earthly and fleshly, because they could not make themselves heavenly and spiritual; they began to draw down all the divine intercourse betwixt God and the soul, yea, the very shape of God himself, into an exterior and bodily form ; . . . they hallowed it, they fumed up, they sprinkled it, they bedecked it, not in robes of pure innocency, but of pure linen, with other deformed and fantastic dresses, in palls and mitres, and gewgaws fetched from Aaron's old wardrobe,

[1] *Of Reformation in England*, second book, Mitford, i. 42.

or the flamins vestry: then was the priest set to con his motions and his postures, his liturgies and his lurries, till the soul by this means, of overbodying herself, given up justly to fleshly delights, bated her wing apace downward; and finding the ease she had from her visible and sensuous colleague, the body in performance of religious duties, her pinions now broken, and flagging, shifted off from herself the labour of high soaring any more, forgot her heavenly flight, and left the dull and droiling carcase to plod on in the old road, and drudging trade of outward conformity."[1]

If we did not discern here the traces of theological coarseness, we might fancy we were reading an imitator of the *Phædo,* and under the fanatical anger recognise the images of Plato. There is one phrase which for manly beauty and enthusiasm recalls the tone of the *Republic:*—" I cannot praise a fugitive and cloistered virtue unexercised and unbreathed, that never sallies out and sees her adversary, but slinks out of the race where that immortal garland is to be run for, not without dust and heat." [2] But Milton is only Platonic by his richness and exaltation. For the rest, he is a man of the Renaissance, pedantic and harsh; he insults the Pope, who, after the gift of Pepin le Bref, " never ceased baiting and goring the successors of his best lord Constantine, what by his barking curses and excommunications;"[3] he is mythological in his defence of the press, showing that formerly " no envious Juno sat cross-legged over the nativity of any man's intellectual offspring." [4] It matters little: these learned, familiar, grand images, whatever they be, are powerful and natural. Super-

[1] *Of Reformation in England,* book first, Mitford, i. 3.
[2] *Areopagitica,* ii. 411-12.
[3] *Of Reformation in England,* book second, 40.
[4] *Areopagitica,* ii. 406. "Whatsoever time, or the heedless hand of

abundance, like crudity, here only manifests the vigour and lyric dash which Milton's character had foretold.

Passion follows naturally; exaltation brings it with the images. Bold expressions, exaggeration of style, cause us to hear the vibrating voice of the suffering man, indignant and determined.

"For books are not absolutely dead things, but do contain a potency of life in them to be as active as that soul was whose progeny they are; nay, they do preserve as in a vial the purest efficacy and extraction of that living intellect that bred them. I know they are as lively, and as vigorously productive, as those fabulous dragon's teeth: and being sown up and down, may chance to spring up armed men. And yet, on the other hand, unless wariness be used, as good almost kill a man as kill a good book; who kills a man kills a reasonable creature, God's image; but he who destroys a good book, kills reason itself, kills the image of God, as it were, in the eye. Many a man lives a burden to the earth; but a good book is the precious life-blood of a master-spirit, embalmed and treasured up on purpose to a life beyond life. It is true, no age can restore a life, whereof, perhaps there is no great loss; and revolutions of ages do not oft recover the loss of a rejected truth, for the want of which whole nations fare the worse. We should be wary, therefore, what persecution we raise against the living labours of public men, how we spill that seasoned life of man, preserved and stored up in books; since we see a kind of homicide may be thus committed, sometimes a martyrdom; and if it extend to the whole impression, a kind of massacre, whereof the execution ends not in the slaying of an elemental life, but strikes at the ethereal and fifth essence, the breath of reason itself; slays an immortality rather than a life." [1]

blind chance, hath drawn down from of old to this present, in her huge drag-net, whether fish or sea-weed, shells or shrubs, unpicked, unchosen, those are the fathers." (*Of Prelatical Episcopacy*, Mitford, i. 73.)

[1] *Areopagitica, ibid.* ii. 400.

This energy is sublime; the man is equal to the cause, and never did a loftier eloquence match a loftier truth. Terrible expressions overwhelm the book-tyrants, the profaners of thought, the assassins of liberty. "The council of Trent and the Spanish inquisition, engendering together, brought forth or perfected those catalogues and expurging indexes, that rake through the entrails of many an old good author, with a violation worse than any that could be offered to his tomb."[1] Similar expressions lash the carnal minds which believe without thinking, and make their servility into a religion. There is a passage which, by its bitter familiarity, recalls Swift, and surpasses him in all loftiness of imagination and genius:—

"A man may be an heretic in the truth, and if he believes things only because his pastor says so, . . . the very truth he holds becomes his heresy. . . . A wealthy man, addicted to his pleasure and to his profits, finds religion to be a traffic so entangled, and of so many piddling accounts, that of all mysteries he cannot skill to keep a stock going upon that trade. . . . What does he therefore, but resolves to give over toiling, and to find himself out some factor, to whose care and credit he may commit the whole managing of his religious affairs; some divine of note and estimation that must be. To him he adheres, resigns the whole warehouse of his religion, with all the locks and keys, into his custody; and indeed makes the very person of that man his religion. . . . So that a man may say his religion is now no more within himself, but is become a dividual movable, and goes and comes near him, according as that good man frequents the house. He entertains him, gives him gifts, feasts him, lodges him; his religion comes home at night, prays, is liberally supped, and sumptuously laid to sleep; rises, is saluted, and after the malmsey, or some well-spiced bruage, . . .

[1] *Areopagitica*, Mitford, ii. 404.

his religion walks abroad at eight, and leaves his kind entertainer in the shop trading all day without his religion."[1]

He condescended to mock for an instant, with what piercing irony we have seen. But irony, piercing as it may be, seems to him weak.[2] Hear him when he comes to himself, when he returns to open and serious invective, when after the carnal believer he overwhelms the carnal prelate:—

"The table of communion, now become a table of separation, stands like an exalted platform upon the brow of the quire, fortified with bulwark and barricado, to keep off the profane touch of the laics, whilst the obscene and surfeited priest scruples not to paw and mammoc the sacramental bread, as familiarly as his tavern biscuit."[3]

He triumphs in believing that all these profanations are to be avenged. The horrible doctrine of Calvin has once more fixed men's gaze on the dogma of reprobation and everlasting damnation. Hell in hand, Milton menaces; he is drunk with justice and vengeance amid the abysses which he opens, and the brands which he wields:—

"They shall be thrown downe eternally into the *darkest* and *deepest Gulfe* of HELL, where, under the *despightfull controule*, the trample and spurne of all the other *Damned*, that in the anguish of their *Torture* shall have no other ease than to exercise a *Raving* and *Bestiall Tyranny* over them as their *Slaves* and

---

[1] *Areopagitica*, Mitford ii. 431-2.

[2] When he is simply comic, he becomes, like Hogarth and Swift, eccentric, rude, and farcical. "A bishop's foot that has all his toes, maugre the gout, and a linen sock over it, is the aptest emblem of the prelate himself; who, being a pluralist, may, under one surplice, which is also linen, hide four benefices, besides the great metropolitan toe."—*An Apology*, etc., i. 275.

[3] *Of Reformation in England*, Mitford, i. 17.

Negro's, they shall remaine in that plight for ever, the *basest*, the *lowermost*, the *most dejected*, most *underfoot*, and *downe trodden Vassals* of *Perdition*.[1]

Fury here mounts to the sublime, and Michael Angelo's Christ is not more inexorable and vengeful.

Let us fill the measure; let us add, as he does, the prospects of heaven to the visions of darkness; the pamphlet becomes a hymn:

"When I recall to mind at last, after so many dark ages, wherein the huge overshadowing train of error had almost swept all the stars out of the firmament of the church; how the bright and blissful Reformation (by divine power) struck through the black and settled night of ignorance and antichristian tyranny, methinks a sovereign and reviving joy must needs rush into the bosom of him that reads or hears; and the sweet odour of the returning gospel imbathe his soul with the fragrancy of heaven." [2]

Overloaded with ornaments, infinitely prolonged, these periods are triumphant choruses of angelic alleluias sung by deep voices to the accompaniment of ten thousand harps of gold. In the midst of his syllogisms, Milton prays, sustained by the accent of the prophets, surrounded by memories of the Bible, ravished with the splendours of the Apocalypse, but checked on the brink of hallucination by science and logic, on the summit of the calm clear atmosphere, without rising to the burning tracts where ecstasy dissolves reason, with a majesty of eloquence and a solemn grandeur never surpassed, whose perfection proves that he has entered his domain, and gives promise of the poet beyond the prose-writer:—

---

[1] *Of Reformation in England*, Mitford, i. 71. [The old spelling has been retained in this passage.—Tr.] [2] *Ibid.* 4.

"Thou, therefore, that sittest in light and glory unapproachable, parent of angels and men! next, thee I implore, omnipotent King, Redeemer of that lost remnant whose nature thou didst assume, ineffable and everlasting Love! and thou, the third subsistence of divine infinitude, illumining Spirit, the joy and solace of created things! one Tri-personal Godhead! look upon this thy poor and almost spent and expiring church. . . . O let them not bring about their damned designs, . . . to reinvolve us in that pitchy cloud of infernal darkness, where we shall never more see the sun of thy truth again, never hope for the cheerful dawn, never more hear the bird of morning sing."[1]

"O Thou the ever-begotten Light and perfect Image of the Father, . . . Who is there that cannot trace thee now in thy beamy walk through the midst of thy sanctuary, amidst those golden candlesticks, which have long suffered a dimness amongst us through the violence of those that had seized them, and were more taken with the mention of their gold than of their starry light? . . . Come therefore, O thou that hast the seven stars in thy right hand, appoint thy chosen priests according to their orders and courses of old, to minister before thee, and duly to press and pour out the consecrated oil into thy holy and ever-burning lamps. Thou hast sent out the spirit of prayer upon thy servants over all the land to this effect, and stirred up their vows as the sound of many waters about thy throne. . . . O perfect and accomplish thy glorious acts! . . . Come forth out of thy royal chambers, O Prince of all the kings of the earth! put on the visible robes of thy imperial majesty, take up that unlimited sceptre which thy Almighty Father hath bequeathed thee; for now the voice of thy bride calls thee, and all creatures sigh to be renewed."[2]

This song of supplication and joy is an outpouring of

[1] *Of Reformation in England*, Mitford, i. 68-69.
[2] *Animadversions*, etc., *ibid.* 220-2.

splendours; and if we search all literature, we will hardly find a poet equal to this writer of prose.

Is he truly a prose-writer? Entangled dialectics, a heavy and awkward mind, fanatical and ferocious rusticity, an epic grandeur of sustained and superabundant images, the blast and the recklessness of implacable and all-powerful passion, the sublimity of religious and lyric exaltation; we do not recognise in these features a man born to explain, persuade, and prove. The scholasticism and coarseness of the time have blunted or rusted his logic. Imagination and enthusiasm carried him away and enchained him in metaphor. Thus dazzled or marred, he could not produce a perfect work; he did but write useful tracts, called forth by practical interests and actual hate, and fine isolated morsels, inspired by collision with a grand idea, and by the sudden burst of genius. Yet, in all these abandoned fragments, the man shows in his entirety. The systematic and lyric spirit is manifested in the pamphlet as well as in the poem; the faculty of embracing general effects, and of being shaken by them, remains the same in Milton's two careers, and we will see in the *Paradise* and *Comus* what we have met with in the treatise *Of Reformation*, and in the *Animadversions on the Remonstrant*.

VI.

"Milton has acknowledged to me," writes Dryden, "that Spencer was his original." In fact, by the purity and elevation of their morals, by the fulness and connection of their style, by the noble chivalric sentiments, and their fine classical arrangement, they are brothers. But Milton had yet other masters—Beaumont, Fletcher, Burton, Drummond, Ben Jonson, Shakspeare, the whole splendid English Renaissance, and behind it the Italian poesy, Latin antiquity, the fine Greek literature, and all the sources whence the English Renaissance sprang. He continued the great current, but in a manner of his own. He took their mythology, their allegories, sometimes their conceits,[1] and discovered anew their rich colouring, their magnificent sentiment of living nature, their inexhaustible admiration of forms and colours. But, at the same time, he transformed their diction, and employed poetry in a new service. He wrote, not by impulse, and at the mere contact with things, but like a man of letters, a classic, in a scholarlike manner, with the assistance of books, seeing objects as much through previous writings as in themselves, adding to his images the images of others, borrowing and re-casting their inventions, as an artist who unites and multiplies the bosses and driven gold, already entwined on a diadem by twenty workmen. He made thus for himself a composite and brilliant style, less natural than that of his precursors, less fit for effusions, less akin to the lively first glow of sensation, but more solid, more regular, more capable of concentrating in one large patch of light all their sparkle and splendour. He brings together like Æschylus, words of "six cubits," plumed and decked in purple, and makes them pass like a royal train before his idea to exalt and announce it. He introduces to us

"The breathing roses of the wood,
Fair silver-buskin'd nymphs;"[2]

[1] See the *Hymn on the Nativity*; amongst others, the first few strophes. See also *Lycidas*.   [2] *Arcades*, l. 32.

and tells how

> "The gray-hooded Even,
> Like a sad votarist in palmer's weed,
> Rose from the hindmost wheels of Phœbus' wain;"[1]

and speaks of

> "All the sea-girt isles,
> That, like to rich and various gems, inlay
> The unadorned bosom of the deep;"[2]

and

> "That undisturbed song of pure concent,
> Aye sung before the sapphire-colour'd throne,
> To Him that sits thereon,
> With saintly shout, and solemn jubilee;
> Where the bright Seraphim, in burning row,
> Their loud-uplifted angel-trumpets blow."[3]

He gathered into full nosegays the flowers scattered through the other poets:

> "Ye valleys low, where the mild whispers use
> Of shades, and wanton winds, and gushing brooks,
> On whose fresh lap the swart-star sparely looks;
> Throw hither all your quaint enamell'd eyes,
> That on the green turf suck the honied showers,
> And purple all the ground with vernal flowers.
> Bring the rathe primrose that forsaken dies,
> The tufted crow-toe, and pale jessamine,
> The white pink, and the pansy freak'd with jet,
> The glowing violet,
> The musk-rose, and the well-attired woodbine,
> With cowslips wan that hang the pensive head,

---

[1] *Comus*, l. 188-190. [2] *Ibid.* l. 21-23.
[3] *Ode at a Solemn Music*, l. 6-11.

And every flower that sad embroidery wears :
Bid amaranthus all his beauty shed,
And daffadillies fill their cups with tears,
To strew the laureat herse where Lycid lies." [1]

When still quite young, on his quitting Cambridge, he inclined to the magnificent and grand; he wanted a great flowing verse, an ample and sounding strophe, vast periods of fourteen and four-and-twenty lines. He did not face objects on a level, as a mortal, but from on high, like those archangels of Goethe,[2] who embrace at a glance the whole ocean lashing its coasts and the earth rolling on, wrapt in the harmony of the fraternal stars. It was not life that he felt, like the masters of the Renaissance, but grandeur, like Æschylus, and the Hebrew seers,[3] manly and lyric spirits like his own, who, nourished like him in religious emotions and continuous enthusiasm, like him displayed sacerdotal pomp and majesty. To express such a sentiment, images, and poetry addressed only to the eyes, were not enough; sounds also were requisite, and that more introspective poetry which, purged from corporeal shows, could reach the soul. Milton was a musician; his hymns rolled with the slowness of a measured song and the gravity of a declamation; and he seems himself to be describing his art in these incomparable verses, which are evolved like the solemn harmony of an anthem:

" But else, in deep of night, when drowsiness
    Hath lock'd up mortal sense, then listen I
    To the celestial sirens' harmony,

---

[1] *Lycidas, l.* 136-151.   [2] *Faust, Prolog im Himmel.*
[3] See the prophecy against Archbishop Laud in *Lycidas*, l. 130 :
" But that two-handed engine at the door
    Stands ready to smite once, and smite no more."

> That sit upon the nine infolded spheres,
> And sing to those that hold the vital shears,
> And turn the adamantine spindle round,
> On which the fate of Gods and men is wound.
> Such sweet compulsion doth in musick lie,
> To lull the daughters of Necessity,
> And keep unsteady Nature to her law,
> And the low world in measured motion draw
> After the heavenly tune, which none can hear
> Of human mould, with gross unpurged ear." [1]

With his style, his subjects differed; he compacted and ennobled the poet's domain as well as his language, and consecrated his thoughts as well as his words. He who knows the true nature of poetry soon finds, as Milton said a little later, what despicable creatures "libidinous and ignorant poetasters" are, and to what religious, glorious, splendid use poetry can be put in things divine and human. " These abilities, wheresoever they be found are the inspired gift of God, rarely bestowed, but yet to some (though most abuse) in every nation; and are of power, beside the office of a pulpit, to imbreed and cherish in a great people the seeds of virtue and public civility, to allay the perturbations of the mind, and set the affections in right tune; to celebrate in glorious and lofty hymns the throne and equipage of God's almightiness, and what he works, and what he suffers to be wrought with high providence in his church; to sing the victorious agonies of martyrs and saints, the deeds and triumphs of just and pious nations, doing valiantly through faith against the enemies of Christ." [2]

[1] *Arcades*, l. 61–73.
[2] *The Reason of Church Government*, book ii. Mitford, i. 147.

In fact, from the first, at St. Paul's School and at Cambridge, he had written paraphrases of the *Psalms*, then composed odes on the *Nativity, Circumcision,* and the *Passion*. Presently appeared sad poems on the *Death of a Fair Infant, An Epitaph on the Marchioness of Winchester;* then grave and noble verses *On Time, At a solemn Musick,* a sonnet *On his being arrived to the Age of Twenty-three,* " his late spring which no bud or blossom shew'th." At last we have him in the country with his father, and the hopes, dreams, first enchantments of youth, rise from his heart like the morning breath of a summer's day. But what a distance between these calm and bright contemplations and the warm youth, the voluptuous *Adonis* of Shakespeare! He walked, used his eyes, listened; there his joys ended; they are but the poetic joys of the soul:

> " To hear the lark begin his flight,
> And singing, startle the dull night,
> From his watch-tower in the skies,
> Till the dappled dawn doth rise; . . .
> While the plowman, near at hand,
> Whistles o'er the furrow'd land,
> And the milk-maid singeth blithe,
> And the mower whets his sithe,
> And every shepherd tells his tale
> Under the hawthorn in the dale." [1]

To see the village dances and gaiety; to look upon the " high triumphs " and the " busy hum of men " in the " tower'd cities;" above all, to abandon himself to melody, to the divine roll of sweet verse, and the charming dreams which they spread before us in a

[1] *L'Allegro,* l. 41–68.

golden light;—this is all; and presently, as if he had gone too far, to counterbalance this eulogy of visible joys, he summons Melancholy:

> "Come, pensive Nun, devout and pure,
> Sober, stedfast, and demure,
> All in a robe of darkest grain,
> Flowing with majestick train,
> And sable stole of Cypress lawn
> Over thy decent shoulders drawn.
> Come, but keep thy wonted state,
> With even step, and musing gait;
> And looks commercing with the skies,
> Thy rapt soul sitting in thine eyes." [1]

With her he wanders amidst grave thoughts and grave sights, which recall a man to his condition, and prepare him for his duties, now amongst the lofty colonnades of primeval trees, whose "high-embowed roof" retains the silence and the twilight under their shade; now in

> "The studious cloysters pale, . . .
> With antick pillars massy proof,
> And storied windows richly dight,
> Casting a dim religious light;" [2]

now again in the retirement of the study, where the cricket chirps, where the lamp of labour shines, where the mind, alone with the noble minds of the past, may

> "Unsphere
> The spirit of Plato, to unfold
> What worlds or what vast regions hold
> The immortal mind, that hath forsook
> Her mansion in this fleshly nook." [3]

[1] *Il Penseroso, l.* 31–40.   [2] *Ibid. l.* 156–160.   [3] *Ibid. l.* 88–92.

He was filled with this lofty philosophy. Whatever the language he used, English, Italian, or Latin, whatever the kind of verse, sonnets, hymns, stanzas, tragedy or epic, he always returned to it. He praised everywhere chaste love, piety, generosity, heroic force. It was not from scruple, but it was innate in him; his chief need and faculty led him to noble conceptions. He took a delight in admiring, as Shakspeare in creating, as Swift in destroying, as Byron in combating, as Spenser in dreaming. Even on ornamental poems, which were only employed to exhibit costumes and introduce fairy-tales, in Masques, like those of Ben Jonson, he impressed his own character. They were amusements for the castle; he made out of them lectures on magnanimity and constancy: one of them, *Comus,* well worked out, with a complete originality and extraordinary elevation of style, is perhaps his masterpiece, and is simply the eulogy of virtue.

Here at the beginning we are in the heavens. A spirit, descended in the midst of wild woods, repeats this ode:

> "Before the starry threshold of Jove's court
> My mansion is, where those immortal shapes
> Of bright aerial spirits live insphered
> In regions mild of calm and serene air,
> Above the smoke and stir of this dim spot,
> Which men call earth; and, with low-thoughted care
> Confined, and pester'd in this pinfold here,
> Strive to keep up a frail and feverish being,
> Unmindful of the crown that Virtue gives,
> After this mortal change, to her true servants,
> Amongst the enthron'd Gods on sainted seats."[1]

[1] *Comus,* l. 1-II.

Such characters cannot speak: they sing. The drama is an antique opera, composed like the *Prometheus*, of solemn hymns. The spectator is transported beyond the real world. He does not listen to men, but to sentiments. He hears a concert, as in Shakspeare; the *Comus* continues the *Midsummer Night's Dream*, as a choir of deep men's voices continues the glowing and sad symphony of the instruments:

> "Through the perplex'd paths of this drear wood,
> The nodding horror of whose shady brows
> Threats the forlorn and wandering passenger,"[1]

strays a noble lady, separated from her two brothers, troubled by the "sound of riot and ill-managed merriment" which she hears from afar. The son of Circe the enchantress, sensual Comus enters with a charming rod in one hand, his glass in the other, amid the clamour of men and women, with torches in their hands, "headed like sundry sorts of wild beasts;" it is the hour when

> "The sounds and seas, with all their finny drove,
> Now to the moon in wavering morrice move;
> And, on the tawny sands and shelves
> Trip the pert faeries and the dapper elves."[2]

The lady is terrified, and sinks on her knees; and in the misty forms which float above in the pale light, perceives the mysterious and heavenly guardians who watch over her life and honour:

> "O, welcome, pure-eyed Faith; white-handed Hope,
> Thou hovering angel, girt with golden wings;
> And thou, unblemish'd form of Chastity,

[1] *Comus*, l. 37-39.   [2] *Ibid.* l. 115-118.

> I see ye visibly, and now believe
> That He, the Supreme good, t' whom all things ill
> Are but as slavish officers of vengeance,
> Would send a glistering guardian, if need were,
> To keep my life and honour unassail'd.
> Was I deceived, or did a sable cloud
> Turn forth her silver lining on the night?
> I did not err; there does a sable cloud
> Turn forth her silver lining on the night,
> And casts a gleam over this tufted grove."[1]

She calls her brothers in "a soft and solemn-breathing sound," which "rose like a steam of rich distill'd perfumes, and stole upon the air,"[2] across the "violet-embroider'd vale," to the dissolute god whom she enchants. He comes disguised as a "gentle shepherd," and says:

> "Can any mortal mixture of earth's mould
> Breathe such divine, enchanting ravishment?
> Sure something holy lodges in that breast,
> And with these raptures moves the vocal air
> To testify his hidden residence.
> How sweetly did they float upon the wings
> Of silence, through the empty-vaulted night,
> At every fall smoothing the raven down
> Of darkness, till it smiled! I have oft heard
> My mother Circe with the syrens three,
> Amidst the flowery-kirtled Naiades,
> Culling their potent herbs and baleful drugs;
> Who, as they sung, would take the prison'd soul,
> And lap it in Elysium: Scylla wept,
> And chid her barking waves into attention.
> But such a sacred and home-felt delight,
> Such sober certainty of waking bliss,
> I never heard till now."[3]

[1] *Comus*, l. 213–225. [2] *Ibid.* l. 555–557. [3] *Ibid.* l. 244–264.

They were heavenly songs which Comus heard; Milton describes, and at the same time imitates them; he makes us understand the saying of his master Plato, that virtuous melodies teach virtue.

Circe's son has by deceit carried off the noble lady, and seats her, with "nerves all chained up," in a sumptuous palace before a table spread with all dainties. She accuses him, resists, insults him, and the style assumes an air of heroical indignation, to scorn the offer of the tempter.

"When lust,
By unchaste looks, loose gestures, and foul talk,
But most by lewd and lavish act of sin,
Lets in defilement to the inward parts;
The soul grows clotted by contagion,
Imbodies and imbrutes, till she quite lose
The divine property of her first being.
Such are those thick and gloomy shadows damp,
Oft seen in charnel vaults and sepulchres
Lingering, and sitting by a new-made grave,
As loth to leave the body that it loved."[1]

"A cold shuddering dew dips all o'er" Comus; he presents a cup of wine; at the same instant the brothers, led by the attendant Spirit, rush upon him with swords drawn. He flees, carrying off his magic wand. To free the enchanted lady, they summon Sabrina, the benevolent naiad, who sits

"Under the glassy, cool, translucent wave,
In twisted braids of lilies knitting
The loose train of thy (her) amber-dropping hair."[2]

The "goddess of the silver lake" rises lightly from her

[1] *Comus*, *l*. 463-473. It is the elder brother who utters these lines when speaking of his sister.—TR. [2] *Ibid*. *l*. 861-863.

"coral-paven bed," and her chariot "of turkis blue and emerald-green," sets her down

> "By the rushy-fringed bank,
> Where grows the willow, and the osier dank."[1]

Sprinkled by this cool and chaste hand, the lady leaves the "venom'd seat" which held her spell-bound; the brothers, with their sister, reign peacefully in their father's palace; and the Spirit, who has conducted all, pronounces this ode, in which poetry leads up to philosophy; the voluptuous light of an Oriental legend beams on the Elysium of the good, and all the splendours of nature assemble to render virtue more seductive.

> "To the ocean now I fly,
> And those happy climes that lie
> Where day never shuts his eye
> Up in the broad fields of the sky:
> There I suck the liquid air
> All amidst the gardens fair
> Of Hesperus, and his daughters three
> That sing about the golden tree:
> Along the crisped shades and bowers
> Revels the spruce and jocund spring;
> The Graces, and the rosy-bosom'd Hours,
> Thither all their bounties bring;
> There eternal Summer dwells,
> And west winds, with musky wing,
> About the cedar'n alleys fling
> Nard and cassia's balmy smells.
> Iris there with humid bow
> Waters the odorous banks, that blow
> Flowers of more mingled hew
> Than her purfled scarf can shew;

[1] *Comus*, l. 890.

> And drenches with Elysian dew
> (List, mortals, if your ears be true)
> Beds of hyacinth and roses,
> Where young Adonis oft reposes,
> Waxing well of his deep wound
> In slumber soft ; and on the ground
> Sadly sits the Assyrian queen :
> But far above in spangled sheen
> Celestial Cupid, her famed son, advanced
> Holds his dear Psyche sweet entranced
> After her wandering labours long,
> Till free consent the gods among
> Make her his eternal bride,
> And from her fair unspotted side
> Two blissful twins are to be born,
> Youth and Joy ; so Jove hath sworn.
> But now my task is smoothly done,
> I can fly, or I can run
> Quickly to the green earth's end,
> Where the bow'd welkin slow doth bend ;
> And from thence can soar as soon
> To the corners of the moon.
> Mortals, that would follow me,
> Love Virtue, she alone is free :
> She can teach ye how to climb
> Higher than the sphery chime ;
> Or, if Virtue feeble were,
> Heaven itself would stoop to her."[1]

Ought I to have pointed out the awkwardnesses, strangenesses, exaggerated expressions, the inheritance of the Renaissance, a philosophical quarrel, the work of a reasoner and a Platonist ? I did not perceive these faults. All was effaced before the spectacle of the bright

[1] *Comus*, l. 976-1023.

Renaissance, transformed by austere philosophy, and of sublimity worshipped upon an altar of flowers.

That, I think, was his last profane poem. Already, in the one which followed, *Lycidas*, celebrating in the style of Virgil the death of a beloved friend,[1] he suffers Puritan wrath and prepossessions to shine through, inveighs against the bad teaching and tyranny of the bishops, and speaks of "that two-handed engine at the door, ready to smite (but) once, and smite no more." On his return from Italy, controversy and action carried him away; prose begins, poetry is arrested. From time to time a patriotic or religious sonnet breaks the long silence; now to praise the chief Puritans, Cromwell, Vane, Fairfax; now to celebrate the death of a pious lady, or the life of a "virtuous young lady;" once to pray God "to avenge his slaughter'd saints," the unhappy Protestants of Piedmont, "whose bones lie scatter'd on the Alpine mountains cold;" again, on his second wife, dead a year after their marriage, his well-beloved "saint"—"brought to me, like Alcestis, from the grave, . . . came, vested all in white, pure as her mind;" loyal friendships, sorrows bowed to or subdued, aspirations generous or stoical, which reverses did but purify. Old age came; cut off from power, action, even hope, he returned to the grand dreams of his youth. As of old, he went out of this lower world in search of the sublime; for the actual is petty, and the familiar seems dull. He selects his new characters on the verge of sacred antiquity, as he selected his old ones on the verge of fabulous antiquity, because distance adds to their stature; and habit, ceasing to measure, ceases also to depreciate them. Just now we had creatures of fancy:

[1] Edward King died in 1637.

Joy, daughter of Zephyr and Aurora; Melancholy, daughter of Vesta and Saturn; Comus, son of Circe, ivy-crowned, god of echoing woods and turbulent excess. Now we have Samson, the despiser of giants, the elect of Israel's God, the destroyer of idolaters, Satan and his peers, Christ and his angels; they come and rise before our eyes like superhuman statues; and their far removal, rendering vain our curious hands, preserves our admiration and their majesty. We rise further and higher, to the origin of things, amongst eternal beings, to the commencement of thought and life, to the battles of God, in this unknown world where sentiments and existences, raised above the ken of man, elude his judgment and criticism to command his veneration and awe; the sustained song of solemn verse unfolds the actions of these shadowy figures; and then we experience the same emotion as in a cathedral, while the music of the organ rolls along among the arches, and amidst the brilliant light of the tapers clouds of incense hide from our view the colossal columns.

But if the heart remains unchanged, the genius has become transformed. Manliness has supplanted youth. The richness has decreased, the severity has increased. Seventeen years of fighting and misfortune have steeped his soul in religious ideas. Mythology has yielded to theology; the habit of discussion has ended by subduing the lyric flight; accumulated learning by choking the original genius. The poet no more sings sublime verse, he relates or harangues, in grave verse. He no longer invents a personal style; he imitates antique tragedy or epic. In *Samson Agonistes* he hits upon a cold and lofty tragedy, in *Paradise Regained* on a cold and noble epic; he composes an imperfect and sublime poem in *Paradise Lost*.

Would to Heaven he could have written it as he tried, in the shape of a drama, or better, as the *Prometheus* of Æschylus, as a lyric opera! A peculiar kind of subject demands a peculiar kind of style; if you resist, you destroy your work, too happy if, in the deformed medley, chance produces and preserves a few beautiful fragments. To bring the supernatural upon the scene, you must not continue in your every-day mood; if you do, you look as if you did not believe in it. Vision reveals it, and the style of vision must express it. When Spenser writes, he dreams. We listen to the happy concerts of his aerial music, and the varying train of his fanciful apparitions unfolds like a vapour before our accommodating and dazzled gaze. When Dante writes, he is rapt; and his cries of anguish, his transports, the incoherent succession of his infernal or mystical phantoms, carry us with him into the invisible world which he describes. Ecstasy alone renders visible and credible the objects of ecstasy. If you tell us of the exploits of the Deity as you tell us of Cromwell's, in a grave and lofty tone, we do not see God; and as He constitutes the whole of your poem, we do not see anything. We conclude that you have accepted a tradition, that you adorn it with the fictions of your mind, that you are a preacher, not a prophet, a decorator not a poet. We find that you sing of God as the vulgar pray to him, after a formula learnt, not from spontaneous emotion. Change your style, or, rather if you can, change your emotion. Try and discover in yourself the ancient fervour of psalmists and apostles, to recreate the divine legend, to experience the sublime agitations by which the inspired and disturbed mind perceives God; then the grand lyric verse will roll on, laden with splendours. Thus roused, we shall not have to examine whether it be Adam or Messiah who speaks; we shall not have to demand that they shall be real, and constructed by the hand of a psychologist; we shall not trouble ourselves with their puerile or unlooked for actions; we shall be carried away, we shall share in your creative madness; we shall be drawn onward by the flow of bold images, or raised by the combination of gigantic metaphors; we shall be moved like Æschylus, when his thunder-stricken Prometheus hears the universal concert of rivers, seas, forests, and created beings, lament with him,[1] as David before Jehovah, for whom a thousand years are but as yesterday, who "carriest them away as with a flood; in the morning they are like grass which groweth up."[2]

But the age of metaphysical inspiration, long gone by, had not yet reappeared. Far in the past Dante was fading away; far in the future Goethe lay unrevealed. People saw not yet the pantheistic *Faust,* and that incomprehensible nature which absorbs all varying existence in her deep bosom; they saw no longer the mystic paradise and immortal Love, whose ideal light envelopes souls redeemed. Protestantism had neither altered nor renewed the divine nature; the guardian of an accepted creed and ancient tradition, it had only transformed ecclesiastical

---

[1] ὦ δῖος αἰθὴρ καὶ ταχύπτεροι πνοαί
ποταμῶν τε πηγαί, ποντίων τε κυμάτων
ἀνήριθμον γέλασμα, παμμῆτόρ τε γῆ,
καὶ τὸν πανόπτην κύκλον ἡλίου καλῶ,
ἴδεσθέ μ', οἷα πρὸς θεῶν πάσχω θεός.
Prometheus Vinctus, ed. Hermann, p. 487, line 88.—Tr

[2] Ps. xc. 5.

discipline and the doctrine of grace. It had only called the Christian to personal salvation and freedom from priestly rule. It had only remodelled man, it had not re-created the Deity. It could not produce a divine epic, but a human epic. It could not sing the battles and works of God, but the temptations and salvation of the soul. At the time of Christ came the poems of cosmogony; at the time of Milton, the confessions of psychology. At the time of Christ each imagination produced a hierarchy of supernatural beings, and a history of the world; at the time of Milton, every heart recorded the series of its upliftings, and the history of grace. Learning and reflection led Milton to a metaphysical poem which was not the natural offspring of the age, whilst inspiration and ignorance revealed to Bunyan the psychological narrative which suited the age, and the great man's genius was feebler than the tinker's simplicity.

And why? Because Milton's poem, whilst it suppresses lyrical illusion, admits critical inquiry. Free from enthusiasm we judge his characters; we demand that they shall be living, real, complete, harmonious, like those of a novel or a drama. No longer hearing odes, we would see objects and souls: we ask that Adam and Eve should act in conformity with their primitive nature; that God, Satan, and Messiah should act and feel in conformity with their superhuman nature. Shakspeare would scarcely have been equal to the task; Milton, the logician and reasoner, failed in it. He gives us correct solemn discourse, and gives us nothing more; his characters are speeches, and in their sentiments we find only heaps of puerilities and contradictions.

Adam and Eve, the first pair! I approach, and it seems as though I discovered the Adam and Eve of

Raphael Sanzio, imitated by Milton, so his biographers tell us, glorious, strong voluptuous children, naked in the light of heaven, motionless and absorbed before grand landscapes, with bright vacant eyes, with no more thought than the bull or the horse on the grass beside them. I listen, and I hear an English household, two reasoners of the period—Colonel Hutchinson and his wife. Good Heavens! dress them at once. People with so much culture should have invented before all a pair of trousers and modesty. What dialogues! Dissertations capped by politeness, mutual sermons concluded by bows. What bows! Philosophical compliments and moral smiles. I yielded, says Eve,

> "And from that time see
> How beauty is excell'd by manly grace
> And wisdom, which alone is truly fair." [1]

Dear learned poet, you would have been better pleased if one of your three wives, as an apt pupil, had uttered to you by way of conclusion the above solid theoretical maxim. They did utter it to you; this is a scene from your own household:

> "So spake our general mother; and, with eyes
> Of conjugal attraction unreproved
> And meek surrender, half-embracing lean'd
> On our first father; half her swelling breast
> Naked met his, under the flowing gold
> Of her loose tresses hid; he, in delight
> Both of her beauty and submissive charms,
> Smiled with superiour love, . . . and press'd her matron lip
> With kisses pure." [2]

[1] *Paradise Lost*, book iv. l. 489.   [2] *Ibid.* l. 492-502.

This Adam entered Paradise *via* England. In that country he learned respectability, and studied moral speechifying. Let us hear this man before he has tasted of the tree of knowledge. A bachelor of arts, in his inaugural address, could not utter more fitly and nobly a greater number of pithless sentences:

> " Fair consort, the hour
> Of night, and all things now retired to rest,
> Mind us of like repose; since God hath set
> Labour and rest, as day and night, to men
> Successive; and the timely dew of sleep,
> Now falling with soft slumbrous weight, inclines
> Our eyelids; other creatures all day long
> Rove idle, unemploy'd, and less need rest:
> Man hath his daily work of body or mind
> Appointed, which declares his dignity,
> And the regard of Heaven on all his ways;
> While other animals unactive range,
> And of their doings God takes no account." [1]

A very useful and excellent Puritanical exhortation! This is English virtue and morality; and at evening, in every family, it can be read to the children like the Bible. Adam is your true paterfamilias, with a vote, an M.P., an old Oxford man, consulted at need by his wife, dealing out to her with prudent measure the scientific explanations which she requires. This night, for instance, the poor lady had a bad dream, and Adam, in his trencher-cap, administers this learned psychological draught: [2]

---

[1] *Paradise Lost*, book iv. *l.* 610-622.
[2] It would be impossible that a man so learned, so argumentative, should spend his whole time in gardening and making up nosegays.

> "Know, that in the soul
> Are many lesser faculties that serve
> Reason as chief; among these Fancy next
> Her office holds; of all external things,
> Which the five watchful senses represent,
> She forms imaginations, aery shapes
> Which Reason, joining or disjoining, frames
> All what we affirm or what deny, and call
> Our knowledge or opinion. . . .
> Oft in her absence mimic fancy wakes
> To imitate her; but, misjoining shapes,
> Wild work produces oft, and most in dreams;
> Ill matching words and deeds long past or late." [1]

Here was something to send Eve off to sleep again. Her husband noting the effect, adds like an accredited casuist:

> "Yet be not sad:
> Evil into the mind of God or man
> May come and go, so unapproved; and leave
> No spot or blame behind." [2]

We recognise the Protestant husband, his wife's confessor. Next day comes an angel on a visit. Adam tells Eve:

> "Go with speed,
> And, what thy stores contain, bring forth, and pour
> Abundance, fit to honour and receive
> Our heavenly stranger.[3]

She, like a good housewife, talks about the *menu*, and rather proud of her kitchen-garden, says:

> He
> Beholding shall confess, that here on earth
> God hath dispensed his bounties as in heaven." [4]

---

[1] *Paradise Lost*, book v. *l.* 100–113. [2] *Ibid. l.* 116–119.
[3] *Ibid. l.* 313-316. [4] *Ibid. l.* 328–330.

Mark this becoming zeal of a hospitable lady. She goes "with dispatchful looks, in haste":

> "What choice to choose for delicacy best;
> What order, so contrived as not to mix
> Tastes, not well join'd, inelegant; but bring
> Taste after taste upheld with kindliest change." [1]

She makes sweet wine, perry, creams; scatters flowers and leaves under the table. What an excellent housewife! What a great many votes she will gain among the country squires, when Adam stands for Parliament. Adam belongs to the Opposition, is a Whig, a Puritan.

> He "walks forth; without more train
> Accompanied than with his own complete
> Perfections: in himself was all his state,
> More solemn than the tedious pomp that waits
> On princes, when their rich retinue long
> Of horses led, and grooms besmeared with gold,
> Dazzles the crowd." [2]

The epic is changed into a political poem, and we have just heard an epigram against power. The preliminary ceremonies are somewhat long; fortunately, the dishes being uncooked, "no fear lest dinner cool." The angel, though ethereal, eats like a Lincolnshire farmer:

> "Nor seemingly
> The angel, nor in mist, the common gloss
> Of theologians; but with keen dispatch
> Of real hunger, and concoctive heat
> To transubstantiate: what redounds, transpires
> Through spirits with ease." [3]

At table Eve listens to the angel's stories, then dis-

---

[1] *Paradise Lost*, book v. l. 333-336.
[2] *Ibid.* l. 351-357.   [3] *Ibid.* l. 434-439.

creetly rises at dessert, when they are getting into politics. English ladies may learn by her example to perceive from their lord's faces when they are "entering on studious thoughts abstruse." The sex does not mount so high. A wise lady prefers her husband's talk to that of strangers. "Her husband the relater she prefered." Now Adam hears a little treatise on astronomy. He concludes, like a practical Englishman:

> "But to know
> That which before us lies in daily life,
> Is the prime wisdom: what is more, is fume,
> Or emptiness, or fond impertinence;
> And renders us, in things that most concern,
> Unpractised, unprepared, and still to seek." [1]

The angel gone, Eve, dissatisfied with her garden, wishes to have it improved, and proposes to her husband to work in it, she on one side, he on the other. He says, with an approving smile:

> "Nothing lovelier can be found
> In woman, than to study household good,
> And good works in her husband to promote." [2]

But he fears for her, and would keep her at his side. She rebels with a little prick of proud vanity, like a young lady who mayn't go out by herself. She has her way, goes alone and eats the apple. Here interminable speeches come down on the reader, as numerous and cold as winter showers. The speeches of Parliament after Pride's Purge were hardly heavier. The serpent seduces Eve by a collection of arguments worthy of

[1] *Paradise Lost*, book viii. *l.* 192–197.
[2] *Ibid.* book ix. *l.* 232.

the punctilious Chillingworth, and then the syllogistic mist enters her poor brain:

> "His forbidding
> Commends thee more, while it infers the good
> By thee communicated, and our want:
> For good unknown sure is not had; or, had
> And yet unknown, is as not had at all. . . .
> Such prohibitions bind not."[1]

Eve is from Oxford too, has also learned law in the inns about the Temple, and wears, like her husband, the doctor's trencher-cap.

The flow of dissertations never ceases; from Paradise it gets into heaven: neither heaven nor earth, nor hell itself, would swamp it.

Of all characters which man could bring upon the scene, God is the finest. The cosmogonies of peoples are sublime poems, and the artists' genius does not attain perfection until it is sustained by such conceptions. The Hindoo sacred poems, the Biblical prophecies, the Edda, the Olympus of Hesiod and Homer, the visions of Dante, are glowing flowers from which a whole civilisation blooms, and every emotion vanishes before the terrible feeling through which they have leapt from the bottom of our heart. Nothing then can be more depressing than the degradation of these noble ideas, settling into the regularity of formulas, and under the discipline of a popular worship. What is smaller than a god sunk to the level of a king and a man? what more repulsive than the Hebrew Jehovah, defined by theological pedantry, governed in his actions by the last manual of doctrine, petrified by literal interpretation?

[1] *Paradise Lost*, book ix. *l.* 753–760.

Milton's Jehovah is a grave king, who maintains a suitable state, something like Charles I. When we meet him for the first time, in Book III., he is holding council, and setting forth a matter of business. From the style we see his grand furred cloak, his pointed Vandyke beard, his velvet-covered throne and golden dais. The business concerns a law which does not act well, and respecting which he desires to justify his rule. Adam is about to eat the apple: why have exposed Adam to the temptation? The royal orator discusses the question, and shows the reason;

> " I made him just and right,
> Sufficient to have stood, though free to fall.
> Such I created all the ethereal powers
> And spirits, both them who stood and them who fail'd. . . .
> Not free, what proof could they have given sincere
> Of true allegiance, constant faith, or love?
> Where only, what they needs must do, appear'd,
> Not what they would: what praise could they receive?
> What pleasure I from such obedience paid?
> When will and reason (reason also is choice),
> Useless and vain, of freedom both despoil'd,
> Made passive both, had served necessity,
> Not me. They therefore, as to right belong'd,
> So were created, nor can justly accuse
> Their Maker, or their making, or their fate;
> As if predestination over-ruled
> Their will, disposed by absolute decree
> Or high foreknowledge: they themselves decreed
> Their own revolt, not I: if I foreknew,
> Foreknowledge had no influence on their fault,
> Which had no less proved certain unforeknown.
> So without least impulse or shadow of fate,
> Or aught by me immutably foreseen,

> They trespass, authors to themselves in all,
> Both what they judge and what they choose."[1]

The modern reader is not so patient as the Thrones, Seraphim, and Dominations; this is why I stop halfway in the royal speech. We perceive that Milton's Jehovah is connected with the theologian James I., versed in the arguments of Arminians and Gomarists, very clever at the *distinguo*, and, before all, incomparably tedious. He must pay his councillors of state very well if he wishes them to listen to such tirades. His son answers him respectfully in the same style. Goethe's God, half abstraction, half legend, source of calm oracles, a vision just beheld after a pyramid of ecstatic strophes,[2] greatly excels this Miltonic God, a business man, a schoolmaster, an ostentatious man! I honour him too much in giving him these titles. He deserves a worse name, when he sends Raphael to warn Adam that Satan intends him some mischief:

> "This let him know,
> Lest, wilfully transgressing, he pretend
> Surprisal, unadmonish'd, unforewarn'd."[3]

This Miltonic Deity is only a schoolmaster, who, foreseeing the fault of his pupil, tells him beforehand the grammar rule, so as to have the pleasure of scolding him without discussion. Moreover, like a good politician, he had a second motive, just as with his angels, "For state, as Sovran King; and to inure our prompt obedience." The word is out; we see what Milton's heaven is: a Whitehall filled with bedizened footmen. The

---

[1] *Paradise Lost*, book iii. *l*. 98–123.
[2] End of the continuation of *Faust*. *Prologue in Heaven*.
[3] *Paradise Lost*, book v. *l*. 243.

angels are the choristers, whose business is to sing cantatas about the king and before the king, keeping their places as long as they obey, alternating all night long to sing "melodious hymns about the sovran throne." What a life for this poor king! and what a cruel condition, to hear eternally his own praises![1] To amuse himself, Milton's Deity decides to crown his son king—partner-king, if you prefer it. Read the passage, and say if it be not a ceremony of his time that the poet describes:

> "Ten thousand thousand ensigns high advanced,
> Standards and gonfalons 'twixt van and rear
> Stream in the air, and for distinction serve
> Of hierarchies, of orders, and degrees;
> Or in their glittering tissues bear imblazed
> Holy memorials, acts of zeal and love
> Recorded eminent;"[2]

doubtless the capture of a Dutch vessel, the defeat of the Spaniards in the Downs. The king brings forward his son, "anoints" him, declares him "his great vicegerent:"

> "To him shall bow
> All knees in heaven. . . . Him who disobeys,
> Me disobeys;"[3]

and such were, in fact, expelled from heaven the same

[1] We are reminded of the history of Ira in Voltaire, condemned to hear without intermission or end the praises of four chamberlains, and the following hymn:
> "Que son mérite est extrême!
> Que de grâces, que de grandeur.
> Ah! combien monseigneur
> Doit être content de lui-même!

[2] *Paradise Lost,* book v. *l.* 588–594. [3] *Ibid. l.* 607–612.

day. "All seem'd well pleased; all seem'd, but were not all." Yet

> "That day, as other solemn days, they spent
> In song and dance about the sacred hill. . . .
> Forthwith from dance to sweet repast they turn
> Desirous."[1]

Milton describes the tables, the dishes, the wine, the vessels. It is a popular festival; I miss the fireworks, the bell-ringing, as in London, and I can fancy that all would drink to the health of the new king. Then Satan revolts; he takes his troops to the other end of the country, like Lambert or Monk, toward "the quarters of the north," Scotland perhaps, passing through well-governed districts, "empires," with their sheriffs and lord-lieutenants. Heaven is partitioned off like a good map. Satan holds forth before his officers against royalty, opposes in a word-combat the good royalist Abdiel, who refutes his "blasphemous, false, and proud" arguments, and quits him to rejoin his prince at Oxford. Well armed, the rebel marches with his pikemen and artillery to attack the fortress.[2] The two parties slash each other with the sword, mow each other down with cannon, knock each other down with political arguments. These sorry angels have their mind as well disciplined as their limbs; they have passed their

---

[1] *Paradise Lost*, book v. l. 617–631.

[2] The Miltonic Deity is so much on the level of a king and man, that he uses (with irony certainly) words like these :
> "Lest unawares we lose
> This our high place, our Sanctuary, our Hill."

His son, about to flesh his maiden sword, replies :
> "If I be found the worst in heaven," etc.
> Book v. 731-742.

youth in a class of logic and in a drill school. Satan holds forth like a preacher:

> "What heaven's Lord had powerfulest to send
> Against us from about his throne, and judged
> Sufficient to subdue us to his will,
> But proves not so : then fallible, it seems,
> Of future we may deem him, though till now
> Omniscient thought."[1]

He also talks like a drill-sergeant. "Vanguard, to right and left the front unfold." He makes quips as clumsy as those of Harrison, the former butcher turned officer. What a heaven! It is enough to disgust a man with Paradise; any one would rather enter Charles I.'s troop of lackeys, or Cromwell's Ironsides. We have orders of the day, a hierarchy, exact submission, extra-duties, disputes, regulated ceremonials, prostrations, etiquette, furbished arms, arsenals, depots of chariots and ammunition. Was it worth while leaving earth to find in heaven carriage-works, buildings, artillery, a manual of tactics, the art of salutations, and the Almanac de Gotha? Are these the things which "eye hath not seen, nor ear heard, nor hath entered into the heart to conceive?" What a gap between this monarchical frippery[2] and the visions of Dante, the souls floating like stars amid the harmonies, the mingled splendours, the mystic roses radiating and vanishing in the azure, the impalpable world in which

---

[1] *Paradise Lost*, book vi. *l*. 425-430.

[2] When Raphael comes on earth, the angels who are "under watch," "in honour rise." The disagreeable and characteristic feature of this heaven is, that the universal motive is obedience, while in Dante's it is love. "Lowly reverent they bow. . . . Our happy state we hold, like yours, while our obedience holds."

all the laws of earthly life are dissolved, the unfathomable abyss traversed by fleeting visions, like golden bees gliding in the rays of the deep central sun! Is it not a sign of extinguished imagination, of the inroad of prose, of the birth of practical genius, replacing metaphysics by morality? What a fall! To measure it, read a true Christian poem, the Apocalypse. I copy half-a-dozen verses; think what it has become in the hands of the imitator:

"And I turned to see the voice that spake with me. And being turned, I saw seven golden candlesticks;

"And in the midst of the seven candlesticks, one like unto the Son of man, clothed with a garment down to the foot, and girt about the paps with a golden girdle.

"His head and his hairs were white like wool, as white as snow; and his eyes were as a flame of fire;

"And his feet like unto fine brass, as if they burned in a furnace; and his voice as the sound of many waters.

"And he had in his right hand seven stars: and out of his mouth went a sharp two edged sword: and his countenance was as the sun shineth in his strength.

"And when I saw him, I fell at his feet as dead."[1]

When Milton was arranging his celestial show, he did not fall as dead.

But if the innate and inveterate habits of logical argument, joined with the literal theology of the time, prevented him from attaining to lyrical illusion or from creating living souls, the splendour of his grand imagination, combined with the passions of Puritanism, furnished him with an heroic character, several sublime hymns, and scenery which no one has surpassed. The finest

---

[1] Rev. i. 12.

thing in connection with this Paradise is hell; and in this history of God, the chief part is taken by the devil. The ridiculous devil of the middle-age, a horned enchanter, a dirty jester, a petty and mischievous ape, band-leader to a rabble of old women, has become a giant and a hero. Like a conquered and banished Cromwell, he remains admired and obeyed by those whom he has drawn into the abyss. If he continues master, it is because he deserves it; firmer, more enterprising, more scheming than the rest, it is always from him that deep counsels, unlooked-for resources, courageous deeds, proceed. It was he who invented "deep-throated engines . . . disgorging, . . . chained thunderbolts, and hail of iron globes," and won the second day's victory; he who in hell roused his dejected troops, and planned the ruin of man; he who, passing the guarded gates and the boundless chaos, amid so many dangers, and across so many obstacles, made man revolt against God, and gained for hell the whole posterity of the new-born. Though defeated, he prevails, since he has won from the monarch on high the third part of his angels, and almost all the sons of his Adam. Though wounded, he triumphs, for the thunder which smote his head left his heart invincible. Though feebler in force, he remains superior in nobility, since he prefers suffering independence to happy servility, and welcomes his defeat and his torments as a glory, a liberty, and a joy. These are the proud and sombre political passions of the constant though oppressed Puritans; Milton had felt them in the vicissitudes of war, and the emigrants who had taken refuge amongst the wild beasts and savages of America, found them strong and energetic in the depths of their hearts.

"Is this the region, this the soil, the clime,
Said then the lost Archangel, this the seat
That we must change for heaven? this mournful gloom
For that celestial light? Be it so, since he,
Who now is Sovran, can dispose and bid
What shall be right: farthest from him is best,
Whom reason has equal'd, force hath made supreme
Above his equals. Farewell, happy fields,
Where joy for ever dwells! Hail, horrours; hail,
Infernal world! and thou, profoundest hell,
Receive thy new possessor; one who brings
A mind not to be changed by place or time.
The mind is its own place, and in itself
Can make a heaven of hell, a hell of heaven.
What matter where, if I be still the same,
And what I should be; all but less than he
Whom thunder hath made greater? Here at least
We shall be free; the Almighty hath not built
Here for his envy; will not drive us hence:
Here we may reign secure; and in my choice
To reign is worth ambition, though in hell:
Better to reign in hell, than serve in heaven."[1]

This sombre heroism, this harsh obstinacy, this biting irony, these proud stiff arms which clasp grief as a mistress, this concentration of invincible courage which, cast on its own resources, finds everything in itself, this power of passion and sway over passion,—

"The unconquerable will,
And study of revenge, immortal hate,
And courage never to submit or yield,
And what is else not to be overcome,"[2]

are features proper to the English character and to

[1] *Paradise Lost*, book i. *l.* 242-263.   [2] *Ibid. l.* 106-109.

English literature, and you will find them later on in Byron's Lara and Conrad.

Around the fallen angel, as within him, all is great. Dante's hell is but a hall of tortures, whose cells, one below another, descend to the deepest wells. Milton's hell is vast and vague.

> " A dungeon horrible on all sides round
> As one great furnace flamed, yet from those flames
> No light, but rather darkness visible
> Served only to discover sights of woe,
> Regions of sorrow, doleful shades.[1] . . .
>
> Beyond this flood a frozen continent
> Lies dark and wild, beat with perpetual storms
> Of whirlwind and dire hail, which on firm land
> Thaws not, but gathers heap, and ruin seems
> Of ancient pile."[2]

The angels gather, innumerable legions:

> " As when heaven's fire
> Hath scathed the forest oaks or mountain pines,
> With singed top their stately growth, though bare,
> Stands on the blasted heath."[3]

Milton needs the grand and infinite; he lavishes them. His eyes are only content in limitless space, and he produces colossal figures to fill it. Such is Satan wallowing on the surges of the livid sea:

> "In bulk as huge . . . as . . . that sea-beast
> Leviathan, which God of all his works
> Created hugest that swim the ocean stream:
> Him, haply, slumbering on the Norway foam,

---

[1] *Paradise Lost*, book i. *l.* 61-65.
[2] *Ibid.* book ii. *l.* 587-591.   [3] *Ibid.* book i. *l.* 612-615.

>   The pilot of some small night-founder'd skiff,
>   Deeming some island, oft, as seamen tell,
>   With fixed anchor in his scaly rind
>   Moors by his side under the lee, while night
>   Invests the sea, and wished morn delays." [1]

Spenser has discovered images just as fine, but he has not the tragic gravity which the idea of hell impresses on a Protestant. No poetic creation equals in horror and grandeur the spectacle that greeted Satan on leaving his dungeon:

>   " At last appear
>   Hell bounds, high reaching to the horrid roof,
>   And thrice threefold the gates; three folds were brass,
>   Three iron, three of adamantine rock,
>   Impenetrable, impaled with circling fire,
>   Yet unconsumed. Before the gates there sat
>   On either side a formidable shape;
>   The one seem'd woman to the waist, and fair,
>   But ended foul in many a scaly fold
>   Voluminous and vast, a serpent arm'd
>   With mortal sting: about her middle round
>   A cry of hell hounds never ceasing bark'd
>   With wide Cerberean mouths full loud, and rung
>   A hideous peal: yet, when they list, would creep,
>   If aught disturb'd their noise, into her womb,
>   And kennel there; yet there still bark'd and howl'd
>   Within unseen. . . . The other shape,
>   If shape it might be call'd, that shape had none
>   Distinguishable in member, joint, or limb,
>   Or substance might be call'd that shadow seem'd,
>   For each seem'd either: black it stood as night,
>   Fierce as ten furies, terrible as hell,
>   And shook a dreadful dart; what seem'd his head

---

[1] *Paradise Lost*, book i. *l.* 196-208.

> The likeness of a kingly crown had on.
> Satan was now at hand, and from his seat
> The monster moving onward came as fast,
> With horrid strides; hell trembled as he strode.
> The undaunted fiend what this might be admired,
> Admired, not fear'd."[1]

The heroic glow of the old soldier of the Civil Wars animates the infernal battle; and if anyone were to ask why Milton creates things greater than other men, I should answer, because he has a greater heart.

Hence the sublimity of his scenery. If I did not fear the paradox, I should say that this scenery was a school of virtue. Spenser is a smooth glass, which fills us with calm images. Shakspeare is a burning mirror, which overpowers us, repeatedly, with multiplied and dazzling visions. The one distracts, the other disturbs us. Milton raises our mind. The force of the objects which he describes passes into us; we become great by sympathy with their greatness. Such is the effect of his description of the Creation. The calm and creative command of the Messiah leaves its trace in the heart which listens to it, and we feel more vigour and moral health at the sight of this great work of wisdom and will:

> " On heavenly ground they stood; and from the shore
> They view'd the vast immeasurable abyss
> Outrageous as a sea, dark, wasteful, wild,
> Up from the bottom turn'd by furious winds
> And surging waves, as mountains, to assault
> Heaven's highth, and with the centre mix the pole.
> ' Silence, ye troubled waves, and thou deep, peace,'
> Said then the omnific Word: ' your discord end !' . . .

[1] *Paradise Lost*, book ii. *l.* 643-678.

> Let there be light, said God; and forthwith light
> Ethereal, first of things, quintessence pure,
> Sprung from the deep; and from her native east
> To journey through the aery gloom began,
> Sphered in a radiant cloud. . . .
> The earth was form'd; but in the womb as yet
> Of waters, embryon immature involved,
> Appear'd not: over all the face of earth
> Main ocean flow'd, not idle, but, with warm
> Prolific humour softening all her globe,
> Fermented the great mother to conceive,
> Satiate with genial moisture, when God said,
> 'Be gather'd now, ye waters under heaven,
> Into one place, and let dry land appear.'
> Immediately the mountains huge appear
> Emergent, and their broad bare backs upheave
> Into the clouds, their tops ascend the sky:
> So high as heaved the tumid hills, so low
> Down sunk a hollow bottom broad and deep,
> Capacious bed of waters: thither they
> Hasted with glad precipitance, uproll'd,
> As drops on dust conglobing from the dry."[1]

This is primitive scenery; immense bare seas and mountains, as Raphael Sanzio outlines them in the background of his biblical paintings. Milton embraces the general effects, and handles the whole as easily as his Jehovah.

Let us quit superhuman and fanciful spectacles. A simple sunset equals them. Milton peoples it with solemn allegories and regal figures, and the sublime is born in the poet, as just before it was born from the subject:—

[1] *Paradise Lost*, book vii. *l.* 210-292.

> "The sun, now fallen . . .
> Arraying with reflected purple and gold
> The clouds that on his western throne attend :
> Now came still evening on, and twilight gray
> Had in her sober livery all things clad ;
> Silence accompanied, for beast and bird,
> They to their grassy couch, these to their nests,
> Were slunk, all but the wakeful nightingale ;
> She all night long her amorous descant sung ;
> Silence was pleased : now glowed the firmament
> With living sapphires : Hesperus, that led
> The starry host, rode brightest, till the moon,
> Rising in clouded majesty, at length,
> Apparent queen, unveiled her peerless light,
> And o'er the dark her silver mantle threw." [1]

The changes of the light become here a religious procession of vague beings who fill the soul with veneration. So sanctified, the poet prays. Standing by the "inmost bower" of Adam and Eve, he says :—

> "Hail wedded love, mysterious law, true source
> Of human offspring, sole propriety
> In Paradise of all things common else !
> By thee adulterous lust was driven from men
> Among the bestial herds to range by thee,
> Founded in reason, loyal, just, and pure,
> Relations dear, and all the charities
> Of father, son, and brother, first were known." [2]

He justifies it by the example of saints and patriarchs. He immolates before it "the bought smile" and "court-amours, mix'd dance, or wanton mask, or midnight ball, or serenate." We are a thousand miles from Shakspeare; and in this Protestant eulogy of the

---

[1] *Paradise Lost*, book iv. *l.* 591-609. [2] *Ibid. l.* 750-757.

family tie, of lawful love, of "domestic sweets," of orderly piety and of home, we perceive a new literature and an altered time.

A strange great man, and a strange spectacle! He was born with the instinct of noble things; and this instinct, strengthened in him by solitary meditation, by accumulated knowledge, by stern logic, becomes changed into a body of maxims and beliefs which no temptation could dissolve, and no reverse shake. Thus fortified, he passes life as a combatant, as a poet, with courageous deeds and splendid dreams, heroic and rude, chimerical and impassioned, generous and calm, like every self-contained reasoner, like every enthusiast, insensible to experience and enamoured of the beautiful. Thrown by the chance of a revolution into politics and theology, he demands for others the liberty which his powerful reason requires, and strikes at the public fetters which impede his personal energy. By the force of his intellect, he is more capable than any one of accumulating science; by the force of his enthusiasm, he is more capable than any of experiencing hatred. Thus armed, he throws himself into controversy with all the clumsiness and barbarism of the time; but this proud logic displays its arguments with a marvellous breadth, and sustains its images with an unwonted majesty: this lofty imagination, after having spread over his prose an array of magnificent figures, carries him into a torrent of passion even to the height of the sublime or excited ode—a sort of archangel's song of adoration or vengeance. The chance of a throne preserved, then re-established, led him, before the revolution took place, into pagan and moral poetry, after the revolution into Christian and moral verse.

In both he aims at the sublime, and inspires admiration; because the sublime is the work of enthusiastic reason, and admiration is the enthusiasm of reason. In both, he arrives at his point by the accumulation of splendours, by the sustained fulness of poetic song, by the greatness of his allegories, the loftiness of his sentiments, the description of infinite objects and heroic emotions. In the first, a lyrist and a philosopher, with a wider poetic freedom, and the creator of a stronger poetic illusion, he produces almost perfect odes and choruses. In the second, an epic writer and a Protestant, enslaved by a strict theology, robbed of the style which makes the supernatural visible, deprived of the dramatic sensibility which creates varied and living souls, he accumulates cold dissertations, transforms man and God into orthodox and vulgar machines, and only regains his genius in endowing Satan with his republican soul, in multiplying grand landscapes and colossal apparitions, in consecrating his poetry to the praise of religion and duty.

Placed, as it happened, between two ages, he participates in their two characters, as a stream which, flowing between two different soils, is tinged by both their hues. A poet and a Protestant, he receives from the closing age the free poetic afflatus, and from the opening age the severe political religion. He employed the one in the service of the other, and displayed the old inspiration in new subjects. In his works we recognise two Englands: one impassioned for the beautiful, devoted to the emotions of an unshackled sensibility and the fancies of pure imagination, with no law but the natural feelings, and no religion but natural belief; willingly pagan, often immoral; such as it is exhibited by Ben Jonson, Beaumont, Fletcher, Shakspeare, Spenser, and the superb harvest of poets which covered the ground for a space of fifty years; the other fortified by a practical religion, void of metaphysical invention, altogether political worshipping rule, attached to measured, sensible, useful, narrow opinions, praising the virtues of the family, armed and stiffened by a rigid morality, driven into prose, raised to the highest degree of power, wealth, and liberty. In this sense, this style and these ideas are monuments of history; they concentrate, recall, or anticipate the past and the future; and in the limits of a single work are found the events and the feelings of several centuries and of a whole nation.

BOOK III.
THE CLASSIC AGE.

CHAPTER I.

The Restoration.

1. The Roisterers.

When we alternately look at the works of the court painters of Charles I. and Charles II., and pass from the noble portraits of Van Dyck to the figures of Lely, the fall is sudden and great; we have left a palace, and we light on a bagnio.

Instead of the proud and dignified lords, at once cavaliers and courtiers, instead of those high-born yet simple ladies who look at the same time princesses and modest maidens, instead of that generous and heroic company, elegant and resplendent, in whom the spirit of the Renaissance yet survived, but who already displayed the refinement of the modern age, we are confronted by perilous and importunate courtesans, with an expression either vile or harsh, incapable of shame or of remorse.[1] Their plump smooth hands toy

---

[1] See especially the portraits of Lady Morland, Lady Williams, the countess of Ossory, the Duchess of Cleveland, Lady Price, and many others.

fondlingly with dimpled fingers; ringlets of heavy hair fall on their bare shoulders; their swimming eyes languish voluptuously; an insipid smile hovers on their sensual lips. One is lifting a mass of dishevelled hair which streams over the curves of her rosy flesh; another falls down with languor, and uncloses a sleeve whose soft folds display the full whiteness of her arms. Nearly all are half-draped; many of them seem to be just rising from their beds; the rumpled dressing-gown clings to the neck, and looks as though it were soiled by a night's debauch; the tumbled under-garment slips down to the hips: their feet tread the bright and glossy silk. With bosoms uncovered, they are decked out in all the luxurious extravagance of prostitutes; diamond girdles, puffs of lace, the vulgar splendour of gilding, a superfluity of embroidered and rustling fabrics, enormous head-dresses, the curls and fringes of which, rolled up and sticking out, compel notice by the very height of their shameless magnificence. Folding curtains hang round them in the shape of an alcove, and the eyes penetrate through a vista into the recesses of a wide park, whose solitude will not ill serve the purpose of their pleasures.

I.

All this came by way of contrast; Puritanism had brought on an orgie, and fanatics had talked down virtue. For many years the gloomy English imagination, possessed by religious terrors, had desolated the life of men. Conscience had become disturbed at the thought of death and dark eternity; half-expressed doubts stealthily swarmed within like a bed of thorns, and the sick heart, starting at every motion, had ended by taking a disgust at all its pleasures, and abhorred all its natural instincts. Thus poisoned at its very beginning, the divine sentiment of justice became a mournful madness. Man, confessedly perverse and condemned, believed himself pent in a prison-house of perdition and vice, into which no effort and no chance could dart a ray of light, except a hand from above should come by free grace, to rend the sealed stone of this tomb. Men lived the life of the condemned, amid torments and anguish, oppressed by a gloomy despair, haunted by spectres. People would frequently imagine themselves at the point of death; Cromwell himself, according to Dr. Simcott, physician in Huntingdon, " had fancies about the Town Cross;"[1] some would feel within them the motions of an evil spirit; one and all passed the night with their eyes glued to the tales of blood and the impassioned appeals of the Old Testament, listening to the threats and thunders of a terrible God, and renewing in their own hearts the ferocity of murderers and the exaltation of seers. Under such a strain reason gradually left them. They continually were seeking after the Lord, and found but a dream. After long hours of exhaustion, they laboured under a warped and overwrought imagination. Dazzling forms, unwonted ideas, sprang up on a sudden in their heated brain; these men were raised and penetrated by extraordinary emotions. So transformed, they knew themselves no longer; they did not ascribe to themselves these violent and sudden inspirations which were forced upon them, which compelled them to leave the beaten tracks, which had no connection one with another, which shook and enlightened them when least expected, without being able

[1] Oliver Cromwell's *Letters and Speeches*, ed. by Carlyle, 1866, i. 39.—Tr.

either to check or to govern them; they saw in them the agency of a supernatural power, and gave themselves up to it with the enthusiasm of madness and the stubbornness of faith.

To crown all, fanaticism had become an institution; the sectary had laid down all the steps of mental transfiguration, and reduced the encroachment of his dream to a theory: he set about methodically to drive out reason and enthrone ecstasy. George Fox wrote its history, Bunyan gave it its laws, Parliament presented an example of it, all the pulpits lauded its practice. Artisans, soldiers, women discussed it, mastered it, excited one another by the details of their experience and the publicity of their exaltations. A new life was inaugurated which had blighted and excluded the old. All secular tastes were suppressed, all sensual joys forbidden; the spiritual man alone remained standing upon the ruins of the past, and the heart, debarred from all its natural safety-valves, could only direct its views or aspirations towards a sinister Deity. The typical Puritan walked slowly along the streets, his eyes raised towards heaven, with elongated features, yellow and haggard, with closely cropt hair, clad in brown or black, unadorned, clothed only to cover his nakedness. If a man had round cheeks, he passed for lukewarm.[1] The whole body, the exterior, the very tone of voice, all must wear the sign of penitence and divine grace. A Puritan spoke slowly, with a solemn and somewhat nasal tone of voice, as if to destroy the vivacity of conversation and the melody of the natural voice. His speech stuffed with scriptural quotations, his style borrowed from the prophets, his name and the

[1] Colonel Hutchinson was at one time held in suspicion because he wore long hair and dressed well.

names of his children drawn from the Bible, bore witness that his thoughts were confined to the terrible world of the seers and ministers of divine vengeance. From within, the contagion spread outwards. The fears of conscience were converted into laws of the state. Personal asceticism grew into public tyranny. The Puritan proscribed pleasure as an enemy, for others as well as for himself. Parliament closed the gambling-houses and theatres, and had the actors whipped at the cart's tail; oaths were fined; the May-trees were cut down; the bears, whose fights amused the people, were put to death; the plaster of Puritan masons reduced nude statues to decency; the beautiful poetic festivals were forbidden. Fines and corporal punishments shut out, even from children, games, dancing, bell-ringing, rejoicings, junketings, wrestling, the chase, all exercises and amusements which might profane the Sabbath. The ornaments, pictures, and statues in the churches were pulled down or mutilated. The only pleasure which they retained and permitted was the singing of psalms through the nose, the edification of long sermons, the excitement of acrimonious controversies, the harsh and sombre joy of a victory gained over the enemy of mankind, and of the tyranny exercised against the demon's supposed abettors. In Scotland, a colder and sterner land, intolerance reached the utmost limits of ferocity and pettiness, instituting a surveillance over the private life and home devotions of every member of a family, depriving Catholics of their children, imposing the abjuration of Popery under pain of perpetual imprisonment or death, dragging crowds of witches[1] to the

[1] 1648; thirty in one day. One of them confessed that she had been at a gathering of more than five hundred witches.

stake.[1] It seemed as though a black cloud had weighed down the life of man, drowning all light, wiping out all beauty, extinguishing all joy, pierced here and there by the glitter of the sword and by the flickering of torches, beneath which one might perceive the indistinct forms of gloomy despots, of bilious sectarians, of silent victims.

II.

After the Restoration a deliverance ensued. Like a checked and choked up stream, public opinion dashed with all its natural force and all its acquired momentum, into the bed from which it had been debarred. The

---

[1] In 1652, the kirk-session of Glasgow "brot boyes and servants before them, for breaking the sabbath, and other faults. They had clandestine censors, and gave money to some for this end."—Note 28, taken from *Wodrow's Analecta;* Buckle, *History of Civilization in England*, 3 vols. 1867, iii. 208.

Even early in the eighteenth century, "the most popular divines" in Scotland affirmed that Satan "frequently appears clothed in a corporeal substance."—*Ibid.* iii. 233, note 76, taken from *Memoirs of C. L. Lewes.*

"No husband shall kiss his wife, and no mother shall kiss her child on the Sabbath day."—Note 135. *Ibid.* iii. 253; from Rev. C. J. Lyon's *St. Andrews*, vol. i. 458, with regard to government of a colony. [It would have been satisfactory if Mr. Lyon had given his authority.]—Tr.

"(Sept. 22, 1649) The quhilk day the Sessioune caused mak this act, that ther sould be no pypers at brydels," etc.—*Ibid.* iii. 258, note 153. In 1719, the Presbytery of Edinburgh indignantly declares: "Yea, some have arrived at that height of impiety, as not to be ashamed of washing in waters, and swimming in rivers upon the holy Sabbath."—Note 187. *Ibid.* iii. 266.

"I think David had never so sweet a time as then, when he was pursued as a partridge by his son Absalom."—Note 190. Gray's *Great and Precious Promises.*

See the whole of Chapter iii. vol. iii., in which Buckle has described, by similar quotations, the condition of Scotland, chiefly in the seventeenth century.

outburst carried away the dams. The violent return to the senses drowned morality. Virtue had the semblance of Puritanism. Duty and fanaticism became mingled in common disrepute. In this great reaction, devotion and honesty, swept away together, left to mankind but the wreck and the mire. The more excellent parts of human nature disappeared; there remained but the animal, without bridle or guide, urged by his desires beyond justice and shame.

When we see these manners through the medium of a Hamilton or a Saint-Évremond, we can tolerate them. Their French varnish deceives us. Debauchery in a Frenchman is only half disgusting; with him, if the animal breaks loose, it is without abandoning itself to excess. The foundation is not, as with the Englishman, coarse and powerful. You may break the glittering ice which covers him, without bringing down upon yourself the swollen and muddy torrent that roars beneath his neighbour;[1] the stream which will issue from it will only have its petty dribblings, and will return quickly and of itself to its accustomed channel. The Frenchman is mild, naturally refined, little inclined for great or gross sensuality, liking a sober style of talk, easily armed against filthy manners by his delicacy and good taste. The Count de Grammont has too much wit to love an orgie. After all an orgie is not pleasant; the breaking of glasses, brawling, lewd talk, excess in eating and drinking,—there is nothing in this very tempting to a rather delicate taste: the Frenchman, after Grammont's type, is born an epicurean, not a glutton or a drunkard. What he seeks is amusement, not unre-

[1] See, in Richardson, Swift, and Fielding, but particularly in Hogarth, the delineation of brutish debauchery.

strained joy or bestial pleasure. I know full well that he is not without reproach. I would not trust him with my purse, he forgets too readily the distinction between *meum* and *tuum;* above all, I would not trust him with my wife: he is not over-delicate; his escapades at the gambling-table and with women smack too much of the sharper and the briber. But I am wrong to use these big words in connection with him; they are too weighty, they crush so delicate and so pretty a specimen of humanity. These heavy habits of honour or shame can only be worn by serious-minded men, and Grammont takes nothing seriously, neither his fellowmen, nor himself, nor vice, nor virtue. To pass his time agreeably is his sole endeavour. "They had said good-bye to dulness in the army," observed Hamilton, "as soon as he was there." That is his pride and his aim; he troubles himself, and cares for nothing beside. His valet robs him; another would have brought the rogue to the gallows; but the theft was clever, and he keeps his rascal. He left England forgetting to marry the girl he was betrothed to; he is caught at Dover; he returns and marries her: this was an amusing *contre-temps;* he asks for nothing better. One day, being penniless, he fleeces the Count de Caméran at play. "Could Grammont, after the figure he had once cut, pack off like any common fellow? By no means; he is a man of feeling; he will maintain the honour of France." He covers his cheating at play with a joke; in reality, his notions of property are not over-clear. He regales Caméran with Caméran's own money; would Caméran have acted better or otherwise? What matter if his money be in Grammont's purse or his own? The main point is gained, since there is pleasure in getting the money, and there is pleasure in spending it. The hateful and the ignoble vanish from such a life. If he pays his court to princes, you may be sure it is not on his knees; so lively a soul is not weighed down by respect, his wit places him on a level with the greatest; under pretext of amusing the king, he tells him plain truths.[1] If he finds himself in London, surrounded by open debauchery, he does not plunge into it; he passes through on tiptoe, and so daintily that the mire does not stick to him. We do not recognise any longer in his anecdotes the anguish and the brutality which were really felt at that time; the narrative flows on quickly, raising a smile, then another, and another yet, so that the whole mind is brought by an adroit and easy progress to something like good humour. At table, Grammont will never stuff himself; at play, he will never grow violent; with his mistress, he will never give vent to coarse talk; in a duel, he will not hate his adversary. The wit of a Frenchman is like French wine; it makes men neither brutal, nor wicked, nor gloomy. Such is the spring of these pleasures: a supper will destroy neither delicacy, nor good nature, nor enjoyment. The libertine remains sociable, polite, obliging; his gaiety culminates only in the gaiety of others;[2] he is attentive to them as naturally as to himself; and in addition, he is ever on the alert and intelligent: repartees, flashes of brilliancy, witticisms,

---

[1] The king was playing at backgammon; a doubtful throw occurs: "Ah, here is Grammont, who'll decide for us; Grammont, come and decide." "Sire, you have lost." "What: you do not yet know."... "Ah, Sire, if the throw had been merely doubtful, these gentlemen would not have failed to say you had won."

[2] Hamilton says of Grammont, "He sought out the unfortunate only to succour them."

sparkle on his lips; he can think at table and in company, sometimes better than if alone or fasting. It is clear that with him debauchery does not extinguish the man; Grammont would say that it perfects him; that wit, the heart, the senses, only arrive at excellence and true enjoyment, amid the elegance and animation of a choice supper.

III.

It is quite the contrary in England. When we scratch the covering of an Englishman's morality, the brute appears in its violence and its deformity. One of the English statesmen said that with the French an unchained mob could be led by words of humanity and honour,[1] but that in England it was necessary, in order to appease them, to throw to them raw flesh. Insults, blood, orgie, that is the food on which the mob of noblemen, under Charles II., precipitated itself. All that excuses a carnival was absent; and, in particular, wit. Three years after the return of the king, Butler published his *Hudibras;* and with what *éclat* his contemporaries only could tell, while the echo of applause is kept up even to our own days. How low is the wit, with what awkwardness and dulness he dilutes his revengeful satire. Here and there lurks a happy picture, the remnant of a poetry which has just perished; but the whole work reminds one of a Scarron, as unworthy as the other, and more malignant. It is written, people say, on the model of Don Quixote; Hudibras is a Puritan knight, who goes about, like his antitype, redressing wrongs, and pocketing beatings. It would be truer to say that it

[1] This saying sounds strange after the horrors of the Commune.—Tr.

resembles the wretched imitation of Avellaneda.[1] The short metre, well suited to buffoonery, hobbles along without rest and limpingly, floundering in the mud which it delights in, as foul and as dull as that of the *Enéide Travestie*.[2] The description of Hudibras and his horse occupies the best part of a canto; forty lines are taken up by describing his beard, forty more by describing his breeches. Endless scholastic discussions, arguments as long as those of the Puritans, spread their wastes and briars over half the poem. No action, no simplicity, all is would-be satire and gross caricature; there is neither art, nor harmony, nor good taste to be found in it; the Puritan style is converted into an absurd gibberish; and the engalled rancour, missing its aim by its mere excess, spoils the portrait it wishes to draw. Would you believe that such a writer gives himself airs, wishes to enliven us, pretends to be funny? What delicate raillery is there in this picture of Hudibras' beard!

> " His tawny beard was th' equal grace
> Both of his wisdom and his face ;
> In cut and die so like a tile,
> A sudden view it would beguile :
> The upper part whereof was whey,
> The nether orange, mix'd with grey.
> This hairy meteor did denounce
> The fall of sceptres and of crowns :

[1] A Spanish author, who continued and imitated Cervantes' *Don Quixote*.

[2] A work by Scarron. *Hudibras*, ed. Z. Grey, 1801, 2 vols., i. canto i. *l*. 289, says also :
> " For as Æneas bore his sire
> Upon his shoulders through the fire,
> Our knight did bear no less a pack
> Of his own buttocks on his back.

>With grisly type did represent
>Declining age of government,
>And tell with hieroglyphic spade
>Its own grave and the state's were made."[1]

Butler is so well satisfied with his insipid fun, that he prolongs it for a good many lines:

>"Like Samson's heart-breakers, it grew
>In time to make a nation rue;
>Tho' it contributed its own fall,
>To wait upon the public downfall. . . .
>'Twas bound to suffer persecution
>And martyrdom with resolution;
>T' oppose itself against the hate
>And vengeance of the incens'd state,
>In whose defiance it was worn,
>Still ready to be pull'd and torn,
>With red-hot irons to be tortur'd,
>Revil'd, and spit upon, and martyr'd.
>Maugre all which, 'twas to stand fast
>As long as monarchy should last;
>But when the state should hap to reel,
>'Twas to submit to fatal steel,
>And fall, as it was consecrate,
>A sacrifice to fall of state,
>Whose thread of life the fatal sisters
>Did twist together with its whiskers,
>And twine so close, that time should never,
>In life or death, their fortunes sever;
>But with his rusty sickle mow
>Both down together at a blow."[2]

The nonsense increases as we go on. Could any one have taken pleasure in humour such as this?—

[1] *Hudibras*, part i. canto i. *l.* 241-250. [2] *Ibid. l.* 253-280.

> "This sword a dagger had, his page,
> That was but little for his age;
> And therefore waited on him so
> As dwarfs upon knights-errant do. . . .
> When it had stabb'd, or broke a head,
> It would scrape trenchers, or chip bread. . . .
> 'Twould make clean shoes, and in the earth
> Set leeks and onions, and so forth." [1]

Everything becomes trivial; if any beauty presents itself, it is spoiled by burlesque. To read those long details of the kitchen, those servile and crude jokes, people might fancy themselves in the company of a common buffoon in the market-place; it is the talk of the quacks on the bridges, adapting their imagination and language to the manners of the beer-shop and the hovel. There is filth to be met with there; indeed, the rabble will laugh when the mountebank alludes to the disgusting acts of private life.[2] Such is the grotesque stuff in which the courtiers of the Restoration delighted; their spite and their coarseness took a

[1] *Hudibras*, part i. canto i. *l.* 375–386.

[2] "Quoth Hudibras, I smell a rat.
  Ralpho, thou dost prevaricate;
  For though the thesis which thou lay'st
  Be true *ad amussim* as thou say'st
  (For that bear-baiting should appear
  Jure divino lawfuller
  Than Synods are, thou do'st deny,
  Totidem verbis; so do I),
  Yet there is fallacy in this;
  For if by sly *homœosis,*
  Tussis pro crepitu, an art
  . . .
  Thou wouldst sophistically imply,
  Both are unlawful, I deny."
  Part i. canto i. *l.* 821–834.

pleasure in the spectacle of these bawling puppets; even now, after two centuries, we hear the ribald laughter of this audience of lackeys.

IV.

Charles II., when at his meals, ostentatiously drew Grammont's attention to the fact that his officers served him on their knees. They were in the right; it was their fit attitude. Lord Chancellor Clarendon, one of the most honoured and honest men of the Court, learns suddenly and in full council that his daughter Anne is *enceinte* by the Duke of York, and that the Duke, the king's brother, has promised her marriage. Listen to the words of this tender father; he has himself taken care to hand them down:

"The Chancellor broke out into a very immoderate passion against the wickedness of his daughter, and said with all imaginable earnestness, 'that as soon as he came home, he would turn her (his daughter) out of his house as a strumpet to shift for herself, and would never see her again.'"[1]

Observe that this great man had received the news from the king unprepared, and that he made use of these fatherly expressions on the spur of the moment. He added, "that he had much rather his daughter should be the duke's whore than his wife." Is this not heroical? But let Clarendon speak for himself. Only such a true monarchical heart can surpass itself:

"He was ready to give a positive judgment, in which he hoped their lordships would concur with him; that the king should immediately cause the woman to be sent to the Tower,

[1] *The Life of Clarendon*, ed. by himself, new ed., 1827, 3 vols., i. 378.

and to be cast into a dungeon under so strict a guard, that no person living should be admitted to come to her; and then that an act of Parliament should be immediately passed for the cutting off her head, to which he would not only give his consent, but would very willingly be the first man that should propose it." [1]

What Roman virtue! Afraid of not being believed he insists; whoever knew the man, will believe that all this came from the very bottom of his heart. He is not yet satisfied; he repeats his advice; he addresses to the king different conclusive reasonings, in order that they might cut off the head of his daughter:

"I had rather submit and bear it (this disgrace) with all humility, than that it should be repaired by making her his wife, the thought whereof I do so much abominate, that I had much rather see her dead, with all the infamy that is due to her presumption." [2]

In this manner, a man, who is in difficulty, can keep his salary and his Chancellor's robes. Sir Charles Berkley, captain of the Duke of York's guards, did better still; he solemnly swore "that he had lain with the young lady," and declared himself ready to marry her "for the sake of the duke, though he knew well the familiarity the duke had with her." Then, shortly afterwards, he confessed that he had lied, but with a good intention, in all honour, in order to save the royal family from such a *mésalliance*. This admirable self-sacrifice was rewarded; he soon had a pension from the privy purse, and was created Earl of Falmouth. From the first, the baseness of the public corporations rivalled that of individuals. The House

[1] *The Life of Clarendon*, i. 379. [2] *Ibid.* i. 380.

of Commons, but recently master of the country, still full of Presbyterians, rebels, and conquerors, voted "that neither themselves nor the people of England could be freed from the horrid guilt of the late unnatural rebellion, or from the punishment which that guilt merited, unless they formally availed themselves of his majesty's grace and pardon, as set forth in the declaration of Breda." Then all these heroes went in a body and threw themselves with contrition at the sacred feet of their monarch. In this universal prostration it seemed that no one had any courage left. The king became the hireling of Louis XIV., and sold his country for a large pension. Ministers, members of Parliament, ambassadors, all received French money. The contagion spread even to patriots, to men noted for their purity, to marytrs. Lord William Russell intrigued with Versailles; Algernon Sidney accepted 500 guineas. They had not discrimination enough to retain a show of spirit; they had not spirit enough to retain a show of honour.[1]

In men thus laid bare, the first thing that strikes you is the bloodthirsty instinct of brute beasts. Sir John

[1] "Mr. Evelyn tells me of several of the menial servants of the Court lacking bread, that have not received a farthing wages since the King's coming in."—*Pepys' Diary*, ed. Lord Braybrooke, 3d ed., 1848, 5 vols., iv. April 26, 1667.

"Mr. Povy says that to this day the King do follow the women as much as he ever did ; that the Duke of York . . . . hath come out of his wife's bed, and gone to others laid in bed for him ; . . . . that the family (of the Duke) is in horrible disorder by being in debt by spending above £60,000 per annum, when he hath not £40,000" (*Ibid.* iv. June 23, 1667).

"It is certain that, as it now is, the seamen of England, in my conscience, would, if they could, go over and serve the king of France or Holland rather than us" (*Ibid.* iv. June 25, 1667).

Coventry, a member of Parliament, let some word escape him, which was construed into a reproach of the royal amours. His friend, the Duke of Monmouth, contrived that he should be treacherously assaulted under the king's command, by respectable men devoted to his service, who slit his nose to the bone. A vile wretch of the name of Blood tried to assassinate the Duke of Ormond, and to stab the keeper of the Tower, in order to steal the crown jewels. Charles II., considering that this was an interesting and distinguished man of his kind, pardoned him, gave him an estate in Ireland, and admitted him to his presence, side by side with the Duke of Ormond, so that Blood became a sort of hero, and was received in good society. After such splendid examples, men dared everything. The Duke of Buckingham, a lover of the Countess of Shrewsbury, slew the Earl in a duel; the Countess, disguised as a page, held Buckingham's horse, while she embraced him, covered as he was with her husband's blood; and the murderer and adulteress returned publicly, and as triumphantly, to the house of the dead man. We can no longer wonder at hearing Count Königsmark describe as a "peccadillo" an assassination which he had committed by waylaying his victim. I transcribe a duel out of Pepys, to give a notion of the manners of these bloodthirsty cut-throats. Sir H. Bellassis and Tom Porter, the greatest friends in the world, were talking together:

"and Sir H. Bellassis talked a little louder than ordinary to Tom Porter, giving of him some advice. Some of the company standing by said, 'What! are they quarrelling, that they talk so high?' Sir H. Bellassis, hearing it, said, 'No!' says he: 'I would have you know I never quarrel, but I strike: and take that as a rule of mine!' 'How?' says Tom Porter, 'strike! I would I could see the man in England that durst give me a blow!' with that Sir H. Bellassis did give him a box of the ears; and so they were going to fight there, but were hindered. . . . Tom Porter, being informed that Sir H. Bellassis' coach was coming, went down out of the coffee-house where he staid for the tidings, and stopped the coach, and bade Sir H. Bellassis come out. 'Why,' says H. Bellassis, 'you will not hurt me coming out, will you?' 'No,' says Tom Porter. So out he went, and both drew. . . . They wounded one another, and Sir H. Bellassis so much that it is feared he will die"—[1] which he did ten days after.

Bull-dogs like these took no pity on their enemies. The Restoration opened with a butchery. The Lords conducted the trials of the republicans with a shamelessness of cruelty and an excess of rancour that were extraordinary. A sheriff struggled with Sir Harry Vane on the scaffold, rummaging his pockets, and taking from him a paper which he attempted to read. During the trial of Major-General Harrison, the hangman was placed by his side, in a black dress, with a rope in his hand; they sought to give him a full enjoyment of the foretaste of death. He was cut down alive from the gibbet, and disembowelled; he saw his entrails cast into the fire; he was then quartered, and his still beating heart was torn out and shown to the people. The cavaliers gathered round for amusement. Here and there one of them would do worse even than this. Colonel Turner, seeing them quarter John Coke, the lawyer, told the sheriff's men to bring Hugh Peters, another of the condemned, nearer; the executioner came up, and rubbing his bloody hands, asked the unfortunate man

[1] *Pepys' Diary*, vol. iv., 29th July 1667.

if the work pleased him. The rotting bodies of Cromwell, Ireton and Bradshaw were dug up in the night, and their heads fixed on poles over Westminster Hall. Ladies went to see these disgusting sights; the good Evelyn applauded them; the courtiers made songs on them. These people were fallen so low, that they did not even turn sick at it. Sight and smell no longer aided humanity by producing repugnance; their senses were as dead as their hearts.

From carnage they threw themselves into debauchery. You should read the life of the Earl of Rochester, a courtier and a poet, who was the hero of the time. His manners were those of a lawless and wretched mountebank; his delight was to haunt the stews, to debauch women, to write filthy songs and lewd pamphlets; he spent his time between gossiping with the maids of honour, broils with men of letters, the receiving of insults, the giving of blows. By way of playing the gallant, he eloped with his wife before he married her. Out of a spirit of bravado, he declined fighting a duel, and gained the name of a coward. For five years together he was said to be drunk. The spirit within him failing of a worthy outlet, plunged him into adventures more befitting a clown. Once with the Duke of Buckingham he rented an inn on the Newmarket road, and turned innkeeper, supplying the husbands with drink and defiling their wives. He introduced himself, disguised as an old woman, into the house of a miser, robbed him of his wife, and passed her on to Buckingham. The husband hanged himself; they made very merry over the affair. At another time he disguised himself as a chairman, then as a beggar, and paid court to the gutter-girls. He ended by turning a quack astrologer, and vendor of drugs for procuring abortion, in the suburbs. It was the licentiousness of a fervid imagination, which fouled itself as another would have adorned it, which forced its way into lewdness and folly as another would have done into sense and beauty. What can come of love in hands like these? We cannot copy even the titles of his poems; they were written only for the haunts of vice. Stendhal said that love is like a dried up bough cast into a mine; the crystals cover it, spread out into filagree work, and end by converting the worthless stick into a sparkling tuft of the purest diamonds. Rochester begins by depriving love of all its adornment, and to make sure of grasping it, converts it into a stick. Every refined sentiment, every fancy; the enchantment, the serene, sublime glow which transforms in a moment this wretched world of ours; the illusion which, uniting all the powers of our being, shows us perfection in a finite creature, and eternal bliss in a transient emotion,—all has vanished; there remain but satiated appetites and palled senses. The worst of it is, that he writes without spirit, and methodically enough. He has no natural ardour, no picturesque sensuality; his satires prove him a disciple of Boileau. Nothing is more disgusting than obscenity in cold blood. We can endure the obscene works of Giulio Romano, and his Venetian voluptuousness, because in them genius sets off sensuality, and the loveliness of the splendid coloured draperies transforms an orgie into a work of art. We pardon Rabelais, when we have entered into the deep current of manly joy and vigour, with which his feasts abound. We can hold our nose and have done with it, while we follow with admiration, and even sympathy, the torrent of ideas and fancies which flows through his mire. But to see a man trying to be elegant and remaining obscene, endeavouring to paint the sentiments of a navvy in the language of a man of the world, who tries to find a suitable metaphor for every kind of filth, who plays the blackguard studiously and deliberately, who, excused neither by genuine feeling, nor the glow of fancy, nor knowledge, nor genius, degrades a good style of writing to such work,—it is like a rascal who sets himself to sully a set of gems in a gutter. The end of all is but disgust and illness. While La Fontaine continues to the last day capable of tenderness and happiness, this man at the age of thirty insults the weaker sex with spiteful malignity:

> "When she is young, she whores herself for sport;
> And when she's old, she bawds for her support....
> She is a snare, a shamble, and a stews;
> Her meat and sauce she does for lechery chuse,
> And does in laziness delight the more,
> Because by that she is provoked to whore.
> Ungrateful, treacherous, enviously inclined,
> Wild beasts are tamed, floods easier far confined,
> Than is her stubborn and rebellious mind....
> Her temper so extravagant we find,
> She hates, or is impertinently kind.
> Would she be grave, she then looks like a devil,
> And like a fool or whore, when she be civil...
> Contentious, wicked, and not fit to trust,
> And covetous to spend it on her lust." [1]

What a confession is such a judgment! what an abstract of life! You see the roisterer stupified at the end of his career, dried up like a mummy, eaten away

[1] Rochester's works, edited by St. Evremond.

by ulcers. Amid the choruses, the crude satires, the remembrance of plans miscarried, the sullied enjoyments which are heaped up in his wearied brain as in a sink, the fear of damnation is fermenting; he dies a devotee at the age of thirty-three.

At the head of all, the king sets the example. This "old goat," as the courtiers call him, imagines himself a man of gaiety and elegance. What gaiety! what elegance! French manners do not suit men beyond the Channel. When they are Catholics, they fall into narrow superstition; when epicureans, into gross debauchery; when courtiers, into base servility; when sceptics, into vulgar atheism. The court of England could only imitate French furniture and dress. The regular and decent exterior which public taste maintained at Versailles was here dispensed with as troublesome. Charles and his brother, in their state dress, would set off running as in a carnival. On the day when the Dutch fleet burned the English ships in the Thames, the king supped with the Duchess of Monmouth, and amused himself by chasing a moth. In council, while business was being transacted, he would be playing with his dog. Rochester and Buckingham insulted him by insolent repartees or dissolute epigrams; he would fly into a passion and suffer them to go on. He quarrelled with his mistress in public; she called him an idiot, and he called her a jade. He would leave her in the morning, "so that the very sentrys speak of it."[1] He suffered her to play him false before the eyes of all; at one time she received a couple of actors, one of whom was a mountebank. If need were, she would use abusive language to him.

[1] *Pepys' Diary*, ii. January 1, 1662–1663.

"The King hath declared that he did not get the child of which she is conceived at this time. But she told him, "... ! but you shall own it."[1] Whereupon he did acknowledge the child, and took to himself a couple of actresses for consolation. When his new wife, Catherine of Braganza, arrived, he drove away her attendants, used coarse language to her, that he might force on her the familiarities of his mistress, and finished by degrading her to a friendship such as this. The good Pepys, notwithstanding his loyal feelings, ends by saying, having heard the king and the duke talk, and seeing and observing their manner of discourse, "God forgive me! though I admire them with all the duty possible, yet the more a man considers and observes them, the less he finds of difference between them and other men, though, blessed be God! they are both princes of great nobleness and spirits."[2] He heard that, on a certain day, the king was so besotted with Mrs. Stewart that he gets "into corners, and will be with her half an hour together kissing her to the observation of all the world."[3] Another day, Captain Ferrers told him "how, at a ball at Court, a child was dropped by one of the ladies in dancing." They took it off in a handkerchief, "and the King had it in his closet a week after, and did dissect it, making great sport of it."[4] These ghastly freaks and these lewd events make us shudder. The courtiers went with the stream. Miss Jennings, who became Duchess of Tyrconnel, disguised herself one day as an orange girl, and cried her wares in the street.[5] Pepys recounts festivities in which lords and ladies smeared one another's

---

[1] *Pepys' Diary*, iv. July 30, 1667.
[2] *Ibid.* iii. July 26, 1665.   [3] *Ibid.* ii. Nov. 9, 1663.
[4] *Ibid.* ii. Feb. 8, 17, 1662-3.   [5] *Ibid.* Feb. 21, 1664-1665.

faces with candle-grease and soot, " till most of us were like devils." It was the fashion to swear, to relate scandalous adventures, to get drunk, to prate against the preachers and Scripture, to gamble. Lady Castlemaine in one night lost £25,000. The Duke of St. Albans, a blind man, eighty years old, went to the gambling-house with an attendant at his side to tell him the cards. Sedley and Buckhurst stripped nearly naked, and ran through the streets after midnight. Another, in the open day, stood naked at the window to address the people. I let Grammont keep to himself his accounts of the maids of honour brought to bed, and of unnatural lusts. We must either exhibit or conceal them, and I have not the courage lightly to insinuate them, after his fashion. I end by a quotation from Pepys, which will serve for example: " Here I first understood by their talk the meaning of company that lately were called Ballers; Harris telling how it was by a meeting of some young blades, where he was among them, and my Lady Bennet and her ladies; and their dancing naked, and all the roguish things in the world."[1] The marvellous thing is, that this fair is not even gay; these people were misanthropic, and became morose; they quote the gloomy Hobbes, and he is their master. In fact, the philosophy of Hobbes shall give us the last word and the last characteristics of this society.

V.

Hobbes was one of those powerful, limited, and, as they are called, positive minds, so common in England, of the school of Swift and Bentham, efficacious and

---

[1] The author has inadvertently confounded "my Lady Bennet" with the Countess of Arlington. See *Pepys' Diary*, iv. May 30, 1668, *footnote.*—Tr.

remorseless as an iron machine. Hence we find in him a method and style of surprising dryness and vigour, most adapted to build up and pull down; hence a philosophy which, by the audacity of its teaching, has placed in an undying light one of the indestructible phases of the human mind. In every object, every event, there is some primitive and constant fact, which forms, as it were, the nucleus around which group themselves the various developments which complete it. The positive mind swoops down immediately upon this nucleus, crushes the brilliant growth which covers it; disperses, annihilates it; then, concentrating upon it the full force of its violent grasp, loosens it, raises it up, shapes it, and lifts it into a conspicuous position, from whence it may henceforth shine out to all men and for all time like a crystal. All ornament, all emotions, are excluded from the style of Hobbes; it is a mere aggregate of arguments and concise facts in a small space, united together by deduction, as by iron bands. There are no tints, no fine or unusual word. He makes use only of words most familiar to common and lasting usage; there are not a dozen employed by him which, during two hundred years, have grown obsolete; he pierces to the root of all sensation, removes the transient and brilliant externals, narrows the solid portion which is the permanent subject-matter of all thought, and the proper object of common intelligence. He curtails throughout in order to strengthen; he attains solidity by suppression. Of all the bonds which connect ideas, he retains but one, and that the most stable; his style is only a continuous chain of reasoning of the most stubborn description, wholly made up of additions and subtractions, reduced to a combination of certain simple ideas, which added on to or diminishing from one another, make up, under various names, the totals or differences, of which we are for ever either studying the formation or unravelling the elements. He pursued beforehand the method of Condillac, beginning with tracing to the original fact, palpably and clearly, so as to pursue step by step the filiation and parentage of the ideas of which this primary fact is the stock, in such a manner that the reader, conducted from total to total, may at any moment test the exactness of his operation, and verify the truth of his results. Such a logical system cuts across the grain of prejudice with a mechanical stiffness and boldness. Hobbes clears science of scholastic words and theories. He laughs down quiddities, he does away with rational and intelligible classifications, he rejects the authority of references.[1] He cuts, as with a surgeon's knife, at the heart of the most living creeds. He denies the authenticity of the books of Moses, Joshua, and the like. He declares that no argument proves the divinity of Scripture, and that, in order to believe it, every man requires a supernatural and personal revelation. He upsets in half-a-dozen words the authority of this and every other revelation.[2] He reduces man to a mere body, the soul

[1] Though I reverence those men of ancient times that either have written truth perspicuously, or set it in a better way to find it out ourselves, yet to the antiquity itself, I think nothing due; for if we reverence the age, the present is the oldest.—Hobbes' *Works*, Molesworth, 11 vols. 8vo, 1839-45, iii. 712.

[2] "To say he hath spoken to him in a dream, is no more than to say he dreamed that God spake to him. . . . To say he hath seen a vision or heard a voice, is to say that he has dreamed between sleeping and waking. . . . To say he speaks by supernatural inspiration, is to say he finds an ardent DESIRE to speak, or some strong opinion of himself for which he can allege no sufficient and natural reason."—*Ibid.* iii. 361-2.

to a function, God, to an unknown existence. His phrases read like equations or mathematical results. In fact it is from mathematics [1] that he derives the idea of all science. He would reconstitute moral science on the same basis. He assigns to it this foundation when he lays down that sensation is an internal movement caused by an external shock; desire, an internal movement toward an external object; and he builds upon these two notions the whole system of morals. Again, he assigns to morals a mathematical method, when he distinguishes, like the geometrician, between two simple ideas, which he transforms by degrees into two more complex; and when on the basis of sensation and desire he constructs the passions, the rights, and institutions of man, just as the geometrician out of straight lines and curves constructs all the varieties of figure. To morals he gives a mathematical aspect, by mapping out the incomplete and rigid construction of human life, like the network of imaginary forms which geometricians have conceived. For the first time there was discernible in him, as in Descartes, but exaggerated and standing out more conspicuously, that species of intellect which produced the classic age in Europe: not the independence of inspiration and genius which marked the Renaissance; not the mature experimental methods and conceptions of aggregates which distinguish the present age, but the independence

[1] "From the principal parts of Nature, Reason, and Passion, have proceeded two kinds of learning, *mathematical* and *dogmatical*. The former is free from controversy and dispute, because it consisteth in comparing figure and motion only, in which things *truth* and *the interest of men* oppose not each other. But in the other there is nothing undisputable, because it compares men, and meddles with their right and profit."—Hobbes' *Works*, Molesworth, 11 vols. 8vo, 1839-45, iv. Epis. ded.

of argumentative reasoning, which dispensing with the imagination, liberating itself from tradition, badly practising experience, acknowledges its queen in logic, its model in mathematics, its instrument in ratiocination, its audience in polished society, its employment in average truth, its subject-matter in abstract humanity, its formula in ideology, and in the French Revolution at once its glory and its condemnation, its triumph and its close.

But whereas Descartes, in the midst of a purified society and religion, noble and calm, enthroned intelligence and elevated man, Hobbes, in the midst of an overthrown society and a religion run mad, degraded man and enthroned matter. Through disgust of Puritanism, the courtiers reduced human existence to an animal licentiousness; through disgust of Puritanism, Hobbes reduced human nature to its merely animal aspect. The courtiers were practically atheists and brutish, as he was atheistic and brutish in the province of speculation. They had established the fashion of instinct and egotism; he wrote the philosophy of egotism and instinct. They had wiped out from their hearts all refined and noble sentiments; he wiped out from the heart all noble and refined sentiment. He arranged their manners into a theory, gave them the manual of their conduct, wrote down beforehand the maxims which they were to reduce to practice.[1] With him, as with them, "the greatest good is the preservation of life and limb; the greatest evil is death, especially with pain." Other goods and other evils are only the means of these. None seek or wish for anything but that which is pleasurable. "No man gives except

[1] His chief works were written between 1646 and 1655.

for a personal advantage." Why are friendships good things? "Because they are useful; friends serve for defence and otherwise." Why do we pity one another? "Because we imagine that a similar misfortune may befall ourselves." Why is it noble to pardon him who asks it? "Because thus one proves confidence in self." Such is the background of the human heart. Consider now what becomes of the most precious flowers in these blighting hands. "Music, painting, poetry, are agreeable as imitations which recall the past, because if the past was good, it is agreeable in its imitation as a good thing; but if it was bad, it is agreeable in its imitation as being past." To this gross mechanism he reduces the fine arts; it was perceptible in his attempt to translate the *Iliad*. In his sight, philosophy is a thing of like kind. "Wisdom is serviceable, because it has in it some kind of protection; if it is desirable in itself, it is because it is pleasant." Thus there is no dignity in knowledge. It is a pastime or an assistance; good, as a servant or a puppet is a good thing. Money being more serviceable, is worth more. "Not he who is wise is rich, as the Stoics say; but, on the contrary, he who is rich is wise."[1] As to religion, it is but "the fear of an in-

[1] Nemo dat nisi respiciens ad bonum sibi.
Amicitiæ bonæ, nempe utiles. Nam amicitiæ cum ad multa alia, tum ad præsidium conferunt.
Sapientia utile. Nam præsidium in se habet nonnullum. Etiam appetibile est per se, id est jucundum. Item pulchrum, quia acquisitu difficilis.
Non enim qui sapiens est, ut dixere stoici, dives est, sed contra qui dives est sapiens est dicendus est.
Ignoscere veniam petenti pulchrum. Nam indicium fiduciæ sui.
Imitatio jucundum: revocat enim præterita. Præterita autem si bona fuerint, jucunda sunt repræsentata, quia bona; si mala, quia præterita. Jucunda igitur musica, poesis pictura.—Hobbes' *Opera Latina*, Molesworth, vol. ii. 98-102.

visible power, whether this be a figment, or adopted from history by general consent."[1] Indeed, this was true for a Rochester or a Charles II.; cowards or bullies, superstitious or blasphemers, they conceived of nothing beyond. Neither is there any natural right. "Before men were bound by contract one with another, each had the right to do what he would against whom he would." Nor any natural friendship. "All association is for the cause of advantage or of glory, that is, for love of one's self, not of one's associates. The origin of great and durable associations is not mutual well-wishing but mutual fear. The desire of injuring is innate in all. Man is to man a wolf. . . . Warfare was the natural condition of men before societies were formed; and this not incidentally, but of all against all: and this war is of its own nature eternal."[2] Sectarian violence let loose, the conflict of ambitions, the fall of governments, the overflow of soured imaginations and malevolent passions, had raised up this idea of society and of mankind. One and all, philosophers and people, yearned for monarchy and repose. Hobbes, an inexorable logician, would have it absolute; repression would

[1] Metus potentiarum invisibilium, sive fictæ illæ sint, sive ab historiis acceptæ sint publice, religio est si publice acceptæ non sint, superstitio.—Hobbes' *Opera Latina*, Molesworth, iii. 45.

[2] Omnis igitur societas vel commodi causa vel gloriæ, hoc est, sui, non sociorum amore contrahitur.—*Ibid.* ii. 161.

Statuendum igitur est, originem magnarum et diuturnarum societatum non a mutua hominum benevolentia, sed a mutuo metu exstitisse.—*Ibid.* ii. 161.

Voluntas lædendi omnibus quidem inest in statu naturæ.—*Ibid.* ii. 162.

Status hominum naturalis antequam in societatem coiretur bellum fuerit; neque hoc simpliciter, sed bellum omnium in omnes.—*Ibid.* ii. 166.

Bellum sua natura sempiternum.—See 166, *l*. 16.

thus be more stern, peace more lasting. The sovereign should be unopposed. Whatsoever he might do against a subject, under whatever pretext, would not be injustice. He ought to decide upon the canonical books. He was pope, and more than pope. Were he to command it, his subjects should renounce Christ, at least with their mouth; the original contract has given up to him, without any reservation, all responsibility of external actions; at least, according to this view, the sectarian will no longer have the pretext of his conscience in harassing the state. To such extremities had the intense weariness and horror of civil war driven a narrow but logical intellect. Upon the secure den in which he had with every effort imprisoned and confined the evil beast of prey, he laid as a final weight, in order that he might perpetuate the captivity of humanity, the whole philosophy and theory not simply of man, but of the remainder of the universe. He reduced judgment to the "combination of two terms," ideas to conditions of the brain, sensations to motions of the body, general laws to simple words, all substance to corporeality, all science to the knowledge of sensible bodies, the human being to a body capable of motion given or received; so that man, recognising himself and nature only under this despised form, and degraded in his conception of himself and of the world, might bow beneath the burden of a necessary authority, and submit in the end to the yoke which his rebellious nature rejects, yet is forced to tolerate.[1] Such, in brief, is the aim which this spec-

[1] Corpus et substantia idem significant, et proinde vox composita substantia incorporea est insignificans æque ac si quis diceret corpus incorporeum.—Hobbes' *Opera Latina*, Molesworth, iii. 281.

Quidquid imaginamur finitum est. Nulla ergo est idea neque conceptus qui oriri potest a voce hac, infinitum.—*Ibid.* iii. 20.

tacle of the English Restoration suggests. Men deserved then this treatment, because they gave birth to this philosophy; they were represented on the stage as they had proved themselves to be in theory and in manners.

VI.

When the theatres, which Parliament had closed, were re-opened, the change of public taste was soon manifested. Shirley, the last of the grand old school, wrote and lived no longer. Waller, Buckingham, and Dryden were compelled to dish up the plays of Shakspeare and Beaumont and Fletcher, and to adapt them to the modern style. Pepys, who went to see *Midsummer Night's Dream,* declared that he would never go there again; "for it is the most insipid, ridiculous play that ever I saw in my life."[1] Comedy was transformed; the fact was, that the public was transformed.

What an audience was that of Shakspeare and Beaumont and Fletcher! What youthful and delightful souls! In this evil-smelling room in which it was necessary to burn juniper, before that miserable half-lighted stage, before decorations worthy of an alehouse, with men playing the women's parts, illusion enchained them. They scarcely troubled themselves about probabilities; they could be carried in an instant over forest and ocean, from clime to clime, across twenty years of time, through

Recidit itaque ratiocinatio omnis ad duas operationes animi, additionem et substractionem.—Hobbes' *Opera Latina,* Molesworth, i. 3.

Nomina signa sunt non rerum sed cogitationem.—*Ibid.* i. 15.

Veritas enim in dicto non in re consistit.—*Ibid.* i. 31.

Sensio igitur in sentiente nihil aliud esse potest præter motum partium aliquarum intus in sentiente existentium, quæ partes motæ organorum quibus sentimus partes sunt.—*Ibid.* i. 317.

[1] *Pepys' Diary,* ii. Sept. 29, 1662.

ten battles and all the hurry of adventure. They did not care to be always laughing; comedy, after a burst of buffoonery, resumed its serious or tender tone. They came less to be amused than to muse. In these fresh minds, amidst a woof of passions and dreams, there were hidden passions and brilliant dreams whose imprisoned swarm buzzed indistinctly, waiting for the poet to come and lay bare to them the novelty and the splendour of heaven. Landscapes revealed by a lightning flash, the gray mane of a long and overhanging billow, a wet forest nook where the deer raise their startled heads, the sudden smile and purpling cheek of a young girl in love, the sublime and various flight of all delicate sentiments, a cloak of ecstatic and romantic passion over all,— these were the sights and feelings which they came to seek. They raised themselves without any assistance to the summit of the world of ideas; they desired to contemplate extreme generosity, absolute love; they were not astonished at the sight of fairy-land; they entered without an effort into the region of poetical transformation, whose light was necessary to their eyes. They took in at a glance its excesses and its caprices; they needed no preparation; they followed its digressions, its whimsicalities, the crowding of its abundant creations, the sudden prodigality of its high colouring, as a musician follows a symphony. They were in that transient and strained condition in which the imagination, adult and pure, laden with desire, curiosity, force, develops man all at once, and in that man the most exalted and exquisite feelings.

The roisterers took the place of these. They were rich, they had tried to deck themselves with the polish of Frenchmen; they added to the stage moveable decorations, music, lights, probability, comfort, every external aid; but they wanted heart. Imagine those foppish and half-intoxicated men, who saw in love nothing beyond desire, and in man nothing beyond sensuality; Rochester in the place of Mercutio. What part of his soul could comprehend poesy and fancy? The comedy of romance was altogether beyond his reach; he could only seize the actual world, and of this world but the palpable and gross externals. Give him an exact picture of ordinary life, commonplace and probable occurrences, literal imitations of what he himself was and did; lay the scene in London, in the current year; copy his coarse words, his brutal jokes, his conversation with the orange girls, his rendezvous in the park, his attempts at French dissertation. Let him recognise himself, let him find again the people and the manners he had just left behind him in the tavern or the antechamber; let the theatre and the street reproduce one another. Comedy will give him the same entertainment as real life; he will wallow equally well there in vulgarity and lewdness; to be present there will demand neither imagination nor wit; eyes and memory are the only requisites. This exact imitation will amuse him and instruct him at the same time. Filthy words will make him laugh through sympathy; shameless imagery will divert him by appealing to his recollections. The author, too, will take care to arouse him by his plot, which generally has the deceiving of a father or a husband for its subject. The fine gentlemen agree with the author in siding with the gallant; they follow his fortunes with interest, and fancy that they themselves have the same success with the fair. Add to this, women debauched, and willing to be debauched;

and it is manifest how these provocations, these manners of prostitutes, that interchange of exchanges and surprises, that carnival of rendezvous and suppers, the impudence of the scenes only stopping short of physical demonstration, those songs with their double meaning, that coarse slang shouted loudly and replied to amidst the *tableaux vivants*, all that stage-imitation of orgie, must have stirred up the innermost feelings of the habitual practisers of intrigue. And what is more, the theatre gave its sanction to their manners. By representing nothing but vice, it authorised their vices. Authors laid it down as a rule, that all women were impudent hussies, and that all men were brutes. Debauchery in their hands became a matter of course, nay more, a matter of good taste; they profess it. Rochester and Charles II. could quit the theatre highly edified; more convinced than they were before that virtue was only a pretence, the pretence of clever rascals who wanted to sell themselves dear.

VII.

Dryden, who was amongst the first[1] to adopt this view of the matter, did not adopt it heartily. A kind of hazy mist, the relic of the former age, still floated over his plays. His wealthy imagination half bound him to the comedy of romance. At one time he adapted Milton's *Paradise*, Shakspeare's *Tempest*, and *Troilus and Cressida*. Another time he imitated, in *Love in a Nunnery,* in *Marriage à la Mode,* in *The Mock Astrologer*, the imbroglios and surprises of the Spanish stage. Sometimes he displays the sparkling images

[1] His *Wild Gallant* dates from 1662.

and lofty metaphors of the older national poets, sometimes the affected figures of speech and cavilling wit of Calderon and Lope de Vega. He mingles the tragic and the humorous, the overthrow of thrones and the ordinary description of manners. But in this awkward compromise the poetic spirit of ancient comedy disappears; only the dress and the gilding remain. The new characters are gross and immoral, with the instincts of a lackey beneath the dress of a lord; which is the more shocking, because by it Dryden contradicts his own talents, being at bottom grave and a poet; he follows the fashion, and not his own mind; he plays the libertine with deliberate forethought, to adapt himself to the taste of the day.[1] He plays the blackguard awkwardly and dogmatically; he is impious without enthusiasm, and in measured periods. One of his gallants cries:

> "Is not love love without a priest and altars?
> The temples are inanimate, and know not
> What vows are made in them; the priest stands ready
> For his hire, and cares not what hearts he couples;
> Love alone is marriage."[2]

Hippolita says, "I wished the ball might be kept perpetually in our cloister, and that half the handsome

---

[1] "We love to get our mistresses, and purr over them, as cats do over mice, and let them get a little way; and all the pleasure is to pat them back again."—*Mock Astrologer*, ii. 1.

Wildblood says to his mistress: "I am none of those unreasonable lovers that propose to themselves the loving to eternity. A month is commonly my stint." And Jacintha replies: "Or would not a fortnight serve our turn?"—*Mock Astrologer*, ii. 1.

Frequently one would think Dryden was translating Hobbes, by the harshness of his jests.

[2] *Love in a Nunnery*, ii. 3.

nuns in it might be turned to men, for the sake of the other."[1] Dryden has no tact or contrivance. In his *Spanish Friar*, the queen, a good enough woman, tells Torrismond that she is going to have the old dethroned king put to death, in order to marry him, Torrismond, more at her ease. Presently she is informed that the murder is completed. "What hinders now," says she, "but that the holy priest, in secret joins our mutual vows? and then this night, this happy night, is yours and mine."[2] Side by side with this sensual tragedy, a comic intrigue, pushed to the most indecent familiarity, exhibits the love of a cavalier for a married woman, who in the end turns out to be his sister. Dryden discovers nothing in this situation to shock him. He has lost the commonest repugnances of natural modesty. Translating any pretty broad play, *Amphitryon* for instance, he finds it too pure; he strips off all its small delicacies, and enlarges its very improprieties.[3] Thus Jupiter says:

> "For kings and priests are in a manner bound,
> For reverence sake, to be close hypocrites."[4]

And he proceeds thereupon boldly to lay bare his own

---

[1] *Love in a Nunnery*, iii. 3.

[2] *Spanish Friar*, iii. 3. And jumbled up with the plot we keep meeting with political allusions. This is a mark of the time. Torrismond, to excuse himself from marrying the queen, says, "Power which in one age is tyranny is ripen'd in the next to true succession. She's in possession."—*Spanish Friar*, iv. 2.

[3] Plautus' *Amphitryon* has been imitated by Dryden and Molière. Sir Walter Scott, in the introduction to Dryden's play, says: "He is, in general, coarse and vulgar, where Molière is witty; and where the Frenchman ventures upon a double meaning, the Englishman always contrives to make it a single one."—Tr.

[4] *Amphitryon*, i. 1.

despotism. In reality, his sophisms and his shamelessness serve Dryden as a means of decrying by rebound the arbitrary Divinity of the theologians. He lets Jupiter say:

> "Fate is what I,
> By virtue of omnipotence, have made it;
> And power omnipotent can do no wrong!
> Not to myself, because I will it so;
> Nor yet to men, for what they are is mine.—
> This night I will enjoy Amphitryon's wife;
> For when I made her, I decreed her such
> As I should please to love."[1]

This open pedantry is changed into open lust as soon as Jupiter sees Alcmena. No detail is omitted: Jupiter speaks his whole mind to her, and before the maids; and next morning, when he is going away, she outdoes him: she hangs on to him, and indulges in the most familiar details. All the noble externals of high gallantry are torn off like a troublesome garment; it is a cynical recklessness in place of aristocratic decency; the scene is written after the example of Charles II. and Castlemaine, not of Louis XIV. and Mme. de Montespan.[2]

---

[1] *Amphitryon*, i. 1.

[2] As Jupiter is departing, on the plea of daylight, Alcmena says to him:

> "But you and I will draw our curtains close,
> Extinguish daylight, and put out the sun.
> Come back, my lord. . . .
> You have not yet laid long enough in bed
> To warm your widowed side."—Act ii. 2.

Compare Plautus' Roman matron and Molière's honest French woman with this expansive female. [Louis XIV. and Made. de Montespan were not very decent either. See *Mémoires de Saint Simon*.]—Tr.

VIII.

I pass over several writers: Crowne, author of *Sir Courtly Nice;* Shadwell, an imitator of Ben Jonson; Mrs. Aphra Behn, who calls herself Astræa, a spy and a courtesan, paid by government and the public. Etherege is the first to set the example of imitative comedy in his *Man of Fashion,* and to depict only the manners of his age; for the rest he is an open roisterer, and frankly describes his habits:

> "From hunting whores, and haunting play,
> And minding nothing all the day,
> And all the night too, you will say." . .

Such were his pursuits in London; and further on, in a letter from Ratisbon to Lord Middleton,

> "He makes grave legs in formal fetters,
> Converses with fools and writes dull letters;"

and gets small consolation out of the German ladies. In this grave mood Etherege undertook the duties of an ambassador. One day, having dined too freely, he fell from the top of a staircase, and broke his neck; a death of no great importance. But the hero of this society was William Wycherley, the coarsest writer who ever polluted the stage. Being sent to France during the Revolution, he there became a Roman Catholic; then on his return abjured; then in the end, as Pope tells us, abjured again. Robbed of their Protestant ballast, these shallow brains ran from dogma to dogma, from superstition to incredulity or indifference, to end in a state of fear. He had learnt at M. de Montausier's[1] residence

---

[1] Himself a Huguenot, who had become a Roman Catholic, and the husband of Julie d'Angennes, for whom the French poets composed the celebrated *Guirlande.*—Tr.

the art of wearing gloves and a peruke, which sufficed in those days to make a gentleman. This merit, and the success of a filthy piece, *Love in a Wood*, drew upon him the eyes of the Duchess of Cleveland, mistress of the king and of anybody. This woman, who used to have amours with a rope-dancer, picked him up one day in the very midst of the Ring. She put her head out of her carriage-window, and cried to him before all, "Sir, you are a rascal, a villain, the son of a ———." Touched by this compliment, he accepted her favours, and in consequence obtained those of the king. He lost them, married the Countess of Drogheda, a woman of bad temper, ruined himself, remained seven years in prison, passed the remainder of his life in pecuniary difficulties, regretting his youth, losing his memory, scribbling bad verses, which he got Pope to correct, amidst many twitches of wounded self-esteem, stringing together dull obscenities, dragging his worn out body and enervated brain through the stages of misanthropy and libertinage, playing the miserable part of a toothless roisterer and a white-haired blackguard. Eleven days before his death he married a young girl, who turned out to be a strumpet. He ended as he had begun, by stupidity and misconduct, having succeeded neither in becoming happy nor honest, having used his vigorous intelligence and real talent only to his own injury and the injury of others.

The reason was, that Wycherley was not an epicurean born. His nature, genuinely English, that is to say, energetic and sombre, rebelled against the easy and amiable carelessness which enables one to take life as a pleasure-party. His style is laboured, and troublesome to read. His tone is virulent and bitter. He frequently forces his comedy in order to get at spiteful satire. Effort and animosity mark all that he says or puts into the mouths of others. It is Hobbes, not meditative and calm, but active and angry, who sees in man nothing but vice, yet feels himself man to the very core. The only fault he rejects is hypocrisy; the only virtue he preaches is frankness. He wants others to confess their vice, and he begins by confessing his own. "Though I cannot lie like them (the poets), I am as vain as they; I cannot but publicly give your Grace my humble acknowledgments. . . . This is the poet's gratitude, which in plain English is only pride and ambition."[1] We find in him no poetry of expression, no glimpse of the ideal, no settled morality which could console, raise, or purify men. He shuts them up in their perversity and uncleanness, and installs himself among them. He shows them the filth of the lowest depths in which he confines them; he expects them to breathe this atmosphere; he plunges them into it, not to disgust them with it as by an accidental fall, but to accustom them to it as if it were their natural element. He tears down the partitions and decorations by which they endeavour to conceal their state, or regulate their disorder. He takes pleasure in making them fight, he delights in the hubbub of their unfettered instincts; he loves the violent changes of the human mass, the confusion of their wicked deeds, the rawness of their bruises. He strips their lusts, sets them forth at full length, and of course feels them himself; and whilst he condemns them as nauseous,

[1] *The Dramatic Works of Wycherley, Congreve, Vanbrugh, and Farquhar*, ed. Leigh Hunt, 1840. Dedication of *Love in a Wood* to her Grace the Duchess of Cleveland.

he enjoys them. People take what pleasure they can get: the drunkards in the suburbs, if asked how they can relish their miserable liquor, will tell you it makes them drunk as soon as better stuff, and that is the only pleasure they have.

I can understand that an author may dare much in a novel. It is a psychological study, akin to criticism or history, having almost equal license, because it contributes almost equally to explain the anatomy of the heart. It is quite necessary to expose moral diseases, especially when this is done to add to science, coldly, accurately, and in the fashion of a dissection. Such a book is by its nature abstruse; it must be read in the study, by lamp-light. But transport it to the stage, exaggerate the bed-room liberties, give them additional life by a few disreputable scenes, bestow bodily vigour upon them by the energetic action and words of the actresses; let the eyes and the senses be filled with them, not the eyes of an individual spectator, but of a thousand men and women mingled together in the pit, excited by the interest of the story, by the correctness of the literal imitation, by the glitter of the lights, by the noise of applause, by the contagion of impressions which run like a shudder through fiery and longing minds. That was the spectacle which Wycherley furnished, and which the court appreciated. Is it possible that a public, and a select public, could come and listen to such scenes? In *Love in a Wood*, amidst the complications of nocturnal rendezvous, and violations effected or begun, we meet with a witling, named Dapperwit, who desires to sell his mistress Lucy to a fine gentleman of that age, Ranger. With what minuteness he bepraises her! He knocks at her door; the intended purchaser meantime, growing impatient, is treating him like a slave. The mother comes in, but wishing to sell Lucy herself and for her own advantage, scolds them and packs them off. Next appears an old puritanical usurer and hypocrite, named Gripe, who at first will not bargain :—

"*Mrs. Joyner.* You must send for something to entertain her with. . . . Upon my life a groat! what will this purchase?

Gripe. Two black pots of ale and a cake, at the cellar.—Come, the wine has arsenic in't. . . .

Mrs. J. A treat of a groat! I will not wag.

G. Why dont you go? Here, take more money, and fetch what you will; take here, half-a-crown.

Mrs. J. What will half-a-crown do?

G. Take a crown then, an angel, a piece;—begone!

Mrs. J. A treat only will not serve my turn; I must buy the poor wretch there some toys.

G. What toys? what? speak quickly.

Mrs. J. Pendants, necklaces, fans, ribbons, points, laces, stockings, gloves. . . .

G. But here, take half a piece for the other things.

Mrs. J. Half a piece!—

G. Prithee, begone!—take t'other piece then—two pieces—three pieces—five! here; 'tis all I have.

Mrs. J. I must have the broad-seal ring too, or I stir not."[1]

She goes away at last, having extorted all, and Lucy plays the innocent, seems to think that Gripe is a dancing-master, and asks for a lesson. What scenes, what double meanings! At last she calls out, her mother, Mrs. Crossbite, breaks open the door, and enters with men placed there beforehand; Gripe is

[1] Act iii. 3.

caught in the trap; they threaten to call in the constable, they swindle him out of five hundred pounds.

Need I recount the plot of the *Country Wife?* It is useless to wish to skim the subject only; we sink deeper and deeper. Horner, a gentleman returned from France, spreads the report that he is no longer able to trouble the peace of husbands. You may imagine what becomes of such a subject in Wycherley's hands, and he draws from it all that it contains. Women converse about Horner's condition, even before him; they suffer themselves to be undeceived, and boast of it. Three of them come to him and feast, drink, sing—such songs! The excess of orgie triumphs, adjudges itself the crown, displays itself in maxims. "Our virtue," says one of them, "is like the statesman's religion, the quaker's word, the gamester's oath, and the great man's honour; but to cheat those that trust us."[1] In the last scene, the suspicions which had been aroused, are set at rest by a new declaration of Horner. All the marriages are polluted, and the carnival ends by a dance of deceived husbands. To crown all, Horner recommends his example to the public, and the actress who comes on to recite the epilogue, completes the shamefulness of the piece, by warning gallants that they must look what they are doing; for that if they can deceive men, "we women —there's no cozening us."[2]

But the special and most extraordinary sign of the times is, that amid all these provocatives, no repellent circumstance is omitted, and that the narrator seems to

[1] *The Country Wife*, v. 4.
[2] Read the epilogue, and see what words and details authors dared then to put in the mouths of actresses.

aim as much at disgusting as at depraving us.[1] Every moment the fine gentlemen, even the ladies, introduce into their conversation the ways and means by which, since the sixteenth century, love has endeavoured to adorn itself. Dapperwit, when making an offer of Lucy, says, in order to account for the delay: "Pish! give her but leave to . . . put on . . . the long patch under the left eye; awaken the roses on her cheeks with some Spanish wool, and warrant her breath with some lemon-peel."[2] Lady Flippant, alone in the park, cries out: "Unfortunate lady that I am! I have left the herd on purpose to be chased, and have wandered this hour here; but the park affords not so much as a satyr for me; and no Burgundy man or drunken scourer will reel my way. The rag-women and cinder-women have better luck than I."[3]

Judge by these quotations, which are the best, of the remainder! Wycherley makes it his business to revolt even the senses; the nose, the eyes, everything suffers in his plays; the audience must have had the stomach of a sailor. And from this abyss English literature has ascended to the strict morality, the excessive decency which it now possesses! This stage is a declared war against beauty and delicacy of every kind. If Wycherley borrows a character anywhere, it is only to do violence,

[1] "That spark, who has his fruitless designs upon the bed-ridden rich widow, down to the sucking heiress in her . . . clout."—*Love in a Wood*, i. 2.

Mrs. Flippant: "Though I had married the fool, I thought to have reserved the wit as well as other ladies."—*Ibid.*

Dapperwit: "I will contest with no rival, not with my old rival your coachman."—*Ibid.*

"She has a complexion like a holland cheese, and no more teeth left, than such as give a haut goût to her breath."—*Ibid.* ii. 1.

[2] *Love in a Wood*, iii. 2.   [3] *Ibid.* v. 2.

or degrade it to the level of his own characters. If he imitates the Agnes of Molière,[1] as he does in the *Country Wife*, he marries her in order to profane marriage, deprives her of honour, still more of modesty, still more of grace, and changes her artless tenderness into shameless instincts and scandalous confessions. If he takes Shakespeare's Viola, as in the *Plain Dealer*, it is to drag her through the vileness of infamy, amidst brutalities and surprises. If he translates the part of Molière's Célimène, he wipes out at one stroke the manners of a great lady, the woman's delicacy, the tact of the lady of the house, the politeness, the refined air, the superiority of wit and knowledge of the world, in order to substitute for them the impudence and deceit of a foul-mouthed courtesan. If he invents an almost innocent girl, Hippolita,[2] he begins by putting into her mouth words that will not bear transcribing. Whatever he does or says, whether he copies or originates, blames or praises, his stage is a defamation of mankind, which repels even when it attracts, and which sickens a man while it corrupts.

A certain gift hovers over all—namely, vigour—

[1] The letter of Agnes, in Molière's *l'École des Femmes*, iii. 4, begins thus: "Je veux vous écrire, et je suis bien en peine par où je m'y prendrai. J'ai des pensées que je désirerais que vous sussiez; mais je ne sais comment faire pour vous les dire, et je me défie de mes paroles," etc. Observe how Wycherley translates it: "Dear, sweet Mr. Horner, my husband would have me send you a base, rude, unmannerly letter; but I won't—and would have me forbid you loving me; but I won't—and would have me say to you, I hate you, poor Mr. Horner; but I won't tell a lie for him—for I'm sure if you and I were in the country at cards together, I could not help treading on your toe under the table, or rubbing knees with you, and staring in your face, till you saw me, and then looking down, and blushing for an hour together,' etc. —*Country Wife*, iv. 2.

[2] In the *Gentleman Dancing-Master.*

which is never absent in England, and gives a peculiar character to their virtues as well as to their vices. When we have removed the oratorical and heavily constructed phrases imitated from the French, we get at the genuine English talent—a deep sympathy with nature and life. Wycherley possessed that lucid and vigorous perspicacity which in any particular situation seizes upon gesture, physical expression, evident detail, which pierces to the depths of the crude and base, which hits off, not men in general, and passion as it ought to be, but an individual man, and passion as it is. He is a realist, not of set purpose, as the realists of our day, but naturally. In a violent manner he lays on his plaster over the grinning and pimpled faces of his rascals, in order to bring before our very eyes the stern mask to which the living imprint of their ugliness has stuck on the way. He crams his plays with incident, he multiplies action, he pushes comedy to the verge of dramatic effect; he hustles his characters amidst surprises and violence, and all but stultifies them in order to exaggerate his satire. Observe in Olivia, a copy of Célimène, the fury of the passions which he depicts. She describes her friends as does Célimène, but with what insults! Novel, a coxcomb, says:

"Madam, I have been treated to-day with all the ceremony and kindness imaginable at my lady Autumn's. But the nauseous old woman at the upper end of her table'...

Olivia: "Revives the old Grecian custom, of serving in a death's head with their banquets.... I detest her hollow cherry cheeks: she looks like an old coach new painted.... She is still most splendidly, gallantly ugly, and looks like an ill piece of daubing in a rich frame."[1]

[1] *The Plain Dealer*, ii. 1.

The scene is borrowed from Molière's *Misanthrope* and the *Critique de l'Ecole des Femmes*; but how transformed! Our modern nerves would not endure the portrait Olivia draws of Manly, her lover; he hears her unawares; she forthwith stands before him, laughs at him to his face, declares herself to be married; tells him she means to keep the diamonds which he has given her, and defies him. Fidelia says to her:

"But, madam, what could make you dissemble love to him, when 'twas so hard a thing for you; and flatter his love to you?"

Olivia. "That which makes all the world flatter and dissemble, 'twas his money: I had a real passion for that.... As soon as I had his money, I hastened his departure like a wife, who when she has made the most of a dying husband's breath, pulls away his pillow."[1]

The last phrase is rather that of a morose satirist than of an accurate observer. The woman's impudence is like a professed courtesan's. In love at first sight with Fidelia, whom she takes for a young man, she hangs upon her neck, "stuffs her with kisses," gropes about in the dark, crying, "Where are thy lips?" There is a kind of animal ferocity in her love. She sends her husband off by an improvised comedy; then skipping about like a dancing girl cries out: "Go, husband, and come up, friend; just the buckets in the well; the absence of one brings the other." "But I hope, like them too, they will not meet in the way, jostle, and clash together."[2] Surprised in *flagrante delicto*, and having confessed all to her cousin, as soon as she sees a chance of safety, she swallows her avowal with the effrontery of an actress:—

[1] *The Plain Dealer*, iv. 2.   [2] *Ibid.*

"*Eliza.* Well, cousin, this, I confess, was reasonable hypocrisy; you were the better for 't.

Olivia. What hypocrisy?

E. Why, this last deceit of your husband was lawful, since in your own defence.

O. What deceit? I'd have you know I never deceived my husband.

E. You do not understand me, sure; I say, this was an honest come-off, and a good one. But 'twas a sign your gallant had had enough of your conversation, since he could so dexterously cheat your husband in passing for a woman.

O. What d'ye mean, once more, with my gallant, and passing for a woman?

E. What do you mean? you see your husband took him for a woman!

O. Whom?

E. Heyday! why, the man he found with. . . .

O. Lord, you rave sure!

E. Why, did you not tell me last night. . . . Fy, this fooling is so insipid, 'tis offensive.

O. And fooling with my honour will be more offensive. . . .

E. O admirable confidence! . . .

O. Confidence, to me! to me such language! nay, then I'll never see your face again. . . . Lettice, where are you? Let us begone from this censorious ill woman. . . .

E. One word first, pray, madam; can you swear that whom your husband found you with . . .

O. Swear! ay, that whosoever 'twas that stole up, unknown, into my room, when 'twas dark, I know not, whether man or woman, by heavens, by all that's good; or, may I never more have joys here, or in the other world! Nay, may I eternally—

E. Be damned. So, so, you are damned enough already by your oaths. . . . Yet take this advice with you, in this plain-dealing age, to leave off forswearing yourself. . . .

O. O hideous, hideous advice! let us go out of the hearing of it. She will spoil us, Lettice."[1]

Here is animation; and if I dared to relate the boldness and the asseveration in the night scene, it would easily appear that Mme. Marneffe[2] had a sister, and Balzac a predecessor.

There is a character who shows in a concise manner Wycherley's talent and his morality, wholly formed of energy and indelicacy,— Manly, the "plain dealer," so manifestly the author's favourite, that his contemporaries gave him the name of his hero for a surname. Manly is copied after Alceste, and the great difference between the two heroes shows the difference between the two societies and the two countries.[3] Manly is not a courtier, but a ship-captain, with the bearing of a sailor of the time, his cloak stained with tar, and smelling of brandy,[4] ready with blows or foul oaths, calling those he came across dogs and slaves, and when they displeased him, kicking them down stairs. And he speaks in this fashion to a lord with a voice like a mastiff. Then, when the poor nobleman tries to whisper something in his ear, "My lord, all that you have made me know by your whispering which I knew not before, is that you

[1] *The Plain Dealer*, v. 1.   [2] See note, vol. i. page 41.

[3] Compare with the sayings of Alceste, in Molière's *Misanthrope*, such tirades as this: "Such as you, like common whores and pickpockets, are only dangerous to those you embrace." And with the character of Philinte, in the same French play, such phrases as these: "But, faith, could you think I was a friend to those I hugged, kissed, flattered, bowed to? When their backs were turned, did not I tell you they were rogues, villains, rascals, whom I despised and hated?"

[4] Olivia says: "Then shall I have again my alcove smell like a cabin, my chamber perfumed with his tarpaulin Brandenburgh; and hear vollies of brandy-sighs, enough to make a fog in one's room."— *The Plain Dealer*, ii. 1.

have a stinking breath; there's a secret for your secret." When he is in Olivia's drawing-room, with "these fluttering parrots of the town, these apes, these echoes of men," he bawls out as if he were on his quarter-deck, "Peace, you Bartholomew fair buffoons!" He seizes them by the collar, and says: "Why, you impudent, pitiful wretches, . . . you are in all things so like women, that you may think it in me a kind of cowardice to beat you. Begone, I say. . . . No chattering, baboons; instantly begone, or" . . . Then he turns them out of the room. These are the manners of a plain-dealing man. He has been ruined by Olivia, whom he loves, and who dismisses him. Poor Fidelia, disguised as a man, and whom he takes for a timid youth, comes and finds him while he is fretting with anger:

"*Fidelia.* I warrant you, sir; for, at worst, I could beg or steal for you.

Manly. Nay, more bragging! . . . You said you'd beg for me.

F. I did, sir.

M. Then you shall beg for me.

F. With all my heart, sir.

M. That is, pimp for me.

F. How, sir?

M. D'ye start? . . . No more dissembling: here (I say,) you must go use it for me to Olivia. . . . Go, flatter, lie, kneel, promise, anything to get her for me: I cannot live unless I have her."[1]

And when Fidelia returns to him, saying that Olivia has embraced her, by force, in a fit of love, he exclaims; "Her love!—a whore's, a witch's love!—

[1] *The Plain Dealer*, iii. 1.

But what, did she not kiss well, sir? I'm sure, I thought her lips—but I must not think of 'em more—but yet they are such I could still kiss,—grow to,—and then tear off with my teeth, grind 'em into mammocks, and spit 'em into her cuckold's face."[1] These savage words indicate savage actions. He goes by night to enter Olivia's house with Fidelia, and under her name; and Fidelia tries to prevent him, through jealousy. Then his blood boils, a storm of fury mounts to his face, and he speaks to her in a whispering, hissing voice: "What, you are my rival, then! and therefore you shall stay, and keep the door for me, whilst I go in for you; but when I'm gone, if you dare to stir off from this very board, or breathe the least murmuring accent, I'll cut her throat first; and if you love her, you will not venture her life.—Nay, then I'll cut your throat too, and I know you love your own life at least. . . . Not a word more, lest I begin my revenge on her by killing you."[2] He knocks over Olivia's husband, another traitor seizes from her the casket of jewels he had given her, casts her one or two of them, saying, "Here, madam, I never yet left my wench unpaid," and gives this same casket to Fidelia, whom he marries. All these actions then appeared natural. Wycherley took to himself in his dedication the title of his hero, *Plain Dealer*; he fancied he had drawn the portrait of a frank, honest man, and praised himself for having set the public a fine example; he had only given them the model of an unreserved and energetic brute. That was all the manliness that was left in this pitiable world. Wycherley deprived man of his ill-fitting French cloak,

---

[1] *The Plain Dealer*, iv. 1.   [2] *Ibid.* iv. 2.

and displayed him with his framework of muscles, and in his naked shamelessness.

And in the midst of all these, a great poet, blind, and sunk into obscurity, his soul saddened by the misery of the times, thus depicted the madness of the infernal rout:

> "Belial came last, than whom a spirit more lewd
> Fell not from heaven, or more gross to love
> Vice for itself . . . who more oft than he
> In temples and at altars, when the priest
> Turns atheist, as did Eli's sons, who fill'd
> With lust and violence the house of God?
> In courts and palaces he also reigns,
> And in luxurious cities, where the noise
> Of riot ascends above their loftiest towers,
> And injury, and outrage: and when night
> Darkens the streets, then wander forth the sons
> Of Belial, flown with insolence and wine." [1]

2. THE WORLDLINGS.

I.

In the seventeenth century a new mode of life was inaugurated in Europe, the worldly, which soon took the lead of and shaped every other. In France especially, and in England, it appeared and gained ground, from the same causes and at the same time.

In order to people the drawing-rooms, a certain political condition is necessary; and this condition, which is the supremacy of the king in combination with a regular system of police, was established at the same period on both sides of the Channel. A regular police brings about peace among men, draws them out of their

[1] *Paradise Lost*, book i. *l.* 490–502.

feudal independence and provincial isolation, increases and facilitates intercommunication, confidence, union, comfort, and pleasures. The kingly supremacy calls into existence a court, the centre of intercourse, from which all favours flow, and which calls for a display of pleasure and splendour. The aristocracy thus attracted to one another, and attracted to the throne by security, curiosity, amusement, and interest, meet together, and become at once men of the world and men of the court. They are no longer, like the barons of a preceding age, standing in their lofty halls, armed and stern, possessed by the idea that they might perhaps, when they quit their palace, cut each other to pieces, and that if they fall to blows in the precincts of the court, the executioner is ready to cut off their hand and stop the bleeding with a red-hot iron; knowing, moreover, that the king may probably have them beheaded to-morrow, and ready accordingly to cast themselves on their knees and break out into protestations of submissive fidelity, but counting under their breath the number of swords that will be mustered on their side, and the trusty men who keep sentinel behind the drawbridge of their castles.[1] The rights, privileges, constraints, and attractions of feudal life have disappeared. There is no more need that the manor should be a fortress. These men can no longer experience the joy of reigning there as in a petty state. It has palled on them, and they quit it. Having no further cause to quarrel with the king, they go to him. His court is a drawing-room, most agreeable to the sight, and most serviceable to those who frequent it. Here are festivities, splendid furniture, a decked and

[1] Consult all Shakspeare's historical plays.

select company, news and tittle-tattle; here they find pensions, titles, places for themselves and their friends; they receive amusement and profit; it is all gain and all pleasure. Here they attend the levée, are present at dinners, return to the ball, sit down to play, are there when the king goes to bed. Here they cut a dash with their half-French dress, their wigs, their hats loaded with feathers, their trunk-hose, their cannions, the large rosettes on their shoes. The ladies paint and patch their faces, display robes of magnificent satin and velvet, laced up with silver and very long, and above you may see their white busts, whose brilliant nakedness is extended to their shoulders and arms. They are gazed upon, saluted, approached. The king rides on horseback in Hyde Park; by his side canter the queen, and with her the two mistresses, Lady Castlemaine and Mrs. Stewart: "the queen in a white-laced waistcoate and a crimson short pettycoate, and her hair dressed à la négligence; . . Mrs. Stewart with her hat cocked and a red plume, with her sweet eye, little Roman nose, and excellent taille."[1] Then they returned to Whitehall "where all the ladies walked, talking and fiddling with their hats and feathers, and changing and trying one another's by one another's heads, and laughing."[2] In such fine company there was no lack of gallantry. Perfumed gloves, pocket mirrors, work-cases fitted up, apricot paste, essences, and other little love-tokens, came over every week from Paris. London furnished more substantial gifts, ear-rings, diamonds, brilliants, and golden guineas; the fair ones put up with these, as if they had come from a greater distance.[3]

[1] *Pepys' Diary*, ii. July 13, 1663.   [2] *Ibid.*
[3] *Mémoires de Grammont*, by A. Hamilton.

There were plenty of intrigues—Heaven knows how many or of what kind. Naturally, also, conversation does not stop. They did not mince the adventures of Miss Warmestré the haughty, who, "deceived apparently by a bad reckoning, took the liberty of lying-in in the midst of the court."[1] They spoke in whispers about the attempts of Miss Hobart, or the happy misfortune of Miss Churchill, who, being very plain, but having the wit to fall from her horse, touched the eyes and heart of the Duke of York. The Chevalier de Grammont relates to the king the history of Termes, or of Poussatin the almoner: every one leaves the dance to hear it; and when it is over, they all burst out laughing. We perceive that this is not the world of Louis XIV., and yet it is a world; and if it has more froth, it runs with the identical current. The great object here also is selfish amusement, and to put on appearances; people strive to be men of fashion; a coat bestows a certain kind of glory on its wearer. De Grammont was in despair when the roguery of his valet obliged him to wear the same suit twice over. Another courtier piques himself on his songs and his guitar-playing. "Russell had a collection of two or three hundred quadrilles in tablature, all of which he used to dance without ever having studied them." Jermyn was known for his success with the fair. "A gentleman," said Etherege, "ought to dress well, dance well, fence well, have a talent for love-letters, a pleasant voice in a room, to be always very amorous, sufficiently discreet, but not too constant." These are already the court manners as they continued in France up to the time of Louis XVI. With such manners, words take

---

[1] *Mémoires de Grammont*, by A. Hamilton. ch. ix.

the place of deeds. Life is passed in visits and conversation. The art of conversing became the chief of all; of course, to converse agreeably, to fill up an idle hour, on twenty subjects in an hour, hinting always, without going deep, in such a fashion that conversation should not be a labour, but a promenade. It was followed up by letters written in the evening, by madrigals or epigrams to be read in the morning, by drawing-room tragedies, or caricatures of society. In this manner a new literature was produced, the work and the portrait of the world which was at once its audience and its model, which sprung from it, and ended in it.

II.

The art of conversation being then a necessity, people set themselves to acquire it. A revolution was effected in mind as well as in manners. As soon as circumstances assume new aspects, thought assumes a new form. The Renaissance is ended, the Classic Age begins, and the artist makes room for the author. Man is returned from his first voyage round the world of facts; enthusiasm, the labour of a troubled imagination, the tumultuous crowding of new ideas, all the faculties which a first discovery calls into play, have become satiated, then depressed. The incentive is blunted, because the work is done. The eccentricities, the far vistas, the unbridled originality, the all-powerful flights of genius aimed at the centre of truth through the extremes of folly, all the characteristics of grand inventive genius have disappeared. The imagination is tempered; the mind is disciplined: it retraces its steps; it walks its own domain once more with a satisfied curiosity, an acquired experience. Judgment, as it were, chews the cud and corrects itself. It finds a religion, an art, a philosophy, to reform or to form anew. It is no longer the minister of inspired intuition, but of a regular process of decomposition. It no longer feels or looks for generalities; it handles and observes specialties. It selects and classifies; it refines and regulates. It ceases to be a creator, and becomes a discourser. It quits the province of invention and settles down into criticism. It enters upon that magnificent and confused aggregate of dogmas and forms, in which the preceding age has gathered up indiscriminately its dreams and discoveries; it draws thence the ideas which it modifies and verifies. It arranges them in long chains of simple ratiocination, which descend link by link to the vulgar apprehension. It expresses them in exact terms, which present a graduated series, step by step, to the vulgar reasoning power. It marks out in the entire field of thought a series of compartments and a network of passages, which, excluding all error and digression, lead gradually every mind to every object. It becomes at last clear, convenient, charming. And the world lends its aid; contingent circumstances finish the natural revolution; the taste becomes changed through a declivity of its own, but also through the influence of the court. When conversation becomes the chief business of life, it modifies style after its own image, and according to its peculiar needs. It repudiates digression, excessive metaphor, impassioned exclamations, all loose and overstrained ways. We cannot bawl, gesticulate, dream aloud, in a drawing-room; we restrain ourselves; we criticise and keep watch over ourselves; we pass the time in narration and discussion; we stand in need of concise expression, exact language, clear and connected reasoning; otherwise we cannot fence or comprehend each other. Correct style, good language, conversation, are self-generated, and very quickly perfected; for refinement is the aim of the man of the world: he studies to render everything more becoming and more serviceable, his furniture and his speech, his periods and his dress. Art and artifice are there the distinguishing mark. People pride themselves on being perfect in their mother tongue, never to miss the correct sense of any word, to avoid vulgar expressions, to string together their antitheses, to develop their thoughts, to employ rhetoric. Nothing is more marked than the contrast of the conversations of Shakspeare and Fletcher with those of Wycherley and Congreve. In Shakspeare the dialogue resembles an assault of arms; we could imagine men of skill fencing with words and gestures as it were in a fencing-school. They play the buffoon, sing, think aloud, burst out into a laugh, into puns, into fishwomen's talk and into poet's talk, into quaint whimsicalities; they have a taste for the ridiculous, the sparkling; one of them dances while he speaks; they would willingly walk on their hands; there is not one grain of calculation to more than three grains of folly in their heads. In Wycherley, on the other hand, the characters are steady; they reason and dispute; ratiocination is the basis of their style; they are so perfect that the thing is overdone, and we see through it all the author stringing his phrases. They arrange a tableau, multiply ingenious comparisons, balance well-ordered periods. One character delivers a satire, another serves up a little essay on morality. We might draw from the comedies of the time a volume of sentences; they are charged with literary morsels which foreshadow the *Spectator*.[1] They hunt for clever and suitable expressions, they clothe indecent circumstances with decent words; they glide swiftly over the fragile ice of decorum, and scratch the surface without breaking it. I see gentlemen, seated in gilt arm-chairs, of quiet wit and studied speech, cool in observation, eloquent sceptics, expert in the fashions, lovers of elegance, liking fine talk as much from vanity as from taste, who, while conversing between a compliment and a reverence, will no more neglect their good style than their neat gloves or their hat.

III.

Amongst the best and most agreeable specimens of this new refinement, appears Sir William Temple, a diplomatist and man of the world, cautious, prudent, and polite, gifted with tact in conversation and in business, expert in the knowledge of the times, and in the art of not compromising himself, adroit in pressing forward and in standing aside, who knew how to attract to himself the favour and the expectations of England, to obtain the eulogies of men of letters, of savants, of politicians, of the people, to gain a European reputation, to win all the crowns appropriated to science, patriotism, virtue, genius, without having too much of science, patriotism, genius, or virtue. Such a life is the masterpiece of that age: fine externals on a foundation not so fine; this is its abstract. His manner as an author agrees with his maxims as a politician. His principles and style are homogeneous; a genuine diplomatist, such

---

[1] Take, for example, Farquhar's *Beaux Stratagem*, ii. 1.

as one meets in the drawing-rooms, having probed Europe and touched everywhere the bottom of things; tired of everything, specially of enthusiasm, admirable in an arm-chair or at a levee, a good story-teller, waggish if need were, but in moderation, accomplished in the art of maintaining the dignity of his station and of enjoying himself. In his retreat at Sheen, afterwards at Moor Park, he employs his leisure in writing; and he writes as a man of his rank would speak, very well, that is to say, with dignity and facility, particularly when he writes of the countries he has visited, of the incidents he has seen, the noble amusements which serve to pass his time.[1] He has an income of fifteen hundred a year, and a nice sinecure in Ireland. He retired from public life during momentous struggles, siding neither with the king nor against him, resolved, as he tells us himself, not to set himself against the current when the current is irresistible. He lives peacefully in the country with his wife, his sister, his secretary, his dependants, receiving the visits of strangers, who are anxious to see the negotiator of the Triple Alliance, and sometimes of the new King William, who unable to obtain his services, comes occasionally to seek his counsel. He plants and gardens, in a fertile soil, in a country the climate of which agrees with him, amongst regular flower-beds, by the side of a very straight canal, bordered by a straight terrace; and he lauds himself in set terms, and with suitable discreetness, for the character he possesses and the part he has chosen:—" I have often wondered how such sharp and violent invectives come to be made

[1] Consult especially, *Observations upon the United Provinces of the Netherlands; Of Gardening.*

so generally against Epicurus, by the ages that followed him, whose admirable wit, felicity of expression, excellence of nature, sweetness of conversation, temperance of life and constancy of death, made him so beloved by his friends, admired by his scholars, and honoured by the Athenians."[1] He does well to defend Epicurus, because he has followed his precepts, avoiding every great confusion of the mind, and installing himself, like one of Lucretius' gods, in the interspace of worlds; as he says: "Where factions were once entered and rooted in a state, they thought it madness for good men to meddle with public affairs." And again: "The true service of the public is a business of so much labour and so much care, that though a good and wise man may not refuse it, if he be called to it by his prince or his country, and thinks he may be of more than vulgar use, yet he will seldom or never seek it; but leaves it commonly to men who, under the disguise of public good, pursue their own designs of wealth, power, and such bastard honours as usually attend them, not that which is the true, and only true, reward of virtue."[2] This is how he ushers himself in. Thus presented to us, he goes on to talk of the gardening which he practises, and first of the six grand Epicureans who have illustrated the doctrine of their master—Cæsar, Atticus, Lucretius, Horace, Mæcenas, Virgil; then of the various sorts of gardens which have a name in the world, from the garden of Eden, and the garden of Alcinous, to those of Holland and Italy; and all this at some length, like a man who listens to himself and is listened to by others, who does rather profusely the honours of his house and of his wit to

[1] Temple's Works: *Of Gardening*, ii. 190.   [2] *Ibid.* 184.

his guests, but does them with grace and dignity, not dogmatically nor haughtily, but in varied tones, aptly modulating his voice and gestures. He recounts the four kinds of grapes which he has introduced into England, and confesses that he has been extravagant, yet does not regret it; for five years he has not once wished to see London. He intersperses technical advice with anecdotes; whereof one relates to Charles II., who praised the English climate above all others, saying: "He thought that was the best climate, where he could be abroad in the air with pleasure, or at least without trouble or inconvenience, most days of the year, and most hours of the day." Another about the Bishop of Munster, who, unable to grow anything but cherries in his orchard, had collected all varieties, and so perfected the trees that he had fruit from May to September. The reader feels an inward gratification when he hears an eyewitness relate minute details of such great men. Our attention is aroused immediately; we in consequence imagine ourselves denizens of the court, and smile complacently; no matter if the details be slender they serve passably well, they constitute "a half hour with the aristocracy," like a lordly way of taking snuff, or shaking the lace of one's ruffles. Such is the interest of courtly conversation; it can be held about nothing; the excellence of the manner lends this nothing a peculiar charm; you hear the sound of the voice, you are amused by the half smile, abandon yourself to the fluent stream, forget that these are ordinary ideas; you observe the narrator, his peculiar breeches, the cane he toys with, the be-ribboned shoes, his easy walk over the smooth gravel of his garden paths between the faultless hedges;

the ear, the mind even is charmed, captivated by the appropriateness of his diction, by the abundance of his ornate periods, by the dignity and fulness of a style which is involuntarily regular, which, at first artificial, like good breeding, ends, like true good breeding, by being changed into a real necessity and a natural talent.

Unfortunately, this talent occasionally leads to blunders; when a man speaks well about everything, he thinks he has a right to speak of everything. He plays the philosopher, the critic, even the man of learning; and indeed becomes so actually, at least with the ladies Such a man writes, like Temple, *Essays on the Nature of Government,* on *Heroic Virtue,*[1] on *Poetry*; that is, little treatises on society, on the beautiful, on the philosophy of history. He is the Locke, the Herder, the Bentley of the drawing-room, and nothing else. Now and then, doubtless, his mother wit leads him to fair original judgments. Temple was the first to discover a Pindaric glow in the old chant of Ragnar Lodbrog, and to place Don Quixote in the first rank of modern fictions; moreover, when he handles a subject within his range, like the causes of the power and decline of the Turks, his reasoning is admirable. But otherwise, he is simply a tyro; nay, in him the pedant crops out, and the worst of pedants, who, being ignorant, wishes to seem wise, who quotes the history of every land, hauling in Jupiter, Saturn, Osiris, Fo-hi, Confucius, Manco-Capac, Mahomet, and discourses on all these obscure and unknown civilisations, as if he had laboriously studied them, at the fountain head and not at

---

[1] Compare this essay with that of Carlyle, on *Heroes and Hero-Worship;* the title and subject are similar; it is curious to note the difference of the two centuries.

second hand, through the extracts of his secretary, or the books of others. One day he came to grief; having plunged into a literary dispute, and claimed superiority for the ancients over the moderns, he imagined himself a Hellenist, an antiquarian, related the voyages of Pythagoras, the education of Orpheus, and remarked that the Greek sages "were commonly excellent poets, and great physicians: they were so learned in natural philosophy, that they foretold not only eclipses in the heavens, but earthquakes at land and storms at sea, great droughts and great plagues, much plenty or much scarcity of certain sorts of fruits or grain; not to mention the magical powers attributed to several of them, to allay storms, to raise gales, to appease commotions of people, to make plagues cease."[1] Admirable faculties, which we no longer possess. Again he regretted the decay of music, "by which men and beasts, fishes, fowls, and serpents, were so frequently enchanted, and their very natures changed; by which the passions of men were raised to the greatest height and violence, and then as suddenly appeased, so as they might be justly said to be turned into lions or lambs, into wolves or into ·harts, by the powers and charms of this admirable art."[2] He wished to enumerate the greatest modern writers, and forgot to mention in his catalogue, "amongst the Italians, Dante, Petrarch, Ariosto, and Tasso; in his list of French, Pascal, Bossuet, Molière, Corneille, Racine, and Boileau; in his list of Spaniards, Lope and Calderon; and in his list of English, Chaucer, Spenser, Shakespeare, and Milton;"[3] though, by way of compensation, he inserted

---

[1] Temple's Works, ii.: *An Essay upon the Ancient and Modern Learning*, 155.   [2] *Ibid.* 165.

[3] Macaulay's Works, vi. 319: *Essay on Sir William Temple.*

the names of Paolo Sarpi, Guevara, Sir Philip Sidney, Selden, Voiture, and Bussy-Rabutin, "author of the *Histoire amoureuse des Gaules.*" To cap all, he declared the fables of Æsop, which are a dull Byzantine compilation, and the letters of Phalaris, a wretched sophistical forgery, to be admirable and authentic:—" It may perhaps be further affirmed, in favour of the ancients, that the oldest books we have are still in their kind the best. The two most ancient that I know of in prose, among those we call profane authors, are Æsop's *Fables* and Phalaris' *Epistles*, both living near the same time, which was that of Cyrus and Pythagoras. As the first has been agreed by all ages since for the greatest master in his kind, and all others of that sort have been but imitations of his original; so I think the *Epistles of Phalaris* to have more grace, more spirit, more force of wit and genius, than any others I have ever seen, either ancient or modern." And then, in order to commit himself beyond remedy, he gravely remarked: " I know several learned men (or that usually pass for such, under the name of critics) have not esteemed them genuine, and Politian with some others have attributed them to Lucian; but I think he must have little skill in painting that cannot find out this to be an original: such diversity of passions, upon such variety of actions and passages of life and government, such freedom of thought, such boldness of expression, such bounty to his friends, such scorn of his enemies, such honour of learned men, such esteem of good, such knowledge of life, such contempt of death, with such fierceness of nature and cruelty of revenge, could never be represented but by him that possessed them; and I esteem Lucian to have been no more capable of writing than of acting what Phalaris did.

In all one writ, you find the scholar or the sophist; and in all the other, the tyrant and the commander."[1]

Fine rhetoric truly; it is sad that a passage so aptly turned should cover so many stupidities. All this appeared very triumphant; and the universal applause with which this fine oratorical bombast was greeted demonstrates the taste and the culture, the hollowness and the politeness, of the elegant world of which Temple was the marvel, and which, like Temple, loved only the varnish of truth.

IV.

Such were the ornate and polished manners which gradually pierce through debauchery and assume the ascendant. Gradually the current grows clearer, and marks out its course, like a stream, which forcibly entering a new bed, moves with difficulty at first through a heap of mud, then pushes forward its still murky waters, which are purified little by little. These debauchees try to be men of the world, and sometimes succeed in it. Wycherley writes well, very clearly, without the least trace of euphuism, almost in the French manner. He makes Dapperwit say of Lucy, in measured phrase, "She is beautiful without affectation, amorous without impertinence, . . . frolic without rudeness."[2] When he wishes it he is ingenious, and his gentlemen exchange happy comparisons. "Mistresses," says one, "are like books: if you pore upon them too much, they doze you, and make you unfit for company; but if used discreetly, you are the fitter for conversation by 'em." "Yes," says another, "a mistress should be

[1] *An Essay upon the Ancient and Modern Learning*, 173.
[2] *Love in a Wood*, iii. 2.

like a little country retreat near the town; not to dwell in constantly, but only for a night and away, to taste the town the better when a man returns."[1] These folk have style, even out of place, often not in accordance with the situation or condition of the persons. A shoemaker in one of Etherege's plays says: "There is never a man in the town lives more like a gentleman with his wife than I do. I never mind her motions; she never inquires into mine. We speak to one another civilly, hate one another heartily." There is perfect art in this little speech; everything is complete, even to the symmetrical antithesis of words, ideas, sounds: what a fine talker is this same satirical shoemaker! After a satire, a madrigal. In one place a certain character exclaims, in the very middle of a dialogue, and in sober prose, "Pretty pouting lips, with a little moisture hanging on them, that look like the Provence rose fresh on the bush, ere the morning sun has quite drawn up the dew." Is not this the graceful gallantry of the court? Rochester himself sometimes might furnish a parallel. Two or three of his songs are still to be found in the expurgated books of extracts in use amongst modest young girls. It matters nothing that such men are really scamps; they must be every moment using compliments and salutations: before women whom they wish to seduce they are compelled to warble tender words and insipidities: they acknowledge but one check, the necessity to appear well-bred; yet this check suffices to restrain them. Rochester is correct even in the midst of his filth; if he talks lewdly, it is in the able and exact manner of Boileau. All these roisterers aim at being wits and men of the world. Sir Charles Sedley

[1] *The Country Wife*, i. 1.

ruins and pollutes himself, but Charles II. calls him "the viceroy of Apollo." Buckingham extols "the magic of his style." He is the most charming, the most sought-after of talkers; he makes puns and verses, always agreeable, sometimes refined; he handles dexterously the pretty jargon of mythology; he insinuates into his airy, flowing verses all the dainty and somewhat affected prettinesses of the drawing-room. He sings thus to Chloris:

> "My passion with your beauty grew,
>   While Cupid at my heart,
> Still as his mother favour'd you,
>   Threw a new flaming dart."

And then sums up:

> "Each gloried in their wanton part:
>   To make a lover, he
> Employ'd the utmost of his art;
>   To make a beauty, she."[1]

There is no love whatever in these pretty things: they are received as they are presented, with a smile; they form part of the conventional language, the polite attentions due from gentlemen to ladies. I suppose they would send them in the morning with a nosegay, or a box of preserved fruits. Roscommon indites some verses on a dead lapdog, on a young lady's cold; this naughty cold prevents her singing — cursed be the winter! And hereupon he takes the winter to task, abuses it at length. Here you have the literary amusements of the worldling. They first treat love, then

[1] Sir Charles Sedley's Works, ed. Briscoe, 1778, 2 vols.: *The Mulberry Garden*, ii.

danger, most airily and gaily. On the eve of a naval contest, Dorset, at sea, amidst the pitching of his vessel, addresses a celebrated song to the ladies. There is nothing weighty in it, either sentiment or wit; people hum the couplets as they pass; they emit a gleam of gaiety; the next moment they are forgotten. Dorset at sea writes to the ladies, on the night before an engagement:

> "Let's hear of no inconstancy,
> We have too much of *that* at sea."

And again:

> "Should foggy Opdam chance to know
> Our sad and dismal story,
> The Dutch would scorn so weak a foe,
> And quit their fort at Goree.
> For what resistance can they find
> From men who've left their hearts behind?"

Then come jests too much in the English style:

> "Then if we write not by each post,
> Think not we are unkind; . . .
> Our tears we'll send a speedier way;
> The tide shall bring them twice a day."

Such tears can hardly flow from sorrow; the lady regards them as the lover sheds them, good-naturedly. She is "at a play" (he thinks so, and tells her so):

> "Whilst you, regardless of our woe,
> Sit careless at a play,
> Perhaps permit some happier man
> To kiss your hand, or flirt your fan." [1]

[1] *Works of the Earls of Rochester, Roscommon, and Dorset*, 2 vols., 1731, ii. 54.

Dorset hardly troubles himself about it, plays with poetry without excess or assiduity, just as it flows, writing to-day a verse against Dorinda, to-morrow a satire against Mr. Howard, always easily and without study, like a true gentleman. He is an earl, lord-chamberlain, and rich; he pensions and patronises poets as he would flirts—to amuse himself, without binding himself. The Duke of Buckingham does the same, and also the contrary; caresses one poet, parodies another; is flattered, mocked, and ends by having his portrait taken by Dryden—a *chef d'œuvre*, but not flattering. We have seen such pastimes and such bickerings in France; we find here the same manners and the same literature, because we find here also the same society and the same spirit.

Among these poets, and in the front rank, is Edmund Waller, who lived and wrote in this manner to his eighty-second year: a man of wit and fashion, well-bred, familiar from his youth with great people, endued with tact and foresight, quick at repartee, not easy to put out of countenance, but selfish, with hardly any feelings, having changed sides more than once, and bearing very well the memory of his tergiversations; in short, a good model of the worldling and the courtier. It was he who, having once praised Cromwell, and afterwards Charles II., but the latter more feebly than the former, said by way of excuse: "Poets, your Majesty, succeed better in fiction than in truth." In this kind of existence, three-quarters of the poetry is written for the occasion; it is the small change of conversation or flattery; it resembles the little events or the little sentiments from which it sprang. One piece is written "Of Tea," another on the queen's portrait; it is necessary to pay court; moreover "His Majesty has requested some verses." One lady makes him a present of a silver pen, straight he throws his gratitude into ryhme; another has the power of sleeping at will, straight a sportive stanza; a false report is spread of her being painted, straight a copy of verses on this grave affair. A little further on there are verses to the Countess of Carlisle on her chamber, condolences to my Lord of Northumberland on the death of his wife, a pretty thing on a lady "passing through a crowd of people," an answer, verse for verse, to some rhymes of Sir John Suckling. He seizes anything frivolous, new, or becoming on the wing; and his poetry is only a written conversation,—I mean the conversation which goes on at a ball, when people speak for the sake of speaking, lifting a lock of one's wig, or twisting about a glove. Gallantry holds the chief place here, as it ought to do, and we may be pretty certain that the love is not over-sincere. In reality, Waller sighs on purpose (Sacharissa had a fine dowry), or at least for the sake of good manners: that which is most evident in his tender poems is, that he aims at a flowing style and good rhymes. He is affected, he exaggerates, he strains after wit, he is always an author. Not venturing to address Sacharissa herself, he addresses Mrs. Braughton, her attendant, "his fellow-servant:"

> "So, in those nations which the Sun adore,
> Some modest Persian, or some weak-eyed Moor,
> No higher dares advance his dazzled sight
> Than to some gilded cloud, which near the light
> Of their ascending god adorns the east,
> And, graced with his beam, outshines the rest."[1]

[1] *The English Poets*, ed. A. Chalmers, 21 vols., 1810; Waller, vol. viii. 44.

A fine comparison! That is a well-made courtesy; I hope Sacharissa responds with one equally correct. His despairs bear the same flavour; he pierces the groves of Penshurst with his cries, "reports his flame to the beeches," and the well-bred beeches "bow their heads, as if they felt the same."[1] It is probable that, in these mournful walks, his greatest care was lest he should wet the soles of his high-heeled shoes. These transports of love bring in the classical machinery, Apollo and the Muses. Apollo is annoyed that one of his servants is ill-treated, and bids him depart; and he departs, telling Sacharissa that she is harder than an oak, and that she was certainly produced from a rock.[2]

There is one genuine reality in all this—sensuality; not ardent, but light and gay. There is a certain piece, "The Fall," which an abbé of the court of Louis XV. might have written:

> [1] "Then blush not, Fair! or on him frown, . . .
> How could the youth, alas! but bend
> When his whole Heav'n upon him lean'd;

[1] *The English Poets*, Waller, viii. 44.
[2] "While in this park I sing, the list'ning deer
Attend my passion, and forget to fear;
When to the beeches I report my flame,
They bow their heads, as if they felt the same.
To gods appealing, when I reach their bow'rs
With loud complaints, they answer me in showers.
To thee a wild and cruel soul is giv'n,
More deaf than trees, and prouder than the heav'n!
 . . . The rock,
That cloven rock, produc'd thee. . . .
This last complaint th' indulgent ears did pierce
Of just Apollo, president of verse;
Highly concerned that the Muse should bring
Damage to one whom he had taught to sing."—*Ibid.* p. 44-5

If aught by him amiss were done,
'Twas that he let you rise so soon." [1]

Other pieces smack of their surroundings, and are not so polished:

"Amoret! as sweet as good,
As the most delicious food,
Which but tasted does impart
Life and gladness to the heart." [2]

I should not be pleased, were I a woman, to be compared to a beef-steak, though that be appetising; nor should I like any more to find myself, like Sacharissa, placed on a level with good wine, which flies to the head:

"Sacharissa's beauty's wine,
Which to madness doth incline;
Such a liquor as no brain
That is mortal can sustain." [3]

This is too much honour for port wine and meat. The English back-ground crops up here and elsewhere; for example, the beautiful Sacharissa, having ceased to be beautiful, asked Waller if he would again write verses for her: he answered, "Yes, madame, when you are once more as young and as handsome as you were." Here is something to shock a Frenchman. Nevertheless Waller is usually amiable; a sort of brilliant light floats like a halo round his verses; he is always elegant, often graceful. His gracefulness is like the perfume exhaled from the world; fresh toilettes, ornamented drawing-rooms, the abundance and the pursuit of all those refined and delicate comforts give to the mind a sort of sweetness which is breathed forth in obliging

[1] *English Poets*, Waller, viii. 32.   [2] *Ibid.* 45.   [3] *Ibid.* 45.

compliments and smiles. Waller has many of these compliments and smiles, and those most flattering, apropos of a bud, a girdle, a rose. Such bouquets become his hands and his art. He pays an excellent compliment "To young Lady Lucy Sidney" on her age. And what could be more attractive for a frequenter of drawing-rooms, than this bud of still unopened youth, but which blushes already, and is on the point of expanding?

> " Yet, fairest blossom! do not slight
> That age which you may know so soon.
> The rosy morn resigns her light
> And milder glory to the noon." [1]

All his verses flow with a continuous harmony, clearness, facility, though his voice is never raised, or out of tune, or rough, nor loses its true accent, except by the worldling's affectation, which regularly changes all tones in order to soften them. His poetry resembles one of those pretty, affected, bedizened women, busy in inclining their head on one side, and murmuring with a soft voice commonplace things which they can hardly be said to think, yet agreeable in their be-ribboned dress, and who would please altogether if they did not dream of always pleasing.

It is not that these men cannot handle grave subjects; but they handle them in their own fashion, without gravity or depth. What the courtier most lacks is the genuine sentiment of a true and original idea. That which interests him most is the correctness of the adornment, and the perfection of external form. They care little for the matter itself, much for the outward shape. In fact, it is form which they take for

---

[1] *English Poets*, Waller, viii. 45

their subject in nearly all their serious poetry; they are critics, they lay down precepts, they compose Arts of Poetry. Denham in his "*Preface to the Destruction of Troy*" lays down rules for translating, whilst Roscommon teaches in a complete poem, an *Essay on translated Verse*, the art of translating poetry well. The Duke of Buckinghamshire versified an *Essay on Poetry* and an *Essay on Satire*. Dryden is in the first rank of these pedagogues. Like Dryden again, they turn translators, amplifiers. Roscommon translated the *Ars Poetica* of Horace; Waller the first act of *Pompée*, a tragedy by Corneille; Denham some fragments of Homer and Virgil, and two poems, one *of Prudence* and another *of Justice*. Rochester composed a satire against *Mankind*, in the style of Boileau, and also an epistle upon *Nothing;* the amorous Waller wrote a didactic poem on *The Fear of God*, and another in six cantos on *Divine Love*. These are exercises of style. They take a theological thesis, a commonplace subject of philosophy, a poetic maxim, and develop it in jointed prose, furnished with rhymes; invent nothing, feel little, and only aim at expressing good arguments in classical metaphors, in noble terms, after a conventional model. Most of their verses consist of two nouns, furnished with epithets, and connected by a verb, like college Latin verses. The epithet is good: they had to hunt through the Gradus for it, or, as Boileau wills it, they had to carry the line unfinished in their heads, and had to think about it an hour in the open air, until at last, at the corner of a wood, they found the right word which they could not hit upon before. I yawn, but applaud. After so much trouble a generation ends by forming the sustained style which is necessary to support, make public, and demonstrate grand things. Meanwhile, with their ornate, official diction, and their borrowed thought they are like formal chamberlains, in embroidered coats present at a royal marriage or an imperial baptism, empty of head, grave in manner, admirable for dignity and bearing, with the punctilio and the ideas of a dummy.

V.

One of them only (Dryden always excepted) showed talent, Sir John Denham, Charles the First's secretary. He was employed in public affairs, and after a dissolute youth, turned to serious habits; and leaving behind him satiric verse and party broad-jokes, attained in riper years a lofty oratorical style. His best poem, *Cooper's Hill*, is the description of a hill and its surroundings, blended with the historical ideas which the sight recalls, and the moral reflections which its appearance naturally suggests. All these subjects are in accordance with the nobility and the limitation of the classical spirit, and display his vigour without betraying his weaknesses; the poet could show off his whole talent without forcing it. His fine language exhibits all its beauty, because it is sincere. We find pleasure in following the regular progress of those copious phrases in which his ideas, opposed or combined, attain for the first time their definite place and full clearness, where symmetry only brings out the argument more clearly, expansion only completes thought, antithesis and repetition do not induce trifling and affectation, where the music of verse, adding the breadth of sound to the fulness of sense, conducts the chain of ideas, without effort or disorder, by an appropriate measure to a becoming order and movement. Gratification is united with solidity; the author of "Cooper's Hill," knows how to please as well as to impress. His poem is like a king's park, dignified and level without doubt, but arranged to please the eye, and full of choice prospects. It leads us by easy digressions across a multitude of varied thoughts. It shows us here a mountain, yonder a memorial of the nymphs, a classic memorial, like a portico filled with statues, further on a broad stream, and by its side the ruins of an abbey; each page of the poem is like a distinct alley, with its distinct perspective. Further on, our thoughts are turned to the superstitions of the ignorant middle-ages, and to the excesses of the recent revolution; then comes the picture of a royal hunt; we see the trembling stag make his retreat to some dark covert:

> "He calls to mind his strength, and then his speed,
> His winged heels, and then his armed head;
> With these t' avoid, with that his fate to meet,
> But fear prevails, and bids him trust his feet.
> So fast he flies, that his reviewing eye
> Has lost the chasers, and his ear the cry."[1]

These are the worthy spectacles and the studied diversity of the grounds of a nobleman. Every object, moreover, receives here, as in a king's palace, all the adornment which can be given to it; elegant epithets are introduced to embellish a feeble substantive; the decorations of art transform the commonplace of nature: vessels are "floating towers;" the Thames is "the most loved of all the Ocean's sons;" the airy mountain hides its proud head among the clouds, whilst a shady mantle clothes its sides. Among different kinds of ideas, there

[1] *English Poets*, vii. 237.

is one kingly, full of stately and magnificent ceremonies of self-contained and studied gestures, of correct yet commanding figures, uniform and imposing like the appointments of a palace; hence the classic writers, and Denham amongst them, draw all their poetic tints. From this every object and event takes its colouring, because constrained to come into contact with it. Here the object and events are compelled to traverse other things. Denham is not a mere courtier, he is an Englishman; that is, preoccupied by moral emotions. He often quits his landscape to enter into some grave reflection; politics, religion, disturb the enjoyment of his eyes; in reference to a hill or a forest, he meditates upon man; externals lead him inward; impressions of the senses to contemplations of the soul. The men of this race are by nature and custom esoteric. When he sees the Thames throw itself into the sea, he compares it with "mortal life hasting to meet eternity." The "lofty forehead" of a mountain, beaten by storms, reminds him of "the common fate of all that's high or great." The course of the river suggests to him ideas of inner reformation:

"O could I flow like thee! and make thy stream
My great example, as it is my theme!
Though deep, yet clear, though gentle yet not dull;
Strong without rage, without o'erflowing, full.

But his proud head the airy mountain hides
Among the clouds; his shoulders and his sides
A shady mantle clothes; his curled brows
Frown on the gentle stream, which calmly flows;
While winds and storms his lofty forehead beat,
The common fate of all that's high or great."[1]

[1] *English Poets*, vii. 236-7.

There is in the English mind an indestructible store of moral instincts, and grand melancholy; and it is the greatest confirmation of this, that we can discover such a stock at the court of Charles II.

These are, however, but rare openings, and as it were croppings up of the original rock. The habits of the worldling are as a thick layer which cover it throughout. Manners, conversation, style, the stage, taste, all is French, or tries to be; they imitate France as well as they are able, and go there to mould themselves. Many cavaliers went there, driven away by Cromwell. Denham, Waller, Roscommon, and Rochester resided there; the Duchess of Newcastle, a poetess of the time, was married at Paris; the Duke of Buckinghamshire served for a short time under Turenne; Wycherley was sent to France by his father, who wished to rescue him from the contagion of Puritan opinions; Vanbrugh, one of the best comic playwrights, went thither to contract a polish. The two courts were allied almost always in fact, and always at heart, by a community of interests, and of religious and monarchical ideas. Charles II. accepted from Louis XIV. a pension, a mistress, counsels, and examples; the nobility followed their prince, and France was the model of the English court. Her literature and manners, the finest of the classic age, led the fashion. We perceive in English writings that French authors are their masters, and that they were in the hands of all well-educated people. They consulted Bossuet, translated Corneille, imitated Molière, respected Boileau. It went so far, that the greatest gallants of them tried to be altogether French, to mix some scraps of French in every phrase. "It is as ill-breeding now to speak good English," says Wycherley, "as to write good English, good sense, or a good hand." These Frenchified coxcombs[1] are compliment-mongers, always powdered, perfumed, "eminent for being *bien gantés*." They affect delicacy, they are fastidious; they find Englishmen coarse, gloomy, stiff; they try to be giddy and thoughtless; they giggle and prate at random, placing the reputation of man in the perfection of his wig and his bows. The theatre, which ridicules these imitators, is an imitator after their fashion. French comedy, like French politeness, becomes their model. They copy both, altering without equalling them; for monarchical and classic France is amongst all nations, the best fitted from its instincts and institutions for the modes of worldly life, and the works of an oratorical mind. England follows it in this course, being carried away by the universal current of the age, but at a distance, and drawn aside by its national peculiarities. It is this common direction and this particular deviation which the society and its poetry have proclaimed, and which the stage and its characters will display.

VI.

Four principal writers established this comedy—Wycherley, Congreve, Vanbrugh, Farquhar:[2] the first gross, and in the pristine irruption of vice; the others more sedate, possessing more a taste for urbanity than debauchery; yet all men of the world, and priding themselves on their good breeding, on passing their days at court or in fine company, on having the tastes and bearing of gentlemen. "I am not a literary man," said Congreve

[1] Etherege's *Sir Fopling Flutter;* Wycherley's *The Gentleman Dancing-master,* i. 2.
[2] From 1672 to 1726.

to Voltaire, "I am a gentleman." In fact, as Pope said, he lived more like a man of quality than a man of letters, was noted for his successes with the fair, and passed his latter years in the house of the Duchess of Marlborough. I have said that Wycherley, under Charles II., was one of the most fashionable courtiers. He served in the army for some time, as did also Vanbrugh and Farquhar; nothing is more gallant than the name of Captain which they employed, the military stories they brought back, and the feather they stuck in their hats. They all wrote comedies on the same worldly and classical model, made up of probable incidents such as we observe around us every day, of well-bred characters such as we commonly meet in a drawing-room, correct and elegant conversations such as well-bred men can carry on. This theatre, wanting in poetry, fancy, and adventures, imitative and discursive, was formed at the same time as that of Molière, by the same causes, and on his model, so that in order to comprehend it we must compare it with that of Molière.

"Molière belongs to no nation," said a great English actor (Kemble); "one day the god of comedy, wishing to write, became a man, and happened to fall into France." I accept this saying; but in becoming man he found himself, at the same time, a man of the seventeenth century and a Frenchman, and that is how he was the god of comedy. "To amuse respectable people," said Molière, "what a strange task!" Only the French art of the seventeenth century could succeed in that; for it consists in leading by an agreeable path to general notions; and the taste for these notions, as well as the custom of treading this path, is the peculiar mark of respectable people. Molière, like

Racine, expands and creates. Open any one of his plays that comes to hand, and the first scene in it, chosen at random; after three replies you are carried away, or rather led away. The second continues the first, the third carries out the second, the fourth completes all; a current is created which bears us on, which bears us away, which does not release us until it is exhausted. There is no check, no digression, no episodes to distract our attention. To prevent the lapses of an absent mind, a secondary character intervenes, a lackey, a lady's-maid, a wife, who, couplet by couplet, repeat in a different fashion the reply of the principal character, and by means of symmetry and contrast keep us in the path laid down. Arrived at the end, a second current seizes us and acts like the first. It is composed like the other, and with reference to the other. It throws it out by contrast, or strengthens it by resemblance. Here the valets repeat the dispute, then the reconciliation of their masters. In one place, Alceste, drawn in one direction through three pages by anger, is drawn in a contrary direction, and through three pages, by love. Further on, tradesmen, professors, relatives, domestics, relieve each other scene after scene, in order to bring out in clearer light the pretentiousness and gullibility of M. Jourdain. Every scene, every act, brings out in greater relief, completes, or prepares another. Everything is united, and everything is simple; the action progresses, and progresses only to carry on the idea; there is no complication, no incidents. One comic event suffices for the story. A dozen conversations make up the play of the *Misanthrope*. The same situation, five or six times renewed, is the whole of *l'Ecole des Femmes*. These pieces are made out of nothing.

They have no need of incidents, they find ample space in the compass of one room and one day, without surprises, without decoration, with an arras and four arm-chairs. This paucity of matter throws out the ideas more clearly and quickly; in fact, their whole aim is to bring those ideas prominently forward; the simplicity of the subject, the progress of the action, the linking together of the scenes,—to this everything tends. At every step clearness increases, the impression is deepened, vice stands out: ridicule is piled up, until, before so many apt and united appeals, laughter forces its way and breaks forth. And this laughter is not a mere outburst of physical amusement; it is the judgment which incites it. The writer is a philosopher, who brings us into contact with a universal truth by a particular example. We understand through him, as through La Bruyère or Nicole, the force of prejudice, the obstinacy of conventionality, the blindness of love. The couplets of his dialogue, like the arguments of their treatises, are but the worked out proof and the logical justification of a preconceived conclusion. We philosophise with him on humanity; we think because he has thought. And he has only thought thus in the character of a Frenchman, for an audience of French men of the world. In him we taste a national pleasure. French refined and systematic intelligence, the most exact in seizing on the subordination of ideas, the most ready in separating ideas from matter, the most fond of clear and tangible ideas, finds in him its nourishment and its echo. None who has sought to show us mankind, has led us by a straighter and easier mode to a more distinct and speaking portrait. I will add, to a more pleasing portrait,—and this is the main talent of comedy: it consists in keeping back what is hateful; and observe that which is hateful abounds in the world. As soon as you will paint the world truly, philosophically, you meet with vice, injustice, and everywhere indignation; amusement flees before anger and morality. Consider the basis of *Tartuffe;* an obscene pedant, a red-faced hypocritical wretch, who, palming himself off on a decent and refined family, tries to drive the son away, marry the daughter, corrupt the wife, ruin and imprison the father, and almost succeeds in it, not by clever plots, but by vulgar mummery, and by the coarse audacity of his caddish disposition. What could be more repelling? And how is amusement to be drawn from such a subject, where Beaumarchais and La Bruyère failed?[1] Similarly, in the *Misanthrope,* is not the spectacle of a loyally sincere and honest man, very much in love, whom his virtue finally overwhelms with ridicule and drives from society, a sad sight to see? Rousseau was annoyed that it should produce laughter; and if we were to look upon the subject, not in Molière, but in itself, we should find enough to revolt our natural generosity. Recall his other plots; Georges Dandin mystified, Géronte beaten, Arnolphe duped, Harpagon plundered, Sganarelle married, girls seduced, louts thrashed, simpletons turned financiers. There are sorrows here, and deep ones; many would rather weep than laugh at them. Arnolphe, Dandin, Harpagon, are almost tragic characters; and when we see them in the world instead of the theatre, we are not disposed to sarcasm, but to pity. Picture to yourself the

[1] *Onuphre,* in 'La Bruyère's *Caractères,* ch. xiii. *de la Mode; Begears,* in Beaumarchais *la Mère Coupable.*

originals from whom Molière has taken his doctors. Consider this venturesome experimentalist, who, in the interest of science, tries a new saw, or inoculates a virus; think of his long nights at the hospital, the wan patient carried on a mattress to the operating table, and stretching out his leg to the knife; or again imagine the peasant's bed of straw in the damp cottage, where an old dropsical mother lies choking,[1] while her children grudgingly count up the crowns she has already cost them. You quit such scenes deeply moved, filled with sympathy for human misery; you discover that life, seen near and face to face, is a mass of trivial harshnesses and of grievous passions; you are tempted, if you wish to depict it, to enter into the mire of sorrows whereon Balzac and Shakspeare have built: you see in it no other poetry than that audacious reasoning power which from such a confusion abstracts the master-forces, or the light of genius which flickers over the swarm and the falls of so many polluted and wounded wretches. How everything changes under the hand of a mercurial Frenchman! how all this human ugliness is blotted out! how amusing is the spectacle which Molière has arranged for us! how we ought to thank the great artist for having transformed his subject so well! At last we have a cheerful world, on canvas at least; we could not have it otherwise, but this we have. How pleasant it is to forget truth! what an art is that which divests us of ourselves! what a point of view which converts the contortions of suffering into funny grimaces! Gaiety has come upon us, the dearest possession of a Frenchman. The soldiers of Villars used to dance that they might forget

[1] Consultations of Sganarelle in the *Médecin malgré lui*.

they had no longer any bread. Of all French possessions, too, it is the best. This gift does not destroy thought, but it masks it. In Molière, truth is at the bottom, but concealed; he has heard the sobs of human tragedy, but he prefers not to re-echo them. It is quite enough to feel our wounds smart; let us not go to the theatre to see them again. Philosophy, while it reveals them, advises us not to think of them too much. Let us enliven our condition with the gaiety of easy conversation and light wit, as we would the chamber of sickness. Let us cover Tartuffe, Harpagon, the doctors, with outrageous ridicule: ridicule will make us forget their vices; they will afford us amusement instead of causing horror. Let Alceste be grumpy and awkward. It is in the first place true, because our more valiant virtues are only the outbreaks of a temper out of harmony with circumstances; but, in addition, it will be amusing. His mishaps will cease to make him the martyr of justice; they will only be the consequences of a cross-grained character. As to the mystifications of husbands, tutors, and fathers, I fancy that we are not to see in them a concerted attack on society or morality. We are only entertaining ourselves for one evening, nothing more. The syringes and thrashings, the masquerades and dances, prove that it is a sheer piece of buffoonery. Do not be afraid that philosophy will perish in a pantomime; it is present even in the *Mariage forcé*, even in the *Malade imaginaire*. It is the mark of a Frenchman and a man of the world to clothe everything, even that which is serious, in laughter. When he is thinking, he does not always wish to show it. In his most violent moments he is still the master of the house, the polite host; he conceals from you his thoughts or his suffering. Mirabeau, when in agony, said to one of his friends with a smile, " Come, you who take an interest in plucky deaths, you shall see mine ! " The French talk in this style when they are depicting life ; no other nation knows how to philosophise smartly, and die with good taste.

This is the reason why in no other nation comedy, while it continues comic, affords a moral; Molière is the only man who gives us models without getting pedantic, without trenching on the tragic, without growing solemn. This model is the "respectable man," as the phrase was, Philinte, Ariste, Clitandre, Éraste ;[1] there is no other who can at the same time instruct and amuse us. His talent has reflection for its basis, but it is cultivated by the world. His character has honesty for its basis, but it is in harmony with the world. You may imitate him without transgressing either reason or duty; he is neither a coxcomb nor a roisterer. You can imitate him without neglecting your interests or making yourself ridiculous ; he is neither an ignoramus nor unmannerly. He has read and understands the jargon of Trissotin and Lycidas, but in order to pierce them through and through, to beat them with their own arguments, to set the gallery in a roar at their expense. He will discuss even morality and religion, but in a style so natural, with proofs so clear, with warmth so genuine, that he interests women, and is listened to by men of the world. He knows man, and reasons about him, but in such brief sentences, such living delineations, such pungent humour, that his philosophy is the best of entertainments. He is faithful to his ruined mistress, his

[1] Amongst women, Éliante, Henriette, Élise, Uranie, Elmire.

calumniated friend, but gracefully, without fuss. All his actions, even noble ones, have an easy way about them which adorns them; he does nothing without pleasantness. His great talent is knowledge of the world; he shows it not only in the trivial circumstances of every-day life, but in the most passionate scenes, the most embarrassing positions. A noble swordsman wants to take Philinte, the "respectable man," as his second in a duel; he reflects a moment, excuses himself in a score of phrases, and "without playing the Hector," leaves the bystanders convinced that he is no coward. Armande insults him, then throws herself in his arms; he politely averts the storm, declines the reconciliation with the most loyal frankness, and without employing a single falsehood, leaves the spectators convinced that he is no boor. When he loves Éliante,[1] who prefers Alceste, and whom Alceste may possibly marry, he proposes to her with a complete delicacy and dignity, without lowering himself, without recrimination, without wronging himself or his friend. When Oronte reads him a sonnet, he does not assume in the fop a nature which he has not, but praises the conventional verses in conventional language, and is not so clumsy as to display a poetical judgment which would be out of place. He takes at once his tone from the circumstances; he perceives instantly what he must say and what be silent about, in what degree and in what gradations, what exact expedient will reconcile truth and conventional propriety, how far he ought to go or where to take his stand, what faint line separates decorum from flattery, truth from awkwardness. On

[1] Compare the admirable tact and coolness of Éliante, Henriette, and Elmire.

this narrow path he proceeds free from embarrassment or mistakes, never put out of his way by the shocks or changes of circumstance, never allowing the calm smile of politeness to quit his lips, never omitting to receive with a laugh of good humour the nonsense of his neighbour. This cleverness, entirely French, reconciles in him fundamental honesty and worldly breeding; without it, he would be altogether on the one side or the other. In this way comedy finds its hero half-way between the *roué* and the preacher.

Such a theatre depicts a race and an age. This mixture of solidity and elegance belongs to the seventeenth century, and belongs to France. The world does not deprave, it develops Frenchmen; it polished then not only their manners and their homes, but also their sentiments and ideas. Conversation provoked thought; it was no mere talk, but an inquiry; with the exchange of news, it called forth the interchange of reflections. Theology and philosophy entered into it; morals, and the observation of the heart, formed its daily pabulum. Science kept up its vitality, and lost only its aridity. Pleasantness cloaked reason, but did not smother it. Frenchmen never think better than in society; the play of features excites them; their ready ideas flash into lightning, in their shock with the ideas of others. The varied current of conversation suits their fits and starts; the frequent change of subject fosters their invention; the pungency of piquant speeches reduces truth to small but precious coin, suitable to the lightness of their hands. And the heart is no more tainted by it than the intelligence. The Frenchman is of a sober temperament, with little taste for the brutishness of the drunkard, for violent joviality, for the riot of loose suppers; he is moreover gentle, obliging, always ready to please; in order to set him at ease he needs that flow of goodwill and elegance which polite society creates and cherishes. And in accordance therewith, he shapes his temperate and amiable inclinations into maxims; it is a point of honour with him to be serviceable and refined. Such is the gentleman, the product of society in a sociable race. It was not so with the English. Their ideas do not spring up in chance conversation, but by the concentration of solitary thought; this is the reason why ideas were then wanting. Their gentlemanly feelings are not the fruit of sociable instincts, but of personal reflection; that is why gentlemanly feelings were then at a discount. The brutish foundation remained; the outside alone was smooth. Manners were gentle, sentiments harsh; speech was studied, ideas frivolous. Thought and refinement of soul were rare, talent and fluent wit abundant. There was politeness of manner, not of heart; they had only the set rules and the conventionalities of life, its giddiness and heedlessness.

VII.

The English comedy-writers paint these vices, and possess them. Their talent and their stage are tainted by them. Art and philosophy are absent. The authors do not advance upon a general idea, and they do not proceed by the most direct method. They put together ill, and are embarrassed by materials. Their pieces have generally two intermingled plots, manifestly distinct,[1] combined in order to multiply incidents, and

[1] Dryden boasts of this. With him, we always find a complete comedy grossly amalgamated with a complete tragedy.

because the public demands a multitude of characters and facts. A strong current of boisterous action is necessary to stir up their dense appreciation; they do as the Romans did, who packed several Greek plays into one. They grew tired of the French simplicity of action, because they had not the French refined taste. The two series of actions mingle and jostle one with another. We cannot see where we are going; every moment we are turned out of our path. The scenes are ill connected; they change twenty times from place to place. When one scene begins to develop itself, a deluge of incidents interrupts. An irrelevant dialogue drags on between the incidents, suggesting a book with the notes introduced promiscuously into the text. There is no plan carefully conceived and rigorously carried out; they took, as it were, a plan, and wrote out the scenes one after another, pretty much as they came into their head. Probability is not well cared for. There are poorly arranged disguises, ill simulated folly, mock marriages, and attacks by robbers worthy of the comic opera. In order to obtain a sequence of ideas and probability, we must set out from some general idea. The conception of avarice, hypocrisy, the education of women, ill-assorted marriages, arranges and binds together by its individual power incidents which are to reveal it. But in the English comedy we look in vain for such a conception. Congreve, Farquhar, Vanbrugh, are only men of wit, not thinkers. They skim the surface of things, but do not penetrate. They play with their characters. They aim at success, at amusement. They sketch caricatures, they spin out in lively fashion a vain and bantering conversation; they make answers clash with one another, fling forth paradoxes; their nimble fingers manipulate and juggle with the incidents in a hundred ingenious and unlooked-for ways. They have animation, they abound in gesture and repartee; the constant bustle of the stage and its lively spirit surround them with continual excitement. But the pleasure is only skin-deep; we have seen nothing of the eternal foundation and the real nature of mankind; we carry no thought away; we have passed an hour, and that is all; the amusement teaches us nothing, and serves only to fill up the evenings of coquettes and coxcombs.

Moreover, this pleasure is not real; it has no resemblance to the hearty laughter of Molière. In English comedy there is always an undercurrent of tartness. We have seen this, and more, in Wycherley; the others, though less cruel, joke sourly. Their characters in a joke say harsh things to one another; they amuse themselves by hurting each other; a Frenchman is pained to hear this interchange of mock politeness; he does not go to blows by way of fun. Their dialogue turns naturally to virulent satire; instead of covering vice, it makes it prominent; instead of making it ridiculous, it makes it odious:

"*Clarissa.* Prithee, tell me how you have passed the night ?..

Araminta. Why, I have been studying all the ways my brain could produce to plague my husband.

Cl. No wonder indeed you look so fresh this morning, after the satisfaction of such pleasing ideas all night."[1]

These women are really wicked, and that too openly. Throughout vice is crude, pushed to extremes, served up with material adjuncts. Lady Fidget says: " Our virtue

[1] Vanbrugh, *Confederacy,* ii. 1.

is like the statesman's religion, the quaker's word, the gamester's oath, and the great man's honour; but to cheat those that trust us."[1] Or again: "If you'll consult the widows of this town," says a young lady who does not wish to marry again, "they'll tell you, you should never take a lease of a house you can hire for a quarter's warning."[2] Or again: "My heart cut a caper up to my mouth," says a young heir, "when I heard my father was shot through the head."[3] The gentlemen collar each other on the stage, treat the ladies roughly before spectators, contrive an adultery not far off between the wings. Base or ferocious parts abound. There are furies like Mrs. Loveit and Lady Touchwood. There are swine like parson Bull and the go-between Coupler. Lady Touchwood wants to stab her lover on the stage.[4] Coupler, on the stage, uses gestures which recall the court of Henry III. of France. Wretches like Fainall and Maskwell are unmitigated scoundrels, and their hatefulness is not even cloaked by the grotesque. Even honest women like Silvia and Mrs. Sullen are plunged into the most shocking situations. Nothing shocked the English public of those days; they had no real education, but only its varnish.

There is a forced connection between the mind of a writer, the world which surrounds him, and the characters which he produces; for it is from this world that he draws the materials out of which he composes them. The sentiments which he contemplates in others

[1] Wycherley, *The Country Wife*, v. 4.
[2] Vanbrugh, *Relapse*, ii. end. [3] *Ibid*.
[4] She says to Maskwell, her lover: "You want but leisure to invent fresh falsehood, and soothe me to a fond belief of all your fictions; but I will stab the lie that's forming in your heart, and save a sin, in pity to your soul."—Congreve, *Double Dealer*, v. 17.

and feels himself are gradually arranged into characters; he can only invent after his given model and his acquired experience; and his characters only manifest what he is, or abridge what he has seen. Two features are prominent in this world; they are prominent also on this stage. All the successful characters can be reduced to two classes—natural beings on the one part, and artificial on the other; the first with the coarseness and shamelessness of their primitive inclinations, the second with the frivolities and vices of worldly habits: the first uncultivated, their simplicity revealing nothing but their innate baseness; the second cultivated, their refinement instilling into them nothing but a new corruption. And the talent of the writers is suited to the painting of these two groups: they possess the grand English faculty, which is the knowledge of exact detail and real sentiments; they see gestures, surroundings, dresses; they hear the sounds of voices, and they have the courage to exhibit them; they have inherited, very little, and at a great distance, and in spite of themselves, still they have inherited from Shakspeare; they manipulate freely, and without any softening, the coarse harsh red colour which alone can bring out the figures of their brutes. On the other hand, they have animation and a good style; they can express the thoughtless chatter, the frolicsome affectations, the inexhaustible and capricious abundance of drawing-room stupidities; they have as much liveliness as the maddest, and at the same time they speak as well as the best instructed; they can give the model of witty conversation; they have lightness of touch, brilliancy, and also facility, exactness, without which you cannot draw the portrait of a man of the world. They find naturally on their palette the strong colours which suit their barbarians, and the pretty tints which suit their exquisites.

VIII.

First there is the blockhead, Squire Sullen, a low kind of sot, of whom his wife speaks in this fashion: "After his man and he had rolled about the room, like sick passengers in a storm, he comes flounce into bed, dead as a salmon into a fishmonger's basket; his feet cold as ice, his breath hot as a furnace, and his hands and his face as greasy as his flannel nightcap. O matrimony! He tosses up the clothes with a barbarous swing over his shoulders, disorders the whole economy of my bed, leaves me half naked, and my whole night's comfort is the tuneable serenade of that wakeful nightingale, his nose!"[1] Sir John Brute says: "What the plague did I marry her (his wife) for? I knew she did not like me; if she had, she would have lain with me."[2] He turns his drawing-room into a stable, smokes it foul to drive the women away, throws his pipe at their heads, drinks, swears, and curses. Coarse words and oaths flow through his conversation like filth through a gutter. He gets drunk at the tavern, and howls out, "Damn morality! and damn the watch! and let the constable be married."[3] He cries out that he is a free-born Englishman; he wants to go out and break everything. He leaves the inn with other besotted scamps, and attacks the women in the street. He robs a tailor who was carrying a doctor's gown, puts it on, thrashes the guard. He is seized and taken by the constable; on

---

[1] Farquhar, *The Beaux Stratagem*, ii. 1.
[2] Vanbrugh, *Provoked Wife*, v. 6. [3] *Ibid.* iii. 2.

the road he breaks out into abuse, and ends by proposing to him, amid the hiccups and stupid reiterations of a drunken man, to go and find out somewhere a bottle and a girl. He returns home at last, covered with blood and mud, growling like a dog, with red swollen eyes, calling his wife a slut and a liar. He goes to her, forcibly embraces her, and as she turns away, cries, " I see it goes damnably against your stomach—and therefore—kiss me again. (*Kisses and tumbles her.*) So, now you being as dirty and as nasty as myself, we may go pig together."[1] He wants to get a cup of cold tea out of the closet, kicks open the door, and discovers his wife's and niece's gallants. He storms, raves madly with his clammy tongue, then suddenly falls asleep. His valet comes and takes the insensible burden on his shoulders.[2] It is the portrait of a mere animal, and I fancy it is not a nice one.

That is the husband; let us look at the father, Sir Tunbelly Clumsey, a country gentleman, elegant, if any of them were. Tom Fashion knocks at the door of the mansion, which looks like "Noah's ark," and where they receive people as in a besieged city. A servant appears at a window with a blunderbuss in his hand, who is at last with great difficulty persuaded that he ought to let his master know that somebody wishes to see him. " Ralph, go thy weas, and ask Sir Tunbelly if he pleases to be waited upon. And dost hear? call to nurse that she may lock up Miss Hoyden before the geat's open."[3] Please to observe that in this house they keep a

[1] Vanbrugh, *Provoked Wife*, v. 2.
[2] The valet Rasor says to his master : "Come to your kennel, you cuckoldy drunken sot you."—*Ibid.*
[3] Vanbrugh's *Relapse*, iii. 3.

watch over the girls. Sir Tunbelly comes up with his people, armed with guns, pitchforks, scythes, and clubs, in no amiable mood, and wants to know the name of his visitor. "Till I know your name, I shall not ask you to come into my house; and when I know your name—'tis six to four I don't ask you neither."[1] He is like a watchdog growling and looking at the calves of an intruder. But he presently learns that this intruder is his future son-in-law; he utters some exclamations, and makes his excuses. "Cod's my life! I ask your lordship's pardon ten thousand times. (*To a servant.*) Here, run in a-doors quickly. Get a Scotch-coal fire in the great parlour; set all the Turkey-work chairs in their places; get the great brass candlesticks out, and be sure stick the sockets full of laurel. Run! . . . And do you hear, run away to nurse, bid her let Miss Hoyden loose again, and if it was not shifting-day, let her put on a clean tucker, quick!"[2] The pretended son-in-law wants to marry Hoyden straight off. "Not so soon neither! that's shooting my girl before you bid her stand. . . . Besides, my wench's wedding-gown is not come home yet."[3] The other suggests that a speedy marriage will save money. Spare money? says the father, " Udswoons, I'll give my wench a wedding dinner, though I go to grass with the king of Assyria for't. . . . Ah! poor girl, she'll be scared out of her wits on her wedding-night; for, honestly speaking, she does not know a man from a woman but by his beard and his breeches."[4] Foppington, the real son-in-law, arrives. Sir Tunbelly, taking him for an impostor, calls him a dog; Hoyden proposes

---

[1] Vanbrugh's *Relapse*, iii. 3.   [2] *Ibid.*
[3] *Ibid.* iii. 5.   [4] *Ibid.*

to drag him in the horse-pond; they bind him hand and foot, and thrust him into the dog-kennel; Sir Tunbelly puts his fist under his nose, and threatens to knock his teeth down his throat. Afterwards, having discovered the impostor, he says, "My lord, will you cut his throat? or shall I? . . . Here, give me my dog-whip. . . . Here, here, here, let me beat out his brains, and that will decide all." He raves, and wants to fall upon Tom Fashion with his fists. Such is the country gentleman, of high birth and a farmer, boxer and drinker, brawler and beast. There steams up from all these scenes a smell of cooking, the noise of riot, the odour of a dunghill.

Like father like child. What a candid creature is Miss Hoyden! She grumbles to herself, "It's well I have a husband a-coming, or, ecod, I'd marry the baker; I would so! Nobody can knock at the gate, but presently I must be locked up; and here's the young greyhound bitch can run loose about the house all the day long, she can; 'tis very well." [2] When the nurse tells her her future husband has arrived, she leaps for joy, and kisses the old woman. "O Lord! I'll go put on my laced smock, though I'm whipped till the blood run down my heels for't." [3] Tom comes himself, and asks her if she will be his wife. "Sir, I never disobey my father in anything but eating of green gooseberries." But your father wants to wait . . . "a whole week." "A week!—Why I shall be an old woman by that time." [4] I cannot give all her answers. There is the spirit of a goat behind her kitchen-talk. She marries Tom secretly on the spot, and the chaplain

[1] Vanbrugh's *Relapse*, v. 5.   [2] *Ibid.* iii. 4.
[3] *Ibid.*   [4] *Ibid.* iv. 1.

wishes them many children. "Ecod," she says, "with all my heart! the more the merrier, I say; ha! nurse!"[1] But Lord Foppington, her real intended, turns up, and Tom makes off. Instantly her plan is formed. She bids the nurse and chaplain hold their tongues. "If you two will be sure to hold your tongues, and not say a word of what's past, I'll e'en marry this lord too." "What," says nurse, "two husbands, my dear?" "Why, you had three, good nurse, you may hold your tongue."[2] She nevertheless takes a dislike to the lord, and very soon; he is not well made, he hardly gives her any pocket-money; she hesitates between the two. "If I leave my lord, I must leave my lady too; and when I rattle about the streets in my coach, they'll only say, There goes mistress—mistress—mistress what? What's this man's name I have married, nurse?" "Squire Fashion." "Squire Fashion is it?—Well, 'Squire, that's better than nothing.[3] . . . Love him! why do you think I love him, nurse? ecod, I would not care if he were hanged, so I were but once married to him!—No—that which pleases me, is to think what work I'll make when I get to London; for when I am a wife and a lady both, nurse, ecod, I'll flaunt it with the best of 'em."[4] But she is cautious all the same. She knows that her father has his dog's whip handy, and that he

---

[1] Vanbrugh's *Relapse*, iv. 4. The character of the nurse is excellent. Tom Fashion thanks her for the training she has given Hoyden: "Alas, all I can boast of is, I gave her pure good milk, and so your honour would have said, an you had seen how the poor thing sucked it.—Eh! God's blessing on the sweet face on't! how it used to hang at this poor teat, and suck and squeeze, and kick and sprawl it would, till the belly on't was so full, it would drop off like a leech." This is good, even after Juliet's nurse in Shakspeare.

[2] *Ibid.* iv. 6. [3] *Ibid.* v. 5. [4] *Ibid.* iv. 1.

will give her a good shake. "But, d'ye hear?" she says to the nurse. "Pray take care of one thing: when the business comes to break out, be sure you get between me and my father, for you know his tricks: he'll knock me down."[1] Here is your true moral ascendency. For such a character, there is no other, and Sir Tunbelly does well to keep her tied up, and to let her taste a discipline of daily stripes.[2]

IX.

Let us accompany this modest character to town, and place her with her equals in fine society. All these artless ladies do wonders there, both in the way of actions and maxims. Wycherley's *Country Wife* gives us the tone. When one of them happens to be partly honest,[3] she has the manners and the boldness of a hussar in petticoats. Others seem born with the souls of courtesans and procuresses. "If I marry my lord Aimwell," says Dorinda, "there will be title, place, and precedence, the Park, the play, and the drawing-room, splendour, equipage, noise, and flambeaux.—Hey, my lady Aimwell's servants there! Lights, lights to the stairs! My lady Aimwell's coach put forward! Stand by, make room for her ladyship!—Are not these things moving?"[4] She is candid, and so are others—Corinna, Miss Betty, Belinda, for example. Belinda says to her aunt, whose virtue is tottering: "The sooner you

---

[1] Vanbrugh's *Relapse*, v. 5.
[2] See also the character of a young stupid blockhead, Squire Humphrey. (Vanbrugh's *Journey to London*). He has only a single idea, to be always eating.
[3] Wycherley's Hippolita; Farquhar's Silvia.
[4] Farquhar's *Beaux Stratagem*, iv. 1.

capitulate the better."[1] Further on, when she has decided to marry Heartrree, to save her aunt who is compromised, she makes a confession of faith which promises well for the future of her new spouse; "Were't not for your affair in the balance, I should go near to pick up some odious man of quality yet, and only take poor Heartfree for a gallant."[2] These young ladies are clever, and in all cases apt to follow good instruction. Listen to Miss Prue: "Look you here, madam, then, what Mr. Tattle has given me.—Look you here, cousin, here's a snuff-box: nay, there's snuff in't;—here, will you have any?—Oh, good! how sweet it is!—Mr. Tattle is all over sweet; his peruke is sweet, and his gloves are sweet, and his handkerchief is sweet, pure sweet, sweeter than roses.—Smell him, mother, madam, I mean.—He gave me this ring for a kiss. . . . Smell, cousin; he says, he'll give me something that will make my smocks smell this way. Is not it pure?— It's better than lavender, mun.—I'm resolved I won't let nurse put any more lavender among my smocks— ha, cousin?"[3] It is the silly chatter of a young magpie, who flies for the first time. Tattle, alone with her, tells her he is going to make love:

"*Miss Prue.* Well; and how will you make love to me? come, I long to have you begin. Must I make love too? you must tell me how.

Tattle. You must let me speak, miss, you must not speak first; I must ask you questions, and you must answer.

Miss P. What, is it like the catechism?—come then, ask me.

T. D'ye think you can love me?

Miss P. Yes.

[1] Vanbrugh's *Provoked Wife*, iii. 3.   [2] *Ibid.* v. 2.
[3] Congreve's *Love for Love*, ii. 10.

T. Pooh! pox! you must not say yes already; I shan't care a farthing for you then in a twinkling.

Miss P. What must I say then?

T. Why, you must say no, or you believe not, or you can't tell.

Miss P. Why, must I tell a lie then?

T. Yes, if you'd be well-bred;—all well-bred persons lie.—Besides, you are a woman, you must never speak what you think: your words must contradict your thoughts; but your actions may contradict your words. So, when I ask you, if you can love me, you must say no, but you must love me too. If I tell you you are handsome, you must deny it, and say I flatter you. But you must think yourself more charming than I speak you: and like me, for the beauty which I say you have, as much as if I had it myself. If I ask you to kiss me, you must be angry, but you must not refuse me. . . .

Miss P. O Lord, I swear this is pure!—I like it better than our old-fashioned country way of speaking one's mind;—and must not you lie too?

T. Hum!—Yes; but you must believe I speak truth.

Miss P. O Gemini! well, I always had a great mind to tell lies; but they frighted me, and said it was a sin.

T. Well, my pretty creature; will you make me happy by giving me a kiss?

Miss P. No, indeed; I'm angry at you. (*Runs and kisses him.*)

T. Hold, hold, that's pretty well;—but you should not have given it me, but have suffered me to have taken it.

Miss P. Well, we'll do it again.

T. With all my heart. Now, then, my little angel. (*Kisses her.*)

Miss P. Pish!

T. That's right—again, my charmer! (*Kisses again.*)

Miss P. O fy! nay, now I can't abide you.

T. Admirable! that was as well as if you had been born and bred in Covent Garden."[1]

She makes such rapid progress, that we must stop the quotation forthwith. And mark, what is bred in the bone will come out in the flesh. All these charming characters soon employ the language of kitchen-maids. When Ben, the dolt of a sailor, wants to make love to Miss Prue, she sends him off with a flea in his ear, raves, lets loose a string of cries and coarse expressions, calls him a "great sea-calf." "What does father mean," he says, "to leave me alone, as soon as I come home, with such a dirty dowdy? Sea-calf! I an't calf enough to lick your chalked face, you cheese-curd, you." Moved by these amenities, she breaks out into a rage, weeps, calls him a "stinking tar-barrel."[2] People come and put a stop to this first essay at gallantry. She fires up, declares she will marry Tattle, or the butler, if she cannot get a better man. Her father says, "Hussy, you shall have a rod." She answers, "A fiddle of a rod! I'll have a husband: and if you won't get me one, I'll get one for myself. I'll marry our Robin the butler."[3] Here are pretty and prancing mares if you like; but decidedly, in these

---

[1] Congreve's *Love for Love*, ii. 11.

[2] "*Miss Prue.* Well, and there's a handsome gentleman, and a fine gentleman, and a sweet gentleman, that was here, that loves me, and I love him; and if he sees you speak to me any more, he'll thrash your jacket for you, he will; you great sea-calf.

Ben. What! do you mean that fair-weather spark that was here just now? Will he thrash my jacket? Let'n, let'n, let'n—but an he comes near me, mayhap I may give him a salt-eel for's supper, for all that. What does father mean, to leave me alone, as soon as I come home, with such a dirty dowdy? Sea-calf! I an't calf enough to lick your chalked face, you cheese-curd you."—*Ibid.* iii. 7.

[3] *Ibid.* v. 6.

authors' hands, the natural man becomes nothing but a waif from the stable or the kennel.

Will you be better pleased by the educated man? The worldly life which they depict is a regular carnival, and the heads of their heroines are full of wild imaginations and unchecked gossip. You may see in Congreve how they chatter, with what a flow of words and affectations, with what a shrill and modulated voice, with what gestures, what twisting of arms and neck, what looks raised to heaven, what genteel airs, what grimaces. Lady Wishfort speaks:

"But art thou sure Sir Rowland will not fail to come? or will he not fail when he does come? Will he be importunate, Foible, and push? For if he should not be importunate, I shall never break decorums:—I shall die with confusion, if I am forced to advance.—Oh no, I can never advance!—I shall swoon, if he should expect advances. No, I hope Sir Rowland is better bred than to put a lady to the necessity of breaking her forms. I won't be too coy neither—I won't give him despair—but a little disdain is not amiss; a little scorn is alluring.

Foible. A little scorn becomes your ladyship.

Lady Wishfort. Yes, but tenderness becomes me best—a sort of dyingness—you see that picture has a sort of a—ha, Foible! a swimmingness in the eye—yes, I'll look so—my niece affects it; but she wants features. Is Sir Rowland handsome? Let my toilet be removed—I'll dress above. I'll receive Sir Rowland here. Is he handsome? Don't answer me. I won't know: I'll be surprised, I'll be taken by surprise.[1] . . . And how do I look, Foible?

F. Most killing well madam.

Lady W. Well, and how shall I receive him? in what figure shall I give his heart the first impression? . . . Shall I

[1] Congreve, *The Way of the World*, iii. 5.

sit?—no, I won't sit—I'll walk—ay, I'll walk from the door upon his entrance; and then turn full upon him—no, that will be too sudden. I'll lie—ay, I'll lie down—I'll receive him in my little dressing-room; there's a couch—yes, yes, I'll give the first impression on a couch. I won't lie neither; but loll and lean upon one elbow: with one foot a little dangling off, jogging in a thoughtful way—yes—and then as soon as he appears, start, ay, start, and be surprised, and rise to meet him in a pretty disorder." [1]

These hesitations of a finished coquette become still more vehement at the critical moment. Lady Plyant thinks herself beloved by Mellefont, who does not love her at all, and tries in vain to undeceive her.

"*Mellefont.* For heaven's sake, madam.

Lady Plyant. O, name it no more!—Bless me, how can you talk of heaven! and have so much wickedness in your heart? May be you don't think it a sin.—They say some of you gentlemen don't think it a sin.—May be it is no sin to them that don't think it so; indeed, if I did not think it a sin—but still my honour, if it were no sin.—But then, to marry my daughter, for the conveniency of frequent opportunities, I'll never consent to that; as sure as can be I'll break the match.

Mel. Death and amazement.—Madam, upon my knees.

Lady P. Nay, nay, rise up; come, you shall see my good nature. I know love is powerful, and nobody can help his passion: 'tis not your fault; nor I swear it is not mine. How can I help it, if I have charms? and how can you help it if you are made a captive? I swear it is pity it should be a fault. But my honour,—well, but your honour too—but the sin!—well, but the necessity—O Lord, here is somebody coming, I dare not stay. Well, you must consider of your crime; and strive as much as can be against it,—strive, be sure—but

[1] Congreve, *The Way of the World,* iv.

don't be melancholic, don't despair.—But never think that I'll grant you anything; O Lord, no.—But be sure you lay aside all thoughts of the marriage: for though I know you don't love Cynthia, only as a blind to your passion for me, yet it will make me jealous.—O Lord, what did I say? jealous! no, no; I can't be jealous, for I must not love you—therefore don't hope,—but don't despair neither.—O, they're coming! I must fly."[1]

She escapes and we will not follow her.

This giddiness, this volubility, this pretty corruption, these reckless and affected airs, are collected in the most brilliant, the most worldly portrait of the stage we are discussing, that of Mrs. Millamant, "a fine lady," as the Dramatis Personæ say.[2] She enters, "with her fan spread and her streamers out," dragging a train of furbelows and ribbons, passing through a crowd of laced and bedizened fops, in splendid perukes, who flutter about her path, haughty and wanton, witty and scornful, toying with gallantries, petulant, with a horror of every grave word and all nobility of action, falling in only with change and pleasure. She laughs at the sermons of Mirabell, her suitor: "Sententious Mirabell!—Prithee don't look with that violent and inflexible wise face, like Solomon at the dividing of the child in an old tapestry-hanging.[3] . . . Ha! ha! ha!—pardon me, dear creature, though I grant you 'tis a little barbarous, ha! ha! ha!"[4]

She breaks out into laughter, then gets into a rage, then banters, then sings, then makes faces, and changes at every motion while we look at her. It is a regular whirlpool; all turns round in her brain as

---

[1] Congreve, *The Double-dealer*, ii. 5.
[2] Congreve, *The Way of the World*.   [3] *Ibid.* ii. 6.   [4] *Ibid.* iii. 11.

in a clock when the mainspring is broken. Nothing can be prettier than her fashion of entering on matrimony:

"*Millamant.* Ah! I'll never marry unless I am first made sure of my will and pleasure!... My dear liberty, shall I leave thee? my faithful solitude, my darling contemplation, must I bid you then adieu? Ay—h—adieu—my morning thoughts, agreeable wakings, indolent slumbers, all ye *douceurs* ye *sommeils du matin* adieu?—I can't do it; 'tis more than impossible—positively, Mirabell, I'll lie a-bed in a morning as long as I please.

Mirabell. Then I'll get up in a morning as early as I please.

Mill. Ah! idle creature, get up when you will—and d'ye hear, I won't be called names after I'm married; positively I won't be called names.

Mir. Names!

Mill. Ay, as wife, spouse, my dear, joy, jewel, love, sweet heart, and the rest of that nauseous cant, in which men and their wives are so fulsomely familiar—I shall never bear that—good Mirabell, don't let us be familiar or fond, nor kiss before folks, like my Lady Fadler, and Sir Francis.... Let us never visit together, nor go to a play together; but let us be very strange and well-bred: let us be as strange as if we had been married a great while; and as well bred as if we were not married at all....

Mir. Shall I kiss your hand upon the contract?[1]

Mill. Fainall, what shall I do? shall I have him? I think I must have him.

Fainall. Ay, ay, take him. What should you do?

Mill. Well then—I'll take my death I'm in a horrid fright—Fainall, I shall never say it—well—I think—I'll endure you.

Fain. Fy! fy! have him, have him, and tell him so in plain terms: for I am sure you have a mind to him.

[1] Congreve, *The Way of the World*, iv. 5.

Mill. Are you? I think I have — and the horrid man looks as if he thought so too—well, you ridiculous thing you, I'll have you—I won't be kissed, nor I won't be thanked—here kiss my hand though.—So, hold your tongue now, don't say a word." [1]

The agreement is complete. I should like to see one more article to it—a divorce "*a mensâ et thoro:*" this would be the genuine marriage of the worldlings, that is a decent divorce. And I am sure that in two years Mirabell and Millamant will come to this. Hither tends the whole of this theatre; for, with regard to the women, but particularly with regard to the married women, I have only presented their most amiable aspects. Deeper down it is all gloomy, bitter, above all, pernicious. It represents a household as a prison, marriage as a warfare, woman as a rebel, adultery as the result looked for, irregularity as a right, extravagance as pleasure.[2] A woman of fashion goes to bed in the

---

[1] Congreve, *The Way of the World*, iv. 6.

[2] "*Amanda.* How did you live together? *Berinthia.* Like man and wife, asunder.—He loved the country, I the town. He hawks and hounds, I coaches and equipage. He eating and drinking, I carding and playing. He the sound of a horn, I the squeak of a fiddle. We were dull company at table, worse a-bed. Whenever we met, we gave one another the spleen; and never agreed but once, which was about lying alone."—Vanbrugh, *Relapse*, Act ii. *ad fin.*

Compare Vanbrugh, *A Journey to London*. Rarely has the repulsiveness and corruption of the brutish or worldly nature been more vividly displayed. Little Betty and her brother, Squire Humphry, deserve hanging.

Again. "*Mrs. Foresight.* Do you think any woman honest? *Scandal.* Yes, several very honest; they'll cheat a little at cards, sometimes; but that's nothing. *Mrs. F.* Pshaw! but virtuous, I mean. *S.* Yes, faith; I believe some women are virtuous too; but 'tis as I believe some men are valiant, through fear. For why should a man court danger or a woman shun pleasure?"—Congreve, *Love for Love*, iii. 14.

morning, rises at mid-day, curses her husband, listens to obscenities, frequents balls, haunts the plays, ruins reputations, turns her home into a gambling-house, borrows money, allures men, associates her honour and fortune with debts and assignations. "We are as wicked (as men)," says Lady Brute, "but our vices lie another way. Men have more courage than we, so they commit more bold impudent sins. They quarrel, fight, swear, drink, blaspheme, and the like; whereas we being cowards, only backbite, tell lies, cheat at cards, and so forth."[1] An admirable resumé, in which the gentlemen are included and the ladies too! The world has done nothing but provide them with correct phrases and elegant dresses. In Congreve especially they talk in the best style; above all they know how to hand ladies about and entertain them with news; they are expert in the fence of retorts and replies; they are never out of countenance, find means to make the most ticklish notions understood; they discuss very well, speak excellently, make their bow still better; but to sum up, they are blackguards, systematical epicureans, professed seducers. They set forth immorality in maxims, and reason out their vice. "Give me," says one, "a man that keeps his five senses keen and bright as his sword, that has 'em always drawn out in their just order and strength, with his reason, as commander at the head of 'em, that detaches 'em by turns upon whatever party of pleasure agreeably offers, and commands 'em to retreat upon the least appearance of disadvantage or danger. . . . I love a fine house, but let another keep it; and just so I

[1] Vanbrugh, *Provoked Wife*, v. 2. Compare also in this piece the character of Mademoiselle, the French chambermaid. They represent French vice as even more shameless than English vice.

love a fine woman."[1] One deliberately seduces his friend's wife; another under a false name gets possession of his brother's intended. A third hires false witnesses to secure a dowry. I must ask the reader to consult for himself the fine stratagems of Worthy, Mirabell, and others. They are coldblooded rascals who forge, commit adultery, swindle, as if they had done nothing else all their lives. They are represented here as men of fashion; they are theatrical lovers, heroes, and as such they manage to get hold of an heiress. We must go to Mirabell for an example of this medley of corruption and elegance. Mrs. Fainall, his former mistress, married by him to a common friend, a miserable wretch, complains to him of this hateful marriage. He appeases her, gives her advice, shows her the precise mode, the true expedient for setting things on a comfortable footing. "You should have just so much disgust for your husband, as may be sufficient to make you relish your lover." She cries in despair, "Why did you make me marry this man?" He smiles calmly, "Why do we daily commit disagreeable and dangerous actions? to save that idol, reputation." How tender is this argument! How can a man better console a woman whom he has plunged into bitter unhappiness! What a touching logic in the insinuation which follows: "If the familiarities of our loves had produced that consequence of which you were apprehensive, where could you have fixed a father's name with credit, but on a

[1] Farquhar's *The Beaux Stratagem*, i. 1; and in the same piece here is the catechism of love: "What are the objects of that passion? —youth, beauty, and clean linen." And from the *Mock Astrologer* of Dryden: "As I am a gentleman, a man about town, one that wears good cloths, eats, drinks, and wenches sufficiently."

husband?" He continues his reasoning in an excellent style; listen to the dilemma of a man of feeling: "A better man ought not to have been sacrificed to the occasion; a worse had not answered to the purpose. When you are weary of him, you know your remedy."[1] Thus are a woman's feelings to be considered, especially a woman whom we have loved. To cap all, this delicate conversation is meant to force the poor deserted Mrs. Fainall into a low intrigue which shall obtain for Mirabell a pretty wife and a good dowry. Certainly this gentleman knows the world; no one could better employ a former mistress. Such are the cultivated characters of this theatre, as dishonest as the uncultivated ones: having transformed their evil instincts into systematic vices, lust into debauchery, brutality into cynicism, perversity into depravity, deliberate egotists, calculating sensualists, with rules for their immorality, reducing feeling to self-interest, honour to decorum, happiness to pleasure.

The English Restoration altogether was one of those great crises which, while warping the development of a society and a literature, show the inward spirit which they modify, but which contradicts them. Society did not lack vigour, nor literature talent; men of the world were polished, writers inventive. There was a court, drawing-rooms, conversation, worldly life, a taste for letters, the example of France, peace, leisure, the influence of the sciences, of politics, of theology,—in short, all the happy circumstances which can elevate the mind and civilise manners. There was the vigorous satire of Wycherley, the sparkling dialogue and delicate raillery of Congreve, the frank nature and animation

[1] Congreve, *The Way of the World*, ii. 4.

of Vanbrugh, the manifold invention of Farquhar, in short, all the resources which might nourish the comic element, and offer a genuine theatre to the best constructions of human intelligence. Nothing came to a head; all was abortive. Their age left nothing behind but the memory of corruption; their comedy remains a repertory of viciousness; society had only a soiled elegance, literature a frigid wit. Their manners are gross and trivial; their ideas are futile or incomplete. Through disgust and reaction, a revolution was at hand in literary feeling and moral habits, as well as in general beliefs and political institutions. Man was to change altogether, and to turn completely round at once. The same repugnance and the same experience were to detach him from every aspect of his old condition. The Englishman discovered that he was not monarchical, Papistical, nor sceptical, but liberal, Protestant, and a believer. He came to understand that he was not a roisterer nor a worldling, but reflective and introspective. He possesses a current of animal life too violent to suffer him without danger to abandon himself to enjoyment; he needs a barrier of moral reasoning to repress his outbreaks. There is in him a current of attention and will too strong to suffer himself to rest content with trifles; he needs some weighty and serviceable labour on which to expend his power. He needs a barrier and an employment. He needs a constitution and a religion which shall restrain him by duties which must be performed, and which shall occupy him by rights which must be defended. He is content only in a serious and orderly life; there he finds the natural groove and the necessary outlet for his faculties and his passions. From this time he enters upon it, and this theatre itself exhibits the impress of it. It undoes and transforms itself. Collier threw discredit upon it; Addison condemned it. National sentiment awoke on the stage; French manners are jeered at; the prologues celebrate the defeats of Louis XIV.; the license, elegance, religion of his court, are presented under a ridiculous or odious light.[1] Immorality gradually diminishes, marriage is more respected, the heroines go no further than to the verge of adultery;[2] the roisterers are pulled up at the critical moment; one of them suddenly declares himself purified, and speaks in verse, the better to mark his enthusiasm; another praises marriage;[3] some aspire in the fifth act to an orderly life. We shall soon see Steele writing a moral treatise called *The Christian Hero.* Henceforth comedy declines and literary talent flows into another channel. Essay, novel, pamphlet, dissertation, take the place of the drama; and the English classical spirit, abandoning the kinds of writing which are foreign to its nature, enters upon the great works which are destined to immortalise it and give it expression.

X.

Nevertheless, in this continuous decline of dramatic invention, and in the great change of literary vitality, some shoots strike out at distant intervals towards

---

[1] The part of Chaplain Foigard in Farquhar's *Beaux Stratagem;* of Mademoiselle, and generally of all the French people.

[2] The part of Amanda in Vanbrugh's *Relapse;* of Mrs. Sullen; the conversion of two roisterers, in the *Beaux Stratagem.*

[3] "Though marriage be a lottery in which there are a wondrous many blanks, yet there is one inestimable lot, in which the only heaven upon earth is written."

"To be capable of loving one, doubtless, is better than to possess a thousand."—VANBRUGH.

comedy; for mankind always seeks for entertainment, and the theatre is always a place of entertainment. The tree once planted grows, feebly no doubt, with long intervals of almost total dryness and almost constant barrenness, yet subject to imperfect renewals of life, to transitory partial blossomings, sometimes to an inferior fruitage bursting forth from the lowest branches. Even when the great subjects are worn out, there is still room here and there for a happy idea. Let a wit, clever and experienced, take it in hand, he will catch up a few oddities on his way, he will introduce on the scene some vice or fault of his time; the public will come in crowds, and ask no better than to recognise itself and laugh. There was one of these successes when Gay, in the *Beggars' Opera*, brought out the rascaldom of the great world, and avenged the public on Walpole and the court; another, when Goldsmith, inventing a series of mistakes, led his hero and his audience through five acts of blunders.[1] After all, if true comedy can only exist in certain ages, ordinary comedy can exist in any age. It is too akin to the pamphlet, novels, satire, not to raise itself occasionally by its propinquity. If I have an enemy, instead of attacking him in a brochure, I can take my fling at him on the stage. If I am capable of painting a character in a story, I am not far from having the talent to bring out the pith of this same character in a few turns of a dialogue. If I can quietly ridicule a vice in a copy of verses, I shall easily arrive at making this vice speak out from the mouth of an actor. At least I shall be tempted to try it; I shall be seduced by the wonderful *éclat* which the footlights, declamation,

[1] *She Stoops to Conquer.*

scenery give to an idea; I shall try and bring my own into this strong light; I shall go in for it even when it is necessary that my talent be a little or a good deal forced for the occasion. If need be, I shall delude myself, substitute expedients for artless originality and true comic genius. If on a few points I am inferior to the great masters, on some, it may be, I surpass them; I can work up my style, refine upon it, discover happier words, more striking jokes, a brisker exchange of brilliant repartees, newer images, more picturesque comparisons; I can take from this one a character, from the other a situation, borrow of a neighbouring nation, out of old plays, good novels, biting pamphlets, polished satires, and petty newspapers; I can accumulate effects, serve up to the public a stronger and more appetising stew; above all, I can perfect my machine, oil the wheels, plan the surprises, the stage effects, the see-saw of the plot, like a consummate playwright. The art of constructing plays is as capable of development as the art of clockmaking. The farce-writer of to-day sees that the catastrophe of half of Molière's plays is ridiculous; nay, many of them can produce catastrophes better than Molière; in the long run, they succeed in stripping the theatre of all awkwardness and circumlocution. A piquant style, and perfect machinery; pungency in all the words, and animation in all the scenes; a superabundance of wit, and marvels of ingenuity; over all this, a true physical activity, and the secret pleasure of depicting and justifying oneself, of public self-glorification: here is the foundation of the *School for Scandal,* here the source of the talent and the success of Sheridan.

Richard Brinsley Sheridan was the contemporary of Beaumarchais, and resembled him in his talent and in his life. The two epochs, the two dramatic schools, the two characters, correspond. Like Beaumarchais, he was a lucky adventurer, clever, amiable, and generous, reaching success through scandal, who flashed up in a moment, dazzled everybody, scaled with a rush the empyrean of politics and literature, settled himself, as it were, among the constellations, and, like a brilliant rocket, presently went out completely exhausted. Nothing failed him; he attained all at the first attempt, without apparent effort, like a prince who need only show himself to win his place. He took as his birthright everything that was most surpassing in happiness, most brilliant in art, most exalted in worldly position. The poor unknown youth, the wretched translator of an unreadable Greek sophist, who at twenty walked about Bath in a red waistcoat and a cocked hat, destitute of hope, and ever conscious of the emptiness of his pockets, had gained the heart of the most admired beauty and musician of her time, had carried her off from ten rich, elegant, titled adorers, had fought with the best-hoaxed of the ten, beaten him, had carried by storm the curiosity and attention of the public. Then, challenging glory and wealth, he placed successively on the stage the most diverse and the most applauded dramas, comedies, farce, opera, serious verse; he bought and worked a large theatre without a farthing, inaugurated a reign of successes and pecuniary advantages, and led a life of elegance amid the enjoyments of social and domestic joys, surrounded by universal admiration and wonder. Thence, aspiring yet higher, he conquered power, entered the House of Commons, showed himself a match for the first orators, opposed Pitt, accused Warren Hastings, supported Fox, jeered at Burke; sustained with brilliancy, disinterestedness, and constancy, a most difficult and liberal part; became one of the three or four most noted men in England, an equal of the greatest lords, the friend of the Prince of Wales, in the end even Receiver-General of the Duchy of Cornwall, treasurer to the fleet. In every career he took the lead. As Byron said of him: "Whatsoever Sheridan has done or chosen to do has been, *par excellence*, always the *best* of its kind. He has written the *best* comedy (*The School for Scandal*), the best drama (in my mind far before that St. Giles lampoon *The Beggar's Opera*), the best farce (*The Critic*—it is only too good for a farce), and the best Address (*Monologue on Garrick*), and, to crown all, delivered the very best oration (the famous Begum Speech) ever conceived or heard in this country."[1]

All ordinary rules were reversed in his favour. He was forty-four years old, debts began to accumulate; he had supped and drunk to excess; his cheeks were purple, his nose red. In this state he met at the Duke of Devonshire's a charming young lady with whom he fell in love. At the first sight she exclaimed, "What an ugly man, a regular monster!" He spoke to her; she confessed that he was very ugly, but that he had a good deal of wit. He spoke again, and again, and she found him very amiable. He spoke yet again, and she loved him, and resolved at all hazard to marry him. The father, a prudent man, wishing to end the affair, gave out that his future son-in-law must provide a dowry of fifteen thousand pounds; the fifteen

---

[1] *The Works of Lord Byron*, 18 vols., ed. Moore, 1832, ii. p. 303.

thousand pounds were deposited as by magic in the hands of a banker; the young couple set off into the country; and Sheridan, meeting his son, a fine strapping fellow, not very satisfied with the marriage, persuaded him that it was the most sensible thing a father could do, and the most fortunate event that a son could rejoice over. Whatever the business, whoever the man, he persuaded; none withstood him, every one fell under his charm.

What is more difficult than for an ugly man to make a young girl forget his ugliness? There is one thing more difficult, and that is to make a creditor forget you owe him money. There is something more difficult still, and that is, to borrow money from a creditor who has come to dun you. One day one of his friends was arrested for debt; Sheridan sends for Mr. Henderson, the crabbed tradesman, coaxes him, interests him, moves him to tears, works upon his feelings, hedges him in with general considerations and lofty eloquence, so that Mr. Henderson offers his purse, actually wants to lend two hundred pounds, insists, and finally, to his great joy, obtains permission to lend it. No one was ever more amiable, quicker to win confidence than Sheridan; rarely has the sympathetic, affectionate, and fascinating character been more fully displayed; he was literally seductive. In the morning, creditors and visitors filled the rooms in which he lived; he came in smiling with an easy manner, with so much loftiness and grace, that the people forgot their wants and their claims, and looked as if they had only come to see him. His animation was irresistible; no one had a more dazzling wit; he had an inexhaustible fund of puns, contrivances, sallies, novel ideas. Lord Byron, who was a good judge, said that he had never heard nor conceived of a more extraordinary power of conversation. Men spent nights in listening to him; no one equalled him during a supper; even when drunk he retained his wit. One morning he was picked up by the watch, and they asked him his name; he gravely answered, "Wilberforce." With strangers and inferiors he had no arrogance or stiffness; he possessed in an eminent degree that unreserved character which always exhibits itself complete, which holds back none of its light, which abandons and gives itself up; he wept when he received a sincere eulogy from Lord Byron, or in recounting his miseries as a plebeian parvenu. Nothing is more charming than this openness of heart; it at once sets people on a footing of peace and amity; men suddenly desert their defensive and cautious attitude; they perceive that a man is giving himself up to them, and they give themselves up to him; the outpouring of his innermost feelings invites the outpouring of theirs. A minute later, Sheridan's impetuous and sparkling individuality flashes out; his wit explodes, rattles like a discharge of firearms; he takes the conversation to himself, with a sustained brilliancy, a variety, an inexhaustible vigour, till five o'clock in the morning. Against such a necessity for launching out in unconsidered speech, of indulgence, of self-outpouring, a man had need be well on his guard; life cannot be passed like a holiday; it is a strife against others and against oneself; people must think of the future, mistrust themselves, make provision; there is no subsisting without the precaution of a shopkeeper, the calculation of a tradesman. If we sup too often, we will end by not having wherewithal to dine upon; when our pockets have holes in them, the shillings will fall out; nothing is more of a truism, but it is true. Sheridan's debts accumulated, his digestion failed. He lost his seat in Parliament, his theatre was burned; sheriff's officer succeeded sheriff's officer, and they had long been in possession of his house. At last, a bailiff arrested the dying man in his bed, and was for taking him off in his blankets; nor would he let him go until threatened with a lawsuit, the doctor having declared that the sick man would die on the road. A certain newspaper (the *Examiner*) cried shame on the great lords who suffered such a man to end so miserably; they hastened to leave their cards at his door. In the funeral procession two brothers of the king, dukes, earls, bishops, the first men in England, carried or followed the body. A singular contrast, picturing in abstract all his talent, and all his life; lords at his funeral and bailiffs at his death-bed.

His theatre was in accordance with his life; all was brilliant, but the metal was not all his own, nor was it of the best quality. His comedies were comedies of society, the most amusing ever written, but merely comedies of society. Imagine the exaggerated caricatures artists are wont to improvise, in the drawing-room of a house where they are intimate, about eleven o'clock in the evening. His first play, *The Rivals*, and afterwards his *Duenna*, and *The Critic*, are filled with these, and scarce anything else. There is Mrs. Malaprop, a silly pretentious woman, who uses grand words higgledy-piggledy, delighted with herself, in "a nice derangement of epitaphs" before her nouns, and declaring that her niece is "as headstrong as an allegory on the banks of the Nile." There is Bob Acres, who suddenly becomes a hero, gets engaged in a duel, and being led on the ground, calculates the effect of the balls, thinks of his will, burial, embalmment, and wishes he were at home. There is another caricature in the person of a clumsy and cowardly servant, of an irascible and brawling father, of a sentimental and romantic young lady, of a touchy Irish duellist. All this jogs and jostles on, without much order, amid the surprises of a twofold plot, by aid of appliances and rencontres, without the full and regular control of a dominating idea. But in vain we perceive it is a patchwork; the high spirit carries off everything: we laugh heartily; every single scene has its facetious and rapid movement; we forget that the clumsy valet makes remarks as witty as Sheridan himself,[1] and that the irascible gentleman speaks as well as the most elegant of writers.[2] The playwright is also a man of letters; if, through mere animal and social spirit, he wished to amuse others and to amuse himself, he does not forget the interests of his talent and the care for his reputation. He has taste, he appreciates the refinements of style, the worth of a new image, of a striking contrast, of a witty and well-considered insinuation. He has, above all, wit, a wonderful conversational wit, the art of rousing and sustaining the attention, of

[1] *Acres.* Odds blades! David, no gentleman will ever risk the loss of his honour!
David. I say, then, it would be but civil in honour never to risk the loss of a gentleman.—Look ye, master, this honour seems to me to be a marvellous false friend; ay, truly, a very courtier-like servant.—*The Dramatic Works of Richard Brinsley Sheridan*, 1828: *The Rivals*, iv. 1.

[2] *Sir Anthony.*—Nay, but Jack, such eyes! so innocently wild! so bashfully irresolute! Not a glance but speaks and kindles some thought of love! Then, Jack, her cheeks! so deeply blushing at the insinuations of her tell-tale eyes! Then, Jack, her lips! O Jack, lips, smiling at their own discretion! and if not smiling, more sweetly pouting, more lovely in sullenness!—*The Rivals*, iii. 1.

being biting, varied, of taking his hearers unawares, of throwing in a repartee, of setting folly in relief, of accumulating one after another witticisms and happy phrases. He brought himself to perfection subsequently to his first play, having acquired theatrical experience, writing and erasing; trying various scenes, recasting, arranging them; his desire was that nothing should arrest the interest, no improbability shock the spectator; that his comedy might glide on with the precision, certainty, uniformity of a good machine. He invents jests, replaces them by better ones; he whets his jokes, binds them up like a sheaf of arrows, and writes at the bottom of the last page, " Finished, thank God.—Amen." He is right, for the work costs him some pains; he will not write a second. This kind of writing, artificial and condensed as the satires of La Bruyère, is like a cut phial, into which the author has distilled all his reflections, his reading, his wit, without keeping anything for himself.

What is there in this celebrated *School for Scandal?* And how is it that it has cast upon English comedy, which day by day was being more and more forgotten, the radiance of a last success? Sheridan took two characters from Fielding, Blifil, and Tom Jones; two plays of Molière, *Le Misanthrope* and *Tartuffe;* and from these puissant materials, condensed with admirable cleverness, he has constructed the most brilliant firework imaginable. Molière has only one female slanderer, Célimène; the other characters serve only to give her a cue: there is quite enough of such a jeering woman; she rails on within certain bounds, without hurry, like a true queen of the drawing-room, who has time to converse, who knows that she is listened to, who listens to herself: she is a woman of society, who preserves the tone of refined conversation; and in order to smooth down the harshness, her slanders are interrupted by the calm reason and sensible discourse of the amiable Eliante. Molière represents the malice of the world without exaggeration; but in Sheridan they are rather caricatured than depicted. " Ladies, your servant," says Sir Peter; " mercy upon me! the whole set—a character dead at every sentence."[1] In fact, they are ferocious: it is a regular quarry; they even befoul one another, to deepen the outrage. Mrs. Candour remarks : " Yesterday Miss Prim assured me, that Mr. and Mrs. Honeymoon are now become mere man and wife, like the rest of their acquaintance. She likewise hinted, that a certain widow in the next street had got rid of her dropsy, and recovered her shape in a most surprising manner. . . . I was informed, too, that Lord Flimsy caught his wife at a house of no extraordinary fame; and that Tom Saunter and Sir Harry Idle were to measure swords on a similar occasion."[2] Their animosity is so bitter that they lower themselves to play the part of buffoons. The most elegant person in the room, Lady Teazle, shows her teeth to ape a ridiculous lady, draws her mouth on one side, and makes faces. There is no pause, no softening; sarcasms fly about like pistol-shots. The author had laid in a stock, he had to use them up. He himself is speaking through the mouth of each of his characters; he gives them all the same wit, that is his own, his irony, his harshness, his picturesque vigour; whatever they are, clowns, fops, old maids, no matter, the author's main business is to break out into twenty explosions in a minute :

[1] *The School for Scandal*, ii. 2.   [2] *Ibid*. i. 1.

"*Mrs. Candour.* Well, I will never join in the ridicule of a friend; so I tell my cousin Ogle, and ye all know what pretensions she has to beauty.

Crab. She has the oddest countenance — a collection of features from all the corners of the globe.

Sir Benjamin. She has, indeed, an Irish front.

Crab. Caledonian locks.

Sir B. Dutch nose.

Crab. Austrian lips.

Sir B. The complexion of a Spaniard.

Crab. And teeth *à la Chinoise.*

Sir B. In short, her face resembles a *table d'hôte* at Spa, where no two guests are of a nation.

Crab. Or a congress at the close of a general war, where every member seems to have a different interest, and the nose and chin are the only parties likely to join issue."[1]

Or again:

"*Crab.* Sad news upon his arrival, to hear how your brother has gone on!

Joseph Surface. I hope no busy people have already prejudiced his uncle against him—he may reform.

Sir Benjamin. True, he may; for my part, I never thought him so utterly void of principle as people say, and though he has lost all his friends, I am told nobody is better spoken of amongst the Jews.

Crab. Foregad, if the old Jewry was a ward, Charles would be an alderman, for he pays as many annuities as the Irish Tontine; and when he is sick, they have prayers for his recovery in all the Synagogues.

Sir B. Yet no man lives in greater splendor.—They tell me, when he entertains his friends, he can sit down to dinner with a dozen of his own securities, have a score of tradesmen waiting in the anti-chamber, and an officer behind every guest's chair."[2]

[1] *The School for Scandal,* ii. 2. [2] *Ibid.* i. 1.

And again:

"*Sir B.* Mr. Surface, I did not mean to hurt you, but depend on't, your brother is utterly undone.
Crab. Oh! undone as ever man was—can't raise a guinea.
Sir B. Everything is sold, I am told, that was moveable.
Crab. Not a moveable left, except some old bottles and some pictures, and they seem to be framed in the wainscot, egad.
Sir B. I am sorry to hear also some bad stories of him.
Crab. Oh! he has done many mean things, that's certain.
Sir B. But, however, he's your brother.
Crab. Ay! as he is your brother — we'll tell you more another opportunity." [1]

In this manner has he pointed, multiplied, driven in to the quick the measured epigrams of Molière. And yet is it possible to grow weary of such a well-sustained discharge of malice and witticisms?

Observe also the change which the hypocrite undergoes under Sheridan's treatment. Doubtless all the grandeur disappears from the part. Joseph Surface does not uphold, like Tartuffe, the interest of the comedy; he does not possess, like his ancestor, the nature of a cad, the boldness of a man of action, the manners of a beadle, the neck and shoulders of a monk. He is merely selfish and cautious; if he is engaged in an intrigue, it is rather against his will; he is only halfhearted in the matter, like a correct young man, well dressed, with a fair income, timorous and fastidious by nature, discreet in manners, and without violent passions; all about him is soft and polished, he takes his tone from the times, he makes no display of re-

[1] *The School for Scandal,* i. 1.

ligion, though he does of morality; he is a man of measured speech, of lofty sentiments, a disciple of Dr. Johnson or of Rousseau, a dealer in set phrases. There is nothing on which to construct a drama in this commonplace person; and the fine situations which Sheridan takes from Molière lose half their force through depending on such pitiful support. But how this insufficiency is covered by the quickness, abundance, naturalness of the incidents! how skill makes up for everything! how it seems capable of supplying everything! even genius! how the spectator laughs to see Joseph caught in his sanctuary like a fox in his hole; obliged to hide the wife, then to conceal the husband; forced to run from the one to the other; busy in hiding the one behind the screen, and the other in his closet; reduced, in casting himself into his own snares, in justifying those whom he wished to ruin, the husband in the eyes of the wife, the nephew in the eyes of the uncle, to ruin the only man whom he wished to justify, namely, the precious and immaculate Joseph Surface; to turn out in the end ridiculous, odious, baffled, confounded, in spite of his adroitness, even by reason of his adroitness, step by step, without quarter or remedy; to sneak off, poor fox, with his tail between his legs, his skin spoiled, amid hootings and laughter! And how, at the same time, side by side with this, the naggings of Sir Peter and his wife, the suppers, songs, the picture sale at the spendthrift's house, weave a comedy in a comedy, and renew the interest by renewing the attention! We cease to think of the meagreness of the characters, as we cease to think of the deviation from truth; we are willingly carried away by the vivacity of the action, dazzled by the brilliancy of the dialogue ; we are charmed, applaud ; admit that, after all, next to great inventive faculty, animation and wit are the most agreeable gifts in the world : we appreciate them in their season, and find that they also have their place in the literary banquet ; and that if they are not worth as much as the substantial joints, the natural and generous wines of the first course, at least they furnish the dessert.

The dessert over, we must leave the table. After Sheridan, we leave it forthwith. Henceforth comedy languishes, fails ; there is nothing left but farce, such as Townley's *High Life Below Stairs*, the burlesques of George Colman, a tutor, an old maid, countrymen and their dialect; caricature succeeds painting; Punch raises a laugh when the days of Reynolds and Gainsborough are over. There is nowhere in Europe, at the present time, a more barren stage ; the higher classes abandon it to the people. This is because the form of society and of intellect which had called it into being, have disappeared. Vivacity, and the abundance of original conceptions, had peopled the stage of the Renaissance in England,— a surfeit which, unable to display itself in systematic argument, or to express itself in philosophical ideas, found its natural outlet only in mimic action and talking characters. The wants of polished society had nourished the English comedy of the seventeenth century,—a society which, accustomed to the representations of the court and the displays of the world, sought on the stage a copy of its conversation and its drawing-rooms. With the decline of the court and the check of mimic invention, the genuine drama and the genuine comedy disappeared ; they passed from the stage into books. The reason of it is, that people no longer live in public, like the embroidered dukes of Louis XIV. and Charles II., but in their families, or at the writing-table; the novel replaces the theatre at the same time that citizen life replaces the life of the court.

END OF VOL. II.